PEACEMAKING IN THE MIDDLE AGES

CW00821801

Manchester University Press

MANCHESTER MEDIEVAL STUDIES

SERIES EDITOR   Professor S. H. Rigby
SERIES ADVISERS   Professor John Hatcher and
Professor J. H. Moran Cruz

The study of medieval Europe is being transformed as old orthodoxies are challenged, new methods embraced and fresh fields of inquiry opened up. The adoption of interdisciplinary perspectives and the challenge of economic, social and cultural theory are forcing medievalists to ask new questions and to see familiar topics in a fresh light.

The aim of this series is to combine the scholarship traditionally associated with medieval studies with an awareness of more recent issues and approaches in a form accessible to the non-specialist reader.

MANCHESTER MEDIEVAL STUDIES

PEACEMAKING IN THE MIDDLE AGES

PRINCIPLES AND PRACTICE

Jenny Benham

Manchester University Press

Published by Manchester University Press
Altrincham Street, Manchester M1 7JA, UK
www.manchesteruniversitypress.co.uk

British Library Cataloguing-in-Publication Data is available

ISBN 978 1 5261 1668 0 paperback

First published by Manchester University Press in hardback 2010

This edition first published 2017

Printed by Lightning Source

CONTENTS

LIST OF ABBREVIATIONS

Adam of Bremen, *Gesta*	*Adam Bremensis Gesta Hammaburgensis Ecclesiae Pontificum*, 3rd edn, ed. B. Schmeidler, MGH SRG, 2 (Hanover, 1917)
AHR	*American Historical Review*
Althoff, *SP*	*Spielregeln der Politik im Mittelalter: Kommunikation in Frieden und Fehde* (Darmstadt, 1997)
Ann. Mon.	*Annales Monastici*, 5 vols, ed. H. R. Luard (London, 1864–69)
ANS	*Anglo-Norman Studies* (The first four volumes were published as *Proceedings of the Battle Conference*), ed. R. Allen Brown (1979–89), M. Chibnall (1990–94), C. Harper-Bill (1995–99), J. Gillingham (2000–4)
ARF	*Annales Regni Francorum*, ed. F. Kurze, MGH SRG, 6 (Hanover, 1895)
Arnoldi Chronica Slavorum	*Arnoldi Chronica Slavorum*, tr. J. M. Lappenberg, MGH SS, 21 (Hanover, 1869; repr. Stuttgart, 1988)
A Short History of the Kings of Denmark	*A Short History of the Kings of Denmark*, in *The Works of Sven Aggesen*, tr. Eric Christiansen (London, 1992)
BIHR	*Bulletin of the Institute of Historical Research*
BJRL	*Bulletin of the John Rylands Library*
Brut y Tywysogyon	*Brut y Tywysogyon or the Chronicle of the Princes*, tr. T. Jones (Cardiff, 1952)
Chaplais, *EDP*	Pierre Chaplais, *English Diplomatic Practice in the Middle Ages* (London, 2003)
Chaplais, *EMDP*	Pierre Chaplais, *English Medieval Diplomatic Practice Part I: Documents and Interpretation*, 2 vols (London, 1982)

The Chronicle of John of Worcester	*The Chronicle of John of Worcester*, 3 vols, ed. R. R. Darlington and P. McGurk (Oxford, 1995–98)
Codice Diplomatico della Repubblica di Genova	*Codice Diplomatico della Repubblica di Genova*, 4 vols, ed. C. Imperiale di Santangelo (Genoa, 1936–42)
Coggeshall	*Radulphi de Coggeshall Chronicum Anglicanum*, ed. J. Stevenson, Rolls Series, 66 (London, 1875)
DA	*Deutsches Archiv*
De Nugis Curialium	Walter Map, *De Nugis Curialium*, ed. and tr. M. R. James, revised by C. N. L. Brooke and R. A. B. Mynors (Oxford, 1983)
Diceto	*The Historical Works of Master Ralph de Diceto*, 2 vols, ed. W. Stubbs, Rolls Series, 68 (London, 1876)
Dip. Docs	*Diplomatic Documents Preserved in the Public Record Office, 1101–1272*, i, ed. P. Chaplais (London, 1964)
Draco Normannicus	*Stephani Rotomagensis monachi Beccensis poema cui titulus Draco Normannicus*, in *Chronicles of the Reigns of Stephen, Henry II and Richard I*, 4 vols, ed. R. Howlett, Rolls Series, 82 (London, 1884–89), ii, 589–779.
EHR	*English Historical Review*
Flores Historiarum	*Flores Historiarum Rogeri Wendoveri*, 2 vols, ed. H. G. Hewlett, Rolls Series, 8 (London, 1886–89)
Foedera	*Foedera, Conventiones, Litterae et cuiuscunque generis Acta Publica*, ed. T. Rymer (London, 1704)
Ganshof, *MA*	F.-L. Ganshof, *The Middle Ages – A History of International Relations*, tr. R. I. Hall (London, 1970)
Gervase of Canterbury	*The Historical Works of Gervase of Canterbury*, 2 vols, ed. William Stubbs, Rolls Series, 73 (London, 1879–80)
Gesta Friderici	*Ottonis et Rahewini Gesta Friderici I Imperatoris*, ed. G. Waitz, MGH SRG, 46 (Hanover, 1884)

GND	*The Gesta Normannorum Ducum of William of Jumièges, Orderic Vitalis, and Robert of Torigni*, 2 vols, ed. and tr. Elisabeth M. C. van Houts (Oxford, 1992–95)
GRA	William of Malmesbury, *Gesta Regum Anglorum: The History of the English Kings*, 2 vols, ed. R. A. B. Mynors, R. M. Thomson and M. Winterbottom (Oxford, 1998–99)
Gregory of Tours, *Libri Historiarum X*	*Gregorii Episcopi Turonensis Libri Historiarum X*, MGH SSRM, 1, part I (Hanover, 1951)
Heinrici Chronicon Lyvonie	*Heinrici Chronicon Lyvonie*, ed. Wilhelm Arndt, MGH SS, 23 (Hanover, 1874; repr. Stuttgart, 1986)
Helmoldi Chronica Slavorum	*Helmoldi Presbyteri Bozoviensis Chronica Slavorum*, ed. G. H. Pertz, MGH SS, 21 (Hanover, 1869; repr. Stuttgart, 1988)
HGM	*Histoire de Guillaume le Maréchal*, 3 vols, ed. P. Meyer (Paris, 1891–1907)
Hist. des ducs	*Histoire des ducs de Normandie et des rois d'Angleterre*, ed. F. Michel (Paris, 1840)
Howden, *Chronica*	*Chronica Magistri Rogeri de Hovedene*, 4 vols, ed. W. Stubbs, Rolls Series, 51 (London, 1868–71)
Howden, *Gesta*	*Gesta Regis Henrici Secundi Benedicti Abbatis*, 2 vols, ed. W. Stubbs, Rolls Series, 49 (London, 1867)
HSJ	*Haskins Society Journal*
JMH	*Journal of Medieval History*
Kolb, *Herrscherbegegnungen*	Werner Kolb, *Herrscherbegegnungen im Mittelalter* (Frankfurt, 1988)
Landon, *Itinerary*	L. Landon, *The Itinerary of King Richard I* (London, 1935)
Magna Carta	*Magna Carta*, 2nd edn. ed. J. C. Holt (Cambridge, 1992)
Mauss, *The Gift*	Marcel Mauss, *The Gift: Forms Functions and Exchange in Archaic Societies*, tr. Ian Cunnison (London, 1988)

MGH	Monumenta Germaniae Historica
Ep.	Epistolae Selectae
Leges	Leges
SRG	Scriptores rerum Germanicarum
SS	Scriptores
SSRM	Scriptores rerum Merovingicarum
De Moribus	*De Moribus et Actibus Primorum Normannorum Ducum auctore Dudone Sancti Quintini decano*, ed. J. Lair (Caen, 1865)
MTB	*Materials for the History of Thomas Becket, archbishop of Canterbury*, 7 vols, ed. J. C. Robertson, Rolls Series, 67 (London, 1875–85)
Newburgh	*The Historia Rerum Anglicarum of William of Newburgh*, in *Chronicles of the Reigns of Stephen, Henry II and Richard I*, 4 vols, ed. R. Howlett, Rolls Series (London, 1884–89); i–ii.
Orderic, *HE*	Orderic Vitalis, *The Ecclesiastical History*, 6 vols, ed. and tr. M. Chibnall (Oxford, 1969–81)
PL	*Patrologia Latina*, 221 vols, ed. J.-P. Migne, complete electronic version of first edition of Migne's *PL*, 1844–55 (Cambridge, 1995)
PR	*Pipe Rolls*: citations to Pipe Rolls are to the regnal years of the reigning kings and published by the Pipe Roll Society, London
PRO	Public Record Office, London
Pryce, *The Acts of Welsh Rulers*	*The Acts of Welsh Rulers 1120–1283*, ed. Huw Pryce (Cardiff, 2005)
Queller, *OA*	Donald E. Queller, *The Office of Ambassador in the Middle Ages* (Princeton, 1967)
Rec. des actes de Philippe Auguste	*Recueil des actes de Philippe Auguste*, 4 vols, ed. H. F. Delaborde (Paris, 1916–79)
RHF	*Recueil des Historiens des Gaules et de la France*, 24 vols, ed. M. Bouquet et al. (Paris, 1840–1914)

RIS	*Rerum Italicarum Scriptores*
Rot. Chart.	*Rotuli Chartarum in Turri Londiniensi Asservati*, ed. T. Duffus Hardy (London, 1837)
Rot. Litt. Claus.	*Rotuli Litterarum Clausarum in Turri Londiniensi Asservati*, 2 vols, ed. T. Duffus Hardy (London, 1833–44)
Rot. Litt. Pat.	*Rotuli Litterarum Patentium in Turri Londiniensi Asservati*, ed. T. Duffus Hardy (London, 1835)
Saxo, *DRHH*	Saxo Grammaticus, *Danorum Regum Heroumque Historia*, 3 vols, ed. Eric Christiansen (Oxford, 1981)
SHR	*Scottish Historical Review*
SJH	*Scandinavian Journal of History*
SS	*Scandinavian Studies*
Thietmar, *Chronicon*	*Thietmari Merseburgensis Episcopi Chronicon*, ed. R. Holtzmann, MGH SRG n.s., 9 (Berlin, 1955)
Torigni	*The Chronicle of Robert Torigni, abbot of Mont St Michel*, in *Chronicles of the Reigns of Stephen, Henry II and Richard I*, 4 vols, ed. R. Howlett, Rolls Series, 82 (London, 1884–89), iv.
TRHS	*Transactions of the Royal Historical Society*
Die Urkunden Friedrichs I	*Die Urkunden Friedrichs I*, 4 vols, ed. H. Appelt, (Hanover, 1975–90)
Voss, *Herrschertreffen*	Ingrid Voss, *Herrschertreffen im frühen und hohen Mittelalter* (Cologne, 1987)
WHR	*Welsh History Review*

LIST OF MAPS

PREFACE

In the course of producing this work I have incurred countless debts, many of which it will be impossible to repay. Several people were kind enough to read and comment on earlier drafts of the book and their feedback has gone a long way in helping to improve the final product: Stephen Church, Nicholas Vincent, John Gillingham, Bill Aird, Adam Kosto, Rob Liddiard, John Charmley, Carole Rawcliffe, Liesbeth van Houts and Ann Shopland. I am also indebted to the two anonymous reviewers, whose incisive comments and suggestions provided encouragement and focus. A special thank you goes to the series editor, S. H. Rigby, for ensuring that I clarified my thoughts and for making many stylistic improvements. My sister, Ellinor, kindly made a number of trips to Borås Stadsbibliotek to ask the staff to order several volumes containing the older Scandinavian historiography on twelfth-century Denmark. I am also grateful to the Arts and Humanities Research Council for providing the financial support for my PhD thesis and to Emma Brennan and Kim Walker at Manchester University Press for their efficiency and helpfulness.

In addition I have some personal debts that should be acknowledged. The first is to my family in Sweden, for always providing a warm welcome home and being supportive and encouraging despite never quite knowing what I was doing. My sisters, Ellinor Johansson and Malene Mårtensson, should be specifically mentioned for ensuring that I occasionally read books other than those containing history. The second debt is to my many former and current work colleagues who have over the years provided encouragement, help and convivial places to earn money. The third is to Ann Shopland and Emily Archer, both of whom have provided me with unfailing friendship and numerous cups of tea for more than ten years. Last, but definitely not least, I owe my sanity to my husband, Mel, for his patience, constant support and sense of humour, and to my son, Keiran, for reminding me that football is occasionally more important than medieval peacemaking. It is to my nearest and dearest, rightly, that the dedication of this book belongs.

Introduction

Few historical problems have received so much attention among those studying the modern period and so little attention among medieval scholars as that of peacemaking.[1] Searching the shelves of any university library, it is immediately apparent that the topic of peacemaking has been approached from many angles in the modern period, so that, for instance, the 1919 conference of Paris intended to settle the unresolved issues of the First World War has been studied from the vantage point of almost every individual nation represented on that occasion.[2] Yet a similar search of the literature for the medieval period yields little on the subject of peacemaking.[3] War, by contrast, carries an extensive literature for the medieval period, ranging from the detailed study of battles, foot soldiers, tactics and strategy by Verbruggen to studies of weapons, castles, the chivalric code or even the laws of war in the later Middle Ages.[4] It seems, however, that, in not writing about peace, historians have overlooked a large part of the social and political history of medieval Europe. Inevitably if we encounter war we must also at some point encounter peace: to fully understand the meaning and impact of war and warfare on medieval society we need to consider peace and war equally.

Certainly ancient and medieval thinkers often linked war and peace inextricably. Cicero's *De Officiis*, composed in 44 BC, argued that wars should be undertaken only with the aim of living in peace and security.[5] According to Philip de Souza the declared aim of restoring or imposing peace through warfare was a well-developed ideology in the Late Republic, and peace (*pax*) 'was often achieved as the result of a war'.[6] At the centre of this ideology lay the idea that wars had to be just, i.e. 'fought to bring peace to Rome and her provinces'. The *princeps* was thus 'a peacemaker because he was an *imperator*', a Roman commander who

1

had achieved victory in war.[7] Cicero argued that achievements in peace-
time could be as great as those in time of war, yet he acknowledged that
'most men accord much higher prestige to what is achieved in war than
in peace'.[8] In practice peace could also 'be obtained by direct negotiations without the recourse to war' and the emperors increasingly had to
respond to an elite residing in the provinces for whom the military culture
of Rome was less important.[9]

In the medieval period peace was intrinsically linked to Christianity.[10]
St Augustine was the central authority on ideas of peace as expressed
through his *Civitas Dei*, and his notion of peace strongly influenced
medieval political thought and the image of the peacemaking king.[11]
Christ was the highest peacemaker, reconciler of man to God through
his Incarnation and Crucifixion.[12] Peace was also the bond of charity,
and a breach of peace was a religious matter, a sin. Peace was seen as the
supreme good, as the perfect realisation of the laws of God, and attempts
to justify peace and to infuse its practice with the precepts of the Christian
religion ranged from theoretical treatises with limited applicability to
more practical programmes with an increasingly secular focus.[13] In particular these ecclesiastical notions of peace surfaced in the Peace and
Truce of God movements of the tenth, eleventh and twelfth centuries.
Both movements were characterised by the holding of councils, presided
over by bishops (sometimes with lay lords) and attended by monks (who
often brought relics with them) and large numbers of nobles, knights
and common people.[14] At these councils decrees were issued to protect
churches, churchmen and other non-combatants (and their possessions)
from attack. Sometimes threats of anathema were made against those
who contravened the decrees. Laymen swore peace-oaths on relics and
miracles occurred.[15]

As peace was seen as the perfect realisation of the laws of God, peace
in the medieval period also became a standard justification for war.[16] At
this more pragmatic level, peace was perceived as the absence of violence
and war.[17] Peace was often expressed, especially in legislative works,
in terms of personal security and the protection of goods and property.
Though this is mostly concerned with what one might term internal
peace, it is clear that the issues of personal security as well as that of goods
and property are often also found in a more international context, and
regularly featured in the terms of treaties between rulers.[18] Furthermore,
contemporaries often conflated internal and external ideas about peace
and explained them in relation to a ruler's duty as a Christian prince.
For instance William of Newburgh wrote of Henry II of England that 'he

was most diligent in defending and promoting the peace of the realm', and that 'in wielding the sword for the punishment of evildoers and the maintenance of peace and quiet for honest men, he was a true servant of God'. According to William, Henry also 'abhorred bloodshed and the sacrifice of men's lives, and strove diligently to keep the peace, wherever possible by gifts of money, but with armed force if he could not secure it likewise'.[19] Similarly Gerald of Wales proclaimed that Henry 'dreaded the doubtful arbitrament of war, and with supreme wisdom . . . he essayed every method before resorting to arms'.[20]

The single Latin term *pax* covered personal, internal and external peace, and in an international context encompassed a wide range of scenarios and vastly differing issues.[21] Gina Fasoli has argued that the Latin term *pax* was derived from an Indo-Germanic term *pak*, meaning to conclude an agreement between two parties: an agreement that not only signified the end or suspension of hostilities but also indicated the maintenance of a new situation.[22] Though peace was often seen as an absence of hostilities, goals of peace and order could be, and were, used to justify and to legitimise aggression. Isidore of Seville, for instance, describes peace as one of the four stages of war, while Fasoli has highlighted how peace tended to be perceived as something achieved through victory and hence only as a result of hostilities.[23] Similarly Michael R. Powicke has argued that war and peace in the Middle Ages were indivisible: war could be a means to peace and this meant that war in one area was necessary for peace in another.[24] More recently Ryan Lavelle has supported this by highlighting how the medieval peace often held a multi-layered significance, and how, as with warfare, peace could be a continuation of politics by other means.[25] This elastic use of the term peace (*pax*) is manifest in contemporary descriptions of peace, peacemaking and agreements, an issue dealt with more fully in the penultimate chapter.

Some historians have argued that it is easier to define what peace is *not*, than to explain what it *is*.[26] Certainly the distinction between war and peace was not absolute. The problem for the historian lies perhaps more in the nature of our sources and in the lack of secondary literature on peace in this period than in any real sense of these two ideas being at the opposite ends of the same scale. Those writing about peace and peacemaking in the twelfth century did so primarily from a theological point of view, and there are few instances when we hear the views of the main participants themselves: the kings and the nobility. Moreover, whereas the ecclesiastical notions of peace as realised in the Peace and Truce of God movements and all manner of war and warfare have received much attention in the secondary literature, historians have been less interested in exploring the practicalities of peace and peacemaking.

The lack of secondary literature on the subject of peacemaking in the Middle Ages was highlighted in 1998 by Professor Christopher Holdsworth in an article entitled 'Peacemaking in the Twelfth Century' published in *Anglo-Norman Studies*. Here Holdsworth investigated the practices surrounding the making of peace in agreements concluded during the reigns of Henry I and Henry II, and showed that they all had certain themes in common: envoys and mediators, hostages and the provisions made for keeping the agreed terms. What this book attempts to do is to develop Holdsworth's ideas and to put these, and other, common themes into a wider context by examining two case studies: peacemaking involving the kings of England and their neighbours in Britain and on the continent; and that involving the kings of Denmark and their neighbours. For England the investigation looks at the reigns of Henry II and his sons, Richard I and John, encompassing the period between 1154 and 1216. For Denmark the focus is on the reigns of Valdemar I and his sons, Cnut VI and Valdemar II, thereby covering most of the period between 1157 and 1241.

Why have these two case studies been chosen? There are many ways in which to answer this question: perhaps the most pertinent reason is that the rulers of the two kingdoms faced similar diplomatic challenges but had vastly different resources at their disposal with which to respond to those challenges. Furthermore, the challenges that these rulers faced were born out of more general trends in the medieval West relating to the formation of kingdoms, the struggle between church and state, and the cultural transition termed by Michael Clanchy as 'From Memory to Written Record'.[27] Therefore the approaches taken by the rulers of Denmark and England to the negotiation and making of peace allow us to compare and contrast practices across Europe.

The major challenge that both the Danish and English kings faced at the outset of the period was the restoration and reformation of royal authority. Most historians and students are familiar with the fact that Henry II's reign ended a period of instability and civil war in England, with Henry succeeding to the throne in 1154 as King Stephen's rightful heir as set out in the treaty of Winchester. In 1157 Valdemar I of Denmark also succeeded to his throne following a civil war, but it was one in which Valdemar emerged as a candidate only at a very late stage. Having initially supported King Svein and then another young man with royal aspirations, Cnut Magnusson, Valdemar eventually emerged victorious following the deaths of first Cnut at the Feast of Roskilde and, then, his main rival Svein at the Battle of Grathe Heath in 1157. These civil wars had not only caused havoc at a domestic level England and Denmark alike had also suffered invasions from neighbouring peoples. In consequence both Henry and Valdemar spent the first few years of their reigns consolidating their position both at home and abroad. At home Henry restored and reformed the government, while, abroad, he attempted to deal with the long-standing dispute over Gisors by contracting a marriage alliance with his French counterpart, as well as renewing the Anglo-Flemish alliance of his predecessors and dealing with the Welsh and the Scots.[28] Similarly Valdemar consolidated his position at home by introducing a number of governmental reforms as well as by responding to the external threat of Slav raids, which had plagued the kingdom during the civil wars.[29]

A second diplomatic challenge that both Henry and Valdemar faced involved the church. Henry's troubles with Thomas Becket had far more wide-ranging consequences than a simple dispute between king and archbishop. Not only did their quarrel involve the king of France, Louis VII, it must also be seen in the context of the conflict between Pope Alexander III and the Emperor Frederick Barbarossa. Valdemar also found himself embroiled in the contest between the Pope and the Emperor and, initially finding it more expedient to support his imperial neighbour, he attended the great assembly at Saint-Jean-de-Losne in 1162. Like Henry, Valdemar too had a troublesome archbishop; one who refused to support the Emperor and Valdemar's choice of pope and instead preferred temporary exile at Clairvaux.[30] It is clear that for both kings this period was one of intense diplomacy and one in which they both experienced the tricky task of balancing the aims and goals of the papacy and the church with the secular needs and demands of their kingdoms.

Thirdly, both the Danish and English kings faced the problematical issue of owing allegiance to powerful neighbours: Henry II to the kings of France, and Valdemar to the German emperor. A large part of Henry's military efforts, and therefore also his peacemaking strategies, involved or was directed against his French rival and the interference of successive French kings in Henry's quarrels with his sons. Valdemar's dealings with the Emperor Frederick Barbarossa were less confrontational because he had the 'luxury' of being the ally, though occasionally also the opponent, of Barbarossa's main rival, Henry the Lion, duke of Saxony. Only in the wake of Duke Henry's exile from the Empire in 1180 did the Danish king start to feel the impact of having his overlord as his closest neighbour. While Henry II's successors continued to battle with this issue, eventually resulting in the confiscation of most of King John's continental lands by Philip Augustus, Valdemar's sons preferred to rid themselves of the problem altogether, first by refusing to appear at the imperial diet and then by conquering the Slav lands along the northern border of the Empire. However, the consequences of re-orientating Danish foreign policy would cast a long shadow over the reigns of Valdemar I's successors, with a marriage alliance with France proving abortive and leading to long, drawn-out negotiations involving at least two different popes, and the expansion along the Baltic resulting in clashes with German petty princes, which ultimately caused the disintegration of the 'Danish Empire'.[31]

In a strange twist of fate, both Henry and Valdemar were followed on the throne by two of their sons in succession and their reigns involved a similar series of diplomatic challenges. Richard I's behaviour during the Third Crusade, his capture and captivity in the German empire on the return journey and the huge ransom demanded for his release are all well-documented events.[32] The fact that Valdemar II (1202–41) was also a crusader, not to the Holy Land but to the lands on the east coast of the Baltic Sea, and that he, too, was captured and ransomed, is perhaps less well known among English-speaking historians but, none the less, is well documented.[33] Furthermore, Richard I was faced with a serious challenge to his throne from his brother John, who, in an attempt to carry out his plan, happily involved Richard's French rival, King Philip Augustus. Similarly, Richard's Danish counterpart, Cnut VI (1182–1202), also faced rebellion, not from his brother but from his cousin, Valdemar of Slesvig. This dispute – which at various stages involved the Emperor Henry VI, the two candidates who succeeded him, and eventually Pope Innocent III – was not completely resolved until the second decade of the thirteenth century. Finally, King John's reign ended in the midst of civil war following the loss of most of the continental lands to which he had succeeded and with his opponents being led by the French king's heir, Louis. Valdemar II, known as 'Sejr' ('the Victorious'), likewise saw his Baltic empire being carved up by his neighbours following his defeat at the Battle of Bornhöved in 1227, and his death in 1241 plunged the Danish kingdom into another period in which the throne was contested between his sons.[34]

Prior to John's reign there is little evidence to show any diplomatic relations between Denmark and England, and even during John's reign the evidence is negligible. However, what is significant about these similar series of events is that they were challenges that helped to shape the kings' relations with their neighbouring rulers. From a comparative perspective this is important because we can see how kings with vastly different resources responded to similar situations. England in this period was one of the richest and most highly bureaucratised kingdoms of the medieval West, whereas Denmark is perhaps best described as an upstart. Though Denmark's linguistic heritage and social customs lay closer to those of the other Scandinavian kingdoms than those of Western Europe, the Danish kings certainly looked south and west for the development of their kingdom.[35] At an early stage there were important ecclesiastical links with England, France and the Empire, and during the twelfth century these were extended to include administration and military and cultural development. For instance, it is thought that Valdemar I's chancellor was of English origin, and one of the most influential abbots during the reign of Cnut VI, William of Ebelholt, was French. Furthermore, not only do the *acta* of the Danish kings increase greatly in numbers during this period but their formal introductions (*arengae*) also followed contemporary practice in Europe.[36] The influence of France in particular is perhaps best seen through the coronation of Cnut as co-regent with his father, Valdemar I, in 1170, a ceremony that mimicked Capetian practice and broke with established custom in Denmark.[37] Though it is clear that the kings of Denmark would not have been able to wield the financial sword in the way that, say, King John did in the lead up to the Battle of Bouvines in 1214, they evidently had enough resources to keep strong neighbours at bay, and their expansion along the Baltic was fuelled by their ability and desire to control the Baltic commerce. Hence, these two case studies show two very different kingdoms that none the less were an integral part of what historians know as the medieval West and, as such, they are important beyond their immediate geographical focus of Denmark and England. Comparing and contrasting these two case studies allow historians to see whether there were some general principles behind the making of peace in the high Middle Ages. In particular, it reveals those themes that were common to several instances of peacemaking in this period, themes which not only tell us something important about the process of making peace but also contribute to our knowledge of other important historical questions.

As peace is a complex word, it is difficult to set the parameters for a study of peacemaking. The aspect of peacemaking studied here is international, i.e. peace made between kings, peoples or the rulers of independent polities rather than between local barons or the fellow subjects of one particular polity or legal system. However, since this is a study of agreements made between princes who acted independently, it is apparent that in a period before nation states, international should be taken to mean 'inter-ruler'. Certainly, peacemaking is commonly defined in our sources by the use of specific terminology or phrases that set international negotiations aside from those of a domestic nature. For example, a meeting or a conference between two or more rulers is usually referred to by the noun *colloquium* (conference, parley, colloquy) with the domestic equivalent being *concilium* (council), *curia* (court), *placitum* (plea) or *conventus* (gathering, assembly).[38] However, the terminology used by contemporaries could be subject to great regional and stylistic variation. For instance, the German chronicler Helmold of Bosau uses *colloquium* to denote parleys involving the Danish king, whereas his continuator, Arnold of Lübeck, uses the verb *occurrere* (to hasten to meet). Similarly, whilst Roger of Howden uses *colloquium* almost continuously to denote Anglo-French conferences, he also used the noun *concilium* at least once, without there being any obvious reason for this change in usage.[39] Other contemporaries merely indicated meetings by verbs such as *colloquor* (to negotiate with) or *convenire* (to come together), which can be used to define both domestic meetings and conferences between rulers, and, on these occasions, only the circumstances or the parties involved reveal that the historian is dealing with peacemaking between rulers.

Meetings between rulers were not always solely concerned with peacemaking. As a result it can be difficult to distinguish between negotiations concerned with peace and negotiations concerned with other matters for a number of reasons. Contemporaries may not always have known or divulged why medieval princes met or negotiated, and commonly there was also more than one reason for the negotiations. Furthermore, just like today, peace in the Middle Ages could be achieved in a number of ways: through agreements that were concerned with commerce or marriage, as well as agreements following military engagements or threats thereof. The definition of peace as the absence of violence or war even allows the historian to consider agreements in which one ruler employed the military men of another ruler against a third party as peacemaking in the sense of deterring the third party from making war. There are a number of such examples from the twelfth century, both from our two case studies and elsewhere in the medieval West. For instance in 1201 Sancho of Navarre made peace, friendship and perpetual alliance with King John, promising to aid the English king against any one or all of his enemies.[40] Similarly, the text of the 1198 agreement between Philip Augustus and Philip of Swabia describes it as a treaty for the good of peace and general advantage of the kingdom ('Confederationem propter bonum pacis et publicam utilitatem'). However, the terms of the treaty reveal that this was an alliance invoking practical help against four common enemies: Richard, king of England, the imperial elect Count Otto of Poitou, Count Baldwin of Flanders and Archbishop Adolph of Cologne.[41] In the modern world agreements such as these are perhaps more likely to be regarded as alliances rather than as peace treaties, especially since no direct conflict preceded them. However, not only did medieval rulers view such agreements within the context of peace as we have seen but medieval and ancient thinkers alike often justified war as a means to peace. Thus it seems likely that texts of treaties that perhaps fit more neatly into the context of military alliances often used a language of peace because this was the ultimate goal.[42] Hence it would be wrong to exclude such treaties from a study of peacemaking in the Middle Ages. On many occasions, these agreements also offer insight into the more general principles and practices of making peace.

Diplomacy and negotiations for peace in this period frequently involved reconciliations following rebellion. As rebels often recruited the assistance of neighbouring rulers it is often difficult to treat these as wholly domestic events. For instance, the 1173–74 rebellion against Henry II included not only three of his sons, Henry the Young King, Geoffrey of Brittany and Richard, count of Poitou, but also William, king of Scots, Louis VII, king of France, Count Philip of Flanders and a number of English barons. The resolution of such situations was usually followed by separate agreements for the various parties involved, but the initial negotiations frequently involved all the parties allied against a common enemy. Here such preliminary negotiations are discussed because they are treated as being of an international nature. In terms of the agreements, however, only those concluded between two or more rulers are included. A similar approach has also been adopted for Henry II's dispute with Archbishop Thomas Becket and the French king.

Peacemaking at the highest, international, level has much in common with more localised dispute settlement. However, one important distinction between the two concerns the available evidence. Fouracre has commented that the settlement of disputes in later Merovingian Francia was based on an elaborate customary procedure and that even in cases of a political nature, with a probably predetermined outcome, the losing parties were given several opportunities to defend themselves before the final judgement. This conclusion was based on the evidence of *placita*, documents recording the final composition at the end of a lawsuit.[43] Historians of dispute settlement have a range of similar documents at their disposal, often allowing them to closely follow the whole process. These documents, categorised by Janet Nelson as being either prescriptive and normative (laws, *formulae*) or formal records of particular cases (charters, *notitiae*, *placita*), find few parallels in instances of peacemaking at the highest, international, level.[44] Treaties are rare, or at least only rarely survive, before the thirteenth century. Furthermore, there are few, if any, formal records of the peacemaking process before the year 1200. Most, perhaps all, of the treaties that exist before 1200 are available in printed form, either in collections of the *acta* of various rulers or in printed chronicles.

In contrast to the documentary records of dispute settlement, the historian of peacemaking has to rely heavily upon the evidence of narrative sources. Such evidence has a number of limitations, which have, where possible, been indicated below with reference to particular instances of peacemaking. Some general observations should, however, be noted. The Angevin Empire between 1170 and c.1200 is by far the best-documented geographical area in Europe. This is largely due to the writings of five chroniclers: Roger of Howden, Robert de Torigny, Ralph de Diceto, Gervase of Canterbury and William of Newburgh. It is well known that the first three of these were eyewitnesses to one or more instances of peacemaking and that they held positions that placed them close to the royal court.[45] Howden, Diceto and Gervase, moreover, had access to documents and included copies of agreements in their texts.[46] The works of these five chroniclers span between thirty fifty years each – a long period compared to other European chroniclers such as Otto of Freising, who, though an eyewitness to events long before Frederick Barbarossa's accession to the throne in 1152, comments in detail only upon the events of the early 1150s. Furthermore, the works of these five chroniclers can be supplemented with and compared to other narrative sources also covering all or parts of the reigns of Henry II, Richard I and John, such as Ralph of Coggeshall and the *Histoire de Guillaume le Maréchal*.

Denmark, by contrast provides only the bare modicum of written sources from which to study peacemaking. Only the reign of Valdemar I (1157–82) is contemporary to the two principal Danish sources: the *Danorum Regum Heroumque Historia* of Saxo Grammaticus and the *Short History of the Kings of Denmark* of Sven Aggesen. Although *Knytlingasaga* provides an additional, if late, narrative for the period up to 1185, which supplies many details not found in the histories of Saxo and Sven, the other Danish sources, mostly annals, date from the second decade of the thirteenth century or later, and the entries are usually too short to contain much of value. Furthermore, only four written agreements involving a Danish king survive from this period and they are all concerned with the same matter, namely the release from captivity of Valdemar II and his son during the mid-1220s.[47] The German chroniclers Helmold of Bosau and Arnold of Lübeck provide useful comparative accounts of the period before 1190, even though most German chroniclers and annalists took little notice of events north of the Empire. As a consequence of these differences in the available evidence from England and Denmark, we cannot compare like for like. Instead the case studies are examples of what can be achieved by studying the best-documented kingdom and one of the worst-documented kingdoms in the medieval West.

The available evidence for dispute settlement as opposed to that for international diplomacy shows that disputes were most commonly over property.[48] However, though it is sometimes possible to hazard a guess at the causes of war among rulers, it is often impossible to pinpoint them exactly. To take one example, when war broke out between Henry II and Louis VII of France in 1167, Gervase of Canterbury recorded that this was because of the dispute over the city of Toulouse 'and various other things'.[49] Robert Torigni, however, believed that war broke out because of a quarrel over the money that had been collected for the crusade to the Holy Land.[50] Often several issues blended together and the building of alliances further blurred the reasons for beginning a specific conflict. Perhaps it would be most apt to conclude, as Paul Fouracre has done for the Merovingian period, that the kings and princes of medieval Europe struggled for power and prestige, often, but not always, presented as power based on military might. Fouracre has further commented that it is clear that 'a struggle for power cannot be reduced to the sort of dispute over a limited issue' that we find recorded in the *placita* and other such records.[51] The struggle for power among medieval rulers is yet another example of what gives international peacemaking its particular and peculiar character and which sets it aside from that of dispute settlement.

In the Middle Ages there were generally understood principles of how to negotiate and to make peace. From the evidence, five main issues can be identified: meeting places; symbolic acts; envoys; oaths and hostages; and treaties. Though we rarely find all of these elements in a recorded instance of peacemaking, by and large these are the features which occur most frequently and so must provide the basis for the investigation. Key questions about the peacemaking process thus include: where did medieval rulers meet to make peace? Why did they meet at particular places? Which commonly occurring acts and ceremonies are found surrounding the making of peace? What were their functions? Who were the envoys and negotiators? What powers did they have to conclude and negotiate agreements? By what means were treaties guaranteed? What role did the written word serve in the peacemaking process? What terminology did contemporaries use to define peace, peacemaking and agreements? More general issues include whether there were differences in practices between regions or rulers? Were there differences in practices between successful and unsuccessful peacemaking? How did peacemaking and diplomacy regulate the relationship(s) between individuals or groups of people? For instance, did peacemaking between equals differ from peacemaking between victor and vanquished, or Christian and non-Christian? This book, then, is an exploration of these themes in a context of the kingdoms of Denmark and England and a search for points of similarity and contrast with European trends.

Notes

1 The exception is, of course, the vast literature on the Peace and Truce of God movements. See for example *The Peace of God: Social Violence and Religious Response in France around the Year 1000*, ed. Thomas Head and Richard Landes (Ithaca, 1992); Michel de Bouard, 'Sur les origines de la Trève de Dieu en Normandie', *Annales de Normandie*, 9 (1959), 169–89; Jane Martindale, 'Peace and War in Early Eleventh-century Aquitaine', in *Medieval Knighthood IV: Papers from the Fifth Strawberry Hill Conference 1990*, ed. Christopher Harper-Bill and Ruth Harvey (Woodbridge, 1992), 147–76; T. Bisson, 'The Organized Peace in Southern France and Catalonia, ca. 1140–ca. 1233', *American Historical Review*, 82 (1977), 290–311. Diane Wolfthal has also noted that peace has attracted more scholars from the sciences than from the humanities. Diane Wolfthal, 'Introduction', in *Peace and Negotiation: Strategies for Coexistence in the Middle Ages and the Renaissance*, ed. Diane Wolfthal, Arizona Studies in the Middle Ages and the Renaissance, 4 (Turnhout, 2000), xi–xii.

2 See for example Margaret MacMillan, *Peacemakers: The Paris Conference of 1919 and Its Attempt to End War* (London, 2001); *The Paris Peace Conference, 1919. Peace without Victory?*, ed. Michael Dockrill and John Fisher (Basingstoke, 2001); *The Treaty of Versailles – A Reassessment after 75 Years*, ed. Manfred F. Boemeke, Gerald D. Feldman and Elisabeth Glaser (Cambridge, 1998); Francis Deák, *Hungary at the Paris Peace Conference* (New York, 1972); Alma Maria Luckau, *The German Delegation at the Paris Peace Conference* (New York, 1971); Démétrios Kitsikés, *Propagande et pressions en politique internationale: La Grèce et ses revendications a la Conférence de la Paix* (Paris, 1963); A. Walworth, *Wilson and His Peacemakers: American Diplomacy at the Paris Peace Conference, 1919* (New York, 1991)

3 F.-L. Ganshof, *Le Moyen Âge. Histoire des relations internationale* (Paris, 1953) provides a broad setting to the topic of peacemaking. Ganshof's work is available in English as *The Middle Ages: A History of International Relations*, tr. R. I. Hall

(London, 1970). For peacemaking in the early medieval period, see Ingrid Voss, *Herrschertreffen im frühen und hohen Mittelalter* (Cologne, 1987); Paul Kershaw, 'Rex Pacificus: Studies in Royal Peacemaking and the Image of the Peacemaking King', unpublished Ph.D. thesis (London, 1999). For peacemaking in the later medieval period, see also Werner Kolb, *Herrscherbegegnungen im Mittelalter* (Frankfurt, 1988); J. G. Russell, *Peacemaking in the Renaissance* (London, 1986), 82–3.

4   Good introductions to this topic can be found in J. F. Verbruggen, *The Art of Warfare in Western Europe during the Middle Ages: From the Eighth Century to 1340*, 2nd edn (Woodbridge, 1997); M. H. Keen, *The Laws of War in the Late Middle Ages* (London, 1965); Philippe Contamine, *La guerre au Moyen Âge* (Paris, 1980).

5   'Quare suscipienda quidem bella sunt ob eam causa, ut sine inuiria in pace vivatur.' Cicero, *De Officiis*, I:35.

6   Philip de Souza, '*Parta victoriis pax*: Roman Emperors as Peacemakers', in *War and Peace in Ancient and Medieval History*, ed. Philip de Souza and John France (Cambridge, 2008), 77, 85.

7   De Souza, '*Parta victoriis pax*', 81, 85.

8   Cicero, *De Officiis*, I:74, 77, 79–80.

9   De Souza, '*Parta victoriis pax*', 81, 106. For some examples, see J. W. Rich, 'Augustus, War and Peace', in *The Representation and Perception of Roman Imperial Power*, ed. L. de Blois (Amsterdam, 2003), 329–57; 'Treaties, Allies and the Roman Conquest of Italy', in *War and Peace in Ancient and Medieval History*, ed. Philip de Souza and John France (Cambridge, 2008) 51–75

10 Antony Adolf's recent work contains a brief summary of peace theory in the Middle Ages. His work, however, is primarily useful for the comparisons that can be made with other periods and different cultural traditions. Antony Adolf, *Peace. A World History* (Cambridge, 2009).

11 Kershaw, 'Rex Pacificus', 22–5, 243–4.

12 Thomas Renna, 'The Idea of Peace in the West, 500–1150', *Journal of Medieval History*, 6 (1980), 147; R. P. Martin, *Reconciliation. A Study of Paul's Theology* (London, 1980); Adolf, *Peace*, 103–4.

13 Gina Fasoli, 'Pace e guerra nell'alto medioevo', *Settimane di studio del centro italiano di studi sull'alto medioevo, XV, Ordinamenti militari in Occidente nell'alto medioevo* (Spoleto, 1968), repr. in *Scritti di storia medievale*, ed. G. Fasoli et al. (Bologna, 1974), 86–7; Kiril Petkov, *The Kiss of Peace* (Leiden, 2003) 1. See also discussion in Contamine, *La guerre au Moyen Âge*, 420–433, 462–4; Renna, 'The Idea of Peace', 153–4.

14 Head, *The Peace of God*, 19; Bisson, 'The Organized Peace in Southern France and Catalonia', 290–311; Bouard, 'Sur les origines de la Trève de Dieu en Normandie', 169–89. For a good summary of the developments of these two movements, see the introductory chapter of *The Peace of God*, ed. Head and Landes, 1–20. See also A. Grabois, 'De la trève de Dieu à la paix du roi. Étude sur la transformation du mouvement du paix au XIIe siècle', *Mélanges offert à*

René Crozet, 2 vols, ed. Pierre Gallais et Yves-Jean Riou (Poitiers, 1966), 585–96; Dominique Barthélemy, *L'an mil et la paix de Dieu: la France chrétienne et féodale, 980–1060* (Paris, 1999).

15 Paul Dalton, 'Civil War and Ecclesiastical Peace in the Reign of King Stephen', in *War and Society in Medieval and Early Modern Britain*, ed. Diana Dunn (Liverpool, 2000) 54; Contamine, *La guerre au Moyen Âge*, 434–5.

16 The essential study on the so called 'just war' is F. H. Russell, *The Just War in the Middle Ages* (Cambridge, 1977). On Augustine and the just war, see Renna, 'The Idea of Peace', 148; Augustine, *City of God*, xix.12. On how this translated into peacemaking between Christian kings and non-Christian leaders in the early medieval period, see Richard Abels, 'Paying the Danegeld: Anglo-Saxon Peacemaking with the Vikings', in *War and Peace in Ancient and Medieval History*, ed. Philip de Souza and John France (Cambridge, 2008), 176–7. For the later medieval period, see S. H. Rigby, *Wisdom and Chivalry: Chaucer's Knight's Tale and Medieval Political Theory* (Leiden, 2009), 187.

17 Kershaw, 'Rex Pacificus', 20; N. Lund, 'Peace and Non-peace in the Viking Age – Ottar in Biarmaland, the Rus in Byzantium, and Danes and Norwegians in England', *Proceedings of the Tenth Viking Congress*, ed. J. E. Knirk (Oslo, 1987), 255; Abels, 'Paying the Danegeld', 177–9.

18 For a few such examples, see *Codice diplomatico della repubblica di Genova*, i, nos 76, 105, 139; *ibid.*, ii, nos 25, 48; *Die Urkunden Friedrichs I*, iii, no. 695.

19 *Newburgh*, i, 282.

20 *Giraldi Cambrensis Opera*, v, 303.

21 Kershaw, 'Rex Pacificus', 21; J. Goebel, *Felony and Misdemeanor. A Study in the History of the Criminal Law* (Philadelphia, 1976), 423–4. See also R. I. Moore's comments on peace being a word with many meanings. R. I. Moore, 'Postscript', in Head, *The Peace of God*, 308.

22 Fasoli, 'Pace e guerra nell'alto medioevo', 80.

23 *Isidori Hispalensis Episcopi Etymologiarum sive originum libri XX*, 2 vols, ed. W. M. Lindsay (Oxford, 1911; repr. 1995), XVIII:x; Fasoli, 'Pace e guerra nell'alto medioevo', 85. An interesting comparison can be drawn with John of Worcester's description of King Stephen: 'Stephen is the king of peace. If he were only the king of firm justice, crushing his enemies under foot, assessing all things with the balanced lance of judgement, protecting and strengthening with his mighty power the friends of peace.' Peace was hence something achieved through force, not negotiation. *The Chronicle of John of Worcester*, 3 vols, ed. R. R. Darlington and P. McGurk (Oxford, 1995–98), iii, 268–9.

24 Michael R. Powicke, 'War as a Means to Peace: Some Late Medieval Themes', in *Documenting the Past: Essays in Medieval History Presented to George Peddy Cuttino*, ed. J. S. Hamilton and Patricia J. Bradley (Woodbridge, 1989), 217.

25 Ryan Lavelle, 'Towards a Political Contextualization of Peacemaking and Peace Agreements in Anglo-Saxon England', in Wolfthal, *Peace and Negotiation*, 39.

26 Lund, 'Peace and Non-peace', 255; Fasoli, 'Pace e guerra nell'alto medioevo', 80.

27 Michael Clanchy, *From Memory to Written Record. England 1066–1307*, 2nd edn (London, 1992).

28 W. L. Warren, *Henry II* (New Haven, 2000), 54–81; Jean Dunbabin, 'Henry II
    and Louis VII', in *Henry II: New Interpretations*, ed. Christopher Harper-Bill
    and Nicholas Vincent (Woodbridge, 2007), 49–50, 53–6; A. A. M. Duncan, 'John
    King of England and the Kings of Scots', in *King John: New Interpretations*, ed.
    S. D. Church (Woodbridge, 1999), 249; R. R. Davies, *Conquest, Coexistence, and
    Change. Wales 1063–1415* (Oxford, 1987), 51–2.

29 Erich Hoffman, 'The Unity of the Kingdom and the Provinces in Denmark during
    the Middle Ages', in *Danish Medieval History: New Currents*, ed. Niels Skyum-
    Nielsen and Niels Lund (Copenhagen, 1981), 101–3, 105.

30 Jørgen Qvistgaard Hansen, '*Regnum et sacerdotium*: Forholdet mellem stat og
    kirke i Danmark 1157–70', in *Middelalder studier tilegnede Aksel E. Christensen
    på tresårsdagen* (Copenhagen, 1966), 57–76. For a brief summary of these events
    in English, see Jakob Benediktsson, 'Denmark', in *Medieval Scandinavia: An
    Encyclopedia*, ed. Phillip Pulsiano et al. (New York, 1993), 128; Malcolm Barber,
    The Two Cities: Medieval Europe 1050–1320 (London, 1992), 385. On Archbishop
    Eskil of Lund, see also the brief account in Eric Christiansen, *The Northern
    Crusades* (London, 1980), 60.

31 For an analysis of the Dano-imperial relationship, see Odilo Engels, 'Friedrich
    Barbarossa und Dänemark', in *Friedrich Barbarossa. Handlungsspielräume und
    Wirkungsweisen des staufischen Kaisers*, ed. A. Haverkamp (Sigmaringen, 1992),
    353–85; Alan V. Murray, 'The Danish Monarchy and the Kingdom of Germany,
    1197–1319: the Evidence of Middle High German Poetry', in *Scandinavia and
    Europe 800–1350. Contact, Conflict, and Coexistence*, ed. Jonathan Adams and
    Katherine Holman (Turnhout, 2004), 291–2. On Danish expansion along the
    Baltic and its ultimate failure, see Christiansen, *The Northern Crusades*, 65–8,
    109–13; Grethe Jacobsen, 'Wicked Count Henry: the Capture of Valdemar II
    (1223) and Danish Influence in the Baltic', *Journal of Baltic Studies*, 9 (1978),
    326–38. For the 1193 marriage alliance between Philip Augustus of France and
    Ingeborg of Denmark, see J. E. M. Benham, 'Philip Augustus and the Angevin
    Empire: The Scandinavian Connexion', *Mediaeval Scandinavia*, 14 (2004),
    37–50; Robert Davidsohn, *Philipp II August von Frankreich und Ingeborg*
    (Stuttgart, 1888).

32 For a masterly summary, see John Gillingham, *Richard I* (Yale, 1999), 123–253.

33 See Jacobsen, 'Wicked Count Henry: the Capture of Valdemar II', 326–38, and
    footnotes therein.

34 Murray, 'The Danish Monarchy and the Kingdom of Germany', 294; Christiansen,
    The Northern Crusades, 65–8, 109–13; Jacobsen, 'Wicked Count Henry: the
    Capture of Valdemar II (1223) and Danish Influence in the Baltic', 326–36.

35 For a short introduction to the development and orientation of Scandinavian cul-
    ture in this period, see Sverre Bagge, 'On the Far Edge of Dry Land: Scandinavian
    and European Culture in the Middle Ages', in *Scandinavia and Europe 800–1350*,
    ed. Jonathan Adams and Katherine Holman (Turnhout, 2004), 355–9.

36 For an introduction to the many cultural and ecclesiastical links between Denmark
    and France in the twelfth century, see T. Riis, 'Autour du mariage de 1193:
    l'épouse, son pays et les relations Franco-Danoises', in *La France de Philippe*

15

Auguste: le temps des mutations, ed. R.-H. Bautier (Paris, 1982) 341–61. See also
Barber, *The Two Cities*, 385; Lucien Musset, *Les peuples scandinaves au Moyen
Âge* (Paris, 1951), 181–3; Kai Hørby, 'The Social History of Medieval Denmark', in
Danish Medieval History: New Currents, 39–42.

37 Note also that this event took place in the same year that Henry II crowned his
son, Henry, as king, again breaking with tradition.

38 Timothy Reuter, 'Assembly Politics in Western Europe from the Eighth Century
to the Twelfth', in *The Medieval World*, ed. Peter Linehan and Janet L. Nelson
(London, 2001), 433.

39 Howden, *Gesta*, i, 272.

40 Rymer, *Foedera*, I, i, 126–8. The peacemaking strategies of early medieval
rulers also frequently included such methods. For some examples, see *Annales
Bertiniani*, ed. G. Waitz, MGH SRG, 9 (Hanover, 1883), 57–8; *Annales Xantenses
et Annales Vedastini*, ed. B. de Simson, MGH SRG, 12 (Hanover, 1909), 52. For
a discussion, see also Richard Abels, 'King Alfred's Peace-making Strategies with
the Vikings', *HSJ*, 3 (1991), 30.

41 *Philippi regis constitutiones*, ed. L. Weiland, MGH Const., 2 (Hanover, 1896), 1.
Commercial treaties were also frequently couched in a language of peace and charity. The 1161 treaty between Duke Henry the Lion of Saxony and the Gotlanders
is one such example. K. Jordan, *Urkunden Heinrichs des Löwen* (Stuttgart,
1957–60), no. 48.

42 For an interesting discussion on how political alliances in the late tenth century
used the language of peace and friendship in order to control war and violence,
see Brian Patrick McGuire, 'Friendship and Peace in the Letters of Gerbert,
982–97', in his *War and Peace in the Middle Ages* (Copenhagen, 1987), 29–55.

43 Paul Fouracre, '*Placita* and the Settlement of Disputes in Later Merovingian
Francia', in *The Settlement of Disputes in Early Medieval Europe*, ed. Wendy
Davies and Paul Fouracre (Cambridge, 1992), 37. See also Patrick J. Geary, 'Land,
Language and Memory in Europe 700–1100', *TRHS*, 6th ser., 9 (1999), 170.

44 Janet L. Nelson, 'Dispute Settlement in Carolingian West Francia', in *The
Settlement of Disputes in Early Medieval Europe*, 45; Stephen D. White, 'From
Peace to Power: The Study of Disputes in Medieval France', in *Medieval
Transformations: Texts, Power and Gifts in Context*, ed. E. Cohen and M. B. de
Jong (Leiden, 2001), 205; Geary, 'Land, Language and Memory', 170. Compare
also Adam J. Kosto's investigation of agreements in eleventh- and twelfth-century
Catalonia, which was based on about a thousand *convenientiae*.

45 *Diceto*, i, p. ix, lxxii–lxxvi; *ibid.*, ii, p. xxxii; Antonia Gransden, *Historical
Writing in England, c.55 0 to c.1307* (London, 1996), 223–4, 230–1, 235, 243; J.
Gillingham, 'The Travels of Roger of Howden and His Views of the Irish, Scots
and Welsh', *ANS*, 20 (1998), 151–69.

46 John Gillingham, 'Roger of Howden on Crusade', in his *Richard Coeur de Lion.
Kingship, Chivalry and War in the Twelfth Century* (London, 1994), 143.

47 *Diplomatarium Danicum*, I:5, no. 217; I:6, nos 16, 17, 42.

48 Nelson, 'Dispute Settlement in Carolingian West Francia', 55; Geary, 'Land,
Language and Memory', 170–1. For some examples of disputes, see S. D. White,

'Feuding and Peacemaking in the Touraine around the year 1000', *American Journal of Legal History*, 22 (1978), 281–308; Patrick J. Geary, 'Vivre en conflit dans une France sans état: Typologie des méchanismes de règlement des conflits, 1050–1200', *Annales: Economies, Sociétés, Civilisations*, 41 (1986), 1107–33. See also Petkov's study of the settlement of disputes in the high and late medieval period, which includes some good evidence from urban centres. Petkov, *The Kiss of Peace: Ritual, Self and Society in the High and Late Medieval West*.

49 *Gervase of Canterbury*, i, 203.
50 *Torigni*, 230.
51 Fouracre, '*Placita* and the Settlement of Disputes in Later Merovingian Francia', 38.

PART I

Meeting places

1

Meetings between equals

At the heart of the medieval peacemaking process stood the face-to-face meeting.[1] Conferences between rulers are frequently mentioned in the sources of the period, yet chroniclers often tell us more about where these parleys took place than they do about what was decided. It is only right then that we begin by asking not only where medieval rulers met but also why the issue of location was so important.

In 1202 King John, as count of Aquitaine and Anjou, was summoned by King Philip Augustus to his court at Paris to submit to its judgement, answer for his wrongs and comply with the law, as determined by his peers. In reply to this summons, King John is said to have answered that, as duke of Normandy, he was not obliged to attend a court in Paris, but had only to confer with the king of the French on the boundary between the kingdom and his duchy (*inter utrosque fines*). According to the chronicler who recorded this exchange of opinions, John furthermore claimed that this arrangement had been agreed in ancient times and confirmed in genuine documents.[2] No documents survive today that incontrovertibly prove that the dukes of the Normans had previously met with the kings of the French on the border between their respective territories, but it is clear that King John had strong precedents for such a claim, even if a document confirming it had never existed. Indeed it is clear that the dukes of the Normans and the kings of the French had a traditional meeting place on the border.[3] According to the chronicler Roger of Howden, Philip Augustus in 1188 in a fit of rage and frustration chopped down the elm tree 'between Gisors and Trie where parleys had always been held between the kings of the French and the Norman dukes'.[4] This is only one of a handful of references to this particular elm tree among the sources.[5] Though the elm tree is not frequently mentioned in the sources, meetings between Gisors and Trie are. At least six conferences can thus be seen to have taken place at or near this elm tree. The first of the meetings recorded as having taken place here occurred in 1167, when the exiled archbishop, Thomas Becket, met with Henry II in November, in the presence of two cardinals and numerous supporters of both sides.[6] Another was recorded under the entry for September 1173 when Louis VII tried to mediate between Henry II and his rebellious sons.[7] On St Nicholas's day (6 December) 1183, Henry II did homage to Philip Augustus and promised to give Gisors to the French king's sister, Alice, upon her marriage to one of Henry's sons.[8] In January 1188, when Henry met with King Philip Augustus at the elm tree, the French king renewed his claim to the castle of Gisors and insisted on the marriage between his half-sister, Alice, and Richard, count of Poitou.[9] Later that same year King Philip then decided to chop the tree down in a dramatic display of erasing the spot where peace had been concluded in the past.[10] Yet, despite this disappearance of the tree, the Norman barons seem to have met with Philip, upon his return from the Third Crusade in 1191, at that same traditional meeting place.[11]

There are other pieces of evidence that indicate that there may have been more conferences held at or near the elm tree. In Roger of Howden's entry describing the elm's destruction, the conference held between Philip and Henry was initially referred to as taking place at Gisors.[12] There were several other parleys supposedly held at Gisors. The first of these meetings was recorded as having taken place as early as 965, when King Lothar of the west Franks made an alliance with Duke Richard I near Gisors.[13] Almost 150 years later, in 1113, Gisors was the appointed place for a conference between Henry I and Louis VI 'the Fat'.[14] During Henry II's reign at least seven meetings were recorded as having taken place at Gisors. The first of these took place in 1158, when the arrangements concerning the marriage of Henry (later known as 'the Young King') to Louis VII's daughter were discussed.[15] It would seem that during the 1160s three meetings took place near the town: in 1160, 1161 and 1164.[16] In September 1173 one of two attempts to mediate between Henry II and his sons was also made near that same place.[17] Only two years later another conference took place there, and in 1180, the so-called treaty of Ivry was renewed at Gisors, as was also the alliance between Henry II and the count of Flanders.[18] Next year Henry used this particular meeting place again when he acted as a mediator between Philip Augustus and the count of Flanders, and in 1186, the settlement of the dower of Philip Augustus's sister, Margaret, was also confirmed there.[19]

It is not very likely that these negotiations for peace actually took place at Gisors itself, the ownership of which had been fiercely disputed throughout the twelfth century.[20] A meeting at this stronghold would surely have rubbed salt into wounds instead of providing the setting for negotiating agreements. Furthermore, an entry in the chronicle of Roger of Howden gives historians an insight into how some contemporary commentators recorded the places where conferences were held. In 1200 Philip Augustus and King John held a conference between Boutavant, *castellum regis Anglie*, and Goulet, *castellum regis Francie*.[21] On the strength of this it is possible to suggest that when the English chroniclers stated that the French kings and the Norman dukes met at Gisors, they simply meant that this was a well-known fortress close to the actual site of the meeting.[22] Thus a parley at Gisors could quite possibly have meant a meeting at the elm tree. This would put the total of known conferences at this elm around fourteen, in the twelfth century alone.[23]

There is another meeting place that seems to have been used regularly by the dukes of Normandy and the kings of France. Between 1181 and 1190 a place named by the chroniclers as 'Vadum Sancti Remigii' was associated with parleys at least five times. In 1181 and 1187 it was the setting for conferences between Henry II and Philip Augustus.[24] In 1189, and twice in 1190, peace was made and confirmed in this same place between Richard I and Philip Augustus.[25] Modern historians have often used the direct French translation 'Gué Saint Remy', without indicating that this is the name not only of a place but also of a crossing point on the river Avre.[26] The ford seems to have been near the Norman castle of Nonancourt.[27] This should again alert historians to the fact that some *colloquia* said to have taken place at Nonancourt most probably did not, but instead took place at the ford. On the strength of this the number of meetings at this ford would total seven in the reigns of Henry II and Richard I.

The fact that the elm tree and the ford of St Remigius served as two of the traditional meeting places between the dukes of the Normans and the kings of the French is of immense importance, because it highlights a problem in medieval history that has been much debated among modern historians, that of borders. It is, furthermore, a topic that is of vital importance for how historians view the relationship between the Norman duke and the French king and our views on both of these problems have an impact on how we think these two rulers made peace. The problem of borders has usually been tackled in relation to the question of whether historians should demarcate the political borders of medieval Europe as lines or as so-called 'marches'. There has been a tendency among historians to mark out the boundaries of medieval Europe chiefly through rivers and mountain ranges to create clear territorial units that usually contained a homogenous population with similar religious beliefs, customs and laws.[28] Historical geographers like W. Gordon East and Xavier de Planhol and historians such as Timothy Reuter have commented that the division of 843, for example, saw, in geographical terms, the emergence of France and, to a limited degree, also the emergence of Germany.[29] The division at Verdun set west Frankia within four rivers: the Escaut, the Meuse, the Saône and the Rhône. In the east and north-east this was roughly the border that continued to separate France from the Empire until the sixteenth century.[30] Similarly the duchy of Normandy, as one of the earliest principalities to be formed out of the crumbling Carolingian empire, has often been seen as being contained within the distinctive lines formed by the rivers Epte, Eure and Avre.[31] Several historians and historical geographers have commented on how these medieval political boundaries often followed much older demarcations. Charlemagne's division of his empire into some three hundred *pagi* largely recognised the original *pagi* of Celtic and Roman Gaul, the equivalent in the German lands beyond the Rhine being the *Gaue*, many of which became the counties and duchies of a later period.[32] Some of these divisions still persist as geographical entities and their survival has partly been explained by the fact that many of the original *pagi* were contained within stretches of land of a particular geological character which tended to give them a certain uniformity in natural vegetation and in economic possibilities.[33] Similarly many of the parish boundaries within England have been found to belong to the Roman or Iron Age period.[34]

Despite this it is not at all clear that medieval men and women had this particular concept of territorial units and their borders. Indeed, historians have increasingly tended to criticise descriptions of medieval territorial units enclosed by linear borders. For instance, while Lemarignier saw the duchy of Normandy as having a homogenous population and as being enclosed by definite legal and administrative boundaries, roughly equivalent to the rivers Epte, Eure and Avre, comparable to that of a 'state', Timothy Reuter pointed out that, although historians often speak of medieval kingdoms and duchies as states, to refer to France or even Normandy is a convenience and a far cry from the fully formed modern European nation states.[35] Though descriptions such as *Francia* or *Normannia* often appear in contemporary narrative sources, it is surely significant that, until the thirteenth century, medieval princes defined themselves in charters and treaties not usually as rulers of specific territories but as rulers of people. Thus Philip Augustus was not king of France but king of the French, 'rex Francorum', and Henry II was not king of England and duke of Normandy but king of the English and duke of the Normans, 'rex Anglorum et dux Normannorum'.[36]

Similarly one of Lemarignier's most recent critics, Daniel Power, has conclusively shown the difficulty in trying to locate the boundary of Normandy along the rivers of Epte, Eure and Avre, when both the Norman duke and the French king laid claim to and held patronage on both sides of this dividing line.[37] Power and others, including Léopold Génicot and Michel Bur, two pioneers in the now blossoming genre of frontier studies, have focused their research on describing borders not in terms of lines but in terms of zones. Génicot and Bur described one such zone, that spanning the Franco-imperial border respectively in the Namurois, and between Lorraine and Champagne, as 'blending rights and possessions resulting from marriage, inheritance, purchase and contracts'.[38] The phenomenon can be found in the eleventh-century epic poem *The Ruodlieb*, whose anonymous author described how the friendship with their border neighbours was maintained: 'They went to each other's countries to purchase whatever they wanted, sometimes paying the toll and sometimes collecting it. Our girls married their men, and they gave us their daughters in marriage. They became mutual godparents, and those who were not were called so.'[39] According to Génicot and Bur the effect of these interactions was a 'fringe' where the known points may be precisely defined but where, taken as a whole, the 'frontier' itself remains blurred and difficult to map on account of repeated alterations of individual details.[40] Daniel Power has noted how the waterways running through and surrounding Normandy subjected different parts of the duchy to contradictory influences from England, the Île-de-France and Anjou, influences which were reflected, for instance, in styles of architecture. Thus the aristocracy living around the duchy's borders often had more in common with their immediate neighbours on the 'other side' than with the inhabitants of central Normandy.[41] In a period when kings and dukes were rulers of people and not territorial units, this 'disunity' is of crucial importance. Though Power recognised that the survival of Norman identity, a 'gens Normannorum', into the twelfth century could be seen in instances like the provincial tournament teams described by the author of the *Histoire de Guillaume le Maréchal*, it was clear to him that, in everyday practicality, religious endowments and patronage crossed those rivers that might be seen as the natural boundaries of the duchy.[42] These different influences created divided loyalties among the aristocracies of these marches, and it was these loyalties and customs that were regulated

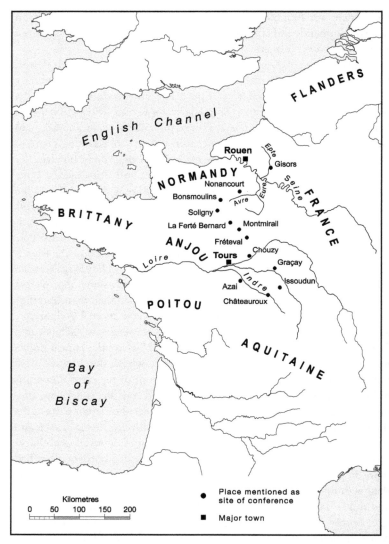

1   Anglo-French peace conferences during the reign of Henry II

in many twelfth-century treaties. For example the 1195 peace between Richard I of England and Philip Augustus does not attempt to set down a record of the political border between the respective territories of the two kings, despite the fact that King Philip had, during Richard's captivity in the Empire, captured several strongholds and thus altered the traditional border. Instead the treaty shows a great concern with unravelling and determining the loyalty and adherence of certain 'marcher lords', such as Hugh de Gournai, and certain 'marcher castles', among them Pacy, Vernon and Vaudreuil.[43] In all of this linear borders seem neither vitally important nor particularly useful.

Lemarignier's study has influenced two generations of historians and, despite some flaws, his definition of a border as something that keeps a well-governed and homogenous population separate from their neighbours is an idea that has been accepted even among his fiercest critics. Whereas Power argued that Lemarignier's theory was untenable because the well-defined boundaries of the duchy did not prevent cultural or political influences from Normandy's neighbours dividing the so-called *Gens Normannorum*, others, such as Robert Helmerichs, have concluded that the duchy had no clearly defined boundaries because the many rivers of the duchy, instead of forming barriers to entry, served as pathways, making it difficult to stop foreign invaders from entering the principality.[44] Helmerichs's and Power's arguments have also been echoed by Michelle Warren who has commented that 'topography does not . . . provide stable grounds for difference'.[45] But no one claims or has claimed that a border or a boundary has to be impregnable. It is perhaps desirable but it is not a prerequisite, for it is arguable that too many historians equate boundaries with barriers. All these historians, including Lemarignier, despite their different theories about frontiers, share the same starting point, a wish to decide firmly whether or not the divisions between the territorial units of medieval Europe should be referred to as 'marches' or borders. Yet this is almost certainly too rigid, since it is quite possible that medieval people themselves made no such distinction.

This is where the evidence of meeting places for conferences can provide an important insight. The evidence of the elm tree and the ford of St Remigius clearly shows that meeting places were a statement by two princes that those two sites were regarded as forming part of the border at the time of meeting. These two rulers did not meet in the 'march' as claimed by Ganshof in his influential work on international relations.[46] They met instead on border sites, just as King John is said to have claimed in 1202.[47] Moreover, conferences were not held in the 'march'. They had to take place in locations that were not controlled by either party, and, as has so convincingly been argued by Daniel Power, 'marches' were places where lordship overlapped; as such they were not places ideally suited for meetings between rulers. The only solution to such a problem would have been to hold parleys on sites that acted as clearly recognisable borders. The border did not have to act as a barrier, it merely needed to be a recognisable feature agreed by two or more parties, and there can be no doubt that such features were often, but not always, along rivers.[48] Thus when Diceto stated that the elm tree was rooted within the limits of France, the chronicler probably meant that it stood on the French side of the bank of the river Epte and not that the Norman duke met with the French king on royal territory.[49] Most importantly, every parley between the duke of the Normans and the French kings at the elm or at the ford near Nonancourt was a mutual agreement that this was a site marking the border at that particular time.

This argument is supported if we trace the sites of conferences between the Norman dukes and the French kings in the period 1154–99. With the accession of Henry II in 1154, the Norman duke was a medieval prince not only in a dual but in a multiple capacity: king of the English, duke of the Normans and the Aquitanians and count of the Angevins. Consequently, the vastness of the territories ruled by Henry II had an impact on where conferences were held. Meetings on the Norman border were prominent, but, given who Henry was, it is hardly surprising to find that his movements shifted further south than his predecessors, as conferences were now also held on the borders of the duchy of Aquitaine.[50] According to Ralph de Diceto, Henry II and Louis VII 'became friends' at a conference near Fréteval in late 1161 or possibly early 1162, after almost engaging in a battle.[51] In November 1177 a conference was held near Graçay on the river Fouzon in Berry, to settle certain issues left over from the negotiations at the ford of St Remigius earlier that year.[52] Châteauroux, on the river Indre, provided the approximate location for the conclusion of a truce in 1187.[53] In 1188 an ineffectual conference took place somewhere between Bonsmoulins and Soligny. It seems likely that the breakdown of the negotiations at this meeting was the direct cause of Richard, count of Poitou, openly siding with Philip Augustus against his father.[54] At least two conferences were held near La Ferté Bernard on the river Huisne, which marked the border between Maine and the territory of the French king, one in 1168 and another in June 1189.[55] On 4 July 1189 one of Henry II's last acts was to conclude a peace with King Philip Augustus on a site near Tours between the rivers Loire and Indre, which the French chroniclers, Rigord and William the Breton, specifically locate at Colombiers ('Colombarium').[56] The use of the Loire for parleys between the dukes of Aquitaine and the French kings seem to have been an old tradition dating back to at least the ninth century, when the duchy had claimed status as a kingdom. We know of at least three conferences on the Loire in the ninth century. In 862 Charles the Bald met with his son at or near Meung and in 867 Charles also met with the leading men of Aquitaine near the '*villa*' of Pouilly.[57] Two years later, he held a further meeting with the Aquitanians on the Loire, this time at Cosne.[58] There also seems to have been a meeting between King Raoul of the west Franks and William of Auvergne (William II, duke of Aquitaine) on the Loire in the tenth century.[59] In the twelfth century, apart from the conference held near Azay in 1189, the river furthermore provided the setting for meetings near Chouzy in 1162 and Vendôme in 1170.[60] Thus when Richard, as count of Poitou, decided finally to give himself up to his father Henry II after the great rebellion of 1174, nothing could be more natural than to hold this conference at a site along that same river.[61]

Conferences held after 1193, during the reign of Richard I, provide a break with this pattern because Philip Augustus's conquest of parts of Normandy during Richard's captivity in the Empire in 1193 had altered the landholdings of the Norman duke and the French king and consequently also altered the traditional border.[62] Between 1194 and 1199 the sites where parleys were held clearly followed the changing pattern of ownership of castles. Thus in June 1194 a conference took place between the intermediaries of both kings at Pont-de-l'Arche, at the junction of the rivers Eure and Seine. This meeting, intended to negotiate peace, was a smokescreen for Philip's intention to lay siege to the castle of Fontaines, and so another meeting had to be set up for later that same month.[63] The second meeting was held near Vaudreuil, a couple of miles south along the river Eure from Pont-de-l'Arche and, again, not along the traditional Norman borders.[64] This conference also failed and a third meeting was set up between Verneuil and Tillières on the river Avre.[65] During 1195 conferences were held near Verneuil on the Avre, near Vaudreuil on the river Eure, and, between Issoudun and Charost on the Arnon in Berry.[66] According to William of Newburgh, at the conference near Issoudun the two kings met in the space between their two armies and verbally agreed a peace, which was formally concluded at or near Louviers in January 1196, a place that stands on the river Eure.[67] In the following three years, at least three conferences were held on the river Seine. The first meeting, in 1197, took place between Gaillon and Les Andelys, where a truce was agreed.[68] The second conference took place between Les Andelys and Vernon in 1199. It would seem that at this second conference there was no bridge or ford between Les Andelys and Vernon, hence Richard attended the conference standing on a boat in the river, while Philip was seated on his horse on the riverbank.[69] The places where peace conferences were held during the reign of Richard I are instructive. If it proved necessary, because land had been won and lost in conflict, meetings shifted from one easily recognisable feature in the landscape to another, i.e. from sites on the rivers Epte, Eure and Avre to sites on the rivers of Eure and Seine. By agreeing to conferences being held near Pont-de-l'Arche and near Vaudreuil on the Eure in 1194, both Philip Augustus and Richard I agreed that sites near these two places marked the border, despite the fact that neither location had ever done so in the past.

The Anglo-French evidence is not unique, even if it is the most abundant. Conferences between rulers were held on border sites in many other areas of Western Europe, including Denmark.[70] Writing his history of the archbishops of Hamburg-Bremen in the late eleventh century, Adam of Bremen commented that the river Eider divided the Danes from the Saxons and the Nordalbingians; in other words that it constituted the border between imperial and Danish territory.[71] There are few reasons to doubt Adam's statement as not only did he have a keen interest in geography but, as noted by Tschan, he was also a familiar of the Danish king, Svein Estrithson, and part of the religious community at the imperial archbishopric of Hamburg-Bremen.[72] Moreover, Adam's statement is corroborated by a similar statement by the tenth-century writer Widukind and by the evidence of where parleys between the Danish kings and the rulers or mediators of their southern neighbours took place.[73] Early on, sites along the Eider seem to have acted as locations for conferences, and it is known that in the ninth century at least three meetings took place along this river.[74] The Danish kings also met with their neighbours along the Eider in the twelfth century. According to Helmold, at least two parleys took place on the Eider between King Valdemar I and Henry the Lion, duke of Saxony.[75] Helmold further lists one other conference at which the two met for peace and for the advantage of both kingdoms, but as no place is specified it is impossible to know whether this meeting also took place on the Eider or whether it occurred at Lübeck, a city on a coastal river once mentioned as a meeting place in his chronicle.[76] Though Helmold was well placed geographically to know about these conferences, he did not supply any dates for them. The only meeting that can be dated with any certainty is the parley that, according to Helmold, took place on 'the feast of the Nativity of Saint John the Baptist [24 June]' before the duke went on his pilgrimage to the Holy Land, which should probably be understood as 1171.[77] In addition, by comparing Helmold's narrative to that of Saxo, it would seem that one of the other conferences should be dated to c. 1166–67.[78] Helmold not only failed to provide dates for these conferences but he also failed to specify exactly where on the Eider they took place. Saxo, however, observed that the 1171 conference was held on a bridge, which Christiansen has identified as being the bridge at Rendsburg.[79] Another parley took place on the Eider in either the summer of, 1173 or the winter of, 1174/75, after the duke's return from Jerusalem. The purpose of this meeting was to confirm the friendship (*amicitiam*) between Henry and Valdemar.[80] In 1180, while Henry the Lion was under military pressure from the Emperor Frederick Barbarossa, he again parleyed with Valdemar at the Rendsburg bridge and, reminding the king of their alliance, he asked for Valdemar's help against the Emperor.[81] Helmold's *Chronicle of the Slavs* ends with events of 1171, but from the narrative of his continuator, Arnold of Lübeck, it is clear that conferences continued to be held on the Eider. In 1182 Sifrid, archbishop of Bremen, and Adolf, count of Holstein, acting as intermediaries for the Emperor Frederick I, met with Cnut VI on a site along that same river.[82] Similarly, when an alliance was concluded in the mid 1180s through the marriage of the dowager queen Sofia, widow of Valdemar I, to Louis (Ludwig), landgrave of Thuringia, Cnut journeyed to the Eider to hand over his mother to her future husband.[83] After 1185, our knowledge of Danish diplomacy is very sparse. We know, however, that in 1214 Frederick II confirmed the Danish conquests of the late twelfth century, and that this document set the division between Danish and imperial lands along the river Elbe rather than the Eider.[84] Certainly at least one conference took place along the Elbe, and a site along this river was the preferred location for the negotiations leading to the release of King Valdemar II in 1224–25.[85] It is also known that, to the north, the Danish kings conferred with the rulers of the other two Scandinavian kingdoms at a site near Kungahälla at the mouth of the Göta river, where the land holdings of these rulers met. Snorri Sturluson knew of at least one such conference at this site, from the 1060s, and it seems that this particular site for centuries thereafter remained a place where kings came to parley.[86]

The crucial point of all of this evidence is that it was the place of meeting, and *only* the place of meeting, which was the agreed border. In short, when it came to relations between rulers, a 'border' meant a specific place as opposed to the modern concept of the border as a line. The fact that princes met at several sites on the same river that does not mean to say that the whole stretch of that river was regarded as the border.[87] What historians must *not* do is to map these meeting places and then draw a solid line, as if to define the boundaries of medieval principalities, because no such practice was in use during this period. One of the oldest Swedish laws, Äldre Västgötalagen, tells of a meeting between the Danish and the Swedish kings, at which it was agreed that the border between the two kingdoms was to be marked by six giant stones.[88] Scandinavian historians cannot agree the exact historical details of this story, but what is of importance here is that, when the text was written down in the 1280s, there was a belief that the border had been agreed and marked in this particular way.[89] Furthermore, in this case, we know that one of the stones mentioned as a boundary marker in the landlaw later marked the place where the Treaty of Brömsebro was agreed between Denmark and Sweden in the seventeenth century. Hence, meeting places, not rivers or lines, marked the boundaries between territories. This view of medieval borders does, if nothing else, have the advantage of reconciling 'marches' and clear boundaries. While not refuting the existence of marches, that is those 'zones' where lordship, culture, language and patronage overlapped, it is important to recognise that medieval rulers also had a concept of borders, not as lines but as specific places or boundary marks. These specific places could be located in the march, yet they were clearly neutral sites where the territories between two or more rulers met and where matters of war and peace should be discussed.

This view of borders can be traced back to ancient Rome. According to Florence Dupont, following Ovid, boundary-stones that identified the owner often marked pieces of land or territories. The space immediately surrounding that boundary-stone was regarded as a zone in which people had to perform rites of passage. On 23 February, at the annual feast of the boundary-stones, owners of neighbouring fields would advance upon one another and hold a banquet together at the stone in order to cement trust and friendship.[90] The similarity between this Roman friendship gathering and the peace meetings between medieval rulers is remarkable. While it may seem strange to modern historians that just an elm tree, or a ford, and not the whole stretch of the river, should have marked the border, this may not have been such a foreign concept to medieval rulers.

There is a good reason why historians should ask whether medieval rulers met to make peace on the border or in the 'marches'. The place of meeting tells us something important about the relationship between the two participants, and, furthermore, it determines what will happen next in the peace process, as each relationship comes with a different set of rites and rules of how to make peace. Conferences on border sites were preferred when two rulers, claiming equal status, feared a loss of face.[91] Meetings on border sites implied equal status amongst the participants, whether perceived or real. This is very clearly shown in the sources. In his description of the meeting on the river Eider in 1171 between Valdemar I and Henry the Lion, Saxo noted that Duke Henry was careful to advance only half-way across the bridge 'in case the man he was approaching should seem to rank higher than him'.[92] Though Saxo scornfully commented that Henry's conduct was insulting and arrogant, because Henry was only a duke while Valdemar was a king, it is significant that the Danish king agreed to meet Henry half-way across the bridge, thereby acknowledging that the two were equals. Why Henry and Valdemar met as equals is open to debate. It could be because they were both vassals of the Emperor, or it could be because in terms of real power, if one imagines this to be something that can be measured in land and patronage, Duke Henry was as powerful as the Danish king.[93] Saxo himself indeed hinted at the latter reason.[94] Here, however, what matters is not why, but the fact that Henry and Valdemar did meet as equals.

This principle also holds true for meetings between the Norman dukes and the French kings. Where these two rulers met and negotiated peace shows the reality of their relationship regardless of their perceived differences. During most of the twelfth century, the dukes of Normandy were also kings of England, and as such the equals of the kings of France. However, on the continent the kings of England did not hold any land by virtue of their royal dignity but merely as dukes of Normandy who were in theory the French kings' inferiors.[95] Despite this, it is clear that, for the most part, parleys between these two medieval rulers took place on border sites, just as King John claimed in 1202.[96] Furthermore, this was a practice that predated the 1066 conquest of England, so that border meetings served as recognition of the *de facto* power of the dukes rather than of their *de jure* status as inferiors of the kings of France. William of Jumièges, following Dudo, in his account of the 911 meeting between the Viking leader Rollo and Charles the Simple, makes it clear that the two leaders treated each other as equals. According to William, neither of the two was prepared to cross the river, or to meet in the middle. To solve the problem, envoys were sent backwards and forwards until a peace had been concluded.[97] What matters here is not whether this meeting took place in exactly the manner described, but that William, writing in the eleventh century, before the Conquest, thought that this was how two princes of equal status would have negotiated peace. The theme of the involved parties lining up on either side of the river and then sending envoys across to negotiate the peace is, furthermore, a recurring one in William of Jumièges's account.[98] Apart from this famous and much

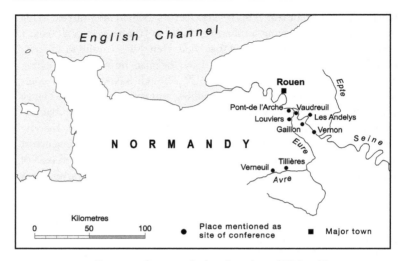

2   Peace conferences during the reign of Richard I

discussed meeting at Saint-Clair in 911, there were at least three other meetings before the dukes of Normandy became kings of England that took place at boundary marks on the river Epte in the tenth century.[99] Thus, just as Henry the Lion in terms of 'real power' considered himself the equal of King Valdemar of Denmark, so the dukes of Normandy may have been considered the equals of the kings of France. Again, as in the example of Henry and Valdemar, the crucial issue is that the Norman dukes and the French kings met to make peace at specific places marking the border, and, that each time they met at those border sites they reasserted their *de facto* equality.

The places where medieval rulers met to confer show a wish to preserve their equality of status not only in terms of princely dignity or in terms of political authority but also in terms of not being seen as victor and vanquished. Clear examples of such meetings are the conferences between Richard I, Philip Augustus and/or their respective negotiators in 1194–96.[100] It was noted earlier how during these years some of Normandy had been conquered by King Philip and consequently parleys could not be held on traditional sites. Yet, despite this, all conferences were held at places along rivers. The reason why they still met on river sites, albeit new ones, is to mark not some equality of status but that neither side had 'won' the war. This is perhaps confirmed by the fact that negotiators conducted four out of five parleys that were held in Normandy between

1194 and 1196.[101] Even more clear-cut, in 1199 Richard attended a conference standing on a boat in the river, while Philip was seated on his horse
on the riverbank.[102] Similarly, in the early twelfth century, Suger noted
of the 1109 meeting near Neaufles that the hosts of Henry I and Louis VI
confronted each other stood on either side of the river, 'at a spot where
neither side could cross'. Mediators were then sent across an old, shaky
bridge to hold discussions.[103] There is also an English example of a parley
taking place under very similar circumstances between King Stephen
and Henry, duke of the Normans. Henry of Huntingdon recorded how,
in 1153, Stephen and Henry talked about arranging a lasting peace, and
stood on either side of a stream.[104] Again this seems to have been in order
to make the clear statement that neither side had, as yet, 'won' the war.[105]

It is clear that medieval rulers met to negotiate and conclude peace at
places that contained features that had been, and would continue to be,
visible in the landscape for generations.[106] The elm tree, for example,
must have been a huge tree, two or three hundred years old, which could
be seen from a long distance.[107] It is thus possible that the elm had marked
the border and been used as a meeting place for a considerable time, possibly already during Carolingian times. It is likely that the use of trees
as meeting places was quite common. The most famous example of this
must be at the battle of Hastings, which was said by the D-redaction of the
Anglo-Saxon Chronicle to have taken place 'near the hoary apple tree'.[108]
Why make any mention of this tree unless it was a feature that the English
knew well? Margaret Gelling has also noted how hundred courts often
met at ash trees, the practice being recorded in names such as Broxash, i.e.
Broc's ash tree, and Bremesesce, i.e. Brēme's ash tree.[109]

Bridges are another example of specific sites of conferences that are visible in the landscape, of which there are some well-known and justifiably
famous meetings that date from the later medieval period. Perhaps the
most famous example is the fifteenth-century meeting between Edward
IV and Louis XI on a bridge over the river Somme, which was divided by
a trellis through which the two kings spoke.[110] A more gruesome fifteenth-
century example is the conference held on a bridge at Montereau, where
John the Fearless, duke of Burgundy, was killed, and his hand was cut
off and held up for all to see.[111] A thirteenth-century example, though
local in character, is the occasion when the Welsh came to parley with
the earl of Pembroke on a bridge near Carmarthen over the river Tywi.[112]
By contrast, the meeting between Henry III and Louis IX at the bridge
of Taillebourg in 1242 serves as an 'international' thirteenth-century
example.[113] However, for the twelfth century, the evidence for meetings

on bridges is rather sparse, despite the fact that Voss argued that in the twelfth century rulers seem to have preferred such topographical sites.[114] Apart from the meeting between Valdemar I and Henry the Lion in 1171, only Philip Augustus's conference with Richard I at Pont-de-l'Arche in 1194 is a possibility. As the name of the place suggests, there was a bridge at this site which may have provided the setting for that particular conference.[115]

Not only were meeting places known points in the landscape, but many were large, open-air locations providing good visibility of what was happening.[116] This is clearly what Saxo had in mind when describing the meeting between the Emperor Frederick Barbarossa and Valdemar I in 1181. According to Saxo, when the tent where the two rulers were holding their meeting collapsed, owing to too many people crowding together to see them, the kings went into an open field 'and there, because of the lack of seats, he [the emperor] stretched out his rod and ordered everyone . . . to sit down in the places where they were standing'. By doing so everyone was able to see the negotiations.[117] The key was clearly that doing things in the open provided witnesses. The events described by Saxo and others appear to be almost as if the participants were performing a play for an audience, though most conferences were not necessarily prenegotiated, calculated or exaggerated, as Gerd Althoff has suggested.[118] Nevertheless, in many ways conferences were open-air shows and they were clearly regarded as such by contemporaries.[119] It also seems likely, as argued by Philippe Buc, that these displays were inspired by practices in ancient Rome, where it had been the mark of the 'public ruler' (*civilis princeps*) to allow himself to be seen by all and to see all citizens.[120] The visual availability of each to each furthermore demonstrated the presence of charity and served to foster unity of mind and the bond of peace. The common phrase 'ore ad os' used by contemporaries to describe the nature of peace conferences bears witness to the importance of this notion. Circles provided spatial metaphors for equality, and seating as opposed to standing signalled participation in authority, on behalf of both the ruler and his followers.[121]

The face-to-face meeting stands at the heart of the peacemaking process in the high Middle Ages. By the late fifteenth century, however, things had seemingly changed and negotiations were not expected to be conducted at face-to-face meetings. For instance, the French chronicler Philip de Commynes commented that it was very imprudent for two great princes of equal power to meet and that it would be much better if they settled their differences by the mediation of wise and loyal servants.[122]

With regards to the English kings and their negotiations with their French colleagues, this development came about much earlier, following the loss of Normandy in 1204. No further conferences took place between King John and Philip Augustus after this date, and the reason is that, had such a meeting taken place, it would have been seen as an acceptance on John's part of the altered landholdings. The practice of meeting face-to-face was also affected by developments in law that gave envoys and mediators greater powers to negotiate and conclude agreements.[123] Nevertheless, the sites of conferences did not cease to be an important part of the peacemaking process. In the seventeenth century, the French and Spanish kings still met on an island in a river running through the Pyrenees, and in the late eighteenth century Russian and Ottoman envoys met on a raft in a stream in order to preserve their equality of status.[124] Even into the twentieth century the issue continued to matter. Who could forget the railway carriage in the forest near Compiègne where the German surrender of 1918 was signed and where, in the summer of 1940, Hitler's armistice terms were read out to the vanquished French?[125] The conference, or the location of the face-to-face meeting, is thus a principle of peacemaking with a great longevity in European history and with immense importance for how historians view the nature of borders and the nature of inter-ruler relationships over a long time span.

Notes

1 Conferences between rulers are the main focus of the works of Voss and Kolb, though neither specifically surveyed those involving the kings of England or those between the kings of Denmark and their neighbouring rulers. Ingrid Voss, *Herrschertreffen im frühen und hohen Mittelalter* (Cologne, 1987); Werner Kolb, *Herrscherbegegnungen im Mittelalter* (Frankfurt, 1988).

2 Ralph of Coggeshall, *Chronicon Anglicanum*, ed. Joseph Stevenson, Rolls Series, 66 (London, 1875), 135–6.

3 For the location of the conferences mentioned in this chapter, see Map 1.

4 'inter Gisortium et Trie, ubi colloquia haberi solebant inter reges Francie et duces Normannie.' Howden, *Gesta*, ii, 47; Howden, *Chronica*, ii, 345. For William the Breton's view on this conference, see *Oeuvres de Rigord et de Guillaume le Breton*, 2 vols, ed. H. F. Delaborde (Paris, 1882–85), i, 188.

5 Howden, *Gesta*, ii, 47; Howden, *Chronica*, ii, 345; *Diceto*, ii, 55; *History of William Marshal*, ed. A. J. Holden and S. Gregory (London, 2002), ll. 7765–78; *Chronique française des rois de France par un anonyme de Béthune*, in *RHF*, xxiv, pt 2, 756.

6 *The Correspondence of Thomas Becket*, i, no. 144; *Gervase of Canterbury*, i, 204; *MTB*, iii, 408–15; *Draco Normannicus*, ii, 677, ll. 475–84; *Torigni*, 224.

7 Howden, *Chronica*, ii, 53–4.

8 Howden, *Gesta*, i, 306; Howden, *Chronica*, ii, 280–1.

9 Howden, *Gesta*, ii, 29–30; Howden, *Chronica*, ii, 334–5; *Diceto*, ii, 51.

10 Howden, *Gesta*, ii, 47; Howden, *Chronica*, ii, 345; *Diceto*, ii, 55.

11 Howden, *Gesta*, ii, 236; Howden, *Chronica*, iii, 167.

12 Howden, *Gesta*, ii, 47: 'Deinde inter eos habito consilio apud Gisortium'.

13 *De Moribus*, 287. For a discussion of the dubious charter that refers to such a meeting at Gisors in 968, see Dudo, *History of the Normans*, ed. E. Christiansen (Woodbridge, 1998), 223, fn. 450.

14 Suger, *Vie de Louis VI, le gros*, ed. Henri Waquet (Paris, 1964), 170–3; Achille Luchaire, *Louis VI, le gros. Annales de sa vie et de son règne (1081–1137)* (Paris, 1890), no. 81.

15 *Continuatio Beccensis*, in *Chronicles of the Reigns of Stephen, Henry II and Richard I*, iv, 318–19.

16 Howden, *Chronica*, i, 217; *Torigni*, 231; Landon, *Itinerary*, 221–2; *Diceto*, i, 303. Torigni records the 1160 peace, but not the place of meeting. *Torigni*, 207–8.

17 Howden, *Gesta*, i, 59; Howden, *Chronica*, ii, 53–4.

18 Howden, *Gesta*, i, 81, 246–7; Howden, *Chronica*, ii, 71, 197.

19 Howden, *Gesta*, i, 277, 343; Howden, *Chronica*, ii, 314–15.

20 Landon, *Itinerary*, 219–34; Suger, *Vie de Louis VI*, 103.

21 Howden, *Chronica*, iv, 114–15.

22 For this see also Voss, *Herrschertreffen*, 72, 82–3, 100, 203.

23 Note that Howden records a conference between Richard and Philip Augustus in 1189 somewhere between Chaumont and Trie, and it is likely that also this should be interpreted as having taken place at the elm tree. The total number of meetings would thus be fifteen. Howden, *Gesta*, ii, 74; Howden, *Chronica*, iii, 3–4.

24 Howden, *Gesta*, i, 272; ii, 5; Howden, *Chronica*, ii, 255, 317.

25 Howden, *Gesta*, ii, 104–5; Howden, *Chronica*, iii, 30; *Diceto*, ii, 74. Landon believes that one of the meetings took place at Dreux, not Nonancourt: for this see Landon, *Itinerary*, 27.

26 Howden, *Gesta*, i 272; ii, 5, 104–5; Howden, *Chronica*, iii, 30, fn. 1; ii, 255.

27 Howden, *Gesta*, i, 272; ii, 5.

28 F. M. Powicke, *The Loss of Normandy*, 2nd edn (Manchester, 1960), 184–5; N. J. G. Pounds, *An Historical Geography of Europe, 450 B.C. – A.D. 1330* (Cambridge, 1973), 173; P. Fouracre, 'Space, Culture and Kingdoms in Early Medieval Europe', in *The Medieval World*, ed. Peter Linehan and Janet L. Nelson (London, 2001), 366; J.-F. Lemarignier, *Recherches sur l'hommage en marches et les frontières féodales* (Lille, 1945), 9–33.

29 W. Gordon East, *An Historical Geography of Europe*, 4th ed. (London, 1962), 230; X. de Planhol and P. Claval, *An Historical Geography of France*, tr. J. Lloyd (Cambridge, 1988), 90–1; T. Reuter, 'The Making of England and Germany, 850–1050: Points of Comparison and Difference', in *Medieval Europeans*, ed. Alfred P. Smyth (Basingstoke, 1998), 55; D. Matthew, *Atlas of Medieval Europe* (Oxford, 1983) 73. Paul Fouracre on the other hand traces this emergence to late antiquity and the period between the fall of Rome and Verdun. P. Fouracre, 'Space, Culture and Kingdoms in Early Medieval Europe', 366.

30 Planhol and Claval, *An Historical Geography of France*, 90–1, 108.
31 Powicke, *The Loss of Normandy*, 184–5.
32 East, *An Historical Geography of Europe*, 155; Pounds, *An Historical Geography of Europe, 450 B.C. – A.D. 1330*, 173; Fouracre, 'Space, Culture and Kingdoms in Early Medieval Europe', 366.
33 East, *An Historical Geography of Europe*, 155.
34 O. Rackham, *The History of the Countryside* (London, 1997), 19.
35 Lemarignier, *Recherches sur l'hommage en marche et les frontières féodales*, 9–33; Reuter, 'The Making of England and Germany', 53–4.
36 *Rec. des actes de Philippe Auguste*, i, no. 7; Howden, *Gesta*, i, 247.
37 D. J. Power, 'What Did the Frontier of Angevin Normandy Comprise?', *ANS*, 17 (1995), 181–201; 'King John and the Norman Aristocracy', in *King John: New Interpretations*, ed. S. D. Church (Woodbridge, 1999), 117–36.
38 M. Bur, 'Recherches sur la frontière dans la région mosane aux XIIe et XIIIe siècles', *Actes du 103e congrès national des sociétés savantes: principautés et territoires et études d'histoire lorraine* (Paris, 1979), 143; L. Génicot, 'La ligne et zone: la frontière des principautés médiévales', *Études sur les principautés lotharingiennes* (Louvain, 1975), 172–85; M. Bur, 'La frontière entre la Champagne et la Lorraine au milieu du Xe siècle la fin du XIIe siècle', *Francia*, 4 (1976), 237–54. See also Marc Suttor, 'Le fleuve, un enjeu politique et juridique', *Médiévales*, 36 (1999), 71–80.
39 *The Ruodlieb*, tr. Gordon B. Ford (Leiden, 1965), 17.
40 Bur, 'Recherches sur la frontière', 143; Génicot, 'La ligne et zone', 172–85; Bur, 'La frontière entre la Champagne et la Lorraine', 237–54.
41 For a good summary of how marriage and suretyship created enduring links between the Norman and French aristocracy living on the frontier, see D. J. Power, *The Norman Frontier in the Twelfth and Early Thirteenth Centuries* (Cambridge, 2004), 242–62.
42 Power, 'King John and the Norman Aristocracy', 120–1. For a summary of the extent of princely power in and around the Norman frontier zone, see also Power, *The Norman Frontier*, 75–80.
43 *Rec. des actes de Philippe Auguste*, ii, no. 517; Powicke, *The Loss of Normandy*, 184–5.
44 R. Helmerichs, '"Ad tutandos patriae fines": the Defence of Normandy, 1135', in *The Normans and Their Adversaries at War*, ed. R. P. Abels and B. S. Bachrach (Woodbridge, 2001), 138–9.
45 Michelle R. Warren, *History on the Edge: Excalibur and the Borders of Britain, 1100–1300*, Medieval Cultures, 22 (Minneapolis, 2000), 4–5.
46 Ganshof, *MA*, 127.
47 *Coggeshall*, 135–6.
48 For a discussion on the significance of rivers as sites for peacemaking in England and Normandy in the tenth and eleventh centuries, see Paul Dalton, 'Sites and Occasions of Peacemaking in England and Normandy, c. 900–c. 1150', *HSJ*, 16 (2005), 15–18.
49 *Diceto*, ii, 55.

50 For a discussion of the sites of Franco-Norman conferences in the tenth, eleventh, and early twelfth centuries, see J. E. M. Benham, 'Anglo-French Peace Conferences in the Twelfth Century', *ANS*, 27 (2005), 58–60.

51 *Diceto*, i, 305.

52 Howden, *Gesta*, i, 196.

53 Howden, *Gesta*, ii, 6–7; Howden, *Chronica*, ii, 317–18. For the miracle said to have brought the parties together, see *Gervase of Canterbury*, i, 370–3.

54 *Newburgh*, i, 276; Howden, *Gesta*, ii, 50.

55 *Torigni*, 237; Howden, *Gesta*, ii, 66; Howden, *Chronica*, ii, 362. John of Salisbury describes the meeting in great detail and from his account it is doubtful if the kings actually met on this occasion. Instead, the negotiations seem to have involved only meetings with the advisers of both kings at separate meetings along the river. *Letters of John of Salisbury*, 2 vols, ed. Millor and H. E. Butler; revised by C. N. L. Brooke (Oxford, 1979–86), ii, no. 279, pp. 602–7.

56 *Oeuvres de Rigord et de Guillaume le Breton*, i, 96, 190; Howden, *Gesta*, ii, 69; Howden, *Chronica*, ii, 372; *The History of William Marshal*, ll. 8941–4.

57 *Annales Bertiniani*, ed. G. Waitz, MGH SRG, 5 (Hanover, 1883), 58, 86.

58 *Annales Bertiniani*, 98.

59 Flodoard, *Annales*, 19–20.

60 *Torigni*, 215; Howden, *Chronica*, ii, 5.

61 Howden, *Gesta*, i, 76; Howden, *Chronica*, ii, 67. Montlouis had also provided the setting for the reconciliation between Henry II and Archbishop Thomas Becket in 1170. Howden, *Chronica*, ii, 10.

62 See map in J. Gillingham, *Richard I* (New Haven, 1999), 351.

63 Howden, *Chronica*, iii, 253.

64 Howden, *Chronica*, iii, 254.

65 Howden, *Chronica*, iii, 257.

66 Howden, *Chronica*, iii, 301–5; *Newburgh*, ii, 456, 459, 461; Landon, *Itinerary*, 106–9.

67 *Newburgh*, ii, 461; Howden, *Chronica*, iii, 305.

68 Howden, *Chronica*, iv, 21, 24

69 Howden, *Chronica*, iv, 79.

70 For Franco-German meetings, see Voss, *Herrschertreffen*, 38–87; Kolb, *Herrscherbegegnungen*, 58–71.

71 Adam of Bremen, *Gesta*, 70, 226–7.

72 Adam of Bremen, *History of the Archbishops of Hamburg-Bremen*, tr. F. J. Tschan (New York, 1959), xiii–xv.

73 Widukind, *Rerum Gestarum Saxonicarum Libri Tres*, ed. H. E. Lohmann and Paul Hirsch, MGH SRG, 60 (Hanover, 1935), 41.

74 *Annales Fuldenses*, 18, 78–9; Adam of Bremen, *Gesta*, 16, 39; *ARF*, 175.

75 *Helmoldi Chronica Slavorum*, 201, 217.

76 *Helmoldi Chronica Slavorum*, 170, 201.

77 *Helmoldi Chronica Slavorum*, 217. According to Christiansen, this meeting could not have taken place in 1170, when King Valdemar attended the large assembly at Ringsted for the crowning of his son, nor could it have been 1172, when Henry's

pilgrimage was already under way. Thus midsummer 1171 is the only possible date for this meeting. Saxo, *DRHH*, iii, 861, fn. 606.

78 Saxo, *DRHH*, ii, 489–91; iii, 831, fn. 461.

79 Saxo, *DRHH*, ii, 544–5; iii, 866 fn. 625; K. Jordan, *Henry the Lion* (Oxford, 1986), 83.

80 Saxo, *DRHH*, ii, 548–9; iii, 868, fn. 639.

81 Saxo, *DRHH*, ii, 580–1; iii, 890, fn. 16.

82 *Arnoldi Chronica Slavorum*, III:ii.

83 *Arnoldi Chronica Slavorum*, III:xvi.

84 *Diplomatarium Danicum*, I:5, no. 48.

85 *Diplomatarium Danicum*, I:6, 34.

86 S. Carlsson and J. Rosén, eds, *Den svenska historien* (Stockholm, 1966), i, 321; R. I. Page, *Chronicles of the Vikings* (London, 1995), 164–5. See also G. Olsson, 'Sverige och landet vid Göta Älvs mynning', *Göteborgs högskolas årsskrift*, 1, ix (1953).

87 Cf. Voss, *Herrschertreffen*, 69. Voss inferred that the sites themselves were not the border but merely locations on it.

88 'Þer sattu ristir mællir Suerikis ok Danmark . . . fyrsti sten a Suntru asi, annær i Danæbæk, þridi Kinnæ sten, fiarði i Vraksnæsi, fæmti Huitæ sten, sætti Brimsæ sten mællir Blekongs ok Møre'. *Äldre Västgötalagen*, ed. Herman Vendell (Helsingfors, 1897), 67.

89 For a summary of the historiography surrounding this particular passage, see Curt Weibull, 'Den äldsta gränsläggningen mellan Sverige och Danmark', *Historisk tidskrift från Skåneland*, 7 (1917–21), 1–18. The precedents for marking boundaries between kingdoms in this way is clearly derived from usage at a local level, for which see Patrick J. Geary, 'Land, Language and Memory in Europe 700–1100', *TRHS*, 6th ser., 9 (1999), 169–84.

90 F. Dupont, *Daily Life in Ancient Rome*, tr. C. Woodall (Oxford, 1992), 83.

91 Voss, *Herrschertreffen*, 38–87, esp. 65–9, 73–7; Russell, *Peacemaking in the Renaissance*, 78.

92 Saxo, *DRHH*, ii, 544–5.

93 For Valdemar's homage to the emperor see *Gesta Friderici*, 158; Saxo, *DRHH*, iii, 866 fn. 625.

94 Saxo, *DRHH*, ii, 544–5.

95 G. Koziol, 'Political Culture', in *France in the Middle Ages*, ed. Marcus Bull (Oxford, 2002), 44.

96 Coggeshall, 135–6.

97 *GND*, i, 52–5, 64–5; Dudo, *History of the Normans*, 48.

98 *GND*, i, 52–5, 64–5, 82–5, 92–3.

99 *De Moribus*, 246–7, 287.

100 Howden, *Chronica*, iii, 253, 254, 257, 301, 302, 304, 305; *ibid.*, iv, 3.

101 Howden, *Chronica*, iii, 253, 254, 257, 304.

102 Howden, *Chronica*, iv, 79.

103 Suger, *Vie de Louis VI*, 104–9.

104 Henry of Huntingdon, *Historia Anglorum*, ed. Diana E. Greenway (Oxford, 1996), 766–7; *Gervase of Canterbury*, i, 154.

105 On this, see also Paul Dalton, 'Sites and Occasions of Peacemaking', 16–18.

106 Voss, *Herrschertreffen*, 75-7.

107 By contrast, the author of the *Histoire de Guillaume le Maréchal* referred to the tree as being young when it was cut down. This may, however, reflect the age of the new tree sprouted from the old, chopped-down elm tree, at the time the author was writing in the 1220s. *History of William Marshal*, ll. 7765–78. William the Breton recalled that in 1188 Henry II and his advisers sat in the shade offered by the branches of the tree, which were some eight feet tall. *Ouevres de Rigord et de Guillaume le Breton*, i, 188.

108 *Two of the Saxon Chronicles Parallel*, 2 vols, ed. C. Plummer (Oxford, 1892–99; repr. 1952), i, 199.

109 M. Gelling, *Signposts to the Past* (London, 1978), 211.

110 Russell, *Peacemaking in the Renaissance*, 78; *Mémoires de sire Philippe de Commynes*, in *Historiens et chroniqueurs du Moyen Âge*, ed. and tr. E. Pognon (Bruges, 1952), IV:x.

111 M. Vale, *Charles VII* (London, 1974), 27–31.

112 R. R. Davies, 'Frontier Arrangements in Fragmented Societies: Ireland and Wales', in *Medieval Frontier Societies*, ed. R. Bartlett and A. MacKay (Oxford, 1989), 86.

113 Matthew Paris, *Chronica Maiora*, 7 vols, ed. H. R. Luard, Rolls Series, 57 (London, 1872–83), iv, 211.

114 Voss, *Herrschertreffen*, 75-6. For other (European) conferences held on bridges see Suger, *Vie de Louis VI*, 99–113; *The Ruodlieb*, 36; Helmold, *Chronica Slavorum*, 178; *Le Liber Pontificalis*, ii, 406; Romuald of Salerno, *Chronicon*, 217. For some early examples, see also Dalton, 'Sites and Occasions of Peacemaking', 14; Gregory of Tours, *Libri Historiarum X*, 216.

115 Howden, *Chronica*, iii, 253. For some historiography on this particular bridge, see M. N. Boyer, *Medieval French Bridges* (Cambridge, 1976), 171–95; C. Gillmor, 'The Logistics of Fortified Bridge Building on the Seine under Charles the Bald', *ANS*, 11 (1988), 88–91.

116 An important comparison can here be made with royal assemblies, for which see Reuter, 'Assembly Politics in Western Europe', 436–41.

117 Saxo, *DRHH*, ii, 594-5. Note also Howden's description of the Anglo-Scottish conference in 1200 taking place 'in conspectu omnis populi'. Howden, *Chronica*, iv, 141.

118 Gerd Althoff, 'Das Privileg der deditio. Formen gütlicher Konfliktbeendigung in der mittelalterlichen Adelsgesellschaft', in Althoff, *SP*, 101–3, 111–12, 124–5. For other examples of conferences 'out in the open', see Raoul Glaber, *Historiarum Libri Quinque*, 108-9. See also discussion in Benham, 'Anglo-French Peace Conferences', 65-6.

119 *Gesta Friderici*, 144.

120 Philippe Buc, 'Martyre et ritualité dans l'Antiquité Tardive. Horizons de l'écriture médiévale des rituels', *Annales*, 48 (1997), 67–70. See also Reuter, 'Assembly Politics', 438–41.

121 R. Reynolds, 'Rites and Signs of Conciliar Decision in the Early Middle Ages', in *Segni e riti*, 2 vols, Centro Italiano di studi sull'alto medioevo, *Settimane*, 33

(1987), 207–78; H. Fichtenau, *Lebensordnungen des 10. Jahrhunderts*, 2 vols (Stuttgart, 1984), i, 30–2. See also one of Walter Map's anecdotes in which a king was said to sit in the centre of a half-circle so that all who sat in the half-circle might be equally near the king's seat. *De Nugis Curialium*, 224–5.

122 *Mémoires de sire Philippe de Commynes*, 1034–5.

123 Chaplais, 'English Diplomatic Documents to the End of Edward III's Reign', in *The Study of Medieval Records: Essays in Honour of Kathleen Major*, ed. D. A. Bullough and R. L. Story (Oxford, 1971), 25.

124 Peter Sahlins, *Boundaries: The Making of France and Spain in the Pyreness* (Berkeley, 1989), 124; *Mubadele*, ed. Norman Itzkowitz and Max Mote (Chicago, 1970), 66–75, 115–17, 125–8, 200–3.

125 Gordon Brook-Shepherd, *November 1918* (London, 1989), 375–7; Alan Palmer, *Victory 1918* (London, 1998), 280–1.

2

Meetings between superior and inferior

In a letter to Hubert de Burgh, justiciar of England, William Brewer, the administrator and justice, announced that a certain messenger had arrived at Beaulieu from Llywelyn, prince of north Wales, bearing news of the prince's refusal to come to a peace conference on the morrow of the feast of Epiphany (7 January) 1220. According to Brewer, the messenger claimed, on behalf of his lord, that Llywelyn 'ought not to come to any conference outside his own boundaries' and that the prince had 'a good and authentic document to that effect from the late King John'.[1] Llywelyn's claim to the right to hold conferences on border sites is similar to that made by King John to Philip Augustus in 1202. Unlike John, however, Llywelyn had no precedent for such a claim. Modern historians often discuss Anglo-Welsh relations in the Middle Ages in terms of domination and conquest, that is, English domination and conquest. The relationship between the English kings and the Welsh rulers has been seen as one of superior to inferior on the basis of, among other things, the evidence of the visits of Welsh rulers to the king's court, an act of inferiority.[2] Contemporary sources are indeed full of tenth-, eleventh- and twelfth-century examples of such meetings at places within the English kingdom such as Shrewsbury, Worcester, Oxford and Gloucester.[3] However, historians need to think carefully about how they compare the evidence for meeting places. This has particular significance in terms of Anglo-Welsh negotiations, because it is difficult to establish a pattern of meetings and meeting places along the lines of those existing between the kings of England and France for the simple reason that the Welsh had more than one ruler at any one time. When historians talk of Anglo-Welsh relations, this is misleading in terms of peacemaking because peace, just like war, was a personal undertaking between two or more rulers and not unified

44

action by a specific nation or race, making it unwise to speak of Anglo-Welsh peacemaking or Anglo-Welsh conferences.

In the late twelfth and early thirteenth centuries three regional Welsh hegemonies are usually identified in English records: Gwynedd (*Nordwallia*), Deheubarth (*Sudwallia*) and Powys. From this, it would be natural to assume that, when the English king met or negotiated with a Welsh ruler, it was usually one who ruled over one of these hegemonies. Yet, as observed by Rowlands, in chancery records the Welsh rulers usually appear to be territorially detached and are commonly only given a simple patronymic, for example Llewelyn ap Iorwerth, which possibly reflects the perception that Welsh lordship was personal before it was territorial.[4] It is also evident that, though certain Welsh rulers appeared to dominate the political arena at various times, there were usually a number of Welsh princes operating within the three regional hegemonies. For instance, in 1175, at least seven different princes obtained peace from Henry II at a conference in Gloucester, even though Rhys ap Gruffudd of Deheubarth was seemingly the pre-eminent Welsh ruler at the time.[5] Consequently there were a number of potential candidates with whom the English king could, and did, meet to negotiate and make peace. Nevertheless, from the myriad of Welsh leaders it is possible to single out certain ones, like Llewelyn ap Iorwerth of Gwynedd, whose dealings with the English kings in matters of war and peace are particularly instructive.

It would seem that during the first eleven years of his reign, John's relations with at least some of the Welsh rulers were on a friendlier basis than during the reigns of previous Angevin kings. Indeed several historians have noted that John, by 1199, had already had a unique experience of dealing with the Welsh through the landholdings of his first wife, Isabella of Gloucester, and we know that John was assisting his brother Richard during the negotiations of 1189.[6] Even so, there is little evidence to support Llywelyn's claim of January 1220 to equality in his dealings with the English king. In July 1201 King John and Llywelyn concluded a treaty, which is the first written agreement to have survived into the modern period between a Welsh ruler and a king of the English.[7] It is unclear, however, whether the Welsh prince actually met with the English king in this year. Although a safe-conduct for Llywelyn was granted in April 1201, it seems likely that John left for Normandy before any parley could take place. The treaty itself was concluded with John's justiciar, Geoffrey fitz Peter, and his archbishop and chancellor, Hubert Walter. The place of this meeting is unknown, though Rowlands considered that Shrewsbury was a possibility.[8] A few years later, in 1204, Llywelyn was betrothed to

King John's illegitimate daughter Joan, and it seems likely, but not certain, that John met with the Welsh prince at Worcester, before the betrothal took place on 15 October.[9] In 1209 Llywelyn received a safe-conduct to meet with the king at Northampton, and he also took part in John's expedition against William, king of Scots, during that same year.[10] By 1211, however, relations between John and Llywelyn had soured and the English king invaded Gwynedd, forcing the Welsh prince to submit and cede north-east Wales, to hand over hostages and to pay a heavy tribute of cattle.[11] It is possible that the harshness of the terms of submission was the reason for Llywelyn's alliance with Philip Augustus, usually dated to 1212 to coincide with the great Welsh uprising of that year.[12] We know that a truce between John and Llywelyn was agreed on 3 June 1213 by the papal legate, which seemingly lasted throughout 1214, and, as late as March 1215, King John referred to Llywelyn in a letter as his beloved son and further stated 'nos et vos boni amici erimus ad invicem' in the hope that Llywelyn would meet his representatives at 'Ruth (=Ruthin, Denbs.?)', or at 'Crucem Griffin (= Gresford, Denbs.?)', where they would try to prevent the prince from joining John's barons in their rebellion.[13] The attempt was futile, however, as Llywelyn fought against King John in 1215 and 1216 as the ally of the rebel barons, and as a party to and a beneficiary of the king's humiliation in Magna Carta.[14]

It is possible that Llywelyn's claim to meet with the English king at a border site stemmed from Magna Carta and that this charter was the document he referred to concerning this point.[15] Certainly article 56 of the charter stipulated that disputes arising over lands disseised or taken from the Welsh would be settled in the 'march'.[16] We know that in the thirteenth century there were certain sites in the 'march' where disputes were settled between the marcher lords and the Welsh – favoured sites included mills and bridges – and it is possible that these agreed places followed a long tradition. However, as R. R. Davies has commented, these thirteenth-century parleys were essentially local in character, being regarded as an obligation of marcher life.[17] Indeed, marcher lords could ask to be, and were, exempted from any general peace concluded between the English king and the native Welsh princes, indicating that meetings between the marcher lords and the Welsh, and how these two parties made peace, were essentially different from meetings between the English kings and the Welsh rulers.[18] If the concessions made in Magna Carta were what Llywelyn was referring to in 1219/20, he was standing on weak ground. The clause in question referred only to the Welsh in general, not to Llywelyn and his successors personally. Nor did it imply that the

English king or his successors had to preside personally at these meetings.[19] Furthermore, on an enrolment of letters patent on 22 July 1215 – that is after Magna Carta had been agreed and sealed – Llywelyn and his advisers were given a safe-conduct to come to the council of Oxford the day after, and it is clear that Llywelyn did indeed meet John there on 23 July.[20]

John's negotiations with Llywelyn were certainly not atypical in their choice of sites. For instance, around the time of Llywelyn and Joan's betrothal in 1204, another Welsh leader, Gwenwynwyn, may have attended a similar meeting, not at Worcester but at Woodstock. He did, at least, receive a safe-conduct for that purpose.[21] A few years later, in October 1208, Gwenwynwyn came to Shrewsbury seeking peace from the English king, but was arrested and imprisoned for his efforts.[22] Going further back, the reigns of Henry II and Richard I are notable for the sheer number of chroniclers who reported on Anglo-Welsh negotiations. For the year 1157, the *Annals of Margam* records how a certain Owain of Wales (presumably Owain ap Gruffydd) became reconciled with the English king ('facti sunt amici'), alas without mentioning the site of any meeting.[23] Gervase of Canterbury describes a disastrous Welsh campaign in 1157, when Henry of Essex had apparently let the royal standard fall, and how a king of Wales ('rege Gualie') eventually gave hostages as the price of peace.[24] The *Annals of Osney* echoes this version of events and the compiler names one of the hostages as being a certain Hywel, whereas Robert of Torigni adds that the Welsh handed back the lands they had taken during the reign of Stephen.[25] The *Brut*, on the other hand, detailed a meeting (at the king's court) and an English expedition in 1158, after which Rhys ap Gruffud of Deheubarth, usually referred to among modern historians as the Lord Rhys, submitted and gave hostages.[26]

These various accounts typify one of the problems with assessing Anglo-Welsh conferences and negotiations. Though we have several sources available for this period, they rarely agree on the exact course of events, their date and the leaders involved, and as a consequence the chroniclers are often better informed about events on the continent than those in Britain.[27] It would in any case seem that events of the late 1150s had ended with the submission and the giving of hostages by at least one Welsh ruler.[28] There is more certainty surrounding the next key event: the conference at Woodstock on 1 July 1163, where all the major Welsh rulers did homage to Henry II and his eldest son Henry following the king's campaign to deal with the troubles between the Welsh and the Anglo-Norman marcher lords.[29] In 1175 another great gathering took place when Henry II

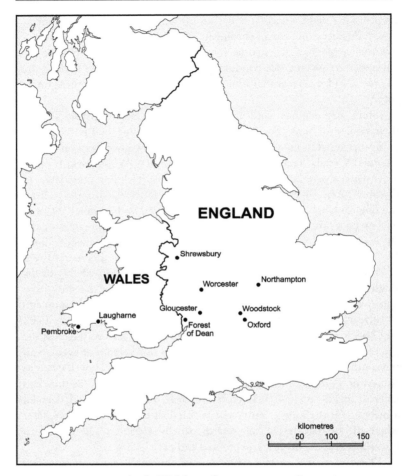

3   Anglo-Welsh conferences 1154–1216

summoned several Welsh princes to Gloucester, and in 1177 the English king negotiated with the Lord Rhys and a certain David ('king of the North Welsh') at Oxford.[30] In 1184 Henry and the Lord Rhys negotiated at Worcester, where it is known that a truce was agreed and hostages were given as a pledge.[31] Only a few months later, the Lord Rhys then came to the king at Gloucester declaring himself unwilling to enter into an agreement with the English king, and, after refusing to give his hostages, he returned to his own country.[32] In 1189 the Lord Rhys was still causing the English some problems and, on Richard I's insistence, the king's brother,

John, was sent to deal with the matter. Having met with some of the Welsh princes at Worcester, Richard then arranged a treaty.[33] However, a little later that same year, the Lord Rhys came to Oxford under a safe-conduct given by John, but, because Richard I did not want to appear, Rhys indignantly returned to his own lands 'sine colloquio regis' and the treaty was seemingly never ratified.[34]

It is clear from this evidence that English and Welsh rulers did not meet as equals. Some of the contemporary sources referred to the fealty and homage of the Welsh rulers to the English kings, though this is, however, of only secondary importance. The fact that the Welsh came to the English kings seeking peace in the twelfth century, as well as the early thirteenth, immediately tells the historian that these were meetings not between equals but between superiors and inferiors. Furthermore, for all his claims to equality in accordance with authentic documents, Llywelyn did eventually attend the appointed meeting at Worcester on 9 February 1220 as well as a further meeting at Shrewsbury in May of the same year and therefore it is clear that his relationship towards the English king had not changed in any way.[35]

Yet if seeing the relationship between the English kings and the Welsh rulers as being that of superior to inferior has some merits, it is important to recognise that there are also problems with such an interpretation. For instance, in the eyes of contemporary writers, rulers such as the Lord Rhys and Llywelyn ap Iorwerth clearly held a higher status vis-à-vis the English kings than other Welsh leaders did. Yet, the evidence of the location of meetings does not seemingly reflect this. Furthermore, it is striking that Anglo-Welsh meetings usually took place on the western side of the English kingdom. At least eight meetings in the period 1154–1216 took place near Welsh territory at Worcester, Shrewsbury and Gloucester. A further five meetings took place in Oxfordshire at Oxford and Woodstock.[36] This is significant in terms of what it tells historians about the collectivity with which the English kings treated Welsh rulers: that is, when it comes to the place of meeting there was little distinction between those rulers with a small territory and following, and those ruling over a larger territory who may have had a greater following. Furthermore, as will become apparent, Anglo-Welsh meetings, being located in areas of western England, often close to Welsh territory, stand in stark contrast to the location of meetings between the English kings and the kings of Scots, which most frequently took place deep within English territory. Thus, on the basis of the evidence of where rulers met to negotiate and make peace, some rulers, like the king of Scots, were evidently more inferior than others because they had to travel much deeper into their enemies' territory.

There are other problems with examining the relationship between the English kings and the Welsh rulers simply in terms of that of superior to inferior. There can be no doubt that there was a shared concept among medieval rulers of what constituted equality and what constituted superiority and inferiority in their relations with each other. It is also evident that the issue of location was an important factor in determining status and that the relationship between two rulers was frequently based on military success or threats thereof.[37] Yet, in this period, the military superiority of the English king vis-à-vis the Welsh cannot to be taken as a fact. It can of course be seen clearly in 1211 when John invaded Wales with a large army, forcing Llewelyn to submit and make peace on humiliating terms.[38] In 1163, the agreement(s) whereby a number of Welsh leaders did homage and gave hostages to Henry II and his son also seemingly followed a military campaign against Rhys ap Gruffudd.[39] However, this campaign has been described by at least one historian as being swift but one that did not curtail Rhys' capacity to wage war.[40] Similarly in 1157–58, Henry's military campaigns against Rhys and Owain ap Gruffudd of Gwynedd, which were ultimately successful, had been blighted by a heavy defeat of the king's fleet and an ambush on part of his forces.[41] Most significant of all, when Henry II launched a large-scale campaign in 1165 in response to attacks on royal castles by a number of Welsh princes, his army ended up returning to England having suffered heavy losses from lack of supplies and bad weather.[42] According to Gerald of Wales and Gervase of Canterbury, the campaign achieved little or nothing, and several other contemporaries gloated at the king's failure at a critical point in his dispute with Archbishop Thomas Becket and the papacy.[43] In the wake of this campaign a few of the lesser Welsh leaders seem to have made their peace with Henry, but, importantly, Rhys and Owain, the two main Welsh leaders, were not among them and they continued to attack castles in the marches over the next five years.[44] It is significant that Henry did not meet with Owain again and, when he next conferred with Rhys, the king was prepared to compromise in order to facilitate his campaign to Ireland in 1171. Peace thus came after a number of military measures had failed to subdue the Welsh – Rhys in particular – and the place of meeting, in the Forest of Dean, was an indication of this and not only a site en route for Ireland.

The unpredictable outcomes of Anglo-Welsh warfare raise some very difficult questions with regards to what characterises a superior and what characterises an inferior when making peace. There could be obvious advantages to appearing to be an inferior, especially when there are several different rulers in a small geographical area all vying for power. For instance R. R. Davies has argued that in 1172 Rhys accepted an inferior position against Henry II in return for securing the office of justiciar in south Wales.[45] Following the conference between Henry II and Rhys at the Forest of Dean, which established peace between the two rulers for the first time after the failed royal campaign of 1165, the two rulers also met at Pembroke, while Henry was en route to Ireland, and then, on Henry's return journey, at Laugharne.[46] It was on this second occasion that Rhys was appointed royal representative in south Wales, though the exact extent of his authority is uncertain. It is clear that after these meetings in 1171–72, Rhys attended the king's court on at least two occasions. Yet the relationship between the Welsh prince and the king during this time cannot be equated with the interchanging periods of hostility and armed neutrality that had existed before 1171 even though the location of these meetings remained the same.[47] It is evident that Rhys's acceptance of an 'inferior' position brought advantages to him, as not only did Henry make him his representative in Wales, he also recognised Rhys's right to the lands he had won in battle. Whether a ruler was a superior or an inferior is therefore an issue dependent on one's vantage point at any one particular time. Hence, superiority and inferiority are in terms of Anglo-Welsh peacemaking not static points at the opposite ends of a scale, but rather a fluid framework guided by *realpolitik*.[48] Although this is reflected in the location of meeting places to a certain extent, the sites do not reflect the relationship between the English kings and the Welsh rulers as clearly as do the meeting places between the English and French kings, or between the English kings and the kings of Scots.

Roger of Howden describes one conference taking place between King John and William, king of Scots, in November 1200, a description that is almost colourful in a work that has otherwise been described as dull and passionless.[49]

> After this, on the same day, he [King John] and William, king of Scots, met for a conference outside the city of Lincoln, which stands on a lofty hill; and there, in sight of all the people, William, king of Scots, became the man of John, king of England, as of his own right, and swore fealty to him.[50]

Two things set this particular conference aside from other Anglo-Scottish meetings that Howden tells us about. Firstly, the revelation that it took place outside the city; and secondly, his statement that it happened in the open for all to see. It must be the combination of these two factors that Howden thought unusual, because the content of the conference and the agreement was not distinct from that of many other Anglo-Scottish meetings in the late twelfth century.[51] Most indistinct of all was the place of meeting: Lincoln – a city well within English territory – and William's attendance at this site reflected his inferior status in the eyes of contemporaries.

There has been a lot of controversy surrounding the relationship between the kings of the English and the kings of Scots, for the most part reflecting the national sentiments of particular historians. Attempts have been made to define a 'border' between the kingdom of the Scots and that of the English and to place some conferences between the two kings or their representatives at certain 'border' sites.[52] Geoffrey Barrow has, for instance, noted how, according to the continuation of Symeon of Durham's *History of the Kings*, the river Tweed divided Lothian from Northumbria, and the castle of Norham, on that river, was similarly described as being on the border between the two kingdoms by the continuation of Symeon's *History of the Church of Durham*.[53] Norham may indeed have been a site for meetings between the kings of the English and the kings of the Scots. There was an ancient ford at Norham, which was referred to as a meeting place in the *Laws of the Marches* of 1249.[54] Barrow has further noted that Norham was the setting for Edward I's court during the deliberation over the Scottish succession in 1291 and 1292, and that King Edgar's 1095 charter to Durham concerning men from both sides of the border was issued in the churchyard of that same place.[55] However, neither of these latter two examples, was an occasion when both an English king and a king of Scots were present and thus they cannot be used as evidence for royal conferences at this particular site. In 1209 King John did meet with William the Lion at Norham, but the English king turned up with his army and the sources describe the event in a manner that makes it seem likely that William came to John asking for peace before the English king could invade his territory.[56]

A second example, Redden Burn, a well-known site used as a meeting place in the later Middle Ages, seems to have been used only three times during the late twelfth and early thirteenth centuries. In 1245 it was the scene of a meeting between English and Scottish representatives, while Roger of Howden refers to two meetings at Redden between Hugh du Puiset, bishop of Durham, and the Scottish king, William the Lion: the first took place in 1174 to arrange a truce in time of war, and the second, occurring in 1181, aimed to solve the disputed election to the bishopric of St Andrews.[57] The 1245 meeting seems to have been a local affair, comparable to those meetings taking place between the Welsh and the English marcher lords during the thirteenth century and which are mentioned in Magna Carta.[58] The meeting was in any case not attended by both kings, and this is true also of the 1174 and the 1181 meetings. It would seem that the evidence of meetings between the Scottish and English kings taking place on border sites like those between equals is at best tenuous.

The twelfth-century evidence of the sites of Anglo-Scottish conferences shows clearly that they were located within the territory of the English kings. By far the best example of the fact that these two kings did not meet as equals can be found in the 1170s. In his metrical chronicle, written shortly after the events it portrays, Jordan Fantosme describes how Brien the messenger came to Henry II in London to recount how Ranulph de Glanville had defeated and captured William the Lion, king of Scots, at the battle of Alnwick in 1174.[59] Henry, who at the time was being threatened by the rebellion of his sons, brought the captive king of Scots with him to the continent, and, after ending the uprising, forced William to make a humiliating peace at Valognes in Normandy in December 1174.[60] The year after, both the peace and the submission were confirmed in a ceremony at York and in 1176 William attended a conference at Northampton intended to confirm the subjection of the Scottish church to that of England just as the treaty specified.[61] A few months after the Northampton gathering, William the Lion met with Henry at Feckenham, just north of Worcester, bringing with him the lord of Galloway for his submission to the English king.[62] Though Richard on his accession to the throne in 1189 released William from the allegiance and submission extracted from the king of Scots by his father, in return for a payment of ten thousand marks, it is significant that this meeting took place in England, at Canterbury.[63] The next conference between Richard and William was also held on English territory. According to Howden, in 1194 William was conducted to Richard's court at Clipston, and thereafter travelled with it to Southwell, Malton, Rutland, Gaitington, Northampton (where Richard arranged for the honourable escort of the Scottish king to and from the English court), before finally attending Richard's second coronation at Winchester on 17 April.[64] There are several other twelfth-century examples of *colloquia* that took place either within England or within the English king's territory on the continent. In 1157 Malcolm, king of Scots, came to a parley with Henry II at Chester, where, according to Torigni, he handed back those towns seized during the reign of King

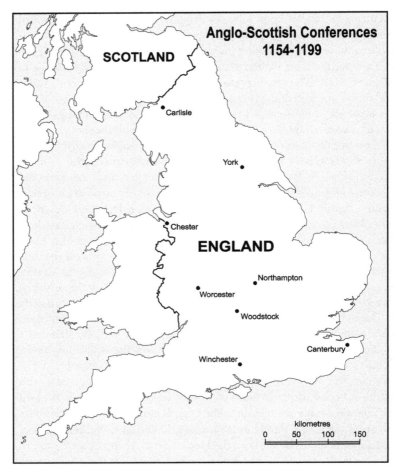

Anglo-Scottish Conferences 1154-1199

SCOTLAND

Carlisle

York

Chester

ENGLAND

Northampton

Worcester

Woodstock

Canterbury

Winchester

kilometres

0   50   100   150

4   Anglo-Scottish conferences 1154–1199

Stephen.[65] At the large gathering at Woodstock in 1163 Malcolm along with other British rulers did homage to Henry the Young King.[66] In addition it is also known that the English and Scottish kings met on at least one other occasion in the 1160s, though the exact location of this meeting is not clear.[67] In 1181 William the Lion attended a peace conference in Normandy with Henry II, Henry the young king and Philip Augustus; and in the mid-1180s William, accompanied by Roland of Galloway, concluded a tripartite treaty with Henry II at Carlisle.[68] It is also evident

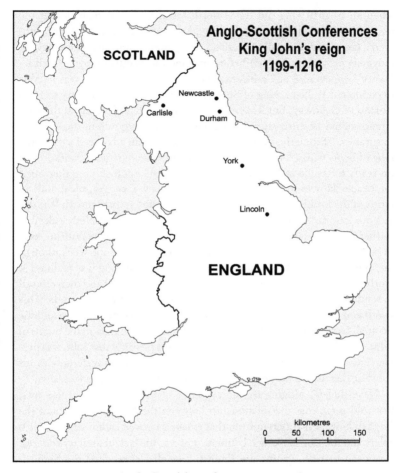

5   Anglo-Scottish conferences 1199–1216

that a large number of Anglo-Scottish conferences took place on English territory in the eleventh and early twelfth centuries, clearly indicating that they were conferences between superiors and inferiors.[69]

If we compare the English kings' meetings with the kings of Scots to those with the Welsh rulers, it is evident that there are significant differences. Whereas Anglo-Welsh conferences were usually held in the western parts of England, close to Welsh territory, the kings of Scots usually had to travel deep into English territory for his meetings. On those occasions

55

when an English king did travel north towards the Scottish border, he tended to be accompanied by an army. For instance, in 1186, Henry gathered a large army from all of England ('magnum congregavit exercitum de universis provinciis Anglie') before meeting the Scottish king at Carlisle. Henry's appearance at Carlisle was clearly a threat. Not only was he able to command William, king of Scots, and his brother David to try to fetch Roland of Galloway, but Roland was convinced that his safety at the conference could be ensured only by Henry committing two hostages to act as sureties.[70] Similarly, in the summer of 1209, John advanced against the king of Scots with a large army ('magno exercitu congregato'), and drew it up ready for battle at Norham. At this threat the Scottish king then sued for peace. However, John's reign certainly saw a geographical shift in terms of the location of meetings. In 1206 and 1207 John met with William at York, and in April 1209 the two kings also parleyed at Newcastle.[71] A further meeting may have taken place in February 1212 when William, king of Scots, met with John at Durham and stayed there for one week, though the only source for this is much later.[72] A further meeting was planned at Norham in January 1213, but the old King William delayed and then refused to send his only heir Alexander to meet the English king on grounds of his youth and inexperience.[73] It is evident that meetings between John and the Scottish king appeared to be taking place further north than in the reigns of John's brother and father. The reason for this is possibly that John was permanently residing in England after 1204 and therefore travelling with his court further across his kingdom than any of his Angevin predecessors.[74]

Nevertheless, judging by the evidence of where the two rulers met, it would seem that the relationship between the kings of Scots and the English kings was different from that existing between some of the Welsh rulers and the English kings. Ultimately, it was the lack of military success, supposed or real, against the English king that compelled the Scottish king to come to the king's court in locations that were much further away from his own lands than those meetings attended by the Welsh rulers. Anglo-Welsh relations in this period are characterised by a constant mixture of loyalty, submission and outright warfare. While the English king negotiated and treated with one Welsh ruler, he was at war with another, and so each party was able to play off one against the other in a seemingly never-ending chain. The Scottish king was not in a position to do this, and his relationship with the English king was further complicated by his claims to various landholdings in the English kingdom, most notably Northumbria.[75]

A parallel for the pattern of location of conferences and also for the relationship between the English kings and the other rulers in Britain can be found on the continent, in the Empire. Here neighbouring kings attended the imperial diets on a regular basis in the tenth to the twelfth centuries; and, occasionally, as part of the reconciliation process after a period of hostility, these neighbouring rulers also took part in particular court ceremonies.[76] The intention of these was obviously not only to foster peace and *caritas* but also to show off the exalted status of the 'German' king who at various times was also the Emperor. One such neighbouring ruler, who appeared at the imperial diet on various occasions, was the Danish king. In making this particular comparison, it is significant that not only is the pattern of the location of peace negotiations similar to those between the English kings and other British rulers, but, more importantly, unlike the Welsh and Scottish rulers, the Danish king had a (native) contemporary commentator, Saxo Grammaticus, who offers significant insight into the importance that contemporaries placed on the location of negotiations for peace.

In the High Middle Ages, the Emperor was widely perceived as a king over kings and it is thus to be expected that the places where he negotiated and made peace with neighbouring kings would not be located on 'border' sites.[77] Though it is known from the works of Voss and Kolb that the German emperors met with the French kings as equals, the relationship with their northern neighbours is more ambiguous.[78] For instance, we know that, in the ninth and tenth centuries, Danish kings met with the emperors both at sites on the border and at sites located within the Empire.[79] By the late eleventh century, however, a pattern clearly emerges whereby the Danish kings were expected to attend the emperors and negotiate at sites located within the Empire, a notion that was very much reinforced in the second half of the twelfth century.[80] In May 1152 two rivals to the Danish throne, Svein and Cnut, came to the diet at Merseburg to receive the 'just arbitration' for their succession dispute by the newly elected Frederick Barbarossa.[81] At this diet Svein, Barbarossa's 'socio militiae' during the reign of Conrad III, received the crown of Denmark from his former ally in return for performing military service. Cnut, Svein's rival, had to renounce his claim to the throne and further agreed to do military service to Svein.[82] Svein's closest supporter, the future King Valdemar I, was Cnut's surety and, according to Otto of Friesing, these terms were approved at the monastery of Corvey.[83] Like Svein in the early 1150s, Valdemar I (1157–82) upon his accession to the throne journeyed to the Empire to receive his crown from Frederick, and in 1162 Valdemar was also summoned to the assembly near Saint-Jean-de-Losne designed to settle the issue of the papal schism.[84] Though these three examples are perhaps not meetings for peacemaking in a traditional sense, it is evident that they set a precedent for where matters of diplomacy would be discussed, i.e. within the Empire. Indeed, the one conference between Valdemar and Frederick Barbarossa designed to discuss matters of peace, namely that of 1181, took place on imperial territory at, or near, Lübeck.[85] Even though this city shortly afterwards became part of the Danish king's territory, it is apparent that the meeting affirmed that the relationship between the Emperor and the Danish king was one of superior to inferior.

Saxo, writing at a time when the Danish king had asserted his independence from the Emperor, did not want to remind his readers of this embarrassing catalogue of events during the early years of Frederick Barbarossa's reign. Instead, Saxo justified the journey of the rivals Svein and Cnut to Merseburg in 1152 by saying that the Emperor was 'unable to make the journey towards Denmark'.[86] Similarly, in his account of the assembly near Saint-Jean-de-Losne, Saxo described several incidents intended to show how Valdemar tried to escape the servitude of the Emperor. According to Saxo, one plan was that, on the pretext of hunting, Valdemar would make a habit of riding over the bridge separating the kingdom of France from that of the Empire, 'and eventually . . . he could head for one of the nearby French towns' with his household and 'be sure that he would be sent back to his country ceremoniously by the king of the Franks'.[87] Saxo then justified the fact that the plan was never executed by saying that the Emperor gave the Danish king the overlordship of Slavia.[88] Eric Christiansen has rightly pointed out that this is unlikely to have been true, as Duke Henry the Lion and Margrave Albert already exercised lordship in Slavia and would hardly have agreed to give this up.[89]

Saxo's concerns about his king's inferiority vis-à-vis the Emperor reached an almost comical height in his description of their next meeting, that of 1181. Here Saxo used every aspect and detail he could possibly think of to show that this was really a meeting between equals. Hence, he described how Valdemar had initially been asked if he wanted the Emperor Frederick to meet him half-way along the river Trave, an offer that the Danish king declined, 'thinking there was very little point in troubling the ruler of the Roman Empire over so trivial a matter'.[90] With this the Danish historian showed the humility of his king, just as Raoul Glaber describes the humility of the Emperor Henry II in the eleventh century and Walter Map that of Edward the Confessor.[91] Saxo next retold how Frederick greeted Valdemar properly with an embrace and a kiss, and, most importantly, by clasping him by the right hand: a sign of equality.[92]

Not happy with his story so far, the Danish historian further commented that the meeting took place in an open field and that the Germans marvelled at the physique and stature of the king, agreeing it to be worthy of that of an emperor.[93] Saxo's account of this meeting cannot wholly be reconciled with that of Arnold of Lübeck, who merely records that the Danish king came to the Emperor ('veniens in presentiam imperatoris') with a large following and boasted loudly of his glory, presumably meaning the Danes' military success against the Slavs.[94] Despite the differences in the two accounts of this meeting, Saxo, by showing his concern over the issue of rank, inadvertently makes it clear that, to contemporaries, Valdemar's presence alongside the Emperor in this location indicated that the Danish king was actually the inferior party. This was not something that the Danes, including Saxo, wanted to remember after the mid-1180s when King Cnut VI had not only asserted his independence from Frederick Barbarossa but also conquered most of the Slav lands.

By the time we arrive at the reigns of Cnut VI (1182–1202) and Valdemar II (1202–41) the question of the locations of Dano-imperial conferences becomes more complicated. Here the sources are very sparse. Saxo, though still alive into the first two decades of the thirteenth century, was busy writing up the glorious past of the Danes and his contemporary section ends with events of 1185. Similarly, Arnold of Lübeck's narrative contains no details of any meetings, even though his *Chronica Slavorum* does not end until 1209. Despite this, we know that some meetings must have taken place. For instance, in early 1202, Otto IV's brother, William of Lüneburg, married Helen, the sister of Cnut VI and Valdemar II. It seems likely that this alliance was agreed at a meeting in Hamburg between Otto IV and Valdemar, then duke. One of the most interesting aspects of this is that Hamburg had recently been captured by the Danish king and so a meeting there in circumstances of military victory is significant in terms of the Danish king's relationship vis-à-vis Otto.[95] There are indications that other conferences had also taken place between the two sides. In a letter to Innocent III of early 1200, Otto IV informed the pope that, owing to the political situation in Germany, Otto had met with Cnut VI and made an agreement whereby the latter had entered Saxony to fight Otto's enemies. Otto then added that no truce had yet been secured.[96] The letter, however, contains no reference to the date or the place of this particular meeting between the kings. Another letter, sent from Innocent III to Valdemar II, probably late in 1203, confirms the alliance concluded with Otto IV and his brothers. Though this second letter makes no specific mention of a meeting, such an occurrence is a possibility.[97] The near-contemporary

Annales Valdemarii mentions the capture and destruction of Byzenburgh by Valdemar II in 1208 and that King Otto met with the Danish king at that place to ask for military help.[98] There can be no doubt that on this occasion the Danish king clearly held the upper hand in the negotiations, as he had also done the year before when he rescued Otto from Brunswick and briskly shipped him over to his uncle, King John of England, from the port of Ribe, all at Valdemar's own expense.[99] As these meetings took place at a time when Otto was on the brink of defeat by his rival Philip of Swabia, they are useful reminders that meeting places could change to fit altered circumstances or fortunes better. It is, furthermore, likely that, had any conferences taken place, their location would have altered again with the ascendancy of Frederick II. We do, of course, know that Valdemar II did not receive his crown from, or perform homage to, Frederick, even after his release from captivity in 1225, and thus it is clear that there was at least no precedent set as to where conferences should take place. Moreover, as the territory extending from the Eider to the river Elbe, conquered during the reigns of Valdemar I and Cnut VI, was confirmed by Frederick in the so-called 'Golden Bull' of 1214, and as a site on the Elbe saw Dano-imperial negotiations in the 1220s, it is perhaps more likely that, if any meetings did take place between Valdemar and Frederick, they would have been located on a border site and not at the imperial court.[100] What is perhaps most significant about this evidence is that the meeting places adapted to the changing fortunes of the rulers involved.

So far the evidence on meeting places has been presented in such a way as to make it obvious that usually participants of peacemaking conferred with each other as equals on border sites or as superior and inferior at sites located within the territory of one or the other of the participants. However, rarely are inter-ruler relations this simple, and it is clear, though the evidence is sparse, that there could be small but significant differences. Take for instance the location of the Anglo-Flemish negotiations of 1163, namely Dover.[101] According to Chaplais, Dover was situated on 'the English fringe of the Anglo-Flemish maritime march'.[102] Chaplais was correct in asserting that the place of meeting needed to be emphasised, but the focus of this must lie in the fact that the count of Flanders agreed to meet the English king on the latter's territory. However, if one compares Dover to the locations of Anglo-Welsh or Anglo-Scottish conferences, it is evident that these latter meetings always took place at the king's court usually at such places as Worcester, Gloucester, Northampton or Oxford. Not only were these sites firmly within English territory but they were, moreover, locations where the English kings commonly held court.[103] Dover, on the other hand, does not seem to have been a site where the king usually held court, and in the first 23 years of his reign Henry is known to have visited Dover only once and this was to embark on a crossing to his continental lands.[104] The king thus had to make a specific journey in order to meet the Flemish count, which would indicate that in 1163 the relationship of the count vis-à-vis the English king may not have been one of equality, but neither was it as inferior as that between the Welsh rulers and the English kings.[105] It is possible that, like Dover, Slesvig served a similar purpose in being the gateway to the heart of the Danish kings' territory. It is at least known that Valdemar II on two occasions met and negotiated with German lords at this site, thereby treating them differently from the Slav princes whose lands he and his predecessors subjugated.[106]

Just as conferences that took place on border sites symbolised the equality of the participants, so the entering of another ruler's territory for the purpose of negotiating tended to be viewed as a weakness. This is not only a medieval phenomenon. Perhaps the best modern comparison is the conference which took place between Hitler and Neville Chamberlain in 1938 at the so-called 'Eagle's Nest' (Berchtesgaden) in Germany. The French ambassador in Berlin, François-Poncet, summed up the problem: 'the fact that the head of the greatest empire in the world should have asked for an audience of the Chancellor of the Reich and agreed to go in person, not even to the German capital, but as far as Berchtesgaden, is considered by Hitler himself, his entourage and by German opinion as an immense success'.[107] It is evident that, to modern and medieval commentators alike, the site of a conference directly influenced the succeeding chain of events and it reflected the relationship between the two rulers making peace, or, for that matter, war. Agreements concluded on border sites tended to be couched in friendship terminology, and they were, as will be shown in succeeding chapters, characterised by exchanges rather than one-sidedness. By contrast, meetings between superior and inferior, or between victor and vanquished, were not located on border sites and they were generally characterised by one-sidedness rather than exchanges. It is clear that what determined the place of meeting was often military force, or threat of military force. Nevertheless, this chapter, more clearly than the first, has shown that not all relationships, and therefore not all sites, fall neatly into a polarised concept of meetings between equals or meetings between superior and inferior. Victory in war would usually see a meeting firmly within the territory of one party as a sign of submission. Yet, we know that the Norman dukes enforced their right to meet on border sites with the French king through victory, or at least through threat of victory. Similarly, a willingness to come to terms or to find allies could also influence the location of meetings as in the case of Henry II's dealings with the Lord Rhys. Meeting places could thus change, as could the relationship between those individuals making peace. Consequently, each meeting started the process anew.

Notes

1 *Calendar of Ancient Correspondence concerning Wales*, ed. J. G. Edwards (Cardiff, 1935), 2.

2 Davies, *Conquest, Coexistence and Change*, 27.

3 See for instance *Two of the Saxon Chronicles Parallel*, i, 119 (s.a. 973), 186 (s.a. 1056), 191 (s.a. 1063), 245 (s.a. 1114); *Brut y Tywysogyon*, 24 (s.a. 1101), 26 (s.a. 1103), 34 (s.a. 1110), 44 (s.a. 1116).

4 Ifor W. Rowlands, 'King John and Wales', in *King John: New Interpretations*, ed. S.D. Church (Woodbridge, 1999), 273.

5 *Brut y Tywysogyon*, 70. Walker has also noted how the Brut names six major Welsh leaders in 1211 and ten or eleven in 1215. David Walker, *Medieval Wales* (Cambridge, 1990), 92.

6 Howden, *Gesta*, ii, 87–8, 97; Walker, *Medieval Wales*, 93; Davies, *Conquest, Coexistence and Change*, 293; A. D. Carr, *Medieval Wales* (Basingstoke, 1995), 54; Ifor W. Rowlands, 'The 1201 Peace between King John and Llywelyn ap Iorwerth', *Studia Celtica*, 24 (2000), 152.

7 Pryce, *The Acts of Welsh Rulers*, no. 221. For a discussion of this treaty, see Rowlands, 'The 1201 Peace', 149–66.

8 Rowlands, 'The 1201 Peace', 155.

9 *Rot. Litt. Pat.*, 44a; *Rot. Litt. Claus*, i, 12. Carr, *Medieval Wales*, 56

10 *Rot. Litt. Pat.*, 89b; Pryce, *The Acts of Welsh Rulers*, 378.

11 *Brut y Tywysogyon*, 85; *Annales Cambriae*, ed. J. Williams ab Ithel (London, 1860), 67–8; *The Annals of Margam*, in *Ann. Mon.*, i, 31; 'The Barnwell Chronicle', in *Memoriale Fratris Walteri de Coventria*, 2 vols, ed. W. Stubbs, Rolls Series, 58 (London, 1872–73), ii, 203; *Flores Historiarum*, ii, 58; Pryce, *The Acts of Welsh Rulers*, no. 233.

12 R. F. Treharne, 'The Franco-Welsh Treaty of Alliance in 1212', *Bulletin of the Board of Celtic Studies*, 18 (1958–60), 64–5.

13 Rymer, *Foedera*, I, i, 196; *Rot. Litt. Pat.*, i, 120b; Treharne, 'The Franco-Welsh Treaty', 66.

14 Treharne, 'The Franco-Welsh Treaty', 66.

15 *Calendar of Ancient Correspondence concerning Wales*, 2.

16 *Magna Carta*, 441ff, cap. 56.

17 Davies, 'Frontier Arrangements in Fragmented Societies', 85 fn. 31, 86–7.

18 *Close Rolls of Henry III, 1231–4* (London, 1902–38), 568–9; Davies, 'Frontier Arrangements in Fragmented Societies', 87. Davies noted that these local

arrangements were distinguished by mutual concessions, not like the royal peace agreements where hostages and tribute were given by the Welsh alone.

19 *Magna Carta*, cap. 56.

20 *Rot. Litt. Pat.*, 150a.

21 *Rot Litt. Pat.*, 45a.

22 Pryce, *The Acts of Welsh Rulers*, no. 576.

23 *Ann. Mon.*, i, 15.

24 *Gervase of Canterbury*, i, 165–6. Gerald of Wales and Jocelyn of Brakelond also make some short comments on this campaign, for which see *Giraldi Cambrensis Opera Omnia*, 8 vols, ed. J. S. Brewer et al., Rolls Series, 21 (London, 1861–91), vi, 130; *The Chronicle of Jocelyn of Brakelond*, ed. H. E. Butler (London, 1949), 70.

25 *Ann. Mon.*, iv, 30; *Torigni*, 195.

26 *Brut y Tywysogyon*, 60. The author of the *Continuatio Beccensis* states that in this year King Henry subjugated the Welsh and made them pay tribute. *Continuatio Beccensis*, 318

27 Paul Latimer has further noted that the Anglo-Norman chroniclers are not very helpful in analysing the Welsh rebellion of 1165, in part owing to some of the chroniclers' attitude to the nature of the Welsh people. Paul Latimer, 'Henry II's Campaign against the Welsh in 1165', *Welsh History Review*, 14 (1989), 527.

28 For a summary of these events, see J. E. Lloyd, *A History of Wales from the Earliest Times to Edwardian Conquest*, 2 vols (London, 1912), ii, 498–500; Davies, *Conquest, Coexistence and Change*, 51; Warren, *Henry II*, 69–70.

29 *Diceto*, i, 311; *Brut y Tywysogyon*, 62–4. For a convenient summary, see Latimer, 'Henry II's Campaign against the Welsh', 525.

30 *Brut y Tywysogyon*, 70; Howden, *Gesta*, i, 92, 162; Gillingham, 'Henry II, Richard I and the Lord Rhys', *Peritia*, 10 (1996), repr. in his *The English in the Twelfth Century* (Woodbridge, 2000), 61.

31 Howden, *Gesta*, i, 314.

32 Howden, *Gesta*, i, 317.

33 Howden, *Gesta*, ii, 87–8. On Richard rather than John meeting the Welsh princes at Worcester see Gilingham, 'Henry II, Richard I and the Lord Rhys', 65–6.

34 Howden, *Gesta*, ii, 97; Howden, *Chronica*, iii, 23.

35 *Calendar of Ancient Correspondence*, 2; J. Beverley Smith, 'Magna Carta and the Charters of the Welsh Princes', *EHR*, 99 (1984), 360.

36 Only the meeting between John and Llywelyn at Northampton in 1209 stands out from this pattern, though this can perhaps be explained by the fact that on that occasion Llywelyn was joining the English king on an expedition against the king of Scots.

37 Medieval writers had a clear sense of these general principles about equals, superiors and inferiors and that the ideal type of peace was that won through victory. For these issues and some examples, see Introduction, 1–3; Saxo, *DRHH*, ii, 544–5; Raoul Glaber, *Historiarum Libri Quinque*, 108–9.

38 *Brut y Tywysogyon*, 85; *Annales Cambriae*, 67–8; *The Annals of Margam*, in *Ann. Mon.*, i, 31; 'The Barnwell Chronicle', in *Memoriale Fratris Walteri de Coventria*, ii, 203; *Flores Historiarum*, ii, 58; Pryce, *The Acts of Welsh Rulers*, no. 233.

39 *Brut y Tywysogyon*, 62.

40 Latimer, 'Henry II's Campaign against the Welsh in 1165', 525.

41 *Gervase of Canterbury*, i, 165–6; *Giraldi Cambrensis Opera Omnia*, vi, 130; *The Chronicle of Jocelyn of Brakelond*, 70.

42 For a good summary, see Latimer, 'Henry II's Campaign against the Welsh in 1165', 530–7.

43 *Gervase of Canterbury*, i, 197; *Giraldi Cambrensis Opera Omnia*, vi, 143; *The Letters of John of Salisbury*, ii, no. 168, 184.

44 Latimer, 'Henry II's Campaign against the Welsh in 1165', 541–2; Davies, *Conquest, Coexistence and Change*, 53.

45 Davies, *Conquest, Coexistence and Change*, 54.

46 It is noteworthy that Davies argues that these meetings were still located in an area which was firmly controlled by the English. Davies, *Conquest, Coexistence and Change*, 51–3, 96–100; Davies, *The First English Empire* (Oxford, 2000), 71–2.

47 The most recent commentator on the relationship between Rhys and Henry II after 1171 aptly describes it as reciprocal. Robert S. Babcock, 'Clients of the Angevin King: Rhys ap Gruffudd and Ruaidri Ua Conchobair Compared', in *Ireland and Wales in the Middle Ages*, ed. Karen Jankulak and Jonathan M. Wooding (Dublin, 2007), 237.

48 Davies, in discussing Anglo-Welsh relations during the reign of Henry I, has made exactly this point: see R. R. Davies, 'Henry I and Wales', in *Studies in Medieval History presented to R. H. C. Davis*, ed. H. Mayr-Harting and R. I. Moore (London, 1985), 138. On English overlordship in general, see Davies, *Conquest, Coexistence and Change*, 290.

49 Howden, *Chronica*, i, lxix; John Gillingham, 'The Travels of Roger of Howden and His Views of the Irish, Scots and Welsh', *ANS* 20 (1998), repr. in his *The English in the Twelfth Century* (Woodbridge, 2000), 69.

50 'Deinde, eodem die, ipse et Willelmus rex Scottorum convenerunt ad colloquium extra civitatem Lincolnie, super montem arduum; et ibi in conspectu omnis populi Willelmus rex Scottorum devenit homo Johannis regis Anglie de juro suo, et juravit ei fidelitatem.' Howden, *Chronica*, iv, 141. Note also that the meeting took place outside Lincoln. According to some sources, there was an old superstition that bad luck and hasty death awaited the king who entered the city. *Newburgh*, i, 57, 117.

51 Howden also details that a meeting had initially been arranged to take place in York, but that the king of Scots had refused to meet John there. Howden, *Chronica*, iv, 107.

52 Though note Ferguson's idea of a fluid border: a frontier zone rather than a 'march'. W. Ferguson, *Scotland's Relations with England. A Survey to 1707* (Edinburgh, 1977), 10.

53 Symeon of Durham, *Opera Omnia*, ed. T. Arnold (London, 1882–85), ii, 278; i, 140; G. W. S. Barrow, *The Kingdom of the Scots* (London, 1973), 155.

54 Barrow, *The Kingdom of the Scots*, 159.
55 Barrow, *The Kingdom of the Scots*, 156.
56 *Flores Historiarum*, ii, 50; *Ann. Mon.*, ii, 80, 262; *Gervase of Canterbury*, ii, 103.
57 Barrow, *The Kingdom of the Scots*, 155; Howden, *Chronica*, ii, 56-7, 263; Howden, *Gesta*, i, 64, 281.
58 *Magna Carta*, cap. 56
59 Jordan Fantosme, *Chronique*, ll. 1954-2018; Howden, *Gesta*, i, 67, 72.
60 Howden, *Gesta*, i, 95-7; *Diceto*, i, 396. Though Howden places this treaty at Falaise, it seems likely that an initial agreement was reached there and a more formal document was drawn up at Valognes as recorded by Diceto. On this see also Gillingham, 'The Travels of Roger of Howden and his Views of the Irish, Scots and Welsh', 76.
61 Howden, *Gesta*, i, 95, 111.
62 Howden, *Gesta*, i, 126.
63 Howden, *Gesta*, ii, 102-3; Howden, *Chronica*, iii, 24-5; *Newburgh*, i, 304.
64 Howden, *Chronica*, iii, 243-50.
65 *Torigni*, 192; *The Chronicle of Melrose*, ed. A. O. and M. O. Anderson (London, 1936), 76.
66 *Torigni*, 218.
67 *Torigni*, 228-9.
68 *Diceto*, ii, 7; Howden, *Gesta*, i, 349.
69 For examples of earlier conferences, see *Two of the Saxon Chronicles Parallel*, i, 157-9, 208, 227; *The Chronicle of John of Worcester*, iii, 20-1, 60-1, 64-5; The *Chronicle of Richard of Hexham*, in *Chronicles of the Reigns of Stephen, Henry II and Richard I*, iii, 145-6.
70 Howden, *Gesta*, i, 349.
71 *Rot. Litt. Pat.*, 69b, 76; *Rot. Litt. Claus.*, i, 86, 90; *The Chronicle of Melrose*, 54.
72 *Johannis de Fordun chronica gentis Scotorum*, ed. W. F. Skene, 2 vols (Edinburgh, 1871-72), i, 278.
73 *Johannis de Fordun chronica gentis Scotorum*, i, 279.
74 Robin Frame, *The Political Development of the British Isles, 1100-1400* (Oxford, 1990), 79.
75 For a summary of this, see Duncan, 'John King of England and the King of Scots', 247-70. On the development of the many cultural, political, ecclesiastical and tenurial links between the two kingdoms in the twelfth century, see K. Stringer, *Earl David of Huntingdon. A Study in Anglo-Scottish History* (Edinburgh, 1985).
76 For a few examples, see Joachim Bumke, *Courtly Culture. Literature and Society in the High Middle Ages*, tr. Thomas Dunlap (London, 2000), 168.
77 For the emperor as a 'king of kings', see Ganshof, *MA*, 64; J. L. Nelson, 'The Lord's Anointed and the People's Choice: Carolingian Royal Ritual', in *Rituals of Royalty*, ed. David Cannadine and Simon Price (Cambridge, 1987),139; *MGH Capitularia Regum Francorum*, i, 270-3, cap. 5.
78 Voss, *Herrschertreffen*, 65-73; Kolb, *Herrscherbegegnungen*, 58-61
79 For meetings on the border see *Annales Fuldenses*, 18, 78-9; Adam of Bremen,

Gesta, 16, 39, 63; *ARF*, 134–5, 141, 167–8, 175. For conferences held at the Frankish court see *ARF*, 141, 162–3, 169–70

80 Adam of Bremen, *Gesta*, 161, 206; *Lamberti Hersfeldensis annales*, MGH SS, 5, ed. G. H. Pertz (Stuttgart, 1985), 194, 202; *Brunonis liber de bello Saxonico*, MGH SS, 5, 335, 341–2 (cap. 20, 36). The best treatment of Dano-imperial relations in the twelfth century is O. Engels, 'Friedrich Barbarossa und Dänemark', in *Friedrich Barbarossa. Handlungsspielräume und Wirkungsweisen des staufischen Kaisers*, ed. A. Haverkamp (Sigmaringen, 1992), 353–85.

81 *Helmoldi Chronica Slavorum*, 67; Saxo, *DRHH*, ii, 379; *Gesta Frederici*, 85.

82 Saxo, *DRHH*, ii, 379.

83 Saxo, *DRHH*, ii, 379–80; *Gesta Frederici*, 85. There is also a charter of Frederick Barbarossa witnessed by 'Sven, king of the Danes, who received his kingdom from the hand of the king [Frederick I]' and Cnut 'who surrendered his right to the same kingdom'. *Diplomatarium Danicum*, I:21, no. 110.

84 *Helmoldi Chronica Slavorum*, 82–3; Saxo, *DRHH*, ii, 462–5; *Annales Stadenses*, ed. J. M. Lappenberg, MGH SS, 16 (Stuttgart, 1994), 344–5.

85 *Arnoldi Chronica Slavorum*, II:xxi; Saxo, *DRHH*, ii, 594–5. The *Annales Ryenses* merely report that the conference took place on the river Trave. *Annales Ryenses*, ed. J. M. Lappenberg, MGH *SS*, 16, 404.

86 Saxo, *DRHH*, ii, 379.

87 Saxo, *DRHH*, ii, 463. This was presumably the same bridge where Barbarossa and King Louis VII had intended to meet in 1162. For this meeting, see *Helmoldi Chronica Slavorum*, 83; *Le Liber Pontificalis*, 3 vols, ed. L. Duchesne (Paris: 1886–92), ii, 406–7.

88 Saxo, *DRHH*, ii, 463.

89 Saxo, *DRHH*, iii, 804 fn. 332.

90 Saxo, *DRHH*, ii, 594–5.

91 Raoul Glaber, *Historiarum Libri Quinque*, 108–9; *De Nugis Curialium*, 192–5.

92 Saxo, *DRHH*, ii, 594–5.

93 Saxo, *DRHH*, ii, 594–5.

94 *Arnoldi Chronica Slavorum*, II:xxi.

95 *Annales Stadenses*, 353; *Arnoldi Chronica Slavorum*, VI:xv; Koch, *Danmarks historie*, iii, 342–3.

96 *Diplomatarium Danicum*, I:4, 11, no. 4.

97 *Diplomatarium Danicum*, I:4, 189, no. 89.

98 *Annales Valdemarii*, 179. Arnold of Lübeck mentions the expedition and in a roundabout way also the alliance between Valdemar and Otto, but not the specific meeting. *Arnoldi Chronica Slavorum*, VII:xii.

99 *Annales Valdemarii*, 179

100 *Diplomatarium Danicum*, I:6, 34; *Annales Stadenses*, 358 For the 'Golden Bull', see *Diplomatarium Danicum*, I:5, no. 48.

101 *Dip. Docs*, i, no. 3.

102 Chaplais, *EDP*, 44.

103 Martin Biddle, 'Seasonal Festivals and Residence: Winchester, Westminster and Gloucester in the Tenth to the Twelfth Centuries', *ANS* 8 (1986), 51–63.

104 Historians have argued that after 1179 Henry II spent a significant amount of money on Dover castle to turn it into the 'show home' of the English king. It certainly seems to have been used specifically for important visitors after this date. John Gillingham, 'The King and the Castle: How Henry II Rebuilt His Reputation', *BBC History Magazine*, August (2009), 35–6; Thomas K. Keefe, 'Shrine Time: King Henry II's Visits to Thomas Becket's Tomb', *HSJ*, 11 (1998), 119–20.

105 It is important to remember that these Anglo-Flemish negotiations followed a tradition too, as at least two and possibly as many as four previous meeting had taken place at Dover. For this see, *Dip. Docs*, i, nos 1, 2, 3; Galbert de Bruges, *Histoire du meurtre de Charles le Bon*, ed. Henri Pirenne (Paris, 1891), 176; *GRA*, i, 730–1. It is also significant that, when Louis VII of France made his pilgrimage to Canterbury in 1179, he too was met at Dover. Howden, *Gesta*, i, 241–2; *Gervase of Canterbury*, i, 293.

106 *Annales Valdemarii*, 179 (s.a. 1206, c. 1218).

107 R. A. C. Parker, *Chamberlain and Appeasement* (Basingstoke, 1993), 162.

PART II

The 'rituals' of peacemaking

3

Gift exchanges and banquets: the symbolism of largesse

Having considered where and in what circumstances medieval rulers met, we now need to examine what they actually did at meetings. Here we need to take into account the role of ritual. But what are rituals? The German historian Gerd Althoff has defined rituals as actions or chains of actions that are repeated by actors 'in certain circumstances in the same or similar ways . . . with the conscious goal of familiarity'.[1] Descriptions of ritual indicate what certain individuals were supposed or expected to do at specific times and occasions. To be a ritual, the actions needed to be easily recognised by those witnessing the event. Althoff further noted that rituals are usually arranged ceremoniously and frequently served to acknowledge the social order or the purpose of commemoration or confirmation.[2] Though the spoken word is not lacking in this ritual communication, the actions alone tell everyone present what has just taken place. The actions indeed suffice to establish obligations and to guarantee appropriate behaviour in the future. Rituals thus provide a universal language that could be understood and witnessed by all. Rather as in watching a television recording of a meeting between two modern statesmen where, at the end of successful negotiations, the two shake hands and smile and, even if one cannot understand or hear what has been agreed, it is clear that the two are friends and allies. Their actions divulge what they wish to present as their relationship. In the medieval period, even more than in the modern era, the public qualities of rituals, even without the spoken word, were essential 'because spectators assumed the role of witnesses and thereby made the action legally binding'.[3] According to historians such as Althoff, rituals created an unambiguous system of communication among the aristocracy, the so-called 'Spielregeln der Politik'. In this context, rituals were not spontaneous acts but were rather scenes that were organised, pre-negotiated, calculated and exaggerated. Although Althoff recognises that it may be doubtful if medieval authors describe the scenes as they actually happened, he argues that these authors had to consider the common rules and customs governing behaviour if they wanted their contemporaries to believe their accounts. 'On the whole', Althoff suggests, 'the description [of ritual] had to correspond to the usual practices of communication', and as such they can be used for the investigation of these practices if not for the history of events.[4]

Recently scholars have started to challenge this view of rituals. Philippe Buc, for example, has argued that, far from providing an unambiguous system of communication, 'rituals', and descriptions of 'rituals', invited cheating and manipulation, which led him to label his monograph on the subject *The Dangers of Ritual*.[5] Buc suggests that as the majority of medieval sources are the products of interpretation or attempts to channel interpretation, and as sources owe their being to purpose and circumstance, the historian cannot establish a linear relationship between ritual and political order in the way that Althoff and others have done. Buc has in this way encouraged medieval scholars to think very carefully about how one can 'cross the bridge to historical reality from the river bank of highly crafted texts produced by a culture of interpretation'.[6] Furthermore, Buc has suggested that, since medieval historians do not have access to ritual practices, but only to texts describing them, it is impossible for them to use anthropological models as these are based on observations of behaviour not on observations of texts.[7]

One anthropological model that has often been used by historians is that of Marcel Mauss on gift giving. In medieval Europe, as in many other civilisations, contracts were fulfilled and exchanges of goods made by means of gifts. Though in theory these gifts were voluntary, Mauss argued that in fact they were given and repaid under obligations. In his celebrated essay on gift giving, Mauss outlined a theory of the so-called *potlatch*. Mauss applied this Chinook word, originally meaning 'to nourish' or 'to consume', to the exchanges of gifts and the rituals surrounding those exchanges taking place at tribal gatherings and by which means political rank within tribes, tribal confederations and nations were settled. Above all, this was a struggle among nobles 'to determine their position in the hierarchy to the ultimate benefit . . . of their own clans'.[8] Mauss noted that, in this *potlatch*, exchanges of gifts were based around three principles: the obligation to give, the obligation to receive and the obligation to repay gifts received. Mauss observed that a king or a chief could keep and maintain his authority among his people, and maintain his position with other chiefs, only if he could prove that he was favourably regarded by the spirits or gods, that he possessed fortune. The only way to demonstrate this fortune was by expending it to the humiliation of others, by putting them in the shadow of his name. To give was to show one's superiority and to refuse to give or to fail to invite was, according to Mauss, a declaration of war; a refusal of friendship and of friendly intercourse.[9] If a ruler had an obligation to give, there was also an obligation to receive and an obligation to repay gifts already given. To refuse a gift showed fear of having to repay and hence of being abased. Consequently, one would receive a gift in order to prove that one was not unworthy, that one was able to repay and able to take one's place in the social order. Mauss noted that the obligation to repay gifts received was the essence of the *potlatch*. Face would be lost for ever if a worthy return of a gift was not made. The person who could not return a gift would lose his rank and, in at least three of the tribes that Mauss observed, the sanction for the obligation to repay was enslavement for debt. Normally the gifts given had to be returned with interest. According to Mauss, if a subject received a blanket from his chief for services rendered, he would have to return two blankets. The chief would in turn redistribute to the subject whatever he received at the next *potlatch* at which rival clans repaid the chief's generosity.[10] Thus a circular arrangement seemingly emerges whereby there is an almost constant exchange of gifts between a chief and his subject, as well as between rival clans or tribes.[11]

Mauss himself tested his model of gift giving against evidence from the medieval period, and it is clear that this has some merits. Medieval writers frequently referred to the generosity of kings, which was clearly based on the notion that liberality was an essential adjunct of great power.[12] For a medieval king the ability to give showed his favour in the eyes of God. Thus giving or generosity was a function that should be performed by a medieval ruler, as noted by the chronicler. The image of the generous ruler is also one that is projected in medieval literature. To take one well-known example, in the Old English poem *Beowulf* the notion of the generous ruler appears primarily in the form of the ring giver.[13] Note also the statement of Arnold of Lübeck that the gifts given by King Cnut VI to the imperial envoys at a conference near the Eider in 1182 were mediocre and not fitting the royal greatness, thereby hinting at the magnificence and generosity expected of rulers.[14] Hence, Mauss's idea of the obligation to give can seemingly be seen to have some parallels in the medieval period. Similarly, the notion that to refuse a gift showed fear of having to repay and hence of being abased was certainly in Saxo's mind when he criticised his master and patron, Archbishop Absalon, for first declining Duke Henry the Lion's offer to spend the night in his camp and then declining an armed escort for his safe return.[15] In Saxo's eyes Absalon had violated etiquette and social order. Within the context of peacemaking, Mauss's model of the three obligations may be useful in general, if not in specifics, because theoretical models cannot account for all variables. In the medieval period, the historian of peacemaking is, furthermore, faced by two other problems. Firstly, contemporary records seldom give a full sequence of events and thus it is difficult to judge to what extent the medieval evidence can be tested against Mauss's model. Secondly, just as Buc has argued, the historian is dealing not with reportage but with highly crafted texts that skilfully reflect the interests and sentiments of the author, his patron or his audience. The effect of these considerations on how historians interpret rituals within the context of peacemaking can be illustrated by an analysis of the gift exchange that took place between Richard I and Tancred of Sicily on the occasion of their conference near Catania in 1191.

At their encounter in Catania, Richard I and Tancred of Sicily exchanged gifts in a ceremony recorded in the *Chronica* and in the *Gesta Regis Henrici Secundi*, both now usually ascribed to Roger of Howden.[16] Roger was in Richard's entourage during the journey to the Holy Land in 1190–91 and may indeed have been an eyewitness to the peace concluded between the English and Sicilian kings.[17] In the *Gesta*, Howden recalls how, following Richard and Tancred's treaty of October 1190, which settled the issue of the dower of Richard's sister Joanna, queen of the late William II of Sicily, King Philip of France suggested to Tancred that the English king could not be trusted and in fact planned to take over Sicily himself. Acting on these suspicions, Tancred decided to block the arrival of Richard's mother, Eleanor of Aquitaine, and his fiancée, Berengaria of Navarre, at Messina.[18] The two kings thus met at Catania amid a certain amount of suspicion and distrust, even if perhaps not outright hostility, and it seems that the event should be seen as a face-to-face confirmation of the earlier treaty.[19] According to the *Gesta*, at this meeting Tancred offered Richard vast presents of gold, silver, horses and silk, though the English king would take only a small ring 'as a sign of mutual affection'. In return Richard then gave Tancred the legendary sword of King Arthur called Caliburn.[20] Michelle R. Warren has recently highlighted this episode and the gift exchanges made, and in her article she argues that Tancred's act of showering the English king with gifts was 'unexplained'.[21] We know, however, from other similar exchanges that Tancred's display of wealth was not at all 'unexplained', but something that contemporaries expected of kings. Voss has for instance argued that Ralph Glaber's account of the meeting between the French king, Robert the Pious, and the Emperor Henry II in 1023 is instructive in analysing gift exchanges at peace conferences.[22] At this meeting Glaber describes how Robert the Pious offered the Emperor Henry II 'vast presents of gold and silver and precious stones, together with one hundred splendidly caparisoned horses each bearing a cuirass and a helmet'. In return, the Emperor then offered the French king one hundred pounds in purest gold.[23] Similarly, in the twelfth century, Arnold of Lübeck, Howden's German contemporary, refers to at least one occasion when the participants came away from a conference laden with presents, and there are several examples in Saxo of the generosity of rulers towards their friends or allies.[24]

Warren argued that Richard's refusal to take any of the economically valuable gifts was because he distinguished them from 'the socially significant ring', restricting the meaning of the exchange to peace. Thus Richard, she argued, was 'not bound to return any material favors'.[25] Comparing this incident to those of other gift exchanges, it would appear, however, that Warren's argument requires modification. For instance, it is not at all clear whether Richard could or would restrict 'the meaning of the exchange to peace'. It is certainly difficult to find a precedent for such usage. In the Middle Ages, rings were commonly given as gifts on all sorts of occasions and in a variety of circumstances. Most helpfully, for this particular argument and occasion, it is evident that rings were sometimes used as gifts in dispute settlements. John of Salisbury's *Historia Pontificalis* tells the story of a divorce case involving Hugh, count of Molise, which came before the papal curia at some point in the 1150s. Pope Eugenius, in reversing the divorce granted by the magnates and prelates of the king of Sicily, confirmed the marriage by the giving of a ring to the count as 'a token of faith and contract'.[26] Here, according to John of Salisbury, the ring – a circular object without a beginning or an end – represented the neverending, unbreakable, nature of the contract (*pactio*). Consequently, it seems likely that in 1191 the ring was symbolic of the agreement – an act of faith – between Richard and Tancred, rather than of peace as a concept.

Contemporaries clearly considered gift giving to be hierarchical and this could pose a problem to medieval rulers, because while both Tancred and Richard had to appear generous, a lordly virtue, they were equally concerned not to be seen to receive too much. Hence Richard took a small, almost token, gift to show that he did not reject the offer of peace and friendship that followed with it, without appearing needy of the other's generosity, which would have indicated inferiority. This same scenario can be seen at the best-known exchange of gifts at a medieval peace conference, that between the Emperor Henry II and the French king Robert the Pious in 1023. Here, the Emperor, among the vast gifts on offer, took only a gospel book set with gold and precious stones and 'a similar reliquary' containing a tooth of St Vincent. Robert the Pious in turn was content with a pair of gold vessels.[27] The principle seems to have also applied to the kings' followers. According to the author of the epic poem *Ruodlieb*, describing a similar eleventh-century meeting, the Emperor instructed his nobles not to accept all of the gifts on offer, saying: 'Do not let it appear that you need his wealth'.[28] The implication given by the author of the poem is that if a noble accepted too many of the gifts that were offered to him, he would be indebted to the French king. Using this precedent, it thus seems unlikely that, as Warren argues, Richard chose the ring because he would not be bound to return any gifts himself. It appears rather that the implication of gift giving remained generally constant. The only real distinction that can be made is between exchanges of gifts between equals, or between superior and inferior. This is the crux of the matter. According to Warren, Tancred's gifts were intended to shift the balance of power between the two kings in favour of the king of Sicily, a balance that Richard then tipped in his favour by giving Tancred the legendary sword of King Arthur, a gift that Warren believed implied lordship.[29] What Warren fails to appreciate is that, although weapons did imply lordship in certain circumstances, this was not such an occasion. The liberal giving of gifts, frequently weapons, by kings to their nobles or underling rulers at specific times of the year were occasions intended to show a ruler's superiority and place in the social hierarchy.[30] In 1191, however, Richard's counter-gift merely redressed the balance between himself and Tancred: both kings offered and both kings reciprocated. Tancred repaid his gift by supplying Richard with ships for his journey to the Holy Land, as attested by the *Gesta*.[31] Richard repaid his gift through the recognition of Tancred as king and rightful heir to his predecessor William II, and through a promise of military aid against any future invader of Sicily – which must in this instance have denoted the German emperor, Henry VI.[32]

Warren argued that the imbalance between the cultural value of the sword and that of the ring, with the sword evoking chivalric rite and the obligation to serve, reveal Richard's 'aggressive effort to dominate Tancred'.[33] However, the sword of King Arthur, Caliburn, also had mythical and heroic connotations. The popularity of the Arthurian tales in the twelfth century ensured that a sword with a reputed Arthurian provenance would convey prestige on its owner and project an image of a born leader, destined to achieve great things.[34] Emma Mason has argued that Tancred, 'facing mounting political pressures', might have welcomed the sword of the legendary hero, while Richard, whose reputation as a war leader was already established, could have afforded to dispense with this particular gift.[35] Richard's capabilities as a military leader was at least such that he realised that he would have more practical need and use of the ships that came with Tancred's good will than of the sword of Arthur. Furthermore, according to Mason, the sword was most likely a valuable item of Richard's regalia rather than a weapon for practical use, and this is of course also true of the ring that Richard chose from among Tancred's gifts.[36] Swords and rings commonly formed part of the regalia symbolising the power and authority of the king. Thus both gifts conferred certain legitimacy on the receiver as well as representing the power of the donor.

Warren has argued that Howden introduced the sword because it was significant in strengthening Richard's sovereignty at a time when it was being challenged by his brother John following Richard's designation of Arthur of Brittany as his heir.[37] However, it is possible that Howden's intention was not only to assert Richard's authority through the giving of a sword but also to show the humility of his king, who accepted only the small gift. In fact, humility is a recurring theme within the context of peacemaking. It can be seen clearly in the 1023 meeting between the Emperor Henry II and Robert the Pious and it also underpins Saxo's accounts of Valdemar I's dealings with Frederick Barbarossa and Henry the Lion.[38] To Howden the real significance of the exchange may not have lain in the cultural value of the sword or the ring, both of which were items that symbolised and conferred royal authority, but rather in the individual actions of the two rulers. Richard was thus portrayed as a true Christian prince, while Tancred appeared as an unworthy successor to his kingdom – a quite significant comment upon the agreement that Richard had concluded with Tancred, as it recognised the latter as the legitimate heir to the throne of Sicily. From all of this, it is obvious that it is difficult to gauge the relationship between two or more rulers just by looking at a specific aspect of one ritual. Howden's account of the gift exchange between Richard and Tancred illustrates aptly Buc's argument that descriptions of rituals were frequently manipulated to reflect the sentiments of individual writers or their patrons. In this case, the problem is not so much whether Howden fabricated or enchanced certain features of this exchange, but rather that the historian simply cannot know if he did. Consequently, while not dismissing the significance of the actual exchange and its various interpretations, it is important to set the event in its immediate context within the process of making peace.

Examining the circumstances surrounding the conclusion of peace corroborates that the 1191 exchange was in fact a mutual exchange of gifts between two kings who treated each other as equals. Firstly, it must be noted that the episode is unique among other similar instances of peacemaking. When Henry II and Robert the Pious met in 1023, their equality was made apparent through their choice of site for the conference; a border site on the river Meuse.[39] In 1191, however, Richard I was clearly within Tancred's territory as a guest so a meeting at a border site was out of the question. Yet, the initial place of meeting and the manner in which Richard and Tancred conferred indicate immediately that the two made a show of being equals. According to the *Gesta*, the two kings met some five miles outside the city of Catania, before riding in to the city together.[40] Richard thus did not come to Tancred, but the two met outside the city in the open. According to Buc, a so-called *occursus* provided medieval political culture with a recognised way – qualitatively and quantitatively – to gauge the relationship between two parties: qualitatively by detailing the nature of the train and its trappings, and quantitatively by evaluating the length an *occursus* travelled to meet its recipients.[41] This is seemingly what Howden was trying to portray in his account of events in 1191. There are several other examples of such meetings outside cities. For instance in 800 Pope Leo met Charlemagne twelve miles outside of Rome, before the two journeyed to the city together, and in the 1150s representatives of the citizens of Rome met Frederick Barbarossa between Rome and Sutri.[42] Furthermore, both Richard and Tancred had journeyed towards each other, echoing the use of meeting places that were roughly equidistant between two royal residences.[43] Indeed it is clear that Catania was some distance away both from Messina, held by Richard, and from Palermo, where Tancred resided.[44] It is also significant that upon meeting the two ran towards each other and exchanged kisses and then rode to and into the city together, a mirroring of each other's actions that again indicates equality.[45]

As with the gift exchange itself, one is struck by the similarity of Howden's account to Glaber's account of the 1023 meeting. According to Glaber, when the French king and the emperor arrived at the agreed site on the river Meuse, 'some from both realms' muttered that it would be improper for either of these kings to cross the river as if to 'aid' the other.[46] This problem was seemingly solved by both parties agreeing to do everything twice. Thus the Emperor, with a small following, first crossed the river to the French king, embraced him warmly, heard mass with him and shared a meal with him. Then followed the act of giving gifts, after which the Emperor took his leave. The morning after, 'King Robert with his bishops crossed the river and went to the camp of the emperor' where he was received with great honour and took a meal with Henry, before in his turn giving gifts.[47] By mirroring each other's actions both kings preserved their equality of status. Despite its unique nature in terms of location it is clear that the gift exchange between Richard I and Tancred of Sicily is comparable to other such instances between equals. Hence, whatever Howden's intentions were in relation to the actual exchange and the specific gifts, he was, nevertheless, keen to show that the two kings made peace as if they were equals.

Descriptions of conferences of the late twelfth and early thirteenth centuries that involved gift exchanges are suprisingly rare, especially in comparison to the large number of exchanges that took place at conferences in earlier centuries. Voss has noted that though Anglo-French conferences are by far the most frequently recorded meetings in the twelfth century, not one contemporary described a gift exchange taking place at such a parley.[48] Although this does not necessarily mean that such exchanges did not take place, the sheer number of available sources for the period 1154–1216 makes the absence of such references suggestive. It is clear that the English and French kings frequently sent gifts to each other even though they may not have exchanged gifts at conferences.[49] This could explain why Howden made so much of the 1191 incident; he, or his source, had simply not witnessed such an event before.[50] The seeming decline in the number of gift exchanges between rulers is echoed across Europe in the twelfth century. For instance Arnold of Lübeck describes in great detail the gifts given at the conference between the Emperor Frederick Barbarossa and King Bela of Hungary in 1189, yet his accounts of other, more frequent, negotiations rarely include such details.[51] However, just as there are no references to ceremonious gift exchanges between the French king and the Norman duke in the twelfth century, neither is there any evidence of such exchanges from the eleventh century, whereas in Europe such references are frequent. Thus it may be that perceived or actual hierarchical differences impacted on when and with whom it was prudent to exchange gifts. For instance, arranging a gift exchange as between equals may have been awkward for the French king, who was, nominally at least, the overlord of the Norman duke. Here, there is clearly a difference between the pragmatism applied to the sites of conferences, often based on military might or threats thereof, and the symbolic nature of certain ceremonies taking place at such meetings.

Nevertheless, it is evident that gifts did still play a significant role in Anglo-French peacemaking in the twelfth century. An interesting comparison can here be drawn with Joachim Bumke's work on feasts; a comparison that perhaps provides the most satisfactory answer to this specific question. In his *Courtly Culture*, Bumke notes that the evidence from the end of the thirteenth century make it seem that the period witnessed fewer feasts than before. Bumke argues, however, that contemporaries did not record fewer feasts, but rather that the feasts gradually lost the character of great public spectacles: 'court society became increasingly a closed society'.[52] It would be be difficult to argue that this was what happened with the conferences between the English and French kings. In fact, we know, to give but two examples, that in 1188 the two parties met outside in the open near the famous elm tree and that in 1195 Richard I and Philip Augustus met in the space between, and in the full view of, their two armies.[53] Nevertheless it is possible that Anglo-French conferences had, like Bumke's thirteenth-century feasts, lost their character of being great public spectacles, simply because there were so many of them. Arranging ceremonial gift exchanges at conferences sometimes occurring as often as three or four times a year does seem, if not impossible, at least impractical and unnecessary between two princes with such familiarity with each other. Part of the spectacle of gift exchanges was to show off the liberality of, and gauge the relationship between, each king to an audience that rarely saw such events and was largely unfamiliar with the other ruler and his followers. Consequently it made sense to have a gift exchange and other festivities surrounding the negotiations between Richard and Tancred, but perhaps not those between Richard and Philip Augustus.

This argument, furthermore, fits the context of those occasions when we know that gifts, though perhaps not specific exchanges, played an important role in Anglo-French diplomacy. They seem to have done so, however, not before or during negotiations or immediately after an agreement had been struck, but more as an affirmation, after a few months or even a year had elapsed, that relations were still cordial.[54] To take one example, in August 1158 Henry II and Louis VII negotiated an agreement (*pactio*) for the marriage of one of Louis's daughters to Henry's oldest son, and sureties ('fidejussores') were given to this effect.[55] A month later, in September, Henry II was received with much ceremony in Paris, in the royal hall, by his French counterpart. At his departure from Paris, Henry II was accompanied by Louis's daughter, whom he was bringing back with him to Normandy, and the French king himself travelled with Henry as far as Mantes, supplying all necessities ('necessariis . . . largiter attributis') during their journey.[56] A few months afterwards, in November, Henry II received Louis in Normandy and a great reception ceremony was arranged for both kings at the abbey of Bec with a procession of bishops and other great men. Henry II then lodged his French counterpart in the great hall of the abbey, while he himself took up quarters in the smaller one. To the author of the *Continuatio Beccensis*, this was a great occasion prompting him to wonder who had ever heard of such cordiality between these two kings? After his sojourn, Louis was taken on a short itinerary of several Norman cities before returning to France, and throughout Henry provided abundant supplies ('inveniens . . . affluenter necessaria').[57] Robert of Torigni adds that Louis had innumerable royal gifts ('innumeris regiis muneribus') with him on the return journey.[58] On another occasion, having concluded the treaty of Goulet with Philip Augustus in May 1200 and confirmed its terms at a conference near Andelys in 1201, King John travelled to France.[59] Here, according to the French chronicler Rigord, he was received by the French king and a procession had been prepared for his reception at the abbey of St Denis. John was then led into Paris by his French colleague, installed in the royal palace and bestowed with abundant supplies of drink and gifts ('Vina . . . liberaliter concessa; preterea munera preciosa . . . et alia carissima dona Philippus rex Johanni regi Anglie liberaliter dedit').[60] It is thus evident from the events of 1158 and 1201 that gifts and giving in Anglo-French diplomacy should be viewed in the wider context of largesse, rather than as specific ritual acts.

If gift exchanges at meetings were seemingly rarely recorded by contemporaries, one similar ceremony does make frequent appearances on the pages of late twelfth-century chronicles, namely feasting. In his article on ritual and ceremony in Ottonian Germany, Karl Leyser noted that banquets 'could be immensely potent rituals both to herald claims and to promote them, to manifest friendship, real or pretended, and acts of reconciliation'.[61] Indeed, that communal meals were a common occurrence within the context of peacemaking throughout medieval Europe, and not only in Ottonian Germany, is evident.[62] For instance several sources describe how after the division of the kingdom of Denmark between the three rivals Cnut, Valdemar and Svein had been confirmed, a great feast was celebrated in Roskilde to signal their reconciliation, and Howden details how, upon concluding their agreement, Tancred of Sicily and Richard I feasted together in Tancred's palace for three days.[63] It is noteworthy, however, that the peace concluded between the Emperor

Frederick Barbarossa and Pope Alexander III in 1177 was not followed by a communal meal. Instead, the pope sent a fatted calf to Frederick, as a symbol of him being the returning prodigal son.[64]

If it is evident that feasting commonly followed peacemaking and diplomacy, it is equally clear that banquets carried with them a number of different ceremonies and gestures. As D. A. Bullough remarked in his article on drama and ritual in medieval Europe, the consumption of food and drink 'is the basic human activity which has the greatest number of ritual acts associated with it'.[65] Saxo's work is full of such descriptions. For instance, in 1160, while on a joint expedition against the Slavs, Henry the Lion and Valdemar I met for a conference during which the Danish king was led into Henry's tent and offered a banquet at which many magnates acted as servitors, prompting Saxo to comment that 'while this dinner was resplendent with many different kinds of dish, the service was even more elegant than the food'. Saxo further added that the retainers were given a separate meal.[66] According to Eric Christiansen, Henry intended this banquet as a 'manifestation of the superiority of host over guests'.[67] Christiansen concluded that a meal could be used in this sense from another of Saxo's passages in which Valdemar, while on his way to the meeting at Saint-Jean-de-Losne in 1162, refused to eat at Count Adolph of Holstein's table, because it would have implied that the count was the Danish king's superior.[68] More recently, Felipe Fernandez-Armesto has noted that food sharing was 'a fundamental form of gift exchange, the cement of societies', and, as such, it would be natural to assume that the acts of feasting in the medieval period followed the same principles of obligation to offer, to receive and to reciprocate found in the Maussian model of gift giving.[69] Saxo certainly took great interest in those of his contemporary princes who showed their generosity through offers of food and feasting. Apart from commenting on the generosity of Count Adolph and Duke Henry the Lion, he also noted how the archbishop of Mainz offered the Danish royal party two nights' entertainment at the great assembly near Saint-Jean-de-Losne in 1162.[70] Furthermore, Esbern, the brother of Saxo's patron Archbishop Absalon, entertained some of the Rugian mediators on board his ship in 1169, an action that was echoed by the archbishop himself in 1185 when he held a feast for Bogiszlav, duke of the Pomeranians, on the occasion of the latter's submission to King Valdemar I.[71] Saxo contrasted these descriptions with a vivid account of Valdemar's treatment by the Emperor Frederick Barbarossa at the assembly of 1162, when Valdemar was not invited to enjoy the emperor's hospitality, or provisioned with supplies, despite pleas from Valdemar's ally, Henry the

Lion.[72] Saxo's aim in retelling some of these events was hence to show that generosity in feasting was a sign of good lordship, indeed an obligation of a ruler's place in the hierarchy, just like the giving of gifts.[73]

However, generous offers of food and its symbolism could make other rulers cautious to accept the offer. In 1162 the Danish king and his court refused the offer of a feast from count Adolph of Holstein because of the symbolic implications of accepting such generosity from a ruler of inferior status. According to Saxo, this problem was solved when Count Adolph, despite Valdemar's unwillingness, had the food brought in to the Danes and 'finally overcame their pride, and obliged them to make use of his generosity'.[74] Clearly a further refusal to eat the food that was now brought in would have been a declaration of enmity and would also have shown a fear of being unable to reciprocate. Moreover, Christiansen has commented that by sending in the food Adolph appeared to have made an offering, which could be seen as a token of submission, just like the paying of tribute. It is also possible that the fact that the Danish king would no longer have to sit at the count's table, as if an equal and ally, might have persuaded him to change his mind. Valdemar preserved his status by eating together with the other Danes, separate from the Holsteiners and their count. A comparison can be made here with the English and French kings, who seem to have been reluctant to share communal meals after their negotiations, and who, even when in the same town or city, feasted at different residences or halls. We know, for instance, that in 1158 Louis VII visited Henry II in Normandy where he was said to have been entertained in the great hall of the abbey of Bec while Henry held a banquet in another, smaller, hall.[75] On another occasion, in 1201, King John was entertained in the palace of Philip Augustus, while the French king himself had taken up residence elsewhere.[76]

Seating arrangements at great feasts were clearly significant in terms of the hierarchy of those present.[77] Normally the host of a feast and the most distinguished guests would sit at a raised dining table, the dais.[78] At royal feasts, the king or emperor tended to sit alone in order to emphasise his highness, whereas two kings sitting together at the high table indicated equality, friendship and solidarity.[79] It is this image that Saxo projects in his description of the famous feast in Roskilde in 1157, where King Svein was apparently given the middle seat at the table, as he was the most honourable in years.[80] Valdemar's refusal, on his way to the meeting at Saint-Jean-de-Losne, to sit at the table of Adolph of Holstein can be contrasted with the Danish king's ready acceptance of the count's hospitality upon his return journey from the great assembly.[81] One must ask what accounted for Valdemar's change of heart. On his journey to the imperial assembly, it would seem from Saxo's narrative that the Danish king was met by the count in order for the latter to escort Valdemar and his entourage safely through his territory, just as the contemporary bishops of Durham were expected to escort the Scottish kings to conferences with the kings of England.[82] At this point Valdemar and Adolph were not princes acting independently, but on the command of the Emperor. This is a significant point because there was 'ancient enmity' between the two that had not been resolved through negotiations by the time Valdemar was escorted by the count.[83] Hence, the relationship between the two was one of hostility, albeit, at the time, not armed. As suggested above, the feast held by Adolph may have symbolised either superiority or equality, neither of which Valdemar found acceptable because this would indicate that their hostility had been settled and replaced by a different relationship.[84] Consequently, the king refused to be entertained. On his return journey, Valdemar and Adolph established a friendship through the mediation of Absalon, the king's adviser, and now feasting was appropriate behaviour, confirming their relationship as allies. Saxo, in describing this second meeting between the count and the Danish king, thought that Adolph had also become Valdemar's man and commented that the count rendered his first service through hospitality.[85] Christiansen thought it possible that the Danish king gave the prince of the Holsteiners a money-fief in return for the treaty of friendship, which would compare favourably with other such arrangements.[86] From this, it is evident that feasting should often be viewed, like the giving of gifts, within the context of largesse. Most importantly this sequence of interactions shows that within peacemaking, feasting was a visual sign of reconciliation that could create, confirm or reconfirm the relationship between the participants. What that relationship was and how the act of feasting should be interpreted depended on where the two parties met and what other acts and ceremonies accompanied the making of peace.

The idea of fostering or restoring good relations with neighbouring rulers by sharing common meals or exchanging gifts was not unique to the Middle Ages. For instance, Eduard Rung has recently highlighted the many occasions when gifts and gift exchanges were an essential part of Graeco-Persian relations in the fifth and fourth centuries BC.[87] In more recent times Winston Churchill, Franklin Roosevelt and Joseph Stalin dined together on the last evening of November 1943 to celebrate the end of three days of gruelling discussions. During the evening Stalin had also kissed the blade of the Sword of Honour presented to him by Churchill on

behalf of King George VI for the people of Stalingrad, who had successfully withstood the German army.[88] Nevertheless, the symbolism of these
occasions clearly altered over time. For instance, historians would not view
Stalin's receipt of the sword of honour in 1943 as the acceptance of a gift
that rendered the Soviet leader an underling to King George VI in the way
that some historians have viewed Richard I's gift of a sword to Tancred
of Sicily as an act of superiority. Despite the fact that some eight hundred
years separate the Conference at Tehran from those of the twelfth century,
it is clear that ceremonies and gestures have continued to be an essential
part of diplomacy and are of immense importance for understanding the
political culture and the power relations between individuals. Although
ceremonies such as feasting and gift exchanges were the public face of
diplomacy – projecting the results of the negotiations and any agreements
to the outside world – it is important to remember that first and foremost
they also had a very real function: the fostering of cordial relations.

Notes

1 Gerd Althoff, 'The Variability of Rituals in the Middle Ages', in *Medieval
   Concepts of the Past: Ritual, Memory, Historiography*, ed. Gerd Althoff, Johannes
   Fried and Patrick J. Geary (Cambridge, 2002), 71.
2 Althoff, 'The Variability of Rituals', 72.
3 Althoff, 'The Variability of Rituals', 71–4.
4 Althoff, 'The Variability of Rituals', 87. For this see also D. A. Warner, 'Ritual and
   Memory in the Ottonian *Reich*: the Ceremony of *Adventus*', *Speculum*, 76 (2001),
   260–1.
5 Philippe Buc, *The Dangers of Ritual* (Princeton, 2001), 8.
6 Buc, *The Dangers of Ritual*, 9, 156.
7 Buc, *The Dangers of Ritual*, 248; 'Political Rituals and Political Imagination in the
   Medieval West from the Fourth to the Eleventh Century', in *The Medieval World*,
   ed. Peter Linehan and Janet L. Nelson (London, 2001), 189–90.
8 Mauss, *The Gift*, 4–5.
9 Mauss, *The Gift*, 10–11, 37.
10 Mauss, *The Gift*, 39–41.
11 For but a few critics of Mauss's theory, see A. Testart, 'Uncertainties of the
   "Obligation to Reciprocate": a Critique of Mauss' in *Marcel Mauss: A Centenary
   Tribute*, ed. W. James and N. J. Allen (New York, 1998); J. Laidlaw, 'A Free Gift
   Makes No Friends', *Journal of the Royal Anthropological Institute*, 6 (2000),
   617–34; Annette Weiner, *Inalienable Possessions: The Paradox of Keeping While
   Giving* (Berkeley, 1992).
12 For instance generosity makes frequent appearances in the poems of Bertran de
   Born. For some examples, see *The Poems of the Troubadour Bertran de Born*,
   ed. W. D. Paden, T. Sankovitch and P. H. Stablein (Berkeley, 1986), nos 14, 15,

33 and 38. For some references to this from the later medieval period, see Rigby, *Wisdom and Chivalry*, 47-8.

13 *Beowulf*, tr. Michael Alexander (London, 2003), ll. 20-5, 34-5, 80-1, 1012, 1486.

14 *Arnoldi Chronica Slavorum*, iii:2.

15 Saxo, *DRHH*, ii, 442-3. Diceto similarly noted how Archbishop William of Rheims during a visit to Canterbury refused the vases given as gifts of hospitality by Henry II, but accepted certain other things which were not offered as part of the gift, as tokens of the king's love. This was clearly not accepted practice, because Diceto commented that the action ran contrary to French custom. *Diceto*, i, 426.

16 Gillingham, 'The Travels of Roger of Howden', 70; 'Roger of Howden on Crusade', in his *Richard Coeur de Lion*, 141-53; D. Corner, 'The *Gesta Regis Henrici Secundi* and *Chronica* of Roger, Parson of Howden', *BIHR*, 56 (1983), 126-44. Voss has made a summary of gift exchanges and their importance for the making of peace that is primarily based on the evidence from the early medieval period. For this, see Voss, *Herrschertreffen*, 151-65.

17 Gillingham, *Richard I*, 130; 'The Travels of Roger of Howden', 72; 'Roger of Howden on Crusade', 143; D. M. Stenton, 'Roger of Howden and Benedict', *EHR*, 68 (1953), 574-82.

18 Howden, *Gesta*, ii, 158-9. On events in Messina, see also Ambroise, *Estoire de la guerre sainte*, in *The History of Holy War*, ed. and tr. Marianne Ailes and Malcolm Barber, 2 vols (Woodbridge, 2003), i, 10-20; ii, 38-48 (ll. 581-1193). For a summary, see Gillingham, *Richard I*, 140-2.

19 The initial agreement had not been made at a face-to-face meeting, but had been negotiated by envoys at Richard's court in Messina.

20 Howden, *Gesta*, ii, 159.

21 Michelle R. Warren, 'Roger of Howden Strikes Back: Investing Arthur of Brittany with the Anglo-Norman Future', *ANS*, 21 (1999), 267.

22 Voss, *Herrschertreffen*, 155.

23 Raoul Glaber, *Historiarum Libri Quinque*, 108-11; *Gesta episcoporum Cameracensium*, 480.

24 *Arnoldi Chronica Slavorum*, iv:8; Saxo, *DRHH*, ii, 440-1, 462-5, 516-17. See also *Knytlingasaga*, c. 119.

25 Warren, 'Roger of Howden Strikes Back', 267-8.

26 'Hic annulus, signaculum fidei et inite pactionis.' John of Salisbury, *Historia Pontificalis*, tr. M. Chibnall (Oxford, 1965), 82.

27 Raoul Glaber, *Historiarum Libri Quinque*, 110-11. For a summary of the most common gifts in the medieval period, see Voss, *Herrschertreffen*, 156-63.

28 *The Ruodlieb*, 36.

29 Warren, 'Roger of Howden Strikes Back', 267-8.

30 To take one example, the *Historia Welforum* reports that Duke Welf VI gave splendid arms and costly vestments to his men 'whenever it seemed appropriate'. Erich König, *Historia Welforum* (Stuttgart, 1938; repr. Sigmaringen, 1978), 72. Similarly, Rigord provides a list of gifts (on this occasion money) handed out by Philip Augustus to his supporters at Christmas 1190, with which the chronicler

clearly intended to show the liberality of the French king. *Oeuvres de Rigord et de Guillaume le Breton*, i, 106–7. Kings were not the only members of the royal family who could hand out gifts of various kinds. For instance Eleanor of Aquitaine was said to have given horses, arms and vestments to William Marshal on at least one occasion. *HGM*, ll. 1876–82.

31 Howden, *Gesta*, ii, 159.

32 Howden, *Gesta*, ii, 134; *Coggeshall*, 58–9; Gillingham, *Richard I*, 136.

33 Warren, 'Roger of Howden Strikes Back', 268.

34 Emma Mason, 'The Hero's Invincible Weapon: an Aspect of Angevin Propaganda', in *The Ideals and Practice of Medieval Knighthood, III*, ed. Christopher Harper-Bill and Ruth Harvey (Woodbridge, 1990), 128.

35 Mason, 'The Hero's Invincible Weapon', 130.

36 Mason, 'The Hero's Invincible Weapon', 130. According to the *Carmen de Hastingae Proelio*, Duke William of Normandy had sent, via Harold Godwineson, a ring and a sword as gifts to King Edward the Confessor, signifying the duke's right to the English throne. *The Carmen de Hastingae Proelio*, ed. Catherine Morton and Hope Muntz (Oxford, 1972), 20–1.

37 Warren, 'Roger of Howden Strikes Back', 268–71.

38 Raoul Glaber, *Historiarum Libri Quinque*, 108–9; Saxo, *DRHH*, ii, 544–5, 594–5. An interesting comparison can also be drawn with Walter Map's description of the meeting between Edward the Confessor and the Welsh ruler Llywelyn. This episode is seemingly based on Glaber, or a common source, and again humility is at its focus. *De Nugis Curialium*, 192–5. For an analysis of the possible origin(s) of these two meetings, see Benham, 'Constructing Memories of Peacemaking' (forthcoming).

39 Raoul Glaber, *Historiarum Libri Quinque*, 108–9. See also discussion by Voss in *Herrschertreffen*, 65–7, 69.

40 Howden, *Gesta*, ii, 158–9.

41 Buc, *The Dangers of Ritual*, 76.

42 *ARF*, 110; *Gesta Friderici*, 108. See also the German examples cited by Joachim Bumke in his *Courtly Culture*, 215–19.

43 *The Annals of St Bertin*, 153.

44 *Itinerarium Peregrinorum et Gesta Regis Ricardi*, in *Chronicles and Memorials of the Reign of Richard I*, 2 vols, ed. W. Stubbs, Rolls Series, 38 (London, 1864) i, 171.

45 Howden, *Gesta*, ii, 158–9.

46 Raoul Glaber, *Historiarum Libri Quinque*, 108–9.

47 Raoul Glaber, *Historiarum Libri Quinque*, 108–9.

48 Voss, *Herrschertreffen*, 164.

49 The excellent work by Schröder provides a good insight into the gifts and gift culture of the English king. Sybille Schröder, *Macht und Gabe: materielle Kultur am Hof Heinrichs II. von England* (Husum, 2004).

50 I am not convinced by Warren's argument that Howden's intent was to focus his description, and hence the interpretation, on the legendary sword Caliburn, rather than the event as a whole. Warren, 'Roger of Howden Strikes Back', 263, 268, 271–2.

51 *Arnoldi Chronica Slavorum*, IV:iii.

52 Bumke, *Courtly Culture*, 210.

53 Howden, *Gesta*, ii, 47; Howden, *Chronica*, ii, 345; *Diceto*, ii, 55; *Oeuvres de Rigord et de Guillaume le Breton*, i, 132–3, 188.

54 It seems likely that it was in this spirit that Philip, count of Flanders, was received in Rouen in 1164, the year after the renewal of the Anglo-Flemish alliance. *Torigni*, 224.

55 *Continuatio Beccensis*, 318–19.

56 *Continuatio Beccensis*, 319.

57 *Continuatio Beccensis*, 320. Robert of Torigni's version of these events is consistent with that of the *Continuatio*. *Torigni*, 196–8.

58 *Torigni*, 198.

59 Howden, *Chronica*, iv, 164; *Gervase of Canterbury*, ii, 93.

60 *Oeuvres de Rigord et de Guillaume le Breton*, i, 150. Roger of Wendover adds that during John's stay at the palace, King Philip was resident elsewhere. *Flores Historiarum*, i, 312.

61 Karl Leyser, 'Ritual, Ceremony and Gesture: Ottonian Germany', in his *Communications and Power in Medieval Europe: The Carolingian and Ottonian Centuries*, ed. Timothy Reuter (London, 1994), 201.

62 For a few examples of feasting in the earlier medieval period, see *ARF*, 144 (s.a. 816); Ermold, *Poème sur Louis le Pieux*, ll. 2338–60, 2426–35 (s.a. 826); *Annales Fuldenses*, 36 (s.a. 847); Raoul Glaber, *Historiarum Libri Quinque*, 108–9 (s.a. 1023); Adam of Bremen, *Gesta*, 161 (s.a. 1052); Rangerius of Lucca, *Vita Metrica*, in MGH SS, 30, ed. E. Sackur, G. Schwartz and B. Schmeidler (Leipzig, 1934), 1224 (s.a. 1077).

63 *Helmoldi Chronica Slavorum*, 78; Saxo, *DRHH*, ii, 405–7; Aggesen, *A Short History of the Kings of Denmark*, 71; Howden, *Gesta*, ii, 158–9. For a discussion of the Danish feast, where one of the rivals was murdered, and the sources, see R. Malmros, 'Blodgildet i Roskilde historiografiskt belyst', *Scandia*, 45 (1979), 43–66.

64 *De Pace Veneta Relatio*, in R. M. Thomson, 'An English Eyewitness Account of the Peace of Venice, 1177', *Speculum*, 50 (1975), 32.

65 D. A. Bullough, 'Games People Played: Drama and Ritual as Propaganda in Medieval Europe, *TRHS*, 5th ser., 24 (1974), 99.

66 Saxo, *DRHH*, ii, 442–3. Bumke has noted that the service at table by nobles was not always done voluntarily and that the practice could be turned on its head by participants wanting to make a demonstration of wealth and power. Bumke, *Courtly Culture*, 188–9. A comparison could here also be made with the 1356 feast held by the Black Prince in the aftermath of his victory at the battle of Poitiers – a feast where the victorious prince himself served the captive French king, Jean II. Froissart, *Chroniques*, in *Historiens et chroniquers du Moyen Âge*, tr. E. Pognon (Paris, 1952), 143–4.

67 Saxo, *DRHH*, iii, 801 fn. 321.

68 Saxo, *DRHH*, ii, 459; iii, 801 fn. 321.

69 F. Fernandez-Armesto, 'Food, Glorious Food', *Sunday Times*, 22, December 2002.

70 Saxo, *DRHH*, ii, 465.

71 Saxo, *DRHH*, ii, 506–7, 622–3.

72 Saxo, *DRHH*, ii, 465.

73 Bumke has drawn a similar conclusion based on German examples from courtly literature. Bumke, *Courtly Culture*, 210.

74 Saxo, *DRHH*, ii, 459.

75 *Continuatio Beccensis*, 320.

76 *Flores Historiarum*, i, 312; *Oeuvres de Rigord et de Guillaume le Breton*, i, 150.

77 For a discussion of some early examples of feasting and the frequent disputes over seating arrangements that accompanied banquets see D. A. Bullough, *Friends, Neighbours and Fellow-drinkers: Aspects of Community and Conflict in the Early Medieval West*, H. M. Chadwick Memorial Lectures 1 (Cambridge, 1991), 13–15. See also M. J. Enright, 'Lady with a Mead-cup: Ritual, Group Cohesion and Hierarchy in the Germanic Warband', *Frühmittelalterliche Studien*, 22 (1988), 170–203; Rigby, *Wisdom and Chivalry*, 40.

78 W. E. Mead, *The English Medieval Feast* (London, 1967), 130.

79 Sergio Bertelli, *The King's Body: Sacred Rituals of Power in Medieval and Early Modern Europe*, tr. R. Burr Litchfield (University Park, Pennsylvania, 2001), 193.

80 Saxo, *DRHH*, ii, 406–7.

81 Saxo, *DRHH*, ii, 466–7.

82 Saxo, *DRHH*, ii, 459–60; Stones, Anglo-*Scottish Relations 1174–1328*, 10.

83 Saxo, *DRHH*, ii, 459.

84 This follows on from Fasoli's definition of peace as something that indicates the maintenance of a new situation, for which see Fasoli, 'La pace e guerra nell'alto medioevo', 80. R. I. Burns in commenting on relations between Christians and Muslims in Valencia, similarly notes how offering food to an enemy, or accepting it, implied a relationship. Robert I. Burns, 'How to End a Crusade: Techniques for Making Peace in the Thirteenth-century Kingdom of Valencia', *Military Affairs*, 35 (1971), 144.

85 Saxo, *DRHH*, ii, 466–7.

86 Saxo, *DRHH*, iii, 807, fn. 349. Among the other examples of 'treaties of friendship' that involved money fiefs could be mentioned the 1163 treaty between Henry II and Thierry of Flanders. *Dip. Docs*, i, 8–11.

87 Eduard Rung, 'War, Peace and Diplomacy in Graeco-Persian Relations from the Sixth to the Fourth Century BC', in *War and Peace in Ancient and Medieval History*, ed. Philip de Souza and John France (Cambridge, 2008), 42, 49.

88 Robin Edmonds, *The Big Three: Churchill, Roosevelt and Stalin* (London, 1991), 29–30.

4

Homage, fealty and gestures of submission

In an often quoted passage in Galbert of Bruges's eyewitness account of the civil war that followed the murder of Count Charles the Good in 1127, the Flemish cleric described how the citizens of Bruges did homage to their new count, William Clito, on a field just outside the town: 'The count asked each one if he wished to become wholly his man, and the latter replied "I so wish", and with his hands clasped and enclosed by those of the count, they were bound together by a kiss. Then with the wand which he held in his hand, the count gave investiture to all'.[1] This is not a description of a ceremony taking place during a meeting between two rulers, but it is the most detailed twelfth-century description of a ritual that is frequently found in peacemaking between rulers. The whole of the ceremony described by Galbert has been termed by some modern historians as an entry into vassalage.[2] The French historian Jacques Le Goff saw in this description three distinct elements; homage, oath of fealty (faith) and investiture. Homage, the first element, normally consisted of two acts. The first was verbal, stating the willingness of the subject to become the count's man. This act is seen clearly in Galbert's account when each of the burghers replied to their count that they wished to become his men.[3] The second act was when the subject placed his joined hands between the hands of the count, the image with which historians traditionally associate homage. The second element of the ritual of vassalage, fealty, was completed by an oath. The oath was symbolically important as it was sworn on the Gospels or certain relics. The third phase of vassalage was investiture, which, again following Le Goff, was accomplished by the count's delivery of a symbolic object to his subjects. Often these objects had some relation to what the subject was being invested with. The most common form was land, which was often transferred by objects like a piece of turf or twigs.[4]

The whole intention of vassalage was to create a social bond through ceremonial or 'ritual'. Le Goff even referred to this as a 'system' that could function only if all elements were present, while at the same time recognising the fact that all three elements are frequently referred to in the sources in a single sentence covering only homage and fealty.[5] The bond or relationship created through the ceremony of vassalage was one of dependence, symbolised in particular through the act of homage.[6] According to Le Goff, this particular act symbolically expressed protection or 'the encounter between power and submission', a notion more recently echoed by Susan Reynolds.[7] Le Goff noted that, in Galbert of Bruges's account of the homage to William Clito, the count's gesture of clasping and enclosing the subjects' hands included a promise of aid and protection, a promise that by its nature implied 'an ostentatious display of a superior . . . power'.[8] Quite simply, to fulfil his role, the protector must have the necessary means and this immediately implies, even before the relationship begins, that the protector is more than his dependent-to-be.[9]

The sort of ceremony described by Galbert of Bruges and interpreted by Le Goff and others has few parallels in peacemaking between rulers, primarily because there are no detailed descriptions of such events.[10] Nevertheless, it is apparent that two of the elements in this ceremony were frequently found in peacemaking, namely the act of homage and the oath of fealty. It would be difficult to argue with the general consensus that the whole intention of the act of performing homage and of taking an oath of fealty was to express a social bond or relationship of dependence. Yet, it is evident that, far from being a system that can be interpreted unambiguously in the same way each time that they are encountered in the sources, homage and fealty were acts that covered a multitude of scenarios. To interpret them all in the same manner would disguise some of the subtlety of medieval diplomacy.[11]

In November 1200 William, king of Scots, held a conference with King John outside the city of Lincoln, and there, in view of all, he became John's man and swore fealty on Archbishop Hubert Walter's cross.[12] Ralph of Coggeshall notes of this same event that William did homage to the English king, which he had until then put off.[13] There is a conflict between these two accounts in that Howden does not specifically record that William did homage (*homagium*), but merely that he became John's man ('devenit homo Johannis regis Anglie'). The historian should not necessarily equate this with homage, as on other occasions Howden specifically used the term *homagium*, in order to refer to actual acts of homage. For instance in 1189 William came to Canterbury where he did homage to

Richard I in order to have his honours in England ('fecit ei [Richard I] homagium pro dignitatibus suis habendis in Anglia').[14] None the less, as Howden does not provide an actual description of the act of homage in his account of the meeting in 1189, the word *homagium* could potentially cover both the act of homage and the oath of fealty, or (n)either of the two acts, as indeed could Coggeshall's description of William's *homagium* in 1200.[15] It seems likely that Howden was an eyewitness to the event at Lincoln. We know from the work of Gillingham that Howden played an important diplomatic role in Anglo-Scottish affairs, and that his narrative is often a reflection of his own travels.[16] The chronicler's presence at the conference of 1200 would explain why he was able to be so specific about it, adding details such as that William's oath was sworn on Archbishop Hubert Walter's cross. It would, furthermore, add strength to the argument that William did not perform homage to King John, i.e. he did not put his hands between those of the English king, but only swore an oath of fealty, just as Howden stated. Even allowing for the possibility that to become someone's man (*devenire homo*) assumes that the act of homage had been, or would be, performed fires wide of the mark of Howden's narrative focus. To him, the most important aspect of this whole chain of events was the oath sworn on Hubert Walter's cross, promising on William's own life and limbs and earthly honour to preserve the peace of King John and his kingdom against all men, saving always his own right.[17]

A. A. M. Duncan has recently suggested that historians do an injustice to both John and William if they seek to explain their relationship in terms of feudal subjection of Scotland. We know that in 1174 the treaty that followed William's capture at Alnwick and his submission to Henry II effectively ended his involvement in the great rebellion of 1173–74, and that this treaty explicitly acknowledged English overlordship and bound William's barons to support the English king against the Scottish king if he rejected Henry's authority.[18] No such undertaking or oath survives from 1189, the year in which Richard absolved the Scottish king from the liege homage exacted by Henry in return for a payment of 10,000 marks, presumably needed for the English king's crusade. Nor does such a document survive from 1200, when the focus of William's oath was simply to preserve John's life and kingdom against all men. One would be inclined to suggest that the man whom the English king most wanted William to give assurances about was Philip Augustus. Indeed it seems clear that the king of Scots, shortly after John's accession to the English throne, had been tempted by the offer of an alliance with the French king and this meddling in Anglo-French politics seems to have been the reason why two proposed meetings of 1199/1200, one at Northampton and another at York, came to nothing.[19] Thus the 'homage' of 1200 did not look back to the treaties of 1174 and 1189, but was a feature of the peacemaking directly responding to the events of 1199–1200. Besides, not even the submission and liege homage of 1174 rendered William a sub-king to Henry II in the way that it did Roderick of Connaught in 1175.[20] Hence, when A. A. M. Duncan commented that the kings of Scots were regarded as neighbours and poor relations, but certainly as masters in their own house, he hit the nail on the head.[21]

As kings were, in theory, equals in terms of social and political status, those occasions when one king performed homage to another, as if to a superior, have usually attracted widespread attention from historians. The homage and (supposed) feudal subjection of the king of Scots to the English king is one such example, but perhaps the best known, and certainly the most discussed, acts of homage in the twelfth century are those of the English king to the king of France. As is well known, the English king did not owe allegiance to the French king in his own right, but rather in his capacity as the duke of Normandy and Aquitaine and as the count of Anjou.[22] There seem to have been two ways in which the Norman dukes overcame the problem of homage and its implications: either they avoided performing it at all, or the heir, rather than the duke himself, did homage. Usually this was to solve the problems of disputed succession.[23] For instance, according to William of Malmesbury, King Henry I's son William did homage to the French king for the duchy of Normandy in 1120 during the negotiations following the battle of Brémule, and Robert of Torigni records how King Stephen's son, Eustace did homage to the French king in 1137.[24] On both of these occasions the act of homage neatly thwarted the French king's support of the English king's rivals for the duchy – William Clito in 1120, and Geoffrey of Anjou and his wife Matilda in 1137.[25] During Henry II's reign the practice of the English king's heir(s) doing homage continued. In 1160 Henry II's son, Henry, then aged five or six, did homage to Louis VII for Normandy, and some nine years later he also did homage for Anjou and Brittany, while his younger brother, Richard, did homage for Aquitaine.[26] There were some occasions when the duke himself performed homage for his continental lands. According to one French chronicler, Richard I performed homage in sight of the English and French armies in 1195, while Howden recorded how John agreed to do homage to Philip Augustus when they met and made the Treaty of Le Goulet on 22 May 1200.[27] It would appear that Henry II also did homage at least once to the French king, in 1183.[28] These occasions when an English king, or his heir, performed homage to the king of France are significant because they were all events that occurred during negotiations for peace.

Klaus van Eickels has suggested that Henry II also did homage in 1177 at a peace conference near Ivry.[29] Van Eickels based his conclusion on the text of the treaty recording the peace, in which the English king called Louis *dominus* (lord) and the French king similarly called Henry *homo* (man) and *fidelis* (faithful).[30] This in itself is not, of course, proof that Henry did homage on that occasion, and it is significant that no contemporary sources record such a ceremony. Klaus van Eickels further argued that during Henry II's reign the act of homage acquired a new function, serving as 'the outward form to conclude a peace treaty between the two kings, who in fact treated each other as equals'. According to van Eickels, the 'mutual feudal obligations' set out in the text were integrated into a larger concept of *amicitia* (friendship), making the 'hierarchically differentiated functions of the ritual (the legitimation of the vassal's possession of his fiefs and his acknowledged subordination to his overlord) recede into the background'. To van Eickels the act of homage was in a sense compensated for by following it up with ritualised feasting and other 'ostentatious gestures' that expressed and confirmed their friendship and stressed their equal rank.[31]

However, van Eickels's conclusions require some modification. Firstly, it is clear from the meeting places that the French and English kings treated each other as equals already before the accession of Henry II and even in the period before the Norman dukes acquired their royal title.[32] Secondly, it seems unlikely that symbolic acts of friendship, like feasting, were necessarily being used to compensate for the subordination of the English king or Norman duke, because we know that feasts could also be employed to manifest a superior to inferior relationship. Van Eickels attempted to use the relationship between the tenth-century, east-Frankish ruler Henry I and his princes as a model, commenting that the parallels were obvious between tenth-century practice and that of the English and French kings in the twelfth century.[33] Though it cannot be denied that Henry I did use friendship pacts to make his kingship acceptable, it is clear that, unless both parties offered the feasts that followed, this offering was seen by contemporaries not as a way of expressing equality but rather as a means to show that there was a hierarchy between the king and his princes. Thus, although van Eickels noted that in 1158 both Henry II and the French king were entertained within the territories of the other, thereby mirroring each other's actions, he failed to mention that this was a form of behaviour that implied equality, not the English king's visit to Paris. Furthermore he suggested that this visit was a continuation of the (supposed) ceremony begun two years earlier, in 1156, whereas they were more likely part and parcel of the peacemaking and marriage negotiations of 1158.[34]

Klaus van Eickels chose to interpret the homage performed by the English king to the king of France in relation to other rituals and ceremonies that often accompanied peacemaking. A different approach to this problem could be to start with the insights provided by John of Worcester. According to this early twelfth-century chronicler, in the 1090s the English king, William II, wanted Malcolm, king of Scots, to come to his court at Gloucester to do homage to William in accordance with the judgement of the English barons. Malcolm refused, saying that he would meet William only somewhere on the frontier between their kingdoms, and would do homage only in accordance with the judgement of the chief men of both realms. It is interesting to note that John of Worcester does not use the term *homagium*, but instead uses the phrase 'in curia sua rectitudinem ei faceret'.[35] Nevertheless, it would seem that what John of Worcester, or Malcolm, was here implying was that performing homage, or having one's rights – whatever those might have been – on the border was less of a subordination than if it had been done at court, because meetings on border sites implied equality. William W. Scott in commenting on this paragraph of John's chronicle has noted that the principle behind this request was probably the homage performed by the Norman dukes to the French king, even though the word homage was in fact not used by John of Worcester and it is uncertain to what extent the Norman dukes had ever performed homage to the French king.[36] Malcolm's (or John of Worcester's) claim is similar to that made by King John in 1202, when he argued that he was not obliged to attend the French king's court, but had only to confer with him on the border between their kingdoms.[37] It is also certain that, on those very few occasions when we can be reasonably certain that an English king did homage to his French counterpart, it was done at border sites.[38] Even the homage of 1195 was said to have taken place in circumstances indicating equality.[39] Thus, even if we allow for the view put forward by Gillingham that Henry II and John did homage in person because they were in weak bargaining positions, the fact remains that they did not have to go to the French king's court to perform the ceremony, and this is significant. Quite simply, when Henry II and John performed homage to the French kings in 1183 and 1200, it indicated a different relationship from that initiated by the homage of a king of Scots to his English colleague, because it was done at border sites. The meeting place clearly indicated the reality of this relationship, not the act of homage.

The location of where homage was performed is clearly important in interpreting this particular ritual, but it is evident that the circumstances surrounding the negotiations must also be taken into consideration. In 1169, Henry II met with King Louis VII of France at Montmirail in the county of Chartres, within French territory. Though the main subject of the conference was the dispute between Archbishop Thomas Becket and Henry II, hence perhaps explaining the location of the meeting, it is clear that the conference was also engineered to facilitate peace between the two kings. According to John of Salisbury, then a member of Thomas Becket's entourage, the restoration of peace included a renewal of homage by Henry II to Louis VII, but the set of gestures that accompanied this act of homage is significantly different from those anticipated by historians such as Le Goff. John of Salisbury relates how Henry came as a suppliant ('supplex accessit') to the French king, offering himself, his children, his lands, his resources and his treasures to be placed under the French king's judgement. Thus, says John, Henry returned to the French king's homage ('in hominium eius reversus est') with a corporal oath that he would keep faith with him as his lord against all men and would give him the aid and service due from a duke of Normandy.[40] Just as in the case of the king of Scots's homage to John in 1200, the oath of fealty stood at the heart of the ceremony in 1169, but the actual gestures were those of a suppliant.

Considering the ecclesiastical focus of this particular meeting, it is perhaps unsurprising that Henry II chose to signal the restoration of peace in this way. Supplication was indeed one of the most commonly occurring symbolic acts accompanying negotiations in the central and high Middle Ages, even though it was usually associated with rebellion.[41] In ancient Rome those who begged the forgiveness of a patron or protector commonly did so with similar gestures of humiliation.[42] Subsequently, the act became one of the most durable aspects of the Christian rite of penitential supplication.[43] Penance was usually a preventative act, designed to protect Christians from the consequences of their sinful mortal life after death. Medieval people sought to atone for their sinful acts through confessing their sins and then undertaking penitential acts such as fasting, flagellation or almsgiving.[44] After the break-up of the Carolingian empire in the ninth century, the ritual of penance became integrated into secular society and was no longer performed just on set days before bishops or priests, but became a part of political order. Geoffrey Koziol has explored this phenomenon in detail with particular reference to early medieval

France. According to Koziol the rules of divine order were essentially the same in kingdom, church and monastery, as each society was regarded as 'a community of *fideles* whose stability rested on its members' humility'. Humility was measured by the willingness of each member of that community to accept his or her role in society. Rejection of one's role in society was 'to reject the very basis of political order'.[45] Consequently, the 'ritual' of supplication became common in acts of reconciliation between kings and rebellious subjects.[46] The act of penance was the same in duchy, kingdom, church and monastery, because rebellion against God's rulers was a sin against God.[47] In all cases the sin was the same: a violation of order and a desire by a subject to set himself above his natural superiors, i.e. the sin of pride. According to the eleventh-century canon lawyer Burchard of Worms, pride was the queen of all evils and as such the act of penance must be the most public and most humiliating of penances.[48] However, the gesture clearly had mutual benefits, as such a show of penitence and complete submission had to be rewarded with forgiveness and absolution, thus allowing the wrongdoer to be received back into the Christian community.[49] For instance, had King Louis VII refused the supplication of Henry II, he would have struck at the heart of his own office. Nevertheless, it is unlikely that Henry with his actions actually conceded anything new at Montmirail. More likely, the king calculated that diplomatically he could have much to gain by the recognition of Louis as his lord in such fulsome terms.[50]

It is possible that the gestures described by John of Salisbury should be labelled as gestures for returning to homage and so should be separated from the more traditional act of homage. We know, for instance, that on the day after Henry's public show of humiliation whereby he returned to the homage of his French counterpart, his two sons, Henry and Richard, themselves did homage ('fecit homagium') for the English king's continental lands.[51] Yet it is clear from the evidence of other negotiations that the act of homage and that of supplication cannot always be separated and it is therefore difficult to interpret these rituals and the relationships they conveyed without considering their broader context. One example of this can be found with the negotiations surrounding the Danish conquest of the Pomeranians in c. 1184/85. According to Saxo, Bogiszlav, prince of the Pomeranians, submitted to Cnut VI outside the fort of Kamien. Bogiszlav obtained peace on the terms that he should pay tribute and receive his hitherto inherited land from the king as a fief (*beneficium*). To guarantee this agreement, he also promised to provide hostages. On the following day the Pomeranian prince bowed the knee and then threw himself at

the king's feet as a suppliant. He, furthermore, gave some of the promised hostages and received his lands from the hand of the king.[52] Saxo's
account of this event is fairly detailed, yet he was probably not an eyewitness to it. We are fortunate, however, in that his account can be complemented by two other writers: Sven Aggesen and Arnold of Lübeck. Sven
Aggesen was a colleague of Saxo, and he probably wrote his passage on
the conquest of the Pomeranians within three years of the event. Sven
confirms the narrative of Saxo, stating that Cnut repressed the wild Slavs
and forced their duke (Bogiszlav) to pay him tribute and homage. The
Danish historian further notes that this was done aboard the king's ship,
glittering with gilding on stem and stern, and lastly he adds: 'and I saw it
done'.[53] The German chronicler, Arnold of Lübeck, likewise records that
the Pomeranians were forced to pay tribute and to hand over the fort of
Wolgast, as well as to give twelve hostages. Thus, Arnold comments, Cnut
subdued the Slavs through tribute and homage, to the indignation of the
Emperor.[54]

Saxo, unlike Sven Aggesen and Arnold of Lübeck, does not use the
term 'homage' to describe this particular event. His narrative is instead
focused on the submission and supplication of the Pomeranian prince and
his family, even though he concedes that Bogiszlav received his land from
the king's hand in an act that must be equated with investiture.[55] Saxo did,
however, refer to the bending of the knee, a gesture that is also echoed by
the French chroniclers recording the homage of King Richard I in 1195,
and it is possible that this was the gesture that Saxo equated with homage,
because it was a gesture of humiliation and hence submission.[56] There
could, in any case, have been a sequence of different acts and gestures,
and perhaps this would best fit Saxo's narrative. It is also noticeable that,
unlike Roger of Howden in 1200 and John of Salisbury in 1169, neither the
Danish chroniclers nor Arnold of Lübeck thought that the oath of fealty
was an important feature of events in 1184/85. It is certainly not mentioned
specifically, which, of course, does not rule out the possibility that it could
have gone under the cover of the term *hominium*. Furthermore, just like
the events described by John of Salisbury at Montmirail, it is clear that this
incident deviates from the act of homage as envisaged by most modern
historians. For example, though Saxo states that Bogiszlav bowed the
knee to, and received his land from, the Danish king, he further states
that Bogiszlav threw himself at the king's feet and gave him hostages and
tribute.[57] Similarly, though Sven and Arnold specifically record that the
Pomeranian prince did homage to Cnut, they also report the giving of
hostages and tribute.[58] These features find no equivalent in the image of

homage as portrayed by modern historians. Neither can they be found at the conference between William, king of Scots, and King John in 1200, nor on those occasions when the English king did homage to his French counterpart in 1183 and in 1200. Although some of the gestures performed by the Slav Duke are similar to those of Henry II in 1169, it is evident that the bond initiated cannot possibly be interpreted as being the same, because the gestures of 1169 had not been forged under circumstances of military defeat. Likewise it would be difficult to compare the homage of Bogiszlav to that of King William in 1200, because, although the king of Scots was negotiating deep within English territory, he had not suffered conquest and he was not asked to surrender any hostages. Again it is evident that there must have been some sort of sliding scale of inferiority, where some participants in peacemaking were more inferior than others. It is, furthermore, evident that what determined where on this sliding scale a ruler ranked when making peace was determined not by a specific set of gestures or rituals but rather by the circumstances in which the ruler performed them. To speak of homage as initiating a specific bond or relationship would hence be very misleading, when the act could clearly encompass a number of different scenarios and relationships.

There are some further examples of the varying interpretations of the use of homage in negotiations for peace, and some of these initially correspond more closely to the model of commendation proposed by Le Goff and others. One example is the 1201 agreement between King John and Llewelyn ap Iorwerth of Gwynedd. The agreement has recently been discussed by Ifor W. Rowlands in the context of Anglo-Welsh relations, in particular of feudal relations. Here our aim is to develop some of the issues raised by Rowlands and to locate the agreement and the relationship between John and Llywelyn in a wider context of peacemaking between rulers.[59] The first thing that sets this example aside from those discussed above is the fact that we know of the homage and fealty of the Welsh prince not through the narrative sources, but through the actual text of the agreement ('forma pacis') as enrolled among the letters patent.[60] According to the text, Llywelyn swore to observe fealty to King John at a meeting with John's representatives, among whom can be found Geoffrey fitz Peter, the king's justiciar, and Hubert Walter, the royal chancellor and archbishop of Canterbury.[61] The agreement further outlines how Llywelyn had received seisin from the justiciar of all the lands of which he was then in possession and that he, upon John's return from the continent, would do homage to him as his liege lord for the aforesaid lands ('homagium ei faciet sicut domino suo ligio de predictis tenementis').[62] The rest of the document then sets out how and where various breaches of the peace would be dealt with.[63] Here we have evidence of a 'ritual' of peacemaking that corresponds to the model of the entry into vassalage set out by modern historians and based on the early twelfth-century description by Galbert of Bruges. If nothing else, the agreement seems to have comprised the three essential elements of the ceremony: the oath of fealty, the act of homage and the investiture.

There are, however, considerable difficulties in interpreting this agreement. Firstly, there is no firm evidence that Llywelyn subsequently did homage to King John. Rowlands has noted that, unlike the oath of fealty, the act of homage could not be done by proxy and it alone created the bond between lord and dependent vassal.[64] In 1201, when the agreement was drawn up, King John was seeing to his affairs on the continent, hence the document's stipulation that Llywelyn would come, after the return and at the command of the king, to perform this act. John returned to England in December 1203 and Huw Pryce has suggested that it is highly likely that Llywelyn fulfilled his undertaking to do homage to the English king at Worcester in 1204 or certainly before his betrothal to John's illegitimate daughter, Joan, in October of that year.[65] Nevertheless, the fact remains that there are no documentary records of such an event and none of the chroniclers mentions it. If, as argued by Rowlands, the key element in the relationship between the Welsh prince and the English king was the act of homage and this fact was 'all too obvious' to the participants, why was it not recorded by any contemporary writers?[66] Though it is always dangerous to argue *ex silentio*, it seems curious that contemporaries omitted such an event when previous acts of homage by the Welsh to an English king had been noted by several contemporaries.[67] Moreover, the oath, and possibly the homage, of William, king of Scots, of November 1200, are reported by contemporaries as diplomatic victories for the English king and the agreement of 1201 must have fallen into a similar category.

Nevertheless, the historian should perhaps not be surprised that this agreement is not mentioned by contemporaries, because the document of 1201 itself contains some discrepancies that throw the validity of the agreement and the ceremonies surrounding it into doubt. As noted by Rowlands, the peace, as it is enrolled, makes it clear that it was formalised at a ceremony on 11 July 1201. It was on this occasion that Llywelyn took his oath of fealty to John's representatives and received seisin of certain lands. Rowlands is furthermore correct in observing that the agreement was not a formal treaty warranted by the king but rather a memorandum of the terms negotiated, which were authenticated by the seals of the chancellor and the justiciar. The text envisaged that King John would at a later date confirm it with his own seal, but there is no evidence that this actually happened. Nor are we aware of any copy that Llywelyn may have had and to which his seal might have been attached.[68] The evidence as it stands, makes it likely that the agreement was never ratified and seems to imply that Llywelyn merely took an oath, in much the same way that William, king of Scots, had done the year before. Indeed, Llywelyn's oath seems to have been very similar to that of William.[69] It is, moreover, certain that it would be difficult to build up a picture of the relationship between the Welsh prince and the English king on the basis of this document alone. It may serve as an indicator of the wishes and aims of the English monarchy vis-à-vis Llywelyn but, in practice, their relationship may have been rather less defined than that set out in the text of the agreement. This is not to dismiss the 'contractual ('feudal') obligations and the practical outcomes of a mutual ('feudal') contract' between John and Llywelyn as 'unhistorical or meaningless' but merely to highlight that historians must base such conclusions on solid evidence.[70] The fact that the agreement was seemingly never ratified probably indicates that, for whatever reason, the oath of fealty was in the end deemed sufficient to secure peace and cordial relations.

Another useful way of looking at this agreement is to compare it with what contemporaries had to say about the relationship between John and Llywelyn. It seems likely that the Welsh hostilities of 1210–11 ended the cordial relations between the two rulers, and all of the contemporary sources record how the English king led an expedition into Wales in 1211 and forced the Welsh prince into submission.[71] In their narratives, however, contemporaries did not detail how Llewelyn had broken his oath or promises to John, nor did they refer to him as being the king's man (*homo*), faithful (*fidelis*), vassal or any other such word now used by historians to denote a dependent relationship.[72] In both the *Annals of Margam* and the *Annals of Waverley*, Llywelyn is recorded as being the son-in-law ('generum') of the English king.[73] The familial bond between the two rulers is furthermore made explicit by another two writers covering the royal expedition to Wales in 1211.[74] John himself, in a letter of an admittedly late date, speaks of Llywelyn as 'his beloved son'.[75] Though all of this may be simply stating a fact, it is curious that contemporaries, rather than detailing the 1201 agreement and the possible subsequent homage of Llywelyn, preferred to remember his marriage in 1205 to Joan, King John's illegitimate daughter.[76] Ifor W. Rowlands has commented that John's initiative in brokering this marriage alliance replicated that of his father, Henry II, in 1175. In that year the English king arranged the marriage between his half-sister, Emma of Anjou, to Dafydd ab Owain of Gwynedd. The Shropshire manor of Ellesmere was her marriage portion as, in 1205, it was to be that of Joan.[77] As suggested by Rowlands, these marriage alliances could have sinister outcomes, as Llywelyn found out in 1211 when his submission charter granted Gwynedd to John as his heir should he not have a child by his wife Joan.[78] It would thus seem that the bond created through homage and oath of fealty could be eclipsed in importance by that created through marriage. It is possible that the marriage between Llywelyn and Joan in 1205 had replaced the original request for homage. It is evident from this that contemporaries were sometimes less concerned with so-called feudo-vassalic rules and relations than modern historians have been. As a consequence it is hardly surprising that historians have often made the 1201 agreement and its implications the focal point of their discussions of Anglo-Welsh relations during King John's reign, whereas the marriage between Llywelyn and the king's daughter is brushed aside in a few sentences.[79] In fact both of these topics need attention. Certainly, a fuller discussion of the implications of the large number of marriage alliances encountered in this period throughout the Angevin Empire and beyond could enhance our knowledge of inter-ruler relations that involved homage and/or oaths of fealty.[80]

If the 1201 Anglo-Welsh treaty is a difficult source with which to establish the relationship between the participants, there are other documents that can serve us better. One such example is the Anglo-Flemish treaty concluded in 1163. Unlike the 1201 agreement, there is no uncertainty surrounding the validity of this agreement. The treaty between Henry II and his son, Henry, on the one hand and Thierry d'Alsace, count of Flanders, and his son, Philip, on the other, was concluded at a ceremony at Dover on 19 March 1163.[81] According to the text of the chirograph, Thierry and his son pledged with faith and an oath ('fide et sacramento assecuraverunt') to the English king and his son, that they would help Henry (and afterwards his son) hold and defend his kingdom against all men, and that they would on the request of King Henry provide annually one thousand soldiers to fight in England, Normandy or Maine.[82] In return the English king would give Count Thierry each year 500 marks in fee ('in feodo'), and his son Philip had for this fee and for the terms of the agreement done homage (*hominium*) to Henry II.[83] Despite the fact that the 1163 treaty, like the 1201 Anglo-Welsh peace, seemingly contains the three elements of oath of fealty, act of homage and investiture, the Anglo-Flemish agreement is very different in its implication for the relationship between the count of Flanders and the English king.

It is evident that the relationship in the Anglo-Flemish treaty is less one-sided than that anticipated with the Anglo-Welsh agreement of 1201. For example, Llywelyn's oath was clearly unilateral, and any reciprocal act of faith that King John was to make is not specified. In 1163, however, mutual acts of faith were made. Thierry and his son assured their contract with Henry through an oath ('sacramento assecuraverunt'), but even if Henry II did not himself take an oath in return, he did at least assure ('assecuravit') them that he would honour his side of the contract as long as they adhered to the terms of the treaty.[84] Furthermore, the 1201 peace stipulated that Llywelyn was to swear an oath of fealty and do homage to John as his liege lord.[85] The count of Flanders, on the other hand, was asked to help Henry II in faith as a friend and lord from whom he holds a fief ('per bonam fidem juvabit sicut amicum et dominum de quo feodum tenet').[86] This is rather interesting because the implication of friendship was commonly that the participants were equals. When, in the eighth century, Alcuin asked his pupil Pippin 'Quid est amicitia?', the correct answer was: 'Aequalitas amicorum'.[87] Though Alcuin was not saying that all friends are equal in status, but rather that friendship requires an equality of love between the two friends, his thoughts provide a useful insight, especially since the 1163 statement of friendship compares favourably with other instances of peacemaking between parties claiming equal status. For example, according to the text of the 1191 treaty concluded at Messina, Philip Augustus had sworn a firm peace with 'amicum et fidelem nostrum', King Richard of England.[88] The French king also described his English counterpart in precisely this way some five years later.[89]

Nonetheless, it would seem that oaths and agreements couched in friendship terminology were commonly used to stabilise or to control lordship. Lords, including kings, could become friends of their vassals, a phenomenon that Althoff has suggested became especially visible during times of crisis.[90] Althoff has also pointed out that friendship could be flexible: it could coexist easily with relationships of superiority and inferiority, and it could at times be perceived as a reward for demonstrable subordination.[91] Julia Barrow has further suggested that the use of the terminology of friendship implies a relative rather than an absolute equality, since in many cases the purpose of a party in seeking friendship was to win the protection of someone more powerful.[92] Whether we choose to view agreements claiming friendship as expressing a bond between absolute or relative equals, or something even less defined, historians have nevertheless argued that in the twelfth and thirteenth centuries the label 'friend' became, increasingly, not simply 'a rhetorical flourish, but rather a serious title expressing a legally fixed position'.[93]

The friendship between the count of Flanders and the English king evidently evolved over time. Two written treaties survives from the period before 1163, one of 1101 and another of 1110, and one later treaty, that of 1197.[94] The texts of the treaties of 1101, 1110 and 1163 are almost identical.[95] Yet there are two significant differences. Firstly, in 1101, unlike the treaty of 1163, it was not recorded that the count of Flanders should help the English king as his friend and lord from whom he held a fief, but merely as his friend ('juvabit sicut suum amicum et de quo feodum tenet').[96] Secondly, although it features in 1163, homage is not referred to in the two preceding agreements. Ganshof considered it likely that such an act had been performed in 1101, but, even if it had not, it is evident that Thierry had none the less done homage to an English king prior to 1163.[97] According to the text of the 1163 treaty, the count's son, Philip, rather than the count, himself did homage to Henry II because Thierry had done homage to Henry's grandfather Henry I.[98] There is no written record of such an agreement between Thierry d'Alsace, who succeeded William Clito as count of Flanders in 1128, and King Henry I, who died in 1135. Galbert of Bruges did, however, note that the Anglo-Flemish alliance was renewed shortly after Thierry's succession to the county.[99] It is thus possible that in 1128 the act of homage was a new aspect of the relationship between the count of Flanders and the English king.[100] In 1163 the inclusion in the written text of the word *dominus* in conjunction with *amicus* and the record of the *hominium* of the count's son could be seen as an attempt to define the relationship between the parties.[101] Nevertheless, even in 1163, the treaty, the act of homage performed by the count's son, and hence the nature of the relationship, was suitably imprecise; there is simply an underlying assumption that both parties understood what it meant to help someone as a friend and a lord from whom one holds a fief. One might imagine that the count's obligations as a friend included the military service outlined in the treaty, but interestingly enough, on the one occasion in the twelfth century when we know that an English king made use of military help from a count of Flanders, a treaty of a different character was concluded. The agreement in question, that of 1197 between Richard I and Baldwin VI, states quite simply that neither party was to make any peace or truce without the other's consent.[102] This treaty makes no mention of friends or friendship.[103] Nowhere is the count of Flanders referred to as Richard's man. The English king is not described as the lord of Baldwin, and homage was not performed. Furthermore, the agreement is characterised by an exchange of oaths and sureties, as if between equals.[104] However, in the text, the count of Flanders is noted as the *consanguineum* of Richard I, a similar if less immediate familial bond to that which later existed between King John and Llywelyn.[105] Over the course of the twelfth century the relationship between the counts of Flanders and the English kings had thus passed from a loose to a more defined friendship and thence to a relationship defined only by kinship and mutuality. Again what seemingly defined the relationship between the count of Flanders and the English king was not the act of homage and its implications but rather the circumstances of the negotiations and the aim of the agreement. The treaty of 1197 was thus more directly tuned to the specific needs and requirements of the war raging between Richard and Philip Augustus. By contrast the relationship between the parties in the earlier Anglo-Flemish agreements was suitably imprecise because they were not negotiated during times of war. Instead, these agreements had a much wider aim of securing peace, friendship and cordial relations.

Despite the fact that the 1163 treaty seems to set out an agreement that defines the obligations of the participants within a so-called feudo-vassalic framework, it clearly shows how different the relationship between Henry II and Thierry d'Alsace was in comparison to those discussed above. Unlike, Bogiszlav's giving of hostages in the 1180s, the Anglo-Flemish agreement of 1163 was characterised by an exchange of sureties, and unlike William the Lion and Llywelyn ap Iorwerth, the Flemish count did not hold his conference with the English king and his representatives at a site that implied English superiority.[106] Moreover, the count did not himself do homage to the English king, just as the Norman duke rarely did homage to the French king. Such 'rituals' of peacemaking, far from providing an unambiguous visual language, instead present the historian with a myriad of different acts and gestures that cannot be viewed in isolation, nor can they always be interpreted without the help of the written word. To speak of homage or the oath of fealty as having one specific meaning is inaccurate when each occasion was clearly unique and should be interpreted only within the context of the circumstances pertinent to that occasion. Quite simply, although the implication of the act of homage and the oath of fealty remained generally constant – that is, they were acts of subordination – the circumstances surrounding these acts and the agreements that accompanied them were not: they were altered and manipulated to fit the ways and wishes of the participants. It is significant that Galbert of Bruges never stated that his description of the homage of the townsmen of Bruges to William Clito was the only way in which one could perform homage. Similarly, the importance of homage in peacemaking did not rest with the individual gestures and ceremonies, but rather in how they fitted together with the process as a whole.[107] To further understand this, we need to investigate those other elements that accompanied the making of peace in the Middle Ages, starting with the role of envoys and mediators.

Notes

1 Galbert of Bruges, *Histoire du meurtre de Charles le Bon*, 89–90 (cap. 56).

2 Jacques Le Goff, 'The Symbolic Ritual of Vassalage', in his *Time, Work and Culture in the Middle Ages*, tr. Arthur Goldhammer (Chicago, 1980), 240.

3 Galbert of Bruges, *Histoire du meurtre de Charles le Bon*, 89 (cap. 56).

4 Le Goff, 'The Symbolic Ritual of Vassalage', 244; cf. Marc Bloch, *Feudal Society*, tr. L. A. Manyon (London, 1965), 145–6; Yannick Carré, *Le baiser sur la bouche au Moyen Âge* (Paris, 1992), 188–91.

5 Le Goff, 'The Symbolic Ritual of Vassalage', 248.

6 H. Mitteis, *Lehnrecht und Staatsgewalt. Untersuchungen zur mittelalterlichen Verfassungsgeschichte* (Weimar, 1958), 479–81; Le Goff, 'The Symbolic Ritual of Vassalage', 241–2, 250–2; Susan Reynolds, 'Some Afterthoughts on Fiefs and Vassals', *HSJ*, 9 (1997), 8–9; C. B. Bouchard, *Strong of Body, Brave and Noble: Chivalry and Society in Medieval France* (London, 1998), 43; J. Maquet, *Pouvoir et société en Afrique* (Paris, 1970), 193; Eickels, *Vom inszenierten Konsens*, 19, 333–41.

7 Le Goff, 'The Symbolic Ritual of Vassalage', 241; Reynolds, 'Some Afterthoughts on Fiefs and Vassals', 8–9.

8 Le Goff, 'The Symbolic Ritual of Vassalage', 250–1.

9 Maquet, *Pouvoir et société en Afrique*, 193.

10 Carré has noted that there are few descriptions of this ceremony in general from the eleventh and twelfth centuries. Carré, *Le baiser sur la bouche*, 188, 206.

11 A number of recent studies have criticised the notion of vassalage and the 'system' it created, for which see E. A. R. Brown, 'The Tyranny of a Construct: Feudalism and Historians of Medieval Europe', *American Historical Review*, 79 (1974), 1063–88; Jean Flori, *L'Essor de la Chevalerie* (Geneva, 1980); Susan Reynolds, *Fiefs and Vassals. The Medieval Evidence Reinterpreted* (Oxford, 1994), especially pp. 18–19, 22–34; D. Barthélemy, 'La mutation féodale a-t-elle eu lieu?', *Annales*, 47 (1992), 767-7; J. O. Prestwich, 'Feudalism: a Critique', in *The Place of War in English History 1066-1214*, ed. Michael Prestwich (Woodbridge, 2004), 83–103. For a specific criticism of the 'ritual' of homage and oath of fealty, see Susan Reynolds, 'Some Afterthoughts on Fiefs and Vassals', 7–9.

12 'Willelmus rex Scottorum devenit homo Johannis regis Anglie de jure suo, et juravit ei fidelitatem super crucem Huberti Cantuariensis archiepiscopi'. Howden, *Chronica*, iv, 141.

13 *Coggeshall*, 107.

14 Howden, *Chronica*, iii, 25–6; Howden, *Gesta*, ii, 98. At this meeting Richard also absolved the Scottish king from doing liege homage to the English king. Howden, *Gesta*, ii, 103; Howden, *Chronica*, iii, 26.

15 Le Goff noted in his article on this subject that such terminology often covered several stages of the ceremony. Le Goff, 'The Symbolic Ritual of Vassalage', 248. Susan Reynolds has further noted that it is not certain whether the word 'homage' always referred to a rite or ceremony. Reynolds, *Fiefs and Vassals*, 29.

16 Gillingham, 'The Travels of Roger of Howden', 72–83.

17 Howden, *Chronica*, iv, 141.

18 Duncan, 'John King of England and the Kings of Scots', 268; Howden, *Gesta*, i, 95–7; *Diceto*, i, 396.

19 *Diceto*, ii, 66; Howden, *Chronica*, iv, 90–2, 107. For a convincing outline of events leading up to the Lincoln meeting, see Duncan, 'John King of England and the Kings of Scots', 251–3.

20 Howden, *Gesta*, i, 102 ('Henricus rex Angliae concessit predicto Roderico, ligio homini suo, regi Connactae, quamdiu ei fideliter serviet, quod sit rex sub eo, paratus ad servitium suum sicut homo suus'). On Henry II and Roderick of Connaucht, see Babcock, 'Clients of the Angevin King', 229–45.

21 Duncan, 'John King of England and the Kings of Scots', 269.

22 F. Lot, *Fidèles ou vassaux? Essai sur la nature juridique du lien qui unissait les grands vassaux à la royauté depuis le milieu du IXe jusqu'à la fin du XIIe siècle* (Paris, 1904), 213; Mitteis, *Lehnrecht und Staatsgewalt*, 324–35; Lemarignier, *Recherches sur l'hommage en marche*, 73–113; C. W. Hollister and T. K. Keefe, 'The Making of the Angevin Empire', *Journal of British Studies*, 12 (1973), repr. in *Monarchy, Magnates and Institutions in the Anglo-Norman World* (London, 1986), 268–71; Bates, *Normandy before 1066*, 8–9, 59–60; van Eickels, *Vom inszenierten Konsens*, 245–86, 297–318; Dieter Berg, *England und der Kontinent* (Bochum, 1987), 264. For a brief discussion of the relationship between the dukes and the French kings in the eleventh century, see also D. C. Douglas, 'The Rise of Normandy', in his *Time and the Hour* (London, 1977), 101–3.

23 Klaus van Eickels, '*Homagium* and *Amicitia*: Rituals of Peace and Their Significance in the Anglo-French Negotiations of the Twelfth Century', *Francia*, 24 (1997), 134; *Vom inszenierten Konsens*, 312–24, 333–4; Jean Dunbabin, *France in the Making 843–1180* (Oxford, 1985), 205.

24 *GRA*, i, 735; *Torigni*, 132. Van Eickels has seen the reign of Henry I, when Normandy and England was held by one person, as the starting point of the problem of homage. Van Eickels, *Vom inszenierten Konsens*, 305–9.

25 John Gillingham, 'Doing Homage to the King of France', in *Henry II: New Interpretations*, ed. Christopher Harper-Bill and Nicholas Vincent (Woodbridge, 2007), 68–9.

26 *Torigni*, 208, 240; *Gervase of Canterbury*, i, 207–8; *The Letters of John of Salisbury*, ii, 636–8. According to Gillingham, Richard's installation as duke of Aquitaine at two ceremonies in 1172 was a ritual expression of 'Aquitaine's de facto independence from the king of France and thus a contrast to events at Montmirail in 1169'. Gillingham, *Richard I*, 39–40.

27 *Oeuvres de Rigord et de Guillaume le Breton*, i, 133, 199; Howden, *Chronica*, iv, 114–15. A fifteenth-century manuscript of the *Grandes Chroniques de France* illustrates well the imagery of the 1195 homage in later medieval thinking. *Les Grandes Chroniques de France*, Châteauroux, Bibliothèque municipale, MS 5, f. 225v. Note that Richard's homage is not mentioned by the English chroniclers. For the view, which one cannot easily dismiss, that the French chroniclers description of the 1195 homage was more firmly based on their perception of Richard's leadership qualities vis-à-vis those of Philip Augustus than on fact, see Gillingham, 'Doing Homage', 82–3.

28 Howden, *Gesta*, i, 306; Howden, *Chronica*, iii, 284. Excluding, of course, the occasion in 1151 when Henry did homage before he became king of England. Howden notes that Henry also did homage in 1156, but he was writing some forty years after this event and his knowledge of events before 1170 is poor. Moreover, such contemporaries as Robert of Torigni do not mention an act of homage in this year. Howden, *Chronica*, i, 215. See also John Gillingham's convincing argument regarding the 1156 incident and others. Gillingham, 'Doing Homage', 63–84.

29 Van Eickels, '*Homagium* and *Amicitia*', 135.

30 Howden, *Gesta*, i, 191; Howden, *Chronica*, ii, 144; *Diceto*, i, 422. This theory was first developed by Lemarignier in 1945 and it was followed by Kolb in 1988: Lemarignier, *Recherches sur l'hommage en marche*, 99; Kolb, *Herrscherbegegnungen im Mittelalter*, 145.

31 Van Eickels, '*Homagium* and *Amicitia*', 135–8. These themes have been developed further in his *Vom inszenierten Konsens*, 19–22, 333–41. In some ways this follows on from Lemarignier's work, in which he made a distinction between the so-called vassalic homage and the 'hommage de paix': Lemarignier, *Recherches sur l'hommage en marche*, 79–83.

32 Benham, 'Anglo-French Peace Conferences in the Twelfth Century', 58–9.

33 Van Eickels, '*Homagium* and *Amicitia*', 136; Gerd Althoff, *Verwandte, Freunde und Getreue* (Darmstadt, 1990), 108–10.

34 *Torigni*, 196–8; *Continuatio Beccensis*, 318–20.

35 *The Chronicle of John of Worcester*, iii, 64–5.

36 Scott, 'The March Laws Reconsidered', 121.

37 *Coggeshall*, 135–6.

38 Howden, *Chronica*, iii, 284; Howden, *Gesta*, i, 306; Howden, *Chronica*, iv, 114–15.

39 *Oeuvres de Rigord et de Guillaume le Breton*, i, 133, 199; *Newburgh*, ii, 461; Howden, *Chronica*, iii, 305. See also Chapter 1, 000.

40 *The Letters of John of Salisbury*, ii, 636–8.

41 One of the most famous examples of this act is Henry IV's appearance before Pope Gregory VII in the snow outside the fortress of Canossa in January 1077. *The Correspondence of Pope Gregory VII*, tr. E. Emerton (New York, 1966), 111–12; *Das Register Gregors VII*, 2 vols, ed. F. Caspar, MGH Ep. 2 (Berlin, 1955), i, 312–14. For two early twelfth-century examples, see *Gesta Friderici*, 27–8; *Annals of Magdeburg*, ed. G. H. Pertz, MGH SS, 16 (Leipzig, 1925), 185; E. F. Vacandard, *Vie de saint Bernard, abbé de Clairvaux*, 4th edn, 2 vols (Paris,

1927), i, 370–2. I am grateful to Professor Christopher Holdsworth for bringing these to my attention. For an Anglo-Norman example of the early twelfth century, see Orderic, *HE*, vi, 278–9. Compare also the contemporary descriptions of John's supplication before his brother, King Richard I, in 1194. *Coggeshall*, 64; *Newburgh*, ii, 424; *Diceto*, ii, 114.

42 Koziol, *Begging Pardon and Favor*, 181.

43 Mary C. Mansfield, *The Humiliation of Sinners* (Ithaca, 1995), 169. Koziol, *Begging Pardon and Favor*, 181.

44 Sarah Hamilton, 'The Unique Favour of Penance: the Church and the People c. 800–c. 1100', in *The Medieval World*, ed. Peter Linehan and Janet L. Nelson (London, 2001), 231. See also Le Goff, *La naissance du purgatoire* (Paris, 1981).

45 Koziol, *Begging Pardon and Favor*, 182, 185.

46 For this aspect of the act of satisfaction, see also Althoff, 'Satisfaction', 270–80.

47 Mansfield, *The Humiliation of Sinners*, 277–8.

48 As quoted in Koziol, *Begging Pardon and Favor*, 187.

49 G. Tellenbach, *Die westliche Kirche vom 10. bis zum frühen 12. Jahrhundert* (Göttingen, 1988), 192–3. According to Althoff, a friendly reception was not always certain. For this see discussion in G. Althoff, 'Satisfaction: Amicable Settlement of Conflicts in the Middle Ages', in *Ordering Medieval Society. Perspectives on Intellectual and Practical Modes of Shaping Social Relations*, ed. Bernhard Jussen, tr. Pamela Selwyn (Philadelphia, 2001), 273–9; 'Das Privileg der deditio', 99–125. In 1077 Henry IV's supplication neatly thwarted the plans of his opponents to remove him from royal office; for this see *Vita Heinrici IV. Imperatoris*, ed. W. Eberhard, MGH SRG 58 (Hanover, 1990), 16; Stefan Weinfurter, *The Salian Century* (Philadelphia, 1999), 149–56.

50 Gillingham, 'Doing Homage to the King of France', 73–4.

51 *The Letters of John of Salisbury*, ii, 636–8; *Torigni*, 240.

52 Saxo, *DRHH*, ii, 622–3.

53 Sven Aggesen, *Brevis Historia*, 141; *A Short History of the Kings of Denmark*, 73.

54 *Arnoldi Chronica Slavorum*, III: vii.

55 Saxo, *DRHH*, ii, 623, 625.

56 *Oeuvres de Rigord et de Guillaume le Breton*, i, 133, 199. Compare this to Lemarignier's discussion of the homage by Rollo to Charles the Simple in c. 911. Lemarignier, *Recherches sur l'hommage en marche*, 83.

57 Saxo, *DRHH*, ii, 622–3. According to Carré, the bending of the knee(s) is not commonly recorded in the sources until the thirteenth century. Carré, *Le baiser sur la bouche*, 192.

58 Sven Aggesen, *Brevis Historia*, 141; *A Short History of the Kings of Denmark*, 73; *Arnoldi Chronica Slavorum*, III:vii.

59 I. W. Rowlands, 'The 1201 Peace between King John and Llywelyn ap Iorwerth', *Studia Celtica*, 34 (2000), 149–66.

60 Pryce, *The Acts of Welsh Rulers*, 372–3, no. 221; *Rot. Litt. Pat.*, 8b–9a.

61 'iuravit . . . fidelitatem domini regis I. contra omnes homines.' Pryce, *The Acts of Welsh Rulers*, 372. Rowlands has noted that the actual place of meeting is uncertain. Rowlands, 'The 1201 Peace', 155.

62 Pryce, *The Acts of Welsh Rulers*, 372.

63 Pryce, *The Acts of Welsh Rulers*, 373.

64 Rowlands, 'The 1201 Peace', 156.

65 Pryce, *The Acts of Welsh Rulers*, 373. Rowlands, very cautiously, echoes this. Rowlands, 'The 1201 Peace', 164.

66 Rowlands, 'The 1201 Peace', 156. Rowlands does, in fact, acknowledge that the absence of references to the actual homage is a fundamental problem in the interpretation of this agreement. *Ibid.*, 164.

67 For a few such examples, see *Gervase of Canterbury*, i, 165–6 (for s.a. 1157–58); *Diceto*, i, 311; *Brut y Tywysogyon*, 62–4; *Newburgh*, i, 145; Howden, *Gesta*, i, 162; Howden, *Chronica*, ii, 134 (for s.a. 1177). Roger of Wendover did, however, report that in 1209 the Welsh did homage to John, which had never been heard of until that time. However, his narrative lacks details and he places the ceremonies at Woodstock, making the description reminiscent of events in 1163. *Flores Historiarum*, ii, 51.

68 Rowlands, 'The 1201 Peace', 155, 164. For the terminology of formal treaties, see Chapter 8, 189–93. Compare also with the terminology of the 1208 agreement with Gwenwynwyn, which begins: 'Hec est conventio facta . . .' Pryce, *The Acts of Welsh Rulers*, 770, no. 576.

69 Llywelyn 'iuravit . . . fidelitatem domini Regis I. contra omnes homines se inperpetuum observaturos de sua vita et membris suis et de suo terreno honore.' Pryce, *The Acts of Welsh Rulers*, 372.

William 'juravit ei [King John] fidelitatem . . . de vita et membris et terreno honore suo, contra omnes homines, et de pace servanda sibi et regno suo'. Howden, *Chronica*, iv, 141.

70 Rowlands, 'The 1201 Peace', 164. Davies did not question the validity of this agreement, but simply assumed it to be a symbol of the intensification of the powers of overlordship. Davies, *Conquest*, 294.

71 *The Annals of Margam*, in *Ann. Mon.*, i, 31; *The Annals of Waverley*, in *Ann. Mon*, ii, 267; The *Annals of Worcester*, in *Ann. Mon.*, iv, 399; *Memoriale Fratris Walteri de Coventria*, ii, 203; *Flores Historiarum*, ii, 58. Though there had been some hostility during 1208, it would seem that this had been patched up by December of that year. *Rot Litt. Pat.*, 88a; Pryce, *The Acts of Welsh Rulers*, no. 228. Llywelyn remained on good terms with John throughout 1209 and took part in the Scottish expedition of that year. Davies, *Conquest*, 241; Pryce, *The Acts of Welsh Rulers*, 378.

72 Reynolds, *Fiefs and Vassals*, 20, 22–3. Le Goff uses the terms vassal and man synonymously. Le Goff, 'The Symbolic Ritual of Vassalage', 240, 244, 249. In his translation of Saxo, Christiansen uses the word vassal for the Latin word *miles*. Saxo, *DRHH*, ii, 466–7, 516–17.

73 *Ann. Mon.*, i, 31; ii, 267.

74 *The Annals of Worcester*, in *Ann. Mon.*, iv, 399; *Brut y Tywysogyon*, 85.

75 *Foedera*, I, i, 127. By contrast, the charter announcing the agreement between John and Renaud de Dammartin in 1212 refers to the count of Boulogne as 'our beloved and faithful'. *Foedera*, I, i, 158.

76 *The Annals of Worcester* in *Ann. Mon.*, iv, 394. For the official document record-
    ing the proposed marriage, see *Rot. Litt. Claus.*, i, 12. Compare also how the
    French chronicler Rigord, in his account of the Treaty of Le Goulet, says nothing
    about King John's homage to the French king, preferring instead to focus on the
    marriage between Prince Louis and John's niece, Blanche of Castile. *Oeuvres de
    Rigord et de Guillaume le Breton*, i, 148.

77 Rowlands, 'King John and Wales', 282; *Diceto*, i, 397–8. On the 1175 marriage,
    see also Warren, *Henry II*, 167. Howden states that Ellesmere was given to
    Dafydd at the conference at Oxford in 1177. Howden, *Gesta*, i, 159, 162.

78 Pryce, *The Acts of Welsh Rulers*, no. 233. Dafydd ab Owain, the husband of
    Emma of Anjou, died an exile in England in 1203, having been handed over to
    Hubert Walter in 1197 by his nephew Llywelyn. Rowlands, 'The 1201 Peace',
    151–2.

79 Davies, *Conquest*, 239, 241, 294–5; Rowlands, 'King John and Wales', 282.
    Althoff argues that the history of alliances in the Middle Ages is one in which
    there was increasingly a hierarchy of bonds and that this hierarchy eventually
    became dominated by the vassal's bond to his lord. Althoff, *Family, Friends and
    Followers*, 90.

80 Finalising a treaty with a marriage was a common practice in medieval peace-
    making and it is a topic to which only a full-length study in its own right can do
    full justice. For some introductory reading, however, see Lindsay Diggelmann,
    'Marriage as a Tactical Response: Henry II and the Royal Wedding of 1160',
    EHR, 119 (2004); John Gillingham, 'Love, Marriage and Politics in the Twelfth
    Century', in his *Richard Coeur de Lion*; Jane Martindale, 'Succession and Politics
    in the Romance-Speaking World, c. 1000–1140', in *England and Her Neighbours,
    1066–1453: Essays in Honour of Pierre Chaplais*, ed. Michael Jones and Malcolm
    Vale (London, 1989); Christopher Brooke, *The Medieval Idea of Marriage*
    (Oxford, 1989); James A. Brundage, *Law, Sex and Christian Society in Medieval
    Europe* (Chicago, 1987).

81 *Dip. Docs*, i, 8. 'Hec conventio facta est et scripta apud Doverham.'

82 *Dip. Docs*, i, 8.

83 *Dip. Docs*, i, 11. Elisabeth van Houts in her translation of the 1101 Anglo-Flemish
    treaty, the text of which is almost exactly replicated in that of 1163, translated
    'feodo' as 'fief', a term that is perhaps too specific. E. van Houts, 'The Anglo-
    Flemish Treaty of 1101', *ANS*, 21 (1999), 173. However, 'in feodo' was commonly
    used in agreements where a money payment, rather than land, was given in return
    for homage and fealty, that is a so-called money-fief. For instance, the term also
    appears in the *conventio* with the Count of Holland, who received an annual
    payment of 400 marks for his fealty and homage. *Foedera*, I, i, 169. On fiefs in
    general, see Reynolds, *Fiefs and Vassals*, 48–74, 276–81.

84 *Dip. Docs*, i, 12. Ganshof considered that this assurance was merely the recipro-
    cation of a lord to his vassal. F.-L. Ganshof, 'Note sur le premier traité Anglo-
    Flamand de Douvres', *Revue du Nord*, 40 (1958), 251. However, none of the
    other treaties examined contains such an assurance and hence its inclusion in the
    treaties of 1101, 1110 and 1163 is significant.

85 Pryce, *The Acts of Welsh Rulers*, 372.
86 *Dip. Docs*, i, 10.
87 Alcuin, *Operum pars septima – opera didascalia*, PL 101, col. 978.
88 *Dip. Docs*, i, 14, no. 5.
89 *Dip. Docs*, i, 16, no. 6.
90 Gerd Althoff, 'Friendship and Political Order', in *Friendship in Medieval Europe*, ed. Julian Haseldine (Stroud, 1999), 93.
91 Althoff, *Verwandte, Freunde und Getreue*, 201–11; 'Friendship and Political Order', 93.
92 Julia Barrow, 'Friends and Friendship in Anglo-Saxon Charters', in *Friendship in Medieval Europe*, 106.
93 Gerd Althoff, '*Amicitiae* [Friendships] as Relationships between States and People', in *Debating the Middle Ages*, ed. Lester K. Little and Barbara H. Rosenwein (Oxford, 1998); Althoff, *Family, Friends and Followers*, 68. See also discussion by Voss on the friendship treaties between the French kings and the emperors. Voss, *Herrschertreffen*, 183–91. For some examples of the rhetoric attached to friendship see also *Adalbertus Samaritanus Praecepta Dictaminum*, ed. Franz-Josef Schmale (Weimar, 1961), 43–6, 68–70.
94 *Dip. Docs*, i, nos 1, 2, 7. It is also clear that an agreement similar to those of 1101, 1110 and 1163 was concluded near Gisors in 1180, even though no such written document has come down to us. Howden outlines almost the exact same terms as in 1163, but he did not insert a copy of the treaty into his narrative. It is, furthermore, clear that the alliance was renewed in 1175 after Philip of Flanders's involvement in the great rebellion of 1173–74, but again no text is extant. Howden, *Gesta*, i, 96, 246.
95 For a discussion of the textual differences, see Chaplais, *EDP*, 42–4.
96 *Dip. Docs*, i, 2. Note that the text of the 1101 agreement printed by Rymer is exactly as that of 1163, that is, it states 'friend and lord'. Rymer, *Foedera*, I, i, 5.
97 Ganshof, 'Note sur le premier traité Anglo-Flamand', 250–1.
98 *Dip. Docs*, i, 11. Note the similarity with the homage of the English king's heir(s) to the French kings. Thierry's request that his son, rather than himself, performed the homage may have deliberately mirrored Henry II's use of Henry (the Young King) in his dealings with Louis VII in 1160. Also, as Thierry left for the Holy Land the year after, leaving his son in charge, the homage by Philip may merely be a practical reflection of the true state of affairs, that is, that Philip would effectively be the person upholding the contract with Henry II.
99 Galbert of Bruges, *Histoire du meurtre de Charles le Bon*, 176 (cap. 122).
100 In light of Gillingham's recent article on homage, it seems likely that in 1128 and possibly even in 1163, the homage was a ceremony conferring right to inheritance. A diplomatic card to be played against the French king. In 1128, the homage of Thierry d'Alsace reinforced his right to rule in the eyes of the powerful Henry I, following the turbulent war and disputed succession of 1127–28 as described by the eyewitness Galbert of Bruges. In 1163, the homage of Philip to Henry II reinforced his right to succeed to Flanders in anticipation of his father's departure for the Holy Land.

101 Chaplais, *EDP*, 51.
102 *Dip. Docs*, i, no. 7. Though note that Howden records that Richard gave the count 5,000 marks of silver for his 'auxilio'. Howden, *Chronica*, iv, 20. This is reminiscent of the agreement set out in previous treaties, but does not correspond to the text of that of 1197.
103 For the terminology of treaties, see Chapter 8, 191–3. Note, however, that the French contemporary Rigord used the term *confederatio* to describe the agreement between Richard and Baldwin, a term which Voss has concluded replaced *amicitia* towards the end of the twelfth century, especially in formal military alliances. Voss, *Herrschertreffen*, 188–90.
104 *Dip. Docs*, i, 19.
105 Dip. Docs, i, 18.
106 *Dip. Docs*, i, 11–12. For a brief discussion of the place of meeting, see Chapter 2, 60–1.
107 See also discussion by Björn Weiler in his 'Knighting, Homage and the Meaning of Ritual: the Kings of England and their Neighbours in the Thirteenth Century', *Viator*, 37 (2006), 275–99, at pp. 296–9.

PART III

The envoys

5

The envoys and negotiators of peace

Face-to-face encounters between rulers stood at the heart of the medieval peacemaking process, yet considerable effort also went into negotiations in the lead up to, during and after such meetings. Most of this work was done by envoys and mediators, that is, those men (and women) who were often in the background of the process but were essential in facilitating it and in moving it forward. Knowing the identity of those who aided rulers in negotiating and making peace, and the role and function of their duties within the process, is hugely important, not only in the context of establishing the rules and practice of making peace but also because of what it can tell us about medieval political culture and about ruling elites.

Much work has been done by historians on envoys and negotiators in the later medieval period. Most notably, Pierre Chaplais has worked on the English diplomatic personnel, and Donald E. Queller has published several studies on the nature of the ambassadorial office in Europe, foremostly in Venice.[1] Both of these historians have had as their starting point the mass of diplomatic documents available from the thirteenth century onwards. According to Chaplais and Queller, the diplomatic personnel of the later Middle Ages generally fell into two categories: *nuncii* and *procuratores*. The distinction, they agree, was based primarily on the legal status of the envoy. According to Roman law, the *nuncius* was essentially a message-bearer and the legal effect of sending such a person was equivalent to sending a letter.[2] By contrast, the role of the procurator 'was to do those things that the principal could have done if he had been present'.[3] Chaplais saw the role of *nuncii* as restricted by concluding that the *nuncius* was not able to negotiate or perform any positive act on behalf of his master: his only purpose was to deliver a message or to make an oral request and bring an answer back.[4] In contrast to this Queller argued that a *nuncius* could both take and receive oaths in place of another or negotiate terms to be referred to his principal for consideration, but he could not bind his principal by an act of his own will.[5] He could negotiate treaties in the form of a draft that would subsequently be referred back to his lord, and, if acceptable, ratified by oath before being sent back to the other party. Should he enter into any treaty in his principal's name, the latter would not be bound, because the negotiator would have exceeded his mandate.[6] Whichever interpretation of the detail one chooses to accept, what unifies Queller's thesis and the view of Chaplais is that the power of the *nuncius* to bind his lord was strictly limited.

Most commonly in the twelfth and early thirteenth centuries *nuncii* carried letters of credence. Letters of credence always included the name and titles of the sender and the recipient of the embassy. Queller concluded that the heart of the letter was the clause of supplication, which named the envoy and requested that his message be received as if from the sender.[7] In England letters of credence were enrolled from the beginning of the reign of King John, probably indicating that these letters were indeed carried by envoys and mediators already in earlier reigns.[8] In an example of January 1200, King John asked the envoys of the king and queen of Castile to believe what Brother P. de Verneuil would say on his behalf.[9] In another example, dating from May 1212, the English king asked the Emperor Otto IV to believe what his 'men of quality', namely Walter de Gray, John's chancellor, Saer de Quency, earl of Winchester, William de Cantilupe, steward of the household, and Robert Tresgoz would say on his behalf.[10]

The *procurator* appeared after the revival of Roman law in the early twelfth century and after the participation of kings and princes in negotiations became less practical, and his role was closely allied to that of papal legates.[11] Queller noted that a *procurator* was an agent whose acts, unlike those of a *nuncius*, bound his principal and were as valid as if the principal himself had performed them. The *procurator* was thus able to both negotiate and conclude.[12] Chaplais similarly described the duties of these envoys as being to negotiate or conclude agreements on the strength of the letters of procuration appointing them.[13] All procurations contained two essential clauses: one named the envoy and defined the type of business which they were empowered to transact. In the other, the clause *de rato*, the king promised to ratify what the envoys would do.[14] One example of this from the early thirteenth century can be found amongst the very first details that Geoffrey de Villehardouin jotted down in his eyewitness account of the Fourth Crusade. According to Geoffrey the six envoys chosen for the embassy to Venice in 1201 had full powers (*plain pooir*) and that 'in confirmation of this they were given charters, duly drawn up and with seals appended, to the effect that all the barons would strictly abide by whatever agreement their envoys might enter into'.[15] Queller concluded that the mission of Geoffrey de Villehardouin and his fellow envoys to Venice in 1201 was a landmark in the development of diplomatic plenipotentiaries sent between secular powers. He has pointed out that it was Geoffrey and his colleagues – not their masters – who decided to treat with Venice and they negotiated and concluded upon terms unforeseen by their principals. Furthermore, the envoys 'redacted and swore to their treaty, sent it off to the pope to be confirmed, and borrowed money to implement it, all without referring their actions to their principals for approval'.[16]

Throughout the thirteenth century the practice of carrying letters of full powers became more frequent, and in England during the reign of John several diplomatic missions carried such letters.[17] One example are the letters patent in which the English king asked Count Ferrand of Flanders to believe what his negotiators William Longsword, earl of Salisbury, and Renaud, count of Boulogne, Hugh de Boves, Henry fitz Count and Brian de Lisle would say. The letter further contained a clause 'de rato' where the king promised to hold firm whatever his envoys would arrange with the count.[18]

While they are largely convincing, there are certain problems with Chaplais's and Queller's definitions of diplomatic personnel. One is that their conclusion that all envoys fall into one of two categories is almost exclusively based on evidence from the thirteenth century onwards and may tell us very little about practices in the preceding century. Queller has noted that though there is evidence of *plena potestas* in the hands of papal legates from the pontificate of Gregory VII, there is no evidence until the late twelfth century for such use among secular princes. Though Queller then cited some twelfth-century examples of procuration, he did not fully explore the significance of the fact that they were all, without exception, either Italian procurations or agreements made in Italy.[19] That such terminology and practice was used in this part of medieval Europe seems not at all surprising, since these practices derived from Roman law.[20] Thus we cannot assume that the diplomatic personnel in the twelfth century were clearly divided between those who were *nuncii* and those who were *procuratores*, because there is no, or very little, evidence upon which to base such a distinction.

The idea that the distinction between a *nuncius* and a *procurator* is based on legal definitions is also problematic. When Chaplais noted that a *procurator* could act only in accordance with the letters of full powers given to him by his master, he made an important point showing that the *procurator* could not act on his own will but only on instructions and within limits set by his principal. One example of this was the letters of procuration that accompanied the envoys sent by Henry III in 1235 to negotiate a marriage alliance between the king and Eleanor of Provence. The envoys had been given several letters instructing them to receive from the count of Provence as Eleanor's dowry a sum of money ranging from 20,000 to 3,000 marks, and then a few days later they received a final procuration ordering them to ignore their powers regarding Eleanor's dowry and bring her to England even without monetary payment.[21] This clearly shows that the envoys themselves were not able to lower the sum of money demanded as dowry, but had to act according to instructions received. This stands in contrast to another English document of 1235 that stressed the usefulness of procuration 'because many things can arise unexpectedly which need a rapid solution and recourse cannot easily be had to us concerning the matters touching us in this country'.[22] If we are to believe the first example, however, *procuratores* could only resolve matters arising that had been thought of beforehand. Clearly, there was some inconsistency as to the exact legal quality of acts of *procuratores*, prompting an increasing specificity of *de rato* clauses over the course of the thirteenth and fourteenth centuries.[23]

Both Chaplais and Queller have noted that in letters of procuration the essential clause was that of the *de rato*, whereby the ruler confirmed that he would ratify everything that his envoys had negotiated and concluded. The question is to what extent this was different from a treaty negotiated by a *nuncius* and then referred to his master for ratification. Queller has noted that any agreements made by *nuncii* became binding only upon subsequent ratification.[24] It would seem however that, following the instructions in letters of full powers, this was also the case with any agreements negotiated by *procuratores*. If this was not the case, why did letters of procuration contain a clause *de rato*? Could an agreement negotiated by *procuratores* be binding without subsequent ratification? According to Queller, in juridical terms there was really no difference between the acts of *nuncii* subsequently ratified and those of *procuratores*, also subsequently ratified, though in practical terms 'one could easily disavow the efforts of the former, while refusal to ratify the acts of the latter, though lawful, was necessarily a matter of diplomatic embarrassment'.[25]

Queller further concluded that covenants made by medieval plenipotentiaries were complete and valid even without subsequent ratification. The
crusader-envoys of 1201 again served as an example for Queller's theory.
After concluding their agreement with Venice, the envoys sent the treaty
to the pope for confirmation and then borrowed money for beginning construction of the desired fleet. Only after that was the treaty ratified by the
envoys' masters at Corbie.[26] This is, of course, not proof that subsequent
ratification was not required but merely shows that, if the agreement had
not been approved, many would have been owed a lot of money. Though
refusal to ratify the acts of plenipotentiaries may have been diplomatically
embarrassing, it did, if nothing else, have the advantage of taking into consideration that political circumstances could change in the time elapsed
between the dispatch of envoys and ratification. In letters of procuration,
the clause requiring subsequent ratification must in many ways have been
a legal loophole, and, by making a strict legal definition between *nuncii*
and *procuratores*, historians may be glossing over some of the subtleties
of medieval international politics, especially in the period before c.1250.

It is clear that letters of procuration also contained other legal loop-
holes. In a letter sent by Pope Innocent III to King John in January 1213,
the pope wrote with some concern about the embassy that he had received
from the English king. According to Innocent, the letter that the emissar-
ies had brought with them affirmed John's intention to ratify any agreement concerning the dispute with the church of Canterbury that might be
concluded by his envoys. However, since only three of an original of six
envoys had reached the papal curia, they were unable to make a settlement
in the sense of John's letter.[27] As John's letter does not survive it is impossible to know the exact reason why the letter became invalid. One possibility is that the mandate became useless simply because of the fact that
not all of those named in the letter reached the intended destination. It is
also possible that one or more of those envoys who did not reach the curia
had been charged with a specific task that could now not be performed. A
third possibility is connected with the political circumstances of the negotiations, because Innocent himself commented that besides the fact that
not all of the original envoys reached him: 'the question at issue concerns
not merely the church of Canterbury but the whole English church which
by your impious persecution you are trying to enslave'. Furthermore, as
John, since the terms of the settlement had been conveyed to him, had
'attempted worse outrages', Innocent no longer considered himself bound
to the terms that he had initially offered to the English king.[28] The likeli-
hood is that this was the real reason behind not accepting the mandate of

the envoys who did arrive, though the capture of half of the embassy on the way to Rome probably provided a convenient excuse. Clearly, legality did not outweigh politics.

When looking at the question of diplomatic personnel in the late twelfth and early thirteenth centuries, a more subtle approach is needed than simply distinguishing between *nuncii* and *procuratores*. There are a number of options available to historians for opening up a discussion and one of these is to look at the role of chancellors and vice-chancellors as envoys in this period, because there is a vast amount of evidence of envoys who were or had been chancellors (or vice-chancellors), and that is significant. One such man was Walter of Coutances (Bishop of Lincoln 1183–84; Archbishop of Rouen 1184–1207). It would appear that Walter had been the royal vice-chancellor, or perhaps rather seal-keeper, prior to becoming archbishop of Rouen in 1184. Though he acted as envoy many times for the English kings Henry II, Richard I and John, there are only three occasions, during the reign of Henry II, when he was also expressly mentioned as the king's vice-chancellor. In 1177 Walter was twice sent on diplomatic missions: first, to Count Philip of Flanders together with the justiciar Ranulph de Glanville; then, in June, to the French king, Louis VII, to discuss the dowries of Louis's daughters.[29] In 1180, Walter was again dispatched by Henry to King Louis VII in an attempt to prevent a French attack.[30] We know that Walter was sent as an envoy at least another five times in the 1180s, although on these occasions he is not referred to as the king's seal-keeper.[31] In 1185, in an attempt to mediate between Philip Augustus and the count of Flanders, Henry sent Walter, together with John, bishop of Norwich, and Godfrey de Lucy, archdeacon of Richmond, into the French kingdom. By the time Henry's embassy arrived, however, Philip and the count of Flanders had arranged a truce through their own envoys.[32] The year after, King Philip demanded the wardship of the heiress of Brittany upon the death of Count Geoffrey, Henry II's son. In response to this, Henry dispatched Walter along with his justiciar Ranulph de Glanville and William de Mandeville, count of Aumale, to the French king to arrange a truce and peace to last until the feast of St Hilary (13 January) 1187. Shortly after negotiating the first truce, Walter of Coutances and William de Mandeville were again sent to the French king: this time in an attempt to prolong the truce until Easter 1187.[33] In 1188 Walter was sent with an embassy to Philip Augustus to ask the French king for the restitution of all damages that the English king had incurred during the hostilities of that year or Henry would renounce his fidelity and declare Philip his mortal enemy.[34] The year after, the archbishop of Rouen was one of many men accompanying Henry II to the conference at La Ferté Bernard to make peace ('ad pacem faciendam') between the English and French kings.[35] Walter was thus a frequently used envoy during the reign of Henry II and for parts of that period he was also a member of the royal chancery.

During the reign of Richard I, Walter of Coutances appears in a number of diplomatic roles. For instance, in November 1190 he stood surety for Richard in the latter's treaty with Tancred of Sicily.[36] During Richard's captivity in the Empire, Walter was one of several negotiators who managed to secure a truce for England with Richard's brother, John, count of Mortain.[37] During this period Walter was also sent to the Empire, and he remained there as one of Richard's hostages to ensure that the king's ransom would be paid.[38] Furthermore, a letter from the Emperor Henry VI to Richard notes how Walter, during his time as a hostage, pleaded with the Emperor to receive Duke Henry the Lion's son, Otto, who was also Richard's nephew, presumably in an attempt to prompt Henry VI to restore some of the duke's lands to his heir.[39] Walter cannot have remained long with the Emperor, however, because, according to Howden, while Philip Augustus was laying siege to the castle of Fontaines in the summer of 1194, a delegation headed by the seneschal of Normandy and Walter of Coutances waited in vain at Pont-de-l'Arche in the expectation of meeting the French king's envoys to discuss peace.[40]

The correspondence of Ralph de Diceto, dean of St Paul's London, with Walter of Coutances often finds its way into the narrative of Diceto's historical work, thereby supplying useful information on Walter's activites and his involvement in Angevin diplomacy. In one of Walter's letters to Diceto, we are told that he was present at the conference held near Issoudun in January 1196 and that he had refused to be one of King Richard's sureties because of a secret agreement with Philip Augustus.[41] For the year 1173 Diceto recorded how a certain Ralph de Warneville was made chancellor and Walter of Coutances vice-chancellor. According to Diceto this Ralph preferred to commit the discharge of his functions in the king's court to his deputy, perhaps explaining Walter's prominent role in Angevin diplomacy over the next few years.[42]

The example of Walter of Coutances is not unique; indeed, there are many other examples of envoys and mediators who had also been chancellors. For instance we know that, as John's chancellor, Hubert Walter was sent with the justiciar, Geoffrey fitz Peter, to treat with Llywelyn ap Iorwerth in July 1201.[43] In November 1200 Hubert also played an important role at the conference between King John and William the Lion, king of Scots, because, according to Howden, William swore fealty to John on Hubert's cross.[44] Moreover, historians know that Hubert Walter, who by the time of his death in 1205 had more than thirty years, experience at court, had frequently accompanied diplomatic missions prior to becoming King John's chancellor in 1199.[45] Another example of a chancellor sent on a diplomatic mission is Thomas Becket, whose mission to the French king in 1158 is well documented in the near-contemporary biography penned by William Fitzstephen.[46] In another example, from 1189, one of Henry II's last acts was to send Roger Malchael, who was at that time in charge of the royal seal, to the French king and have him set down in writing all those who had been turn-coats in the war against Henry II and, in return, to hand over a document with all the names of the men of Philip Augustus who had helped Henry against the French king.[47] During Richard's reign William Longchamps, who was Richard's chancellor even before his accession to the English throne, was active at the French court. In 1189 Longchamps seems to have been sent to Paris by Richard in response to one of Henry II's attempt to drive a wedge between his son and his ally, Philip Augustus.[48] On another occasion, in 1193, Longchamps was one of three envoys equipped with a procuration from the king to negotiate and conclude a peace treaty with Philip Augustus.[49] Similarly, Richard's chancellor during the latter part of his reign, Eustace, bishop of Ely, was in 1199 sent on a diplomatic mission to Philip Augustus in France to declare the truce, which had been agreed earlier in the year, formally broken.[50]

The English kings were not the only medieval princes to have entrusted diplomatic missions to their chancellors in this period. During the Second Crusade a certain Bartholomew acted as the chancellor to Louis VII and was sent on at least three diplomatic missions.[51] According to Otto of Freising, the French king sent another chancellor, Master Aldericus, to a meeting with some imperial envoys in the late 1150s.[52] In another example, Master Laurence, who was involved in the negotiations between King Henry II and Roderic, king of Connaught, in the mid-1170s, was referred to as the latter's chancellor by Roger of Howden.[53] The practice was also current in Denmark, where in the early thirteenth century a certain Peter, bishop of Roskilde and chancellor to Cnut VI and Valdemar II in succession, emerges as a man with a considerable role to play in Danish diplomacy. In 1203 he was said to be negotiating the terms of the release from captivity of Adolph, count of Holstein.[54] A few years later, in 1207, he was sent by Valdemar II to deal with the matter of the election to the see of Bremen of Valdemar of Slesvig, a rival to the Danish throne.[55] We further know that Peter led expeditions for his king(s) on at least two occasions.[56]

The role of the chancellor within the territory of his master is interest-ing and it clearly sheds some light on his possible functions within peace-making and diplomacy. One of the best accounts of the nature of the office of chancellor is that in the *Life of Thomas Becket* by William Fitzstephen. According to William, the chancellor of England was considered:

> second in rank in the realm only to the king. He holds the other part of the king's seal, with which he seals his own orders. He has respon-sibility and care of the king's chapel, and maintains whatever vacant archbishoprics, bishoprics, abbacies and baronies fall into the king's hands. He attends all the king's councils to which he does not even require a summons. All documents are sealed by his clerks, the royal seal-keepers, and everything is carried out according to his advice. Also, if by God's grace the merits of his life allow it, he will be made archbishop or a bishop before he dies.[57]

That William's last statement was true is clear from the great number of European archbishops and bishops who had previously been, and some-times continued to be, chancellors.[58] Apart from this, three statements are particularly interesting for diplomacy in Fitzstephen's description, namely that the chancellor was in charge of the royal seal, the royal writ-ing office and the royal chapel. Within the context of peacemaking and diplomacy the latter is particularly important because the royal chapel, apart from providing clerks to the writing office, contained the royal relics; the very things that oaths were sworn on.[59] Moreover, as the custodian of the king's seal and the man in charge of the royal *scriptorium*, it seems reasonable to assume that one of the reasons why the chancellor was sent on diplomatic missions (or was present at meetings between princes) was that he was in charge of the necessary personnel to draw up and seal agree-ments and other diplomatic correspondence. The question is whether he was able to perform such a duty in unusual circumstances. In the summer of 1193, during the captivity of Richard I in the Empire, a diplomatic mission headed by the chancellor, William Longchamps, bishop of Ely, concluded a peace with the French king, Philip Augustus. Longchamps's inclusion in this embassy may have been not only on account of his close relationship with Richard, but also because he had the authority and the necessary know-how to draft and seal the document confirming the terms of the peace. Indeed the text of the treaty itself confirms this, stat-ing that William had carried with him letters patent authorising him to agree the terms of the peace and that whatever he concluded the English king ratified and held firm.[60] Chaplais has deemed these letters to be the first precise reference to an English procuration.[61] Letters of procuration could, of course, be issued to any member of the king's *familia*, and thus the question that needs to be asked is whether the chancellor, who was the titular custodian of the royal seal, with the actual keeper of the seal, often the vice-chancellor, serving under him, would have been able to draw up diplomatic instruments that required no further ratification even without letters of procuration.[62]

It seems clear that the immediate answer to this question is that neither the cancellor nor his deputy, the seal keeper, could perform such a function and that this was not their role within diplomacy. For instance, according to the text of the treaty concluded with the French king at Mantes in July 1193, the document was sealed with the seals of William Longchamps, William des Roches, John des Preaux and William Brewer.[63] The document consequently required further authentification with Richard's Great Seal, of which, incidentally, Longchamps at the time was not in charge.[64] Since we have little documentary evidence that letters of procuration were widely carried by envoys before the thirteenth century, the seal, or rather the impression of it, could perhaps have given envoys similar powers to that thought to be contained within such letters. Unfortunately there are no exact references to a diplomatic mission carrying the royal seal, or its impression. This is a real problem, because we know that there are many instances prior to c. 1200 when envoys and mediators carried out duties that Chaplais and Queller have considered could be done only by *procuratores*. One such instance is the Anglo-Sicilian marriage negotiations of 1176–77, which were conducted by Sicilian envoys in England who took oaths for King William and by English envoys in Sicily who took similar oaths on Henry II's behalf. According to Chaplais, such duties could be undertaken only by negotiators who had full powers.[65] Much earlier, in 991, a similar example is found in the negotiations between Richard I, duke of the Normans, and King Aethelred II of England, known only from a spurious papal letter confirming the conclusion of peace between the duke and the king. According to the letter, King Aethelred's envoys Aethelsige, bishop of Sherborne, Leofstan and Aethelnoth accompanied the papal legate, Leo of Trevi, to the Norman court, where the peace was confirmed 'by the mark of the oaths' of the envoys on the part of the English king.[66] Did these envoys need to carry something to show that they were empowered to act in the king's name? If they did, it would seem that, in the last example at least, this was again the royal seal. Although the letter does not specifically mention that these envoys carried the seal, its very last sentence stipulated that neither Aethelred nor Richard was to receive men from the other who did not carry the seal of their master, and this makes it likely that the seal was the item empowering the acts of these envoys.[67] Contrary to this, both Keynes and Chaplais have referred to the 991 example as an occasion when the seal was used as credence, that is, it was used to show that the envoys were trusted and came from the English king. However, as the envoys of 991 took oaths, an act that Chaplais believed required full powers in the twelfth century, one must question why he thought that those swearing oaths on behalf of their royal masters in the tenth century did not.[68]

The evidence of envoys and mediators who were able to act in the name of their master is not extensive. Nor can historians be certain that those envoys who did perform such acts needed to carry something that showed the other party that they had the authority to do so. If they did, however, it is difficult to imagine, in the absence of documentary evidence, an item that would better provide such authentication than the seal, or a similar item such as a signet ring.[69] Chaplais has, however, noted that documents intended to aid an envoy's memory could have been, and were, shown to the other principal as a way to empower the acts of envoys, and there is at least one such example from the reign of Henry II.[70] By contrast Huw Pryce and Hoffmann argued that it was the envoy himself who provided the best guarantee of authenticity. However, neither Pryce nor Hoffmann have explained satisfactorily how such an envoy, even one who was a chancellor, would be recognised without his letter of introduction containing any internal or external features, such as the wax impression of a seal.[71] It is in any case not clear whether any such envoys could make binding contracts. Nevertheless, the chancellor was probably one such person to whom Chaplais referred in his recent book as being of such dignity and political stature, with close association to his country's government, that his actions 'could not fail to be ratified'.[72] On reflection then, it would seem that sending a chancellor or a vice-chancellor as envoy had a greater significance than their just being message-bearers.[73]

There is some evidence that indicates that the chancellor had a further function in diplomacy and peacemaking. Two letters sent to the chancellor of Louis VII, Hugh de Champfleury, indicate that, on some occasions at least, the chancellor was the first contact for matters of diplomacy. In one example, of 1162, Rainald, archbishop-elect of Cologne and imperial chancellor, wrote to Hugh concerning a meeting between their respective princes, the Emperor Frederick Barbarossa and King Louis VII, expressing the wish that the conference would take place in August.[74] On another occasion, Owain, 'king of Wales', sent his envoy, Moses, to Hugh so that he could hear the purpose of the embassy and to forward the matter to the French king.[75] It is just possible that, during the last year of Richard's reign or the first year of John's reign, the Norwegian king, Sverre, approached the English archbishop and chancellor, Hubert Walter, in much the same way. We know of the communication between Hubert Walter and King Sverre only from a letter sent by Pope Innocent III to the archbishop in July 1200, warning the archbishop not to receive envoys or gifts from the Norwegian king who was an excommunicate and 'a sacrilegious apostate and perfidious murderer'.[76] Though Innocent's letter does not state the purpose of the Norwegian envoys' mission to Hubert Walter, it seems likely that it was concerned with military and political support for Sverre against the rival *Baglar* faction. Indeed the evidence that such military support was sent by King John can be found in the pipe rolls for 1201.[77] It would thus seem that, within the context of peacemaking and diplomacy, not only were chancellors their kings' most trusted mediators sent on important diplomatic missions, but they were also a first port of call for foreign embassies and for raising any diplomatic matter with their master.

It is clear then that it is difficult to understand the personnel of diplomatic missions in the late twelfth and early thirteenth centuries simply by distinguishing between those who were agents of their masters and those who were merely delivering a message. Probably it is not even important whether such a distinction is possible. The key issue is rather what can be said about those taking part in embassies to foreign rulers in a period before the ready availability of documentary evidence. Firstly, it must be noted that in the absence of diplomatic documents the vast majority of the evidence for diplomatic missions in the period before c. 1220 is derived from narrative sources. One of the problems with this is that chroniclers and historical writers alike recorded many diplomatic missions by referring to those involved as *nuncii*, *legati* or men of wisdom or men of quality. The authors of these sources, furthermore, tend to name only the envoys of those missions that were headed by high-status men or women such as counts, dukes, bishops, abbots and members of the ruler's own family. Moreover, the quality of the evidence from these narrative sources varies greatly. A clear example of how factors such as geographical location, the author's or his informants' closeness to court, patronage and the aim of the work had an impact on what the chronicler knew or recorded about diplomatic missions can be found in the work of the Danish historian Saxo Grammaticus.

According to Saxo, a man of great experience who was frequently used for the most important diplomatic missions by the Danish kings

Valdemar I and Cnut VI was Absalon, bishop of Roskilde (1157–78) and archbishop of Lund (1178–1202). One of the first references in Saxo's text to Absalon's inclusion in negotiations can be found in 1157, when he appears to have been the only mediator admitted into the church of St Albans in Odense for the meeting between two of the rival candidates for the Danish throne.[78] In another example, from the spring of 1160, Absalon, as commander of one of the Danish warships, negotiated with a Rugian envoy by the name of Domborus and, a little later that same year, he was the only person to accompany Valdemar I to his conference with Henry the Lion.[79] Shortly after this meeting, the Danish king sent Absalon to Duke Henry as his envoy, in order to discuss Valdemar's concerns about the ravages of the sons of the recently deceased Slav prince Niklot.[80] The Danish bishop was again at the forefront of diplomacy a few weeks later when asked by a Slav envoy to act as the mediator between the king and the Rugians.[81] Some two years later, during the Emperor Frederick Barbarossa's large gathering at Saint-Jean-de-Losne, Absalon, together with the envoy Ralph, came before the Emperor on a mission to obtain the promises made to King Valdemar in return for his attendance at the meeting.[82] In the late 1160s Absalon was then back to negotiating peace settlements with the Slavs, before mediating between the Norwegian jarl, Erling Skakke, and Valdemar I shortly after the great council at Ringsted in 1170.[83] It would also seem that Absalon was one of the men involved with the negotiations surrounding the conquest of the Pomeranians in 1184/85.[84]

However, there are some good reasons for not wholly believing Saxo's depiction of Absalon's importance as the Danish kings' foremost envoy and mediator. Though Saxo was in a good position to know about Absalon's political role, it is clear that his importance has been greatly enhanced by the Danish historian. After all Saxo had been commissioned to write a history of Denmark by the archbishop himself shortly after the conquest of the Pomeranians in the mid-1180s. Saxo divided his huge work into some sixteen books, of which only the last three deal with events of the twelfth century. According to Eric Christiansen, the most recent editor of Saxo's last three books, these near-contemporary chapters were written first, and the complete absence of references to Cnut VI's brother Valdemar would suggest a date before 1202 when the latter succeeded to the Danish throne.[85] As Book XVI ends with the glorious moment of the submission of Bogiszlav, prince of the Pomeranians, the intention was probably to give the Danes a glorious past to match that of the present day; thus Books I–XII, though composed later, depicted this past.[86] Although Saxo's work is named 'The History of the Danish Kings' (or more precisely 'The History and Heroic Deeds of the Danish Kings'), neither Valdemar I nor his successor Cnut VI is the main character in the near-contemporary chapters: a role which is instead awarded to the archbishop.[87] This is hardly surprising as Saxo's main informant on events after 1134 was Absalon himself.[88] According to Saxo it was Absalon who did everything from implementing church reforms to putting down rebellions, not Valdemar or Cnut. Birgit Sawyer noted some time ago that, while Valdemar is described as undecided, thoughtless, impulsive and weak, Saxo depicts Absalon as resolute, wise, full of initiative and strong.[89] In short Absalon was the person who devised cunning plans, negotiated and undertook dangerous missions, fought battles and generally steered the king in the right direction. Clearly it is impossible to understand what actually happened from such obvious propaganda. Indeed the historical work of Saxo's contemporary Sven Aggesen was written to praise the Danish kings and it mentioned the archbishop only incidentally.

On some occasions there obviously were other envoys present at these negotiations mentioned by Saxo. Indeed Saxo himself records the names of at least four of them: Ralph, Thorbern, Esbern and Henry the Staller.[90] Ralph accompanied Absalon to the court of the Emperor Frederick Barbarossa at Saint-Jean-de-Losne in 1162.[91] Lucien Musset identified this Ralph as the Danish king's English-born chancellor, and, though this would fit with the pattern of chancellors acting as envoys, there is no actual evidence that Ralph the envoy should be identified as Ralph the chancellor.[92] Thorbern was sent as an envoy to Henry the Lion in 1164 to convey the terms offered by some of the Slavs and to let Henry know that Valdemar, as the duke's ally ('militiae socio'), would not be concluding any agreement without his consent.[93] According to Christiansen, Thorbern seems to have lived on an estate near Roskilde and had fostered the daughter of one of the rivals for the Danish throne during the civil wars of the 1140s and 1150s. Upon Valdemar's accession to the throne in 1157, Thorbern went into exile, but was shortly afterwards recalled by Absalon, and for the remainder of Valdemar's reign he served under the king on several expeditions and later became the castellan of Søborg.[94] Esbern was dispatched as an envoy to Erling Skakke, jarl of Norway, around 1170, and remained in Norway as a hostage while the jarl visited the Danish king.[95] As Esbern was Absalon's brother it is surely no accident that he reappears several times in the midst of important affairs. One other example of this can be found in 1168/69, when Esbern can be found as the host of a banquet for some Rugian mediators and nobles, who, in fact, remained with Esbern to ensure

Absalon's safe return from a diplomatic mission to the fort of Karentia in southern Rügen.[96] The final envoy mentioned by Saxo is Henry the Staller. After a rebellion against the Danish king in the mid-1170s, one of the leaders of the revolt, Magnus, went into exile at Henry the Lion's court in Saxony under false pretences. When Duke Henry sent a letter to Valdemar to attempt a reconciliation between the king and Magnus, Valdemar, according to Saxo, thought it best to place his reply not in a letter but with Henry, 'whom he [Valdemar] had put in charge of his stable'.[97] Like Ralph, the envoy who accompanied Absalon to Frederick Barbarossa's court in 1162, Henry the Staller is otherwise unknown. Nevertheless, what makes three of these Danish envoys, Thorbern, Esbern and Ralph, for special mention in Saxo's text is their connection with Absalon.

Unfortunately Sven Aggesen's work is not detailed enough to contain much of value with regards to diplomatic missions. Furthermore, although two German chroniclers, Helmold of Bosau and Arnold of Lübeck, in many instances provide a valuable comparison to Saxo's narrative, like Sven, they contain little or no information on Danish diplomatic missions, or, incidentally, on Absalon. Thus the flaws of Saxo's work, the lack of detail in these matters in the works of Sven Aggesen and the lack of confirmation in the narratives of Arnold of Lübeck and Helmold of Bosau mean that we know little about Danish envoys and mediators in the twelfth century. Most importantly, Saxo's narrative clearly shows the limitation of using evidence from narrative sources to build up a picture of the personnel of diplomatic missions in the period before c. 1220. Having said this, it is clear that Saxo's evidence should not be ignored. Indeed, as noted above, the vast majority of chroniclers recorded only embassies headed by high-status envoys. Thus there is nothing inconsistent in what Saxo tells us about the role of Absalon in Danish diplomacy.

According to Matthew Paris's *Chronica Maiora*, King John, in 1213, sent the household knights Thomas of Erdington and Ralph fitz Nicholas and the royal clerk Robert of London to the emir of Morocco to offer him the crown of England.[98] Though the chronicler claimed that he had heard this from one of the envoys, Robert of London, it is clear that the story should not be taken seriously. The chronicler presents the emir as despising the English king for his willingness to give up his crown and kingdom to another king and religion, thereby achieving Paris's aim of showing with what contempt John was regarded by other rulers as well as his own people.[99] What one historian did pick out from this story was, however, the composition of the embassy: two knights and a royal clerk.[100] Stephen Church saw that this format was usual, as he had found many other instances where such a team had been used. For instance in 1213, the same year as the supposed embassy to the emir, King John redeemed the knights Thomas Erdington and Philip of Worcester, and master Richard of Terrington, who had been taken captive during a diplomatic mission.[101] In 1215 the household knights Thomas Erdington and Geoffrey Luttrell and the abbot of Beaulieu were King John's representatives at the Fourth Lateran Council.[102]

However, Church's conclusion that this format was the norm for diplomatic missions was based on a very small selection of the available evidence, indeed his interest in these embassies was primarily from the perspective of King John's household knights, the focus of his research. By widening Church's inquiry chronologically, geographically and in terms of sources used, it is evident that, while some embassies were composed of two knights and a clerk, many were not.[103] We know, for instance, that Louis VII and Henry the Young King sent an embassy to Henry II during the war of 1174 to ask for peace and that this embassy was headed by the archbishop of Rheims accompanied by a bishop, an abbot and a templar.[104] In another example, King John sent a seven-man mission to the king of Scots with the purpose of bringing William the Lion to the English king at Lincoln in November 1200. Among the dignitaries in this embassy was the Scottish king's brother, earl David.[105]

What is clear from the evidence is that most diplomatic missions were headed by people of high status. Even allowing for the fact that there may have been many embassies made up of envoys of lower rank, which the chroniclers failed to record, most diplomacy would still have been conducted by envoys who held titles like counts or bishops, or who were household officials. According to Chaplais, persons of high standing, such as barons, bishops or royal officials, so-called 'solemn envoys' or 'men of quality', were not normally mere message-bearers.[106] It is clear, however, that his view has to be modified somewhat for the period before 1220, because there are clear examples of high-status envoys who merely negotiated or delivered oral messages, that is they were what both Chaplais and Queller referred to as *nuncii*. Though there were some occasions when such envoys were agents (*procuratores*) rather than message-bearers, the sheer abundance of evidence of embassies composed of well-known and often high-ranking envoys would advise against the conclusion that they were all *procuratores*. The problem is that not only is it not clear from the sources to what extent a distinction between so-called *nuncii* and *procuratores* can be made but, furthermore, the narratives are often not detailed enough on this particular point.

In his work *The Office of Ambassador in the Middle Ages* Queller has highlighted the representative nature of diplomatic missions and, moreover, noted that the *nuncius* 'was more than a simple courier of inferior status'.[107] Queller's interpretation is consistent with the evidence for the earlier period, and it is clear that also contemporary writers noted the representative function of envoys. In his *Life of Saint Thomas* William Fitzstephen recorded the magnificent embassy of Thomas Becket to France in 1158. According to Fitzstephen, Thomas 'prepared to display and lavish the opulence of England's luxury, so that before all men and in all things the person of the sender might be honoured in the one sent'.[108] Thomas was said to have had at least two hundred of his household with him on his journey: 'knights, clerks, stewards, servants, esquires and sons of noblemen serving him in arms', and, like the king himself, he also had dogs and birds of all kinds with him.[109] Fitzstephen was probably not an eyewitness to Thomas's splendid embassy and his account of it was written nearly twenty years after it had taken place, yet it is clear that his description was not necessarily entirely inaccurate. The author of the contemporary poem *Draco Normannicus* described the embassy of Frederick Barbarossa, headed by Duke Henry the Lion, to the English king in Normandy in 1168, in similarly splendid terms with people coming out of their houses to watch the progression of the mission.[110] Alan of Tewkesbury clearly felt that he needed to justify the presence of William d'Aubigny, earl of Arundel, at the council at Sens in November 1164 and consequently put into William's mouth what is, almost certainly, an invented speech addressing Pope Alexander in the following manner:

> we have come for this purpose, that we represent in your presence and that of the whole Roman Church, the devotion and love of our lord king [Henry II], which he has been accustomed to show towards you, and continues to show. Who then, represents the king in this way but the greatest and noblest subjects in all his lands?[111]

The evidence of these writers make it certain that high-ranking envoys were often sent on diplomatic missions as they were seen as suitable to represent the person or the power of their master, and not because they had the authority to conclude agreements.

Using envoys was clearly a more courteous and representative way of conducting diplomacy than merely sending someone a letter. It would, furthermore, seem that envoys had often been given instructions and messages that, for one reason or another, the sender thought inappropriate to put in writing. This reasoning was advanced by Archbishop Thomas

Becket when he sent an envoy to Pope Alexander III to account for his sufferings at the hands of Henry II: 'To enumerate or set down in writing all that we are suffering would be long and wearisome, so we are sending to your paternal kindness Master Henry [of Houghton] . . . in whose mouth we have put each and every detail.'[112] Likewise, King John, on one occasion, instructed his envoy, Walter Mauclerc, to carry a reply to the French legate regarding the private word they had had about the Anglo-French conference and truce.[113] One thing emerges clearly out of these pieces of evidence, namely that much diplomatic activity was conducted face to face and orally, and, on account of this and as much of its purpose was secret, the envoys and mediators chosen had to be the trusted advisers of their patrons. Indeed, both Chaplais and the German historian Hoffmann have concluded that much care had to be taken in the selection of an envoy who had to deliver an oral message.[114] Not only did such an envoy have to be relied upon to refrain from revealing any part of his message to unauthorised persons, the master also had to be sure that the envoy would deliver his message as he had received it, without addition or omission.[115] By contrast, the author of the *Itinerarium Peregrinorum et Gesta Regis Ricardi*, in describing one diplomatic mission during the Third Crusade, referred to Marquis Conrad as a 'disloyal ambassador' who interpreted 'maliciously' the message he had been charged with delivering.[116]

The English documentary evidence of the early thirteenth century is full of examples of embassies composed of the king's most trusted men, and the appearance of Brian de Therefeld as envoy during the reign of King John is but one such example. Brian seems to have been King John's man for all things Scandinavian. For instance, in 1201–2 he journeyed to Norway. The reason for his visit is not stated in the pipe roll, merely that Brian brought with him 500 'summs' of corn. As he travelled not long after King John had sent military aid to the Norwegian king, Sverre, it seems likely that Brian's embassy was connected with this military aid.[117] In 1203 Brian was described as being with the king's birds, thus clearly being responsible for the favoured Scandinavian birds of prey that the English king hunted with, and it would seem that he also held his land at Leatherhead, Surrey, and Therefeld, Hertfordshire, and his office as usher, in return for one goshawk per year for all services.[118] Two years later, Brian took custody of the Norwegian king's lands in Lincolnshire and some eight years later, in 1213, he journeyed to the court of the Danish king, Valdemar II.[119] On his journey to the Danish court Brian carried with him a letter of introduction that stated that the trading of birds between Denmark and England would be in accordance with letters patent made at that time, but again the nature of the actual embassy is not revealed.[120] The letter was sent in early October 1213, around the time of the attempt by the English king's rival, Philip of France, to woo the Danish king back into an alliance. Thus it would seem that, by sending Brian to the Danish court, King John was trying to secure a friendship with the Danes in opposition to his French rival, offering a lucrative trading deal as a prize.[121] The importance of this mission can be seen by the fact that John decided to send Brian, whose career had been at a standstill since c. 1208, but who was clearly the king's most experienced man on Scandinavian matters as a result of the diplomatic dealings of John's early reign. There can be no doubt that Brian was a trusted subject of King John. Indeed he had proved himself to his patron even before John succeeded to the English throne by taking part in the latter's rebellion of 1193/94, and he was subsequently fined 100*s* by Richard I for his involvement.[122] Almost immediately upon his succession, John seems to have installed Brian as his usher. The fact that Brian was twice referred to as *ostiarium nostrum*, and that he remained John's only usher for a large part of the reign, would indicate that he was probably the usher of the king's hall or chamber.[123] In 1203 King John appointed Brian to a forest serjeanty, and between 1203 and 1205 he was also given custody of two royal castles: Pickering in Yorkshire and Harestan in Derbyshire.[124] Brian was hence a household official with direct access to King John.

John's reign is marked for its use of such household officials and knights rather than using high-status envoys for diplomatic missions, or at least the greater availability of administrative sources make it seem more of a watershed. As much of the evidence for the use of household officials and knights as envoys has already been charted by S.D. Church, it is unnecessary to include it here, but the conclusions that Church was able to draw from his investigation are of great interest. Church identified three regions to which embassies containing household knights were frequently sent: Poitou, the Papal Curia, and Germany and the Low Countries.[125] According to Church, Poitou was the destination of several embassies because this was where John was trying to lay the foundations of his intended reconquest of the Angevin continental lands, while Germany and the Low Countries were the focus of much diplomatic activity intended to build alliances against the French king. Towards the end of his reign, many of John's household officials and knights were sent to the Papal Curia to put his case against the barons.[126] The aims of the embassies directed to these regions, the interdict and the turbulence of the latter part of John's reign, meant that the use of independent-minded magnates and ecclesiastics, who may have had axes of their own to grind, was not seen as a suitable option. Household officials, by contrast, owed everything to the largesse of their master and were consequently the ideal candidates for diplomatic missions during which they were expected to explain John's wishes fully without the need to seek his advice.[127] Not only were these men fully trusted and loyal to their king, they were frequently described as such in the letters of introduction that they carried. When Brian de Therefeld journeyed to the court of Valdemar II in Denmark in 1213, the letter he carried referred to him as 'fidelem nostrum'.[128] Similarly, in 1212 King John had sent to Emperor Otto IV his 'fideles et familiares' as envoys, among whom could be found two members of his household: William de Cantilupe, steward of the household, and Robert Tresgoz.[129]

Nevertheless it is in the careers of men like Absalon and Walter of Coutances that one can most clearly see the close relationship to their masters of those who made up embassies in the period before c. 1220. These two men were representing their kings because they were close advisers who accompanied their masters on their itineraries, held important lands and castles, and even led military expeditions. Churchmen leading troops to war might seem anomalous in this period, but it would seem that such practice was not unparalleled elsewhere in Europe. For instance Christian von Buch, archbishop of Mainz and imperial arch-chancellor, was foremostly involved in the negotiations between the Emperor Frederick Barbarossa and Pope Alexander III in the run up to, and during, the peace conference at Venice in 1177, though he had also been sent to England, Constantinople and Sicily.[130] Just like Absalon's, his career as a diplomat ran parallel to that of a warrior, and for over twenty years Christian also led a large number of military campaigns in Barbarossa's name.[131] Munz, in his biography of the Emperor Frederick I, considered that it was more than likely that Frederick had appointed Christian of Mainz his chief negotiator in Venice, because he had 'first-hand knowledge of the extent of Frederick's actual power in that area', and, if we believe Saxo's interpretation of Absalon's role in the Slav wars, this same principle probably holds true for him as well.[132] Munz also suggested that Christian was 'a warrior and not a diplomat' and 'not a man whom we can credit with any great diplomatic astuteness or political inventiveness'.[133] This rather belittles the role of the archbishop of Mainz in Barbarossa's diplomacy, and, moreover, misrepresents the role of diplomatic personnel. Not only is it rather difficult to assess the diplomatic astuteness and political inventiveness of any envoy from the available sources, but, most importantly, these things did not matter in the way that Munz believed. What any medieval prince foremostly required from his envoys and mediators was not political inventiveness but the ability to carry out his wishes fully.[134] The sole requirement for such a function was closeness to the patron in question. Furthermore, recipients of any diplomatic mission would expect that the members of that embassy were the most trusted people of their prince: anything less would have been a grave insult. Quite simply, envoys and mediators were the most trusted servants of their masters.

Notes

1 Donald E. Queller, *The Office of Ambassador in the Middle Ages* (Princeton, 1967); *Early Venetian Legislation on Ambassadors* (Geneva, 1966).
2 Queller, *OA*, 6; Pierre Chaplais, 'English Diplomatic Documents to the End of Edward III's Reign', 39.
3 Queller, *OA*, 26.
4 Chaplais, 'English Diplomatic Documents to the End of Edward III's Reign', 39; James A. Brundage, *Medieval Canon Law* (London, 1995), 116.
5 Queller, 'Thirteenth-century Diplomatic Envoys: *Nuncii* and *Procuratores*', *Speculum*, 35 (1960), 200–1.
6 Queller, *OA*, 112, 225.
7 Queller, *OA*, 110–11.
8 There are, for example, at least two letters of credence from the 1160s, and at least one from King Stephen's reign. Chaplais, *EMDP*, i, no. 34 (a–c).
9 Chaplais, *EMDP*, i, no. 35.
10 Chaplais, *EMDP*, i, no. 36.
11 Queller, *OA*, 26; Brundage, *Medieval Canon Law*, 116–17.
12 Queller, 'Thirteenth-century Diplomatic Envoys: *Nuncii* and *Procuratores*', 202–3.
13 Chaplais, 'English Diplomatic Documents to the End of Edward III's Reign', 41.
14 Chaplais, 'English Diplomatic Documents to the End of Edward III's Reign', 42–3.
15 Villehardouin, *La conquête de Constantinople*, 99.
16 Queller, *OA*, 29–30.
17 Chaplais, *EMDP*, I, nos 80–4. In this I have excluded no. 79 as it does not specifically contain a clause 'de rato'.
18 Chaplais, *EMDP*, i, no. 80; *Rot. Litt. Pat.*, 99; Queller, *OA*, 111.
19 Though note that Philip Augustus's envoy to Genoa in 1190 described himself as procurator, but again the fact that the mission went to Italy is significant. *Codice diplomatico della repubblica di Genova*, ii, no. 191.
20 Queller, *OA*, 27–9. Similar material, all involving at least one contracting party from Italy, has more recently been flagged up by Chaplais in his *English Diplomatic Practice in the Middle Ages*, 57–63.
21 Chaplais, *EMDP*, i, no. 106.
22 Chaplais, *Treaty Rolls*, i, 25, no. 65.

23 For one example see PRO E135/3/25. I am grateful to Professor Nick Vincent for bringing this document to my attention.

24 Queller, *OA*, 210.

25 Queller, *OA*, 210.

26 Robert de Clari, *La conquête de Constantinople*, ed. Ph. Lauer (Paris, 1924), 8; Queller, *OA*, 212–15.

27 *Selected Letters of Pope Innocent III concerning England*, ed. C. R. Cheney and W. H. Semple (London, 1953), 130–1, no. 45.

28 *Selected Letters of Innocent III*, 131, no. 45.

29 Howden, *Gesta*, i, 136, 168.

30 *Diceto*, ii, 4.

31 *Handbook of British Chronology*, 3rd edn, ed. E. B. Fryde et al. (London, 1986), 84. Some historians have concluded that Walter continued to act as keeper of the royal seal, i.e. vice-chancellor, until Henry's death in 1189, but this has now been dismissed by scholars such as Nicholas Vincent.

32 Howden, *Gesta*, i, 334–5. It was during this mission that Walter was translated from the see of Lincoln to that of Rouen.

33 Howden, *Gesta*, i, 353. *Diceto*, ii, 43–4.

34 Howden, *Gesta*, ii, 45–6.

35 Howden, *Gesta*, ii, 66.

36 Howden, *Gesta*, ii, 134.

37 Howden, *Chronica*, iii, 207.

38 Howden, *Chronica*, iii, 233; *Diceto*, ii, 112–13.

39 *Diceto*, ii, 112–13.

40 Howden, *Chronica*, iii, 253.

41 *Diceto*, ii, 135–6. For the circumstances surrounding this episode, see Powicke, *Loss of Normandy*, 113–15.

42 *Diceto*, i, 367.

43 Pryce, *The Acts of Welsh Rulers*, no. 221; Rowlands, 'The 1201 Peace', 150–2.

44 Howden, *Chronica*, iv, 141.

45 In 1197, Diceto informs us that Hubert returned to England, having been involved in negotiating the treaty with Flanders and the settlement between Richard I and the archbishop of Rouen regarding Andeli, and these are just two of very many examples of his diplomatic activity prior to 1199. *Diceto*, ii, 157–8. Hubert's modern biographer, Cheney, commented that his power was indeed measured by his membership of diplomatic missions. C. R. Cheney, *Hubert Walter* (London, 1967), 104. For a brief statement of some of Hubert's role in developing English bureaucracy, see Nicholas Vincent, 'Why 1199? Bureaucracy and Enrolment under John and His Contemporaries', in *English Government in the Thirteenth Century*, ed. Adrian Jobson (Woodbridge, 2004), 41, 43–4. For contemporary opinion about the archbishop, see John Gillingham, 'The Historian as Judge: William of Newburgh and Hubert Walter', *EHR*, 119 (2004), 1277–81.

46 *MTB*, iii, 29–31.

47 *History of William Marshal*, ll. 9051–64.

48 *History of William Marshal*, ll. 8313-34.
49 Howden, *Chronica*, iii, 217-20; Chaplais, *EMDP*, ii, no. 287.
50 Howden, *Chronica*, iv, 80.
51 Odo of Deuil, *De profectione Ludovici VII in orientem*, ed. Virginia Gingerick Berry (New York, 1948), 24-5, 74-5.
52 *Gesta Friderici*, 144; Otto of Freising, *The Deeds of Barbarossa*, 187.
53 Howden, *Gesta*, i, 101
54 *Arnoldi Chronica Slavorum*, VI:xvii.
55 *Arnoldi Chronica Slavorum*, VII:x.
56 *Arnoldi Chronica Slavorum*, VI:ix, VI:xiii.
57 *MTB*, iii, 17.
58 For a recent discussion on this in England in the early twelfth century, see Christelow, 'Chancellors and Curial Bishops', 55-6.
59 H. G. Richardson and G. O. Sayles, *The Governance of Medieval England from the Conquest to Magna Carta* (Edinburgh, 1974), 244; H. A. Cronne, *The Reign of Stephen 1135-54* (London, 1970), 206.
60 Howden, *Chronica*, iii, 217, 220; Chaplais, *EMDP*, ii, no. 287.
61 Chaplais, *EMDP*, ii, no. 287.
62 Chaplais, *English Royal Documents. King John to Henry VI*, 3; Christelow, 'Chancellors and Curial Bishops', 54; N. Vincent, 'The Origins of the Chancellorship of the Exchequer', 105.
63 Howden, *Chronica*, iii, 220; Chaplais, *EMDP*, ii, no. 287.
64 For a discussion of the whereabouts of Richard's seal in 1192-93 and for the making of a new seal in 1194, see Landon, *Itinerary*, 176-9.
65 Chaplais, 'English Diplomatic Documents to the End of Edward III's Reign', 25; Chaplais, *EDP*, 55.
66 *Memorials of Saint Dunstan, Archbishop of Canterbury*, ed. William Stubbs, Rolls Series, 63 (London, 1874), 396-7; *EHD*, i, no. 231. There is also that questionable eleventh-century example of Harold's oath to Duke William. Though Harold would have given an assurance of his own observance of the agreement regarding the succession, he would essentially have acted on behalf of Edward, since the agreement was not between Harold and William but between William and King Edward.
67 Stubbs, *Memorials of Saint Dunstan*, 396-7; *EHD*, i, no. 231.
68 Keynes, *The Diplomas of King Aethelred 'the Unready' 978-1016*, 139-40. Chaplais has, however, highlighted the case of the seal of Cenwulf of Mercia, which came into the possession of the British Museum in the nineteenth century having passed through various Italian collections. Chaplais, 'The Anglo-Saxon Chancery: from the Diploma to the Writ', *Journal of the Society of Archivists*, 3 (1966), 168-9.
69 For a discussion of finger-rings used as credences see Chaplais, *EDP*, 3-6; 'The Anglo-Saxon Chancery', 167.
70 Chaplais, *EDP*, 54-6. For an example of one such aide-memoire, see *MTB*, vii, 204-5.
71 Hoffmann, 'Zur mittelalterlichen Brieftechnik', in *Spiegel der Geschichte: Festgabe für Max Braubach*, ed. Konrad Repgen (Münster, 1964), 141-7; Huw Pryce,

'Owain Gwynedd and Louis VII: the Franco-Welsh Diplomacy of the First Prince of Wales', *Welsh History Review*, 19 (1998), 18.

72 Chaplais, *EDP*, 56.

73 It must be noted that a full-length study of envoys and mediators is much needed for the twelfth century. Certainly, it is evident that the identification of, say, all envoys active during the reigns of Henry I, Stephen, Henry II and Richard I could shed light on some of the questions raised here.

74 *Epistolarum Hugoni de Campo-Florido*, in *RHF*, xvi, 202, no. 11.

75 *Epistolarum Hugoni de Campo-Florido*, 205, no. 29; Pryce, 'Owain Gwynedd and Louis VII', 6, Appendix no. 2.

76 *The Letters of Pope Innocent III concerning England and Wales. A Calendar with an Appendix of Texts*, ed. C. R. Cheney and Mary G. Cheney (Oxford, 1967), no. 254; Cheney, *Hubert Walter*, 123.

77 *PR 3 John*, 128, 137, 264.

78 Saxo, *DRHH*, ii, 402–3.

79 Saxo, *DRHH*, ii, 438–9, 442–3.

80 Saxo, *DRHH* ii, 442–3.

81 Saxo, *DRHH*, ii, 447–9.

82 Saxo, *DRHH*, ii, 462–3.

83 Saxo, *DRHH*, ii, 504–7; 516–17.

84 Saxo, *DRHH*, ii, 622–3.

85 Saxo, *DRHH*, iii, 905.

86 Christiansen, *The Northern Crusades*, 61.

87 Birgit Sawyer, 'Valdemar, Absalon and Saxo: Historiography and Politics in Medieval Denmark', *Revue belge de philologie et d'histoire*, 63 (1985), 689.

88 Saxo, *DRHH*, iii, 710, 886.

89 Sawyer, 'Valdemar, Absalon and Saxo', 691.

90 Saxo, *DRHH*, ii, 462–3, 476–7, 516–17, 556–7.

91 Saxo, *DRHH*, ii, 462–3.

92 Musset, *Les peuples scandinaves au Moyen Âge*, 182. Koch, in his history of twelfth-century Denmark, does not note Ralph's presence at Saint-Jean-de-Losne in 1162, but tells of his mission to the imperial council at Pavia in 1160. Koch, *Danmarks Historie*, iii, 265–8.

93 Saxo, *DRHH*, ii, 476–7.

94 Saxo, *DRHH*, ii, 476–7.

95 Saxo, *DRHH*, ii, 516–17.

96 Saxo, *DRHH*, ii, 506–7.

97 Saxo, *DRHH*, ii, 556–7.

98 Matthew Paris, *Chronica Maiora*, ii, 559–64.

99 S. D. Church, *The Household Knights of King John* (Cambridge, 1999), 66. For a discussion of this mission, see also N. Barbour, 'The Embassy Sent by King John of England to Miramolin, King of Morocco', *Al-Andalus*, 25 (1960), 373–81. For a briefer discussion, based on that of Barbour, see N. Vincent, 'Isabella of Angouleme: John's Jezebel', in *King John: New Interpretations*, ed. S. D. Church (Woodbridge, 1999), 200–1.

100 Church, *The Household Knights of King John*, 66.
101 *Documents Illustrative of English History in the Thirteenth and Fourteenth Centuries*, ed. H. Cole (London, 1844), 256.
102 Matthew Paris, *Chronica Maiora*, ii, 633.
103 Some historians have argued that, in classical times, the Greeks most commonly sent three men per embassy, but that two, five or ten was also a possibility. Eduard Rung, 'War, Peace and Diplomacy', 45.
104 *The History of William Marshal*, ll. 2321-3.
105 Howden, *Chronica*, iv, 107, 140. Similarly, Eduard Rung has argued that, in Athens, personal ties with the Persian royal house were considered in the choice of ambassadors. Rung, 'War, Peace and Diplomacy', 44.
106 Chaplais, *EMDP*, i, no. 36, fn. 5; Chaplais, 'English Diplomatic Documents to the End of Edward III's Reign', 41; Chaplais, *EDP*, 56-8.
107 Queller, *OA*, 7.
108 *MTB*, iii, 29; *The Lives of Thomas Becket*, tr. Michael Staunton (Manchester, 2001), 55.
109 *MTB*, iii, 29-31; Staunton, *The Lives of Thomas Becket*, 55-6.
110 *Draco Normannicus*, ll. 201-4.
111 *MTB*, ii, 339-40; Staunton, *The Lives of Thomas Becket*, 130-1.
112 *The Correspondence of Thomas Becket, Archbishop of Canterbury, 1162-1170*, 2 vols, ed. and tr. Anne Duggan (Oxford, 2000), i, no. 12.
113 *Foedera*, I, i, 190.
114 Chaplais, 'English Diplomatic Documents to the End of Edward III's Reign', 33; Chaplais, *EDP*, 56; H. Hoffmann, 'Zur mittelalterlichen Brieftechnik', 145.
115 Chaplais, 'English Diplomatic Documents to the End of Edward III's Reign', 33; Chaplais, *EDP*, 56.
116 *Itinerarium Peregrinorum et Gesta Regis Ricardi*, in *Chronicles and Memorials of the Reign of Richard I*, 2 vols, ed. William Stubbs, Rolls Series, 38 (London, 1864), i, 94-5; *Chronicle of the Third Crusade*, tr. Helen J. Nicholson (Aldershot, 1997), 100.
117 *PR 4 John*, 104; *PR 3 John*, 128, 137, 264.
118 *PR 5 John*, 235; *Rot Chart.*, i, 106b, 107: 'per unum austurcum pro omni servicio'.
119 *Rot. Litt. Claus.*, i, 26; *PR 6 John*, 63bis.
120 *Rot. Litt. Claus.*, i, 132.
121 A proposal remarkably similar to that made to the Norwegians four years later, which in 1223 led to the conclusion of the first Anglo-Norwegian commercial treaty. *Dip. Docs*, i, nos 132, 138, 155. For full outline of the significance of Brian's embassy to Denmark, see my 'Philip Augustus and the Angevin Empire: the Scandinavian Connexion', *Mediaeval Scandinavia*, 14 (2004), 37-50.
122 *CR 8 Ric. I*, 66; *PR 9 Ric. I*, 21; *PR 10 Ric. I*, 22.
123 *Rot. Lib.*, 12, 85.
124 *Rot. Chart.*, i, 106b; *Rot. Litt. Pat.*, 52b; *Rot. Litt. Claus.*, i, 53b; *PR 5 John*, 198. Harestan in particular emerges as an important castle during this period and had some £700 spent on improvements in these years. *History of the King's Works*, ed. R. Allen Brown (London, 1963), ii, 681-2.

125 Church, *The Household Knights of King John*, 63–5.

126 Church, *The Household Knights of King John*, 63–4.

127 Church, *The Household Knights of King John*, 67; *The Chronicle of the Election of Hugh Abbot of Bury St Edmunds and Later Bishop of Ely*, ed. R. M. Thomson (Oxford, 1974), 162–3.

128 *Rot. Litt. Claus.*, i, 132.

129 Chaplais, *EMDP*, i, no. 36.

130 Romuald of Salerno, *Chronicon*, 265–7, 271–92; *Le Liber Pontificalis*, ii, 431–5, 437; *Codice diplomatico della repubblica di Genova*, ii, nos 71–2; *Chronica Regia Colonienses*, 120; *Draco Normannicus*, ll. 191–8, 235–60. The standard work on Christian of Mainz is still C. Varentrapp, *Erzbischof Christian I. von Mainz* (Berlin, 1867).

131 *The Correspondence of Thomas Becket*, i, no. 55; Peter Munz, *Frederick Barbarossa* (London, 1969), 299, 325, 328, 363; Gina Fasoli, 'Federico Barbarossa e le città lombarde', *Vorträge und Forschungen*, 12 (1967), repr. in *Scritti di storia medievale*, 248–9.

132 Munz, *Frederick Barbarossa*, 328. In Ancient Greece, politicians and prominent generals were similarly used for negotiations as they had specific knowledge of the practical implications of war. Rung, 'War, Peace and Diplomacy', 44.

133 Munz, *Frederick Barbarossa*, 325, 328.

134 Church, *The Household Knights of King John*, 67; *The Chronicle of the Election of Hugh Abbot of Bury St Edmunds and Later Bishop of Ely*, 162–3.

PART IV

Guaranteeing the peace

6

Oaths

I, N., do swear upon these Holy Gospels of God, that my lord Richard, king of England, shall from this hour forward preserve with the lord Tancred, king of Sicily, the dukedom of Apulia and the principality of Capua, and his realm, and all the lands under his dominion, lasting peace, both himself and his, by land and by sea; and that so long as my said lord shall be in the kingdom of King Tancred, he shall give him his assistance in defending his territories wheresoever he shall happen to be in the territories of the lord Tancred, king of Sicily, and what person soever may attempt to invade, or make war, against the same; and that my lord shall, with his own hand, swear to observe this same treaty of peace, if the lord, King Tancred, shall in like manner, with his hand, swear to observe the said treaty of peace. And if at any time, may heaven prevent, my lord shall attempt to break the said peace, I will place myself in the custody of the said lord, King Tancred, wheresoever he shall think fit; and all these things my lord Richard, king of England, and I myself will observe in good faith and without fraud and evil intent, so help us God and these Holy Gospels and the relics of the Saints. Amen.[1]

This text of the oath taken by the men of Richard I accompanies the treaty concluded between the English king and Tancred of Sicily in November 1190, while Richard was residing on the island on his way to the Holy Land. The oath is interesting, not least because it survives as a separate record. No other such examples involving an English king survives from the twelfth century and it is uncertain whether the reason for this is that the oath was usually not recorded or that the record of the oath was simply not preserved. We do know, however, that the practice of recording and preserving the oath(s), either separate to or within the terms of a treaty, was widespread in Italy, which may explain why a separate oath was recorded on this occasion.[2]

The oath of 1190 reveals a common practice in peacemaking of the late twelfth and early thirteenth centuries, namely that of a representative taking an oath in the name of his ruler. According to Chaplais, 'a king never swore personally to keep the terms of a treaty except in the presence of the other king'. Chaplais has also concluded that it was common practice in the Middle Ages for a king never to take an oath in person before, or rather, to, an inferior.[3] The example that Chaplais used to prove his hypothesis was that of the negotiations leading up to the Treaty of Paris in 1259, during which the diplomatic records show that both the oath of Louis IX and that of Henry III were sworn by proxy in the presence of the envoys of the other king.[4] One could compare Chaplais's example of the Anglo-French negotiations of 1259 to that of the Anglo-Sicilian marriage negotiations of 1176. A letter sent by the king of Sicily to Henry II tells us that three trustworthy men had sworn on Henry's behalf and in his presence that the marriage between Henry's daughter Joan and King William would be finalised, and, on the Sicilian side, King William's envoys had taken a similar oath on his behalf.[5] Shortly afterwards an English embassy turned up in Sicily to receive the oath of King William himself.[6] First, the English envoys asked the king of Sicily to swear *manu propria* what his own envoys had sworn in England, a request that was refused on the grounds that the kings of Sicily never swore in person. The envoys then asked that William should appoint deputies to take an oath on his soul, as Henry II had done. As Chaplais has recently pointed out it is unclear whether this second request was granted or not, but William's letter to King Henry clearly stated that he held firm what his envoys had sworn in his name in England, and that he was satisfied with the oath that had been taken on Henry's soul.[7]

The arrangements surrounding the Anglo-Sicilian oath of 1190 were similar to the negotiations of 1176. A meeting had been set up between Richard and his advisers, and Tancred's representatives. Once the treaty had been negotiated and drawn up, the oath was made upon Richard's soul by at least twenty-four of his men in the presence of Tancred's envoys. These envoys then swore to the same effect upon Tancred's soul. The text of the oath further makes the claim that each king would make oath, 'manu sua', if the other was also prepared to do so.[8] It is not clear whether this was ever put into effect, as when the two kings met at Catania in March 1191 Roger of Howden merely says that Richard spent three days and three nights in Tancred's palace.[9]

Though the examples above record the taking of oaths in the pre-liminary, often negotiating, stages of the peace process, there are several recorded instances where a representative swore in the name of his king at an actual meeting between the two parties. One such example is found in 1197 when Count John of Mortain swore on the soul of his brother, Richard I, that the English king would keep the peace and alliance that he had concluded with the count of Flanders.[10] Despite the fact that both the king and the count of Flanders were present at the meeting, it seems likely that, as the count of Flanders was Richard's inferior, it was appropriate that John, and not Richard, took the oath.[11]

It is evident that on occasions of making peace not only did rulers take oaths but so too did their followers. In 1190 all of those required to swear took the oath in the name of their patron, but there are many examples of nobles taking oaths in their own right to keep the terms of a treaty. In 1197, apart from Count John who took the oath in the king's stead, twenty-eight men on Richard's side and twelve men from the county of Flanders took oaths to adhere to the treaty. A few days (or even weeks) later, a further twenty-eight of the English king's men swore to keep the terms of the alliance. According to the text of the treaty, the oaths were taken in Normandy before the king himself as well as before the representatives of the count of Flanders. At some point thereafter, twenty-two of Count Baldwin's men similarly swore to the treaty in the presence of the count and some English representatives at a site in Flanders.[12] This brought the number of men who swore to keep this particular agreement to a rather magnificent total of ninety. Though this seems quite high, there are other contemporary examples where large number of followers took similar oaths. In 1173, for example, the agreement between Henry II and the count of Maurienne had at least forty, and this number does not include those who took oaths at the ratifying stages.[13] It is evident from this that the common practice of twelve men taking oaths, which Kershaw observed in the ninth and tenth centuries, is only occasionally found in the late twelfth and early thirteenth centuries.[14]

It is clear that the practice of oath-taking by both ruler and followers has parallels with, and possibly its origins in, medieval dispute settlement. For instance, Ian Wood has drawn attention to an example from the eighth chapter of the Burgundian *Liber Constitutionum* where the crucial issue is that a man may clear himself by taking an oath in the company of twelve relatives.[15] Similarly, the *Pactus Legis Salicae* contain various references to individuals and groups purging themselves by their own oaths and that of relatives or friends, though with some variations in the number of *iuratores* (oath-takers) required.[16] In the twelfth century the count of Anjou renounced his exactions on land held by a certain Andefredus after the latter had chosen twelve men to swear on relics on his behalf.[17] Just as in disputes between rulers, it would seem that those taking oaths in dispute settlement lower down the social scale occasionally, but certainly not always, numbered twelve.

The oath of 1190 allows the historian to address another issue, namely the verbal connection between an oath and an agreement. Owing to the fact that so few documents recording oaths taken at conferences survive, we rarely know the exact verbal form of any oath taken by the participants of peacemaking. Texts of treaties tend to refer to oaths sworn to adhere to and fulfil the terms 'as written above' and similar statements, such as 'and confirmed this with oaths', are usual in chronicles.[18] Such statements tell historians very little about whether the oaths taken were simply a matter of 'I swear to keep these terms' or a longer oath detailing specific terms. The oath of 1190 certainly outlines the heart of the treaty itself: Richard would aid Tancred, both on land and at sea, against any aggressor for as long as he remained within the latter's territory. Interestingly, the aggressor is not specified in the oath or in the treaty, and though it must be suspected that the Emperor Henry VI was the prime target it seems likely that the text was non-specific in order that Richard would not be able to refuse assistance in case of the attacker being one of Henry's allies and not the Emperor himself. Exactly what Tancred's representatives swore in return is not known as only the oath taken by Richard's advisers is recorded. One could hazard a guess, however, that the Sicilian oath may have outlined the settlement of the dower of Richard's sister Joanna, queen of the late William II of Sicily.[19]

The fact that the text of the 1190 oath is recorded in Latin raises the issue of whether the oath would have been sworn in Latin or in the vernacular. One reason for using ecclesiastical envoys in negotiations was that Latin, the language of the Roman church, was universal. Thus, not only could negotiations be conducted in this language, but at least some of those present at peace conferences would have had little difficulty in understanding an oath sworn in Latin. However, Janet Nelson has suggested that, from at least the ninth century, oaths were actually sworn in a vernacular.[20] The most famous example of this is the oft-quoted passage from Nithard's *Histories* where Charles the Bald and his brother Louis the German made an alliance and swore oaths to guarantee its terms. According to Nithard, Louis swore his oath in Romance and Charles the Bald in turn swore in German.[21] As Charles and Louis each swore in the

language of the followers of the other, there must have been some importance attached to the actual words of the oaths. Chapters 3 and 4 above
showed the importance of visual acts in peacemaking and how these could
be used to convey a message without any words. In this case, however,
it was clearly not enough that those present were witnesses to the act of
taking an oath, they also needed to hear and understand the words of
those oaths.

How did this work in practice? Rosamond McKitterick has concluded
that not only were Charles and Louis bilingual, but so also were many of
their supporters, hence avoiding any problems arising from the unfamili-
arity of the language in which any oath was to be sworn.[22] The example
of Charles and Louis may perhaps be explained by the fact that they had
been brought up in a vast conglomeration of kingdoms spanning parts
that included both Romance-speaking and German-speaking followers.
One assumes that the same could have been true of vernacular oaths taken
in the twelfth and thirteenth centuries by the kings of England, France,
Scotland, Sicily, the counts of Flanders and perhaps even the Welsh
princes: they and their followers would all have spoken, or at least been
familiar with, a form of French.[23] However, this was not the case for oaths
taken to guarantee agreements between the Slavs and the Danish kings
where it is difficult to see how someone unfamiliar with either of these
vernaculars could have taken an oath in it. It is equally uncertain whether,
in this instance, oaths in Latin would have been appropriate, when some
of those Slavs were non-Christians and hence unfamiliar with the language
of the church. Furthermore, if the witnesses had not understood the oath
taken, because it was in an unfamiliar language, it might render it invalid.
This issue does raise some difficult questions about the relationship
between witnessing the act of swearing an oath, the oath itself and the
agreement that the oath guaranteed.[24] Possibly these three elements and
the language(s) in which they were performed were interconnected. All of
these elements may have been necessary because together they provided
something for everyone. The idea of peacemaking, or concluding any
agreement, was hence not that everyone present had to understand everything but that there was something in the whole process that could be
recognised by every single person.[25] Here there is clearly a parallel to be
drawn with examples from dispute settlement where the validity of a claim
tended to be judged after the adjudicator had seen and heard it, hence the
standard phrase in charters recording dispute settlement: 'vidit et audi-
vit'.[26] Thus the question whether an oath was taken in the vernacular or
in Latin is perhaps not crucial, because there were aspects of the process

that were performed in Latin and others that could have been performed in the vernacular, and some may even have contained both.[27] What mattered was that some of these aspects could be understood by the lay and ecclesiastical followers of the rulers involved in making the agreement. Most importantly, the prime function of oaths was that the written word served alongside the spoken word, and acts and gestures, to ensure that they were kept.[28]

In 1190, the last sentence of the oath formula shows that oaths in the medieval period had a clear connection with Christianity: 'so help us God and these Holy Gospels and the relics of the Saints'.[29] The oath in the medieval West was an appeal to God that included actual physical contact with a sacred object, usually a relic or a Gospel book.[30] There seems to have been no preferred choice between these and occasionally oaths were taken on both of these items. For instance, the *conventio* of 1173 between the count of Toulouse and Henry II was confirmed 'touching the Gospels', whereas Howden records how Henry the Young King took many oaths to his father on relics.[31] The whole point of swearing on holy objects was the belief that oath-breakers would suffer divine retribution because perjury was a mortal sin. Similarly, the many oaths sworn by followers on their king's or their own souls were intended to deter through fear of what might happen to one's soul in the afterlife. As Ganshof has pointed out, in an age of faith, the fear of divine retribution meant a great deal.[32] There are many accounts of the fate of oath-breakers. Most famous, of course, is the fate in the eleventh century of Harold Godwineson, whose defeat at the Battle of Hastings was depicted by the Norman sources as divine retribution for having broken his oath to Duke William.[33] Less famously but equally importantly, several contemporaries, in narrating the hostility between Henry II and his sons in the early 1180s, relate a long series of oaths that were broken and how this ultimately led to the death of two of Henry's sons, Henry the Young King and Geoffrey, count of Brittany. In commenting on the death of Henry the Young King for instance, Walter Map recalls how Henry the Young King took an oath against his father at Martel, and was on that same day 'smitten with the hammer of death by the all-righteous avenging hand' as this oath ran contrary to his earlier promises of faith.[34] Richard received a similar treatment by Ralph de Diceto. For the sin of taking up arms against his father in 1188–89, contrary to his oath, Richard had to receive absolution from the archbishops of Canterbury and Rouen once he had become king in July 1189. Diceto does, however, seem to have felt that Richard made up for the way he had treated his father by the honour in which he held his mother.[35] Later, when Richard was a prisoner in the Empire, Ralph reconsidered his position on this matter and noted that perhaps Richard had needed further punishment from God, hence his imprisonment, in order to show true repentance for his sins against his father.[36]

Despite some clear examples where oath-breakers were thought to have suffered divine retribution, it is equally clear that some agreements guaranteed by oaths were broken, and, in some cases, the oath to keep a certain agreement was even sworn in the knowledge that it would be broken. John Gillingham has found at least one example of this. In 1189 and 1190 Richard renewed his earlier promise to marry Alice, the sister of Philip Augustus, and swore oaths to this effect.[37] According to Gillingham, however, it was clear that Richard had no intention of keeping this promise, having already determined upon marrying the daughter of the king of Navarre, an alliance that had been on the cards as early as 1188 if we are to believe Bertran de Born's poem *S'ieu fos aissi segner ni poderos* and Ambroise's *Estoire de la guerre sainte*.[38] Similarly the Anglo-French treaty of 1193, in which Richard, then in captivity in the Empire, allowed the French king to keep the territory captured from him while he had been away, was probably also entered into with the full intention of breaking it as soon as an opportunity arose.[39] It would certainly be difficult to envisage a situation in which Richard, once free, would have allowed Philip to keep his conquests.

Examples such as these raise some important questions about the taking of oaths. Would a medieval ruler break an oath if he believed he would suffer divine retribution? Why guarantee treaties through oaths if they could so easily be broken? Sources frequently record instances of peacemaking where treaties and oaths were broken. This is hardly surprising as ecclesiastics wrote most of our contemporary sources, and many of these were, moreover, monastic writers. These were men whose whole outlook on life, society and politics was religious and who, consequently, often added a moral tone to their narrative. Ultimately, the fate of oath-breakers also made for a better story. As oaths were fundamental to medieval society there would have been many sworn every day that lasted, but almost inevitably those oaths that appear among our sources are those that did not. However, within society, whether a kingdom, duchy, county or even a town, the judicial process gave extra incentive to keep oaths that bound parties to contracts and agreements.[40] The prospect of fines, of having lands or goods confiscated, being maimed or killed, sent into exile and a long list of other punishments served as deterrents on a par with, if not more severe than, suffering divine retribution. However, international relations prior to the late twelfth century did not have any such process to which participants of peacemaking could appeal, and as a consequence *realpolitik* must have guided decisions on whether or not to break an oath.[41] Rulers could justify breaking an oath on the grounds that they were acting in the best interest of themselves, their family, their lands and their followers. One suspects for instance that in 1189 and 1190 Richard's desire to go on crusade guided his actions, ensuring through his oaths and promises to King Philip regarding his sister Alice that the French king would accompany him to the Holy Land and that his continental territory would be safe in his absence.[42] However, the issue is perhaps less that oaths could be broken, but rather that parties took great care to maintain at least a semblance of voluntary oath-taking. Those occasions when an oath was broken tend to follow a claim that the oath had been exacted involuntarily. Canon law stipulated that oaths and promises made under duress had no validity and hence treaties sometimes stipulated that oaths had been sworn voluntarily.[43] Oaths and promises were also an appeal to an individual's sense of honour and again this is commonly found in treaties.[44] Interestingly enough, the former claim seems to have been more common in treaties from Italy, whereas the latter occurs more frequently in treaties from north of the Alps.

Though oaths in the medieval period had a clear connection with Christianity, oaths were not only a Christian concept. There is, after all, evidence of oath-taking in dispute settlement from the Roman period and from ancient Greece, where one could swear oaths invoking the gods as witnesses or as avengers of a promise broken. The number and the names of the gods furthermore varied according to the circumstances of place, time, age and sex of the oath-taker.[45] There are, moreover, several medieval examples of non-Christians taking oaths seemingly under the same fear of retribution as Christians, and, most importantly, there is no notion that Christians considered these oaths as less valid than those they would take themselves. Most commonly in the early medieval period non-Christians would swear on their weapons, 'clashing them together', as described by one Frankish chronicler.[46] Twelfth- and thirteenth-century writers report on similar practices. For instance, according to *The Chronicle of Henry of Livonia*, non-Christian Letts and Livonians confirmed their oaths by trampling on their swords.[47] What is clear from this is that oaths were not 'mere words' among non-Christians but were rather a recognised means of guaranteeing contracts and agreements.[48]

Peacemaking in the medieval period would be unthinkable without the oath. The oath was an essential part of guaranteeing agreements through the appeal to faith, personal honour and obligation that it invoked on behalf of the oath-taker. Often oaths were undertakings not only by rulers but also by their followers, showing a clear emphasis on the need to agree, confirm and guarantee peace collectively. Importantly, oaths were cross-cultural, being recognised among Christians and non-Christians alike, and their importance is not confined to one historical period.[49] Despite this, it is clear that as peacemaking was at times carried out within a context of great mistrust, oaths could require further guarantees, namely hostages and sureties, and it is to these we must now turn.

Notes

1   'Ego N. juro super hec sancta Dei evangelia, quod dominus meus Ricardus, rex Anglie, ab hac hora in antea servabit domino Tancredo regi Sicilie, ducatus Apulie, principatus Capue, et regno ejus, et toti terre dominationis sue, pacem perpetuam per se et per suos, terra et mari: et quamdiu ipse dominus meus erit regno regis Tancredi, dabit ei auxilium ad defendum terram suam, ubicunque ipse fuerit in terra domini Tancredi Regis Sicilie, quicunque vellet eam invadere, aut ei facere guerram: et quod dominus meus pacem istam manu sua jurabit, si dominus rex Tancredus similiter pacem manu sua juraverit. Et si aliquando (quod absit) dominus meus vellet pacem istam infringere, ego ponam me in captione ipsius domini regis Tancredi, ubi ipse voluerit. Et hec omnia dominus Ricardus rex Anglie, et ego, bona fide, et sine fraude, et sine male ingenio tenebimus: sic Deus nos adjuvet et hec sancta Dei evangelia, et sanctorum reliquie. Amen.' Howden, *Chronica*, iii, 64; Howden, *Gesta*, ii, 136.
2   For some examples of this from Genoese diplomacy, see *Codice diplomatico della repubblica di Genova*, i, nos 195, 279, 280, 282; ii, nos 58, 59, 101.
3   Pierre Chaplais, 'The Making of the Treaty of Paris (1259) and the Royal Style', *EHR*, 67 (1952), repr., in his *Essays in Medieval Diplomacy and Administration* (London, 1981), 237. See also, Voss, *Herrschertreffen*, 195–6.
4   Chaplais, 'The Making of the Treaty of Paris (1259) and the Royal Style', 241–4.
5   *Diceto*, i, 413–14.
6   *Diceto*, i, 408.
7   *Diceto*, i, 414; Chaplais, *EDP*, 54–5. Compare also the oaths taken by the envoys of the French king and by William Marshal for Richard I in London in 1189. Howden, *Chronica*, iii, 19; Howden, *Gesta*, ii, 93.
8   'et quod dominus meus pacem istam manu sua jurabit, si dominus rex Tancredus similiter pacem manu sua juraverit'. Howden, *Chronica*, iii, 64; Howden, *Gesta*, ii, 136.
9   Howden, *Chronica*, iii, 97.
10 *Dip. Docs*, i, no. 7.

11 *Ibid.* See also Werner Goez's discussion on oaths taken by the German emperors. W. Goez, '". . .*iuravit in anima regis*": Hochmittelalterliche Beschränkungen königlicher Eidesleistung', *DA*, 42 (1986), 517–54.

12 *Dip. Docs*, i, 19–20.

13 Howden, *Gesta*, i, 38.

14 Kershaw, 'Rex Pacificus', 122–3. In Genoa, jurors frequently exceeded twelve. For some examples of this, see *Codice diplomatico della repubblica di Genova*, i, no. 282; iii, no. 58.

15 Ian Wood, 'Disputes in Late Fifth- and Sixth-century Gaul', in *The Settlement of Disputes in Early Medieval Europe*, 14.

16 Wood, 'Disputes in Late Fifth- and Sixth-century Gaul',15.

17 Jane Martindale, '"His Special Friend"? The Settlement of Disputes and Political Power in the Kingdom of the French (Tenth to Mid-twelfth Century)', *TRHS*, 6th ser., 5 (1995), 50–1.

18 For one such example, see *Helmoldi Chronica Slavorum*, 78.

19 For this see the letter patent of Richard outlining the treaty with Tancred. Howden, *Chronica*, iii, 61–4; Howden, *Gesta*, ii, 134.

20 Nelson, 'Literacy in Carolingian Governement', 268.

21 *Nithard histoire des fils de Louis le pieux*, 100–9.

22 Rosamond McKitterick, 'Latin and Romance: an Historian's Perspective', in *The Frankish Kings and Culture in the Early Middle Ages*, ed. Rosamond McKitterick (Aldershot: 1995), 138.

23 Similarly, Danish diplomacy with the petty princes in the northern parts of the Empire could have been conducted in Middle Low German. We know for instance that it was used extensively for trading purposes in the Scandinavian countries in this period. Murray, 'The Danish Monarchy and the Kingdom of Germany', 296–7.

24 In Italy in the early ninth century, certain men claimed not to be bound by the additions made to Lex Salica by Charlemagne on the grounds that they had not been present to hear them announced by the ruler. This indicates a clear relationship between hearing and understanding an oath and its validity. Janet Nelson, 'Literacy in Carolingian Government', 267.

25 Kosto, *Making Agreements in Medieval Catalonia*, 156; Geary, 'Land, Language and Memory', 178.

26 Geary, 'Land, Language and Memory', 175. See also discussion by Patrick Wormald on royal decrees. Patrick Wormald, 'Lex Scripta and Verbum Regis: Legislation and Germanic Kingship, from Euric to Cnut', in *Early Medieval Kingship*, ed. P. H. Sawyer and I. N. Woods (Leeds, 1977), 105–38.

27 Geary, 'Land, Language and Memory', 178.

28 Geary, 'Land, Language and Memory', 178; Kosto, *Making Agreements in Medieval Catalonia*, 157.

29 Howden, *Chronica*, iii, 64; Howden, *Gesta*, ii, 136.

30 Nicole Hermann-Mascard, *Les reliques des saints. Formation coutumière d'un droit* (Paris, 1975), 236, 254–6; F. L. Ganshof, *Feudalism*, 3rd edn (London, 1979), 28.

31 Howden, *Gesta*, i, 36, 294–301. See also, Hermann-Mascard, *Les reliques des saints*, 256.

32 Ganshof, *Feudalism*, 28.

33 *The Gesta Guillelmi of William of Poitiers*, ed. and tr. R. H. C. Davis and M. Chibnall (Oxford, 1998), 20–1, 68–71, 76–7, 120–1; *The Gesta Normannorum Ducum of William of Jumièges, Orderic Vitalis and Robert of Torigni*, 2 vols, ed. E. M. C. van Houts (Oxford, 1992–95), ii, 158–61.

34 *De Nugis Curialium*, 280–1.

35 *Diceto*, ii, 67–8.

36 *Diceto*, ii, 107.

37 Howden, *Gesta*, ii, 104–5.

38 Gillingham, *Richard I*, 126; *The Poems of the Troubadour Bertran de Born*, no. 35, p. 380; Ambroise, *Estoire de la guerre sainte*, ll. 1148–9.

39 Howden, *Chronica*, iii, 217–20.

40 Little, *Benedictine Maledictions*, 52–3.

41 W. Ullmann, 'The Medieval Papal Court as an International Tribunal', *Virginia Journal of International Law*, 11 (1971), repr. in his *The Papacy and Political Ideas in the Middle Ages* (London, 1976), 356–78.

42 Gillingham, *Richard I*, 123.

43 For examples, see *Rec. des actes de Philippe Auguste*, i, 448; *Guillelmi I. regis diplomata*, 35.

44 For one example, see *The Acts of Welsh Rulers*, 372.

45 Ian Wood, 'Disputes in Late Fifth- and Sixth-century Gaul', 17; Joseph Plescia, *The Oath and Perjury in Ancient Greece* (Tallahassee, 1970), 2–5.

46 *The Fourth Book of the Chronicle of Fredegar*, 63. Lee has recently highlighted several examples where rulers and their followers took oaths according to their 'native ritual'. A. D. Lee, 'Treaty-making in Late Antiquity', in *War and Peace in Ancient and Medieval History*, 114.

47 *Heinrici Chronicon Lyvonie*, ed. W. Arndt, in *MGH SS*, 23 (Hanover, 1874; repr. Stuttgart, 1986), 281.

48 Abels, 'King Alfred's Peacemaking Strategies with the Vikings', 27–8.

49 See for example Plescia, *The Oath and Perjury in Ancient Greece*, 2–5; Russell, *Peacemaking in the Renaissance*, appendix B, 242–5; *Major Peace Treaties of Modern History*, ed. A. Toynbee, F. L. Israel and E. Chill (New York, 1967), i, 70, 113.

7

Hostages and sureties

It should be simplicity itself to define what a hostage was in the medieval period. After all, medieval warfare and high politics still generate more books on the university library bookshelves than any other medieval topics, and hostages are a common feature of both. Often the issue of hostages has been used by contemporary commentators and modern historians alike as a yardstick by which to measure the success or failure of individual kings.[1] A number of historians have recently highlighted the important socio-cultural, symbolic and political uses of hostages in the early medieval period, but few historians have to date devoted more than a passing reference to the role of hostages in the period after 1100.[2] In this period it is not always clear what a hostage was or how to identify them in the sources, because hostages can be confused with the related topic of prisoners of war.[3] Consequently, any discussion of hostages must begin with a definition.

In the post-1100 period, the most common use of hostages in negotiations was those given to secure the release of adversaries captured in war. Probably the two most well-known such examples from the late twelfth century are the release from captivity of William the Lion, king of Scots, and of Richard I, king of England. The Scottish king, captured by Henry II's justiciar at the battle of Alnwick in 1174 and paraded throughout the English king's dominions, was forced to make a humiliating peace. William himself became the man of Henry for his lands as did also any Scots barons or ecclesiastics who might be required to do so by the English king. The Scottish king furthermore promised not to harbour any of Henry's enemies. To guarantee the observance of these terms, William had to deliver four castles to his English captor and for executing ('exequendo') the treaty the king of Scots delivered some twenty-one hostages:

his brother David, Earl Duncan, Earl Waltheof, Earl Gilbert, the earl of Angus, Richard de Morville the constable, Ness son of William, Richard Comyn, Walter Corbet, Walter Olifard, John de Vaux, William Lindsay, Philip de Colleville, Philip of Valognes, Robert Frembert, Robert de Bourneville, Hugh Giffard, Hugh Ridel, Walter of Berkeley, William Hay and William Mortimer. Once the castles had been surrendered, William himself and his brother would be released, though the other hostages would be released only upon giving a hostage of their own.[4]

By contrast the release of Richard I was ensured through the payment of a huge ransom, 100,000 pounds 'of the money of Cologne'.[5] Another 50,000 marks were to be shared between the Emperor Henry VI and the duke of Austria, and hostages would be given to ensure payment. For his share – 30,000 of the 50,000 marks – the Emperor would receive sixty hostages, whereas the duke of Austria would receive seven hostages for his 20,000 marks. According to the treaty, negotiated in late June 1193, King Richard would be set free once Henry VI had received the sum of 100,000 marks and the sixty hostages.[6] In an additional clause Henry then stipulated that, if Richard was successful in his 'promise' regarding Henry the Lion, the exiled duke of Saxony, the Emperor would discharge 50,000 marks of Richard's ransom, pay the 20,000 marks due to Leopold of Austria, and, furthermore, waive the right to the sixty-seven hostages. If Richard was unable to fulfil his promise, the additional 50,000 marks would be due within seven months of his return to his own lands.[7]

In the case of Richard I's agreement with the Emperor Henry VI, the hostages required were essentially to guarantee payment of the ransom. The agreement between Richard and Henry suggests an intention to release all of the hostages once full payment had been received, despite the fact that the written document does not explicitly state this.[8] By contrast, in the 1174 treaty between Henry II and William the Lion there is no suggestion of a release; instead the terms specify the replacement of the original hostages with their heirs.[9] The ultimate fate of the Scots hostages is not referred to in Henry's treaty with William, or in the 1189 agreement by which Richard I restored the status quo as it had been before the capture of the Scottish king.[10] Hence the intention with this treaty was to keep the hostages to ensure the future good behaviour of the Scottish king and his nobles. Moreover, in this particular example, the hostages not only guaranteed the future good behaviour of the person who had been released, they were also symbolic of political submission.[11]

There are other, less well-known, examples of hostages being used to guarantee the release of captured leaders. When Count Adolph of

Holstein, one of the Danish kings' adversaries, was made captive in 1201, his release was secured, some two years later, only upon the promise of high-status hostages to ensure the count's good behaviour. According to Arnold of Lübeck, these hostages were to be released by the Danish king after ten years, or upon the death of the king.[12] Some twenty years earlier, two captured Slav leaders had been released by Cnut VI on condition that they would hand over twenty-four hostages, among whom was the heir of one of the leaders.[13] There is also the example of Valdemar II of Denmark and his eldest son and co-regent Valdemar III, who were captured by Count Henry of Schwerin in May 1223 while on a hunting expedition on the island of Lyø.[14] Following no fewer than three different agreements, Valdemar II was released on Christmas Day 1225 in return for a ransom of 45,000 marks of silver, the jewellery of the queen, and a promise to give up all of his lands between the rivers of Eider and Elbe. Hostages were then given to ensure payment.[15] Valdemar's son, however, was released only the following April, and the Danish king had to give up his younger sons as hostages.[16]

There is some secondary writing on ransom and prisoners of war in the Middle Ages, which, though useful for the general history of warfare, must be set aside from the present discussion of hostages.[17] Prisoners of war and captured knights should not be confused with hostages in the Middle Ages, even though modern terminology often blurs the differences between hostages and prisoners. We now might refer to soldiers or workers captured in a foreign country as hostages, whereas a captured subject of a medieval ruler was not a hostage.[18] It is clear from the primary sources that hostages in the high Middle Ages were essentially guarantors of agreements. Thus, Howden referred to the captive King Richard not as a hostage (*hostagius, obses*), but as *in captionem*.[19] Arnold of Lübeck used a similar terminology (*in custodia*) when denoting captive Slavs, and he distinguished these from the hostages (*obsides*) given as a pledge for their ransom and release.[20] In another example the 1196 treaty between Richard I and Philip Augustus, the terms of the treaty refer to captives (*prisones*) as well as to *ostagii prisonum*, who were surely the hostages that had been pledged for the release of captured knights.[21] Thus one would pay ransom for a captive ruler or a follower, and as part of that agreement hostages might be given as a pledge that the full ransom would be paid.[22]

In the early medieval period hostages are frequently found in Western kings' dealings with their neighbours, chiefly non-Christians and those living on the Celtic fringe. Peacemaking following conflicts where one side had either been conquered or had submitted voluntarily often included the giving of hostages to the superior party and tended to go hand in hand with other familiar acts of submission such as the giving of tribute or appearing before the superior ruler with bare feet.[23] To early medieval writers, the willingness to give or exchange hostages with an enemy was an undesirable quality in a ruler, because it usually followed military defeat or at least indicated a lack of success in war. Consequently, those rulers often received negative comments by contemporaries.[24] Similarly, Saxo, writing at the end of the twelfth century, picked up on this theme and continuously emphasised the ability of the Danish kings to exact hostages and tribute from the Slavs. In one example, from 1160, Saxo describes the meeting between the Slav envoy Domborus and the Danish king's adviser Absalon, recalling how the latter was affronted by the envoy's suggestion of an exchange of hostages. According to Saxo, Absalon declared that the Rugians usually sent not only hostages but money and supplies for the Danish fleet, while the Danes could not recall that they had ever conceded or contributed anything similar to the Rugians.[25] On another occasion, Saxo records how the Slavs rather offered hostages to King Valdemar than to Duke Henry the Lion, thereby attempting to show the exalted status of the king in relation to his German ally.[26] Despite his polemical intentions, the acts of receiving hostages to which he refers are not, for that reason, untruths. Saxo refers to at least six instances when hostages were offered to the Danish kings in the period 1157–85, and some of these can be corroborated by other sources.[27]

The way in which successive English kings made peace with the Welsh rulers in the period 1154–1216 further illustrates the practice of using hostages to enforce submission or to reconfirm a superior–inferior relationship. In 1158, for instance, Rhys ap Gruffudd gave hostages as the price of his peace with Henry II. We also know that at Woodstock in 1163, a large number of Welsh princes gave hostages to the English king.[28] Similarly, after King John's expedition against Llywelyn in 1211, the Welsh prince made peace with the king on condition that he would give John hostages from 'amongst the leading men of the land' along with twenty thousand cattle and forty steeds.[29] These are clear examples of the Welsh rulers giving hostages as part of their submission following military expeditions, or threats thereof, by the English. On other occasions, some Welsh rulers seem to have had a more harmonious relationship with the reigning English king. One example of this is Henry II's dealings with the Lord Rhys. In 1171, when Henry was preparing his expedition to Ireland, he made an agreement with Rhys at a meeting in the Forest of Dean, whereby the Welsh lord agreed to give Henry some fourteen hostages, three hundred horses and four thousand oxen. The two agreed to meet again, shortly afterwards, and on this occasion Rhys was given back his son Hywel 'who had been a hostage with the king for a long time before that', and he was also given a respite until the king's return from Ireland concerning the other hostages and the tribute. Henry and Rhys then met for a third time on Easter Monday 1172 while Henry was on his way back to England, but the compiler of the *Brut* does not mention whether Rhys was compelled to produce his hostages and the tribute during this conference. Interestingly enough, the year after, Rhys, as a conciliatory gesture, sent his son Hywel, the former hostage, to serve Henry II at his court on the continent.[30] Clearly, in these latter examples Rhys did not give hostages as a consequence of military subjugation, but as a voluntary and conscious act to keep the peace, accepting by his actions that he was Henry's political inferior, or at least that it was politically expedient to appear to be so.[31]

Seeing the frequent giving of Slav and Welsh hostages to the English and Danish kings as simply reflecting a relationship of inferior to superior relationship has some merits, and it can be compared to the way in which successive Angevin kings dealt with their subjects.[32] The Welsh and the Slavs were often treated as underlings whose political misbehaviour, both actual and threatened, should be, and was, punished severely. Yet it is also evident from the sources that, when it came to hostages, non-Christians and the peoples of the Celtic fringe, perhaps the Welsh in particular, were treated more harshly than those of the rest of Western Europe. Not only did peacemaking with these specific groups more commonly involve hostages but contemporary attitudes and opinions of their ability to make and keep agreements were also manifestly different from those held of other Western peoples. As noted above, in the early medieval period, the unwillingness to adhere to the terms of a treaty and the willingness to 'write-off' hostages served to illustrate, in the eyes of the Frankish annalists, the immorality of their enemies, and this opinion is echoed by twelfth- and thirteenth-century writers commenting on negotiations with the Welsh and the Slavs.[33] To take one example, in the early twelfth century the author of the *Gesta Stephani* commented that the Welsh were men of an animal type, 'naturally swift-footed, accustomed to war, volatile always in breaking their words as in changing their abodes'.[34] William of Newburgh describes the Welsh in a similar manner when referring to the great Welsh rebellion of c. 1165. According to William the Welsh were lawless and savage, wantonly breaking their treaty with King Henry (II), and thereby also exposing their hostages to danger.[35] Robert of Toringi, in recording the lead up to the hostilities, refers to two of the leaders, Rhys ap Gruffudd (the Lord Rhys) and his uncle, Owain Gwynedd, as men of perversity.[36] Likewise Gerald of Wales, in his *Descriptio Cambriae*, dedicated a whole chapter to the failure of the Welsh to keep their promises.[37] Anglo-Norman chroniclers weren't the only ones to harbour such attitudes and feelings towards the Welsh. In a letter to the exiled Archbishop Thomas Becket, Arnulf of Lisieux referred to the unreliability ('inprobitate') and audacity ('audaciam') of the Welsh.[38] Walter Map makes a similar observation, noting that they were only honest in their dishonesty ('sola scilicet improbitate probi').[39] Similar comments about the Slavs are found in the thirteenth century, in the work of Henry of Livonia, an eyewitness to the Christianisation of the lands around the Baltic Sea. Henry refers to the trickery and deceitfulness of the Baltic Slavs, attributing this, quite naturally, to their non-Christian beliefs.[40] Helmold of Bosau and Arnold of Lübeck, however, seem to have been content with just chronicling the piracy and 'false' baptisms of the Slavs and are surprisingly silent on any oath-breaking or forsaking of hostages.[41] Saxo likewise seems to have made little distinction between the disloyalties of the Slavs and those of other nations. For instance, in recalling the civil war between Cnut and Svein of the 1150s, Saxo reported how supporters of either one of the rivals swapped sides without being hindered 'by their affection for the hostages they had given'.[42] On another occasion, Saxo, in one sentence criticised not only the inconstancy of the king's enemies, the Slavs, but also the treachery of his friend, Duke Henry the Lion.[43] Indeed, most of the Danish sources display a more hostile opinion of the 'Germans' than they do of the Slavs, labelling them as faithless and deceitful.[44]

There are examples of peacemaking between other Western rulers where one side was clearly negotiating from a better vantage point, yet these instances only very rarely involve hostages. For instance in 1193 the French king, Philip Augustus, inevitably held the upper hand in the negotiations, because the treaty was negotiated and concluded by Richard I's envoys during the king's captivity in the Empire. Yet, Philip did not demand or try to press home his advantage by demanding hostages.[45] Another example is the treaty between the dying Henry II and Philip Augustus of July 1189 in which the text clearly divulges Philip's more advantaged position in the negotiations, but again hostages were not requested.[46] Similarly no hostages were demanded by Frederick Barbarossa from Svein, who received the Danish kingdom from the Emperor's hand, or from Valdemar I upon his doing homage to Frederick for his crown in the 1160s.[47] In the case of Anglo-French negotiations, one reason why hostages were not demanded could be because war was controlled by the aristocratic elites who knew or were related to one another.[48] In general there seems to have been an unwritten code regarding the use of hostages among Western rulers that apparently did not apply to certain 'barbarous' people. These attitudes to the Welsh in particular go some way towards explaining why they were more frequently required to give hostages and also explains the harsher treatment that their hostages seem to have received.[49] However, economic, demographic and cultural differences lay behind such views and therefore also underpinned the use of hostages.[50] For instance the role of castles in the medieval West within the context of both warfare and peacemaking is indicated by their frequent use as sureties in Anglo-French negotiations of this period.[51] In Wales, Denmark and the Slav lands, on the other hand, such tactics were not always possible, because although these peoples had fortified sites, the diffusion of a tradition of building in stone was still taking place during the twelfth and thirteenth centuries. Furthermore, it seems likely that the sparsity of population and the difficult terrain of these parts also made it logistically easier to use hostages to guarantee agreements.[52] Gillingham has noted that Scotland started to change during the reign of David I and it was a measure of this transformation that Henry II was able to release William the Lion in return for possession of five key castles.[53] Evidently, though the principles and practice of making peace were generally very similar across the regions covered by this book, the use of hostages offer one exception. It is significant that by the thirteenth century the practice of giving or exchanging hostages had all but disappeared in the rest of Western Europe unless it was for the purpose of ransom. In the later Middle Ages ransom and hostages for payment thereof became an integral part of the terms of treaties. However, in the twelfth century, though negotiations among other Western rulers frequently involved hostages given to guarantee the payment of ransoms, there are no examples where hostages served as a pledge to keep the terms of a final peace agreement (*pax, pax firma, pax et finalis concordia*).

Exchanges of hostages, as opposed to the giving or taking of hostages, occur rarely in the sources of the twelfth and early thirteenth centuries. Occasionally exchanges of hostages were made to ensure the safety of rulers while attending conferences. For instance, before coming to Denmark for a meeting with Valdemar I in 1160, the Norwegian jarl Erling Skakke made his negotiators request that Esbern, the brother of Absalon, would be dispatched to Norway as a hostage to guarantee Erling's safe return. The Danish king, in turn, before sending Esbern, demanded that two Norwegians, Erling and Ivar, be detained in Denmark.[54] This rare example of an exchange of hostages from this period stands in such stark contrast to the numerous references to the giving of hostages that it is worth pondering its significance. Christopher Holdsworth has suggested that the reason why exchanges of hostages were not always mentioned by chroniclers was that they were so common that chroniclers simply took this practice for granted.[55] It is possible, however, that the reverse is closer to the truth; that exchanges of hostages were rarely recorded simply because they were rare occurrences.

There are compelling reasons why exchanges of hostages may have been a rarity. Consider the identity of hostages. In all cases of peacemaking and diplomacy where hostages are mentioned, the intention was to guarantee agreements through the giving of 'valuable' people: men, women or children whom the donor would want to be returned safely. Consequently hostages tended to be the heirs of rulers or the heirs of their closest advisers.[56] For instance, when the author of the *Brut* referred to the Welsh hostages given to Henry II at some point before the rebellion of 1165, he named these as being the 'two sons of Owain's, Rhys and Cadwallon, and Cynwrig and Maredudd, sons of Rhys, and several others'.[57] Similarly Arnold of Lübeck's account of the negotiations for the release of Adolph of Holstein reveals that the count gave the Danish king two of his own sons, a son from each of his allies, Ludolf of Dasle and Henry of Dannenberg, and eight boys from his *ministeriales*.[58] As giving heirs as hostages could jeopardise the position of a ruler and that of his family, and in turn destabilise his territory, the intention in taking hostages was thus to undermine a ruler's ability to take decisive action both on a domestic and on an 'international' level.[59] This can be seen clearly in 1211 when Llywelyn ap Iorwerth was not only forced to give his sole heir, Gruffydd, an illegitimate son, into King John's custody and place him entirely at the king's will, but also had to concede that, should he have no heirs by his wife Joan, he would cede all of his lands to the English king.[60] As Beverley Smith has commented: 'Llywelyn was confronted with the dire prospect that his dominion would escheat to the king at his death'.[61]

This argument becomes more convincing if we also consider the fate of hostages. Most contemporaries tend to note merely that hostages were given or exchanged and then perhaps include some of their names. On rare occasions the sources record how long the hostages were expected to remain with their keepers. For example, according to Arnold of Lübeck, the hostages of Count Adolph of Holstein were to be released by the Danish king after ten years or upon the death of the king, whereas the author who recorded the giving of a hostage to Philip Augustus in 1215 in exchange for the release of the count of Flanders set the term of captivity as five years.[62] Another example can be found in article 58 of Magna Carta which states that King John was to restore at once the son of Llywelyn and all other Welsh hostages.[63] These were presumably the hostages who had been given to John at the time of Llywelyn's submission in 1211, and who had remained with the English king for some four years. It seems likely, however, that no actual period of captivity had initially been agreed. In 1215 John also released two hostages to Gwenwynwyn of Powys, both of whom had been given at the Welsh leader's submission in 1208.[64] As with the hostages of Llywelyn in 1211, no period of captivity is specified for those of Gwenwynwyn in the charter of 1208.[65] Only in one of these instances is reference made to what would happen to the hostages if the ruler who had pledged them died, whereas none of the sources reveals the fate of the hostages if the political circumstances changed in other ways.

It is easy to imagine what happened to hostages if the agreements for which they were guarantors were broken, and indeed this is a topic in which contemporary commentators seem to have taken a great interest. The *Brut* for instance records how, in 1165, Henry II in a fit of rage ordered the eyes of his Welsh hostages to be gouged out.[66] A similar story can be found in the same source some forty-five years later when at least one of the hostages given by Llywelyn in 1211 was killed when the Welsh ruler initiated war again in 1212. According to the author of the *Brut*, King John retaliated by ordering Robert Vieuxpont to hang Rhys ap Maelgwn, a young boy of seven, on the walls of the town of Shrewsbury.[67] According to Wendover, John also ordered the hanging in Nottingham of twenty-eight boys, all Welsh hostages.[68] Hanging, in fact, seems to have been a favourite punishment given to hostages. The author of the *Chronicle of Henry of Livonia* records at least one occasion when the Danish king, Valdemar II, had a large number of Slav hostages hanged.[69] On a another occasion, Duke Henry the Lion, at the outset of his summer campaign of 1163, hanged Vartiszlav, the brother of the Slav prince Pribiszlav, as punishment for the latter making war on the duke. It would seem that Vartiszlav had been a hostage since the campaign of the previous year.[70] In a domestic context, Saxo reports that after besieging a certain stronghold in Denmark on account of his hostility with Archbishop Eskil, Valdemar I received a hostage from the keepers as a promise that the castle would be handed over to him. After the keepers reneged on this promise, Valdemar 'raised up the trunk of a large tree' and brought the hostage to it and pretended that he was about to pay the penalty for the castle's resistance by being hanged. On hearing, and presumably seeing, this, the garrison then surrendered.[71] Other common punishments dished out to hostages include mutilation by the cutting off of ears and noses.[72] There are also some examples where the hostages were returned after having had their hands cut off: a possible reference to the fact that the person pledging the hostages had broken his oath, sworn while touching a relic.[73] There is also the famous example of the five-year-old William Marshal who, having been both placed on a siege catapult and hung out of a window, was eventually spared death by King Stephen, despite the fact that William's father failed to keep the agreement for which his son had been pledged.[74]

Acting as a hostage was a personal obligation based upon the relationship between ruler and subject. In 1193, Robert of Nunant, the brother of Bishop Hugh of Coventry, refused to be a hostage for the ransom of Richard I on the grounds that he was the man of Count John.[75] Potentially the refusal could have ruptured the agreement between Henry VI and Richard I, thereby endangering the personal safety of the English king. We know, of course, that Robert's action did not have dire consequences for Richard, but his refusal to act as a hostage highlights the problem of giving hostages and it also emphasises the consensual nature of giving hostages. To give hostages was not a light undertaking for a ruler or for his subjects, and this must go some way towards explaining why exchanges of hostages occurred so rarely in this period.[76] An exchange of hostages would have been a statement that the two parties making the agreement were in an equally strong bargaining position. It seems likely, that in such circumstances neither side would have been very willing to give hostages and it is important to emphasise again that there are no examples from the period covered by this book when hostages were exchanged as a pledge to keep the terms of a final peace agreement.

The difficulties posed by using hostages may have resulted in a variation of this practice that emerges clearly in this period: the giving or exchanging of sureties or guarantors. Though sureties and guarantors were commonly found in dispute settlement of the early medieval period, they do not seem to have accompanied peacemaking between rulers in the period before c. 1100.[77] That sureties and guarantors in peacemaking developed out of the practice of giving or exchanging hostages is corroborated by terminology. Historians have concluded that there were at least two different types of sureties: real and personal. The first of these was commonly a pledge of property that was not a direct subject of the agreement and control tended to be handed over only in case of forfeit.[78] Personal sureties were individuals as opposed to objects and they operated in a number of ways: 'by using influence to encourage the debtor to perform; by forcing the debtor to perform; by compensating the creditor in case of a debtor's failure to perform; by performing the debtor's obligation itself, whether payment or action'.[79] Unlike a hostage, those acting as sureties were deprived of their liberty only if there was a breach of the agreement. In the documents that Kosto examined, personal sureties were described in a number of ways, some shared with real sureties (*pignus, fidancia, firmantia, guadium*), others referring specifically to people and their actions (*debitor, federator, fideiussor, guarantus, guarantor, manulerator, obses, ostaticum, pagator, plevius, tenedor*).[80] Kosto noted that the terms were not applied with any absolute consistency and, though this applies also to the treaties discussed here, it is clear that guarantors and sureties had similar though fewer designations, most commonly *fideiussor, obses, guarantor* and even a couple not found among those agreements investigated by Kosto (*securitates, hostagius*). Most importantly, two of these terms (*obses, hostagius*) are also used to describe hostages.

A good example of the use of real sureties in peacemaking can be found in the Treaty of Messina concluded between Richard I of England and Philip Augustus of France in 1191. According to this treaty, the French king gave as *fidejussores et obsides* the count of Ponthieu and the whole of his fief. The treaty further set down that all of those who 'subscribed' to this agreement themselves acted as *fidejussores et obsides* that the count of Ponthieu would perform this function and that the treaty in the form of letters patent had been given to the king of the English. The names of those subscribing are then given: Bernard of Saint-Valery, William de Borry (Barris), John de 'Terria', the lord of Corcelles, Count Robert, Hugh de Castello, the count of Perche, and the lord of Issoudun. Just as in the *convenientiae* that Kosto examined, the count of Ponthieu had to hand himself, or his heir, over to the English king, within three weeks, only if Philip actually broke the terms of the treaty.[81] The fact that not only the fief but also the count himself acted as a surety gives further support to Kosto's findings that personal sureties commonly complemented real sureties.[82] Another example of the use of real sureties is found in the 1174 Treaty of Falaise between Henry II and William, king of Scots. According to the text of this treaty, William guaranteed his observance of the terms by delivering the castles of Roxburgh, Berwick, Jedburgh, Edinburgh and Stirling to the English king. It is clear from this that, unlike the 1191 example and just as was the case with hostages, this had to be done immediately and not merely if the agreement was broken. Furthermore, the text of the treaty stipulated that, while these castles were at the disposal of Henry, the king of Scots had to maintain them from his own revenue.[83] This feature cannot be found in 1191, though Kosto noted that among the agreements that he investigated the holder of sureties, whether real or personal, was rarely responsible for the maintenance of the properties held.[84]

According to Kosto, usually only one party provided real sureties and among Kosto's documents these commonly occurred at submissions. The castle sureties of 1174 are clearly one such example. The surety provision of 1191 is a more difficult matter. Here, the count of Ponthieu and his fief had clearly been pledged by the French king and any sureties given by the English king are not mentioned in the text. This is perhaps not surprising because the text of the treaty, as it is now available to us, is in the form of letters patent in the name of the French king.[85] This was the exemplar kept by the English king, and one would assume that Richard had handed over to the French side his letter patent outlining the terms of the treaty and the procedures to ensure that they were kept. Thus it is possible that also the English king had pledged a combination of real and personal sureties to guarantee the terms of the peace.

Though some similar enforcement procedures were made at submissions, it is clear that the 1191 peace should not be interpreted in such a context, despite the fact that at least one historian has viewed the treaty as a humiliation for the French king.[86] A comparison with another contemporary treaty, that concluded between Richard I and Tancred of Sicily in November 1190, makes it evident that in 1191 both Philip Augustus and Richard alike pledged sureties. The treaty between Richard and Tancred, like its Anglo-French contemporary, has come down to us in the form of letters patent in the name of only one of the kings, namely Richard, and, just as in the Treaty of Messina, only the sureties of the king in whose name the letter was issued are revealed.[87] Despite this Howden makes it clear that also Tancred had pledged sureties to keep the terms of the treaty: 'Et si ipse Tancredus rex Sicilie et sui pacem non servaverint, predicti archiepiscopi et ceteri qui sacramentum illud ex parte regis Tancredi juraverunt, ponent se in captione Ricardi Regis Anglie, ubi ipse voluerit'.[88] What we are dealing with in the surety provisions of the Treaty of Messina is thus not one-sided action from an inferior but a specific form of wording in treaties from the early 1190s. It is apparent, furthermore, that this form was to change within a decade of these two treaties. Compare, for instance, the surety provisions of the Treaty of Messina to that of Le Goulet of 1200. The Treaty of Le Goulet survives in both the letters patent issued by the French king and that issued in the name of the English king.[89] The exemplars are almost identical, with the names of each king having been swapped in accordance with which of the kings had issued the letter, and with some minor changes in spellings and word order.[90] Unlike the Treaty of Messina, however, the text of both exemplars of the Treaty of Le Goulet names the sureties of both the English and French kings.[91]

Personal sureties were by far the most common way to ensure that a treaty was kept. The agreement between the English kings and the counts of Flanders, which was renewed on several occasions in the twelfth century, provides a good and seemingly the earliest example of such sureties. The 1101 agreement between Count Robert of Flanders and King Henry I stipulated that twelve guarantors on the side of the count of Flanders were to pay the English king 100 marks each if Robert broke the agreement. Similarly the guarantors of the English king were each to pay the same amount, except Robert fitz Hamo who would pay 200 marks, in case of a breach of the terms by Henry I. The money was to be collected and sent to the other party within 120 days.[92] If any of the count's guarantors were unable to pay, they were to place themselves in the captivity of the English king in the Tower of London or any other place where the king could 'hold them free at his mercy'. King Henry's men were guarantors under these same conditions towards the count of Flanders, though the text of the treaty does not name a specific place to where Henry's men would be held.[93] The 1163 renewal of this alliance, almost an exact copy of the 1101 treaty, similarly gave twelve sureties from each side who each had to pay 100 marks.[94]

The Anglo-Flemish alliance was, or was attempted to be, renewed at least six times in the twelfth century, in 1110, c. 1128, 1154, 1163, 1180 and 1197.[95] At least two of the agreements follow a formula concerning the sureties different from that set out above, namely the 1110 renewal of the agreement between King Henry I and Count Robert of Flanders and the treaty between Richard I and Count Baldwin VII of 1197. The text of the 1110 agreement is almost identical to that of 1101 except for the surety provisions. Not only were there fewer sureties in 1110 than there had been in 1101, ten for the count of Flanders and nine for the king of England, but there were, moreover, no monetary payments attached to them. Furthermore, two of the sureties appear as guarantors for both King Henry and Count Robert, namely Count Eustace of Boulogne and Count Manasse of Guines.[96] Why the 1110 agreement in terms of its sureties is different from that of 1101 and 1163 is not clear. The 1197 agreement, by contrast, is completely different in its character from those of the earlier twelfth century. In 1197 there was no notion of the military service of the count of Flanders and his men in return for a yearly payment. The treaty is simply an agreement not to make any peace or truce with the king of France without having consulted each other.[97] The treaty was then guaranteed by some ninety sureties in total who swore to hand themselves over to the captivity of the other in case of breaches of the terms of the treaty.

Similarly, the marriage agreement made between Henry II and the count of Maurienne in 1173, according to which Henry's son John would marry the count's daughter and be provided with a large amount of land, was guaranteed by the oaths of fifty-one people promising to hand themselves over as hostages if the count broke the terms of the agreement.[98] This can also be seen in 1190 when, according to the text of the oath taken by the sureties of Richard I, each surety swore to hand himself over ('ego ponam me in captione') to Tancred, king of Sicily, if the English king broke the terms of the agreement.[99] In 1200, King John and Philip Augustus provided nine sureties each for the Treaty of Le Goulet. The sureties of the English king, with all their lands 'citra mare', swore to join Philip Augustus if John broke the terms of the peace, and Philip's men were sureties towards the English king under these same conditions.[100] A final example, King John's alliance of 1199 with Renaud de Dammartin, count of Boulogne, was guaranteed by more than thirty nobles on the English king's side, but only by three on behalf of the count.[101] The inequality in the number of guarantors on each side in this case may indicate the relative status and power that each ruler wielded at that time, though note that in 1110 the count of Flanders had more sureties than the English king and it is unlikely that this implicated the lesser status of the English king. Nevertheless, those acting as sureties to the treaties of 1173, 1191, 1199 and 1200 were different from those guaranteeing the agreements of 1101 and 1163 in one respect. Unlike the two Anglo-Flemish agreements, the sureties of the treaties of 1173, 1191, 1199 and 1200 could seemingly not discharge their personal involvement through a payment of money.

There is at least one clear example recorded by contemporaries of how sureties were intended to work. According to Howden, shortly after concluding the treaty of Louviers in January 1196, Philip Augustus resumed hostilities with the English king. Upon this, Richard seized all the property of the sureties that was held within his territory, both on the continent and in England, namely the property of the abbots of Marmoutier, Cluny, Saint Denis, and La Charité. Howden states that the sureties would have to pay Richard 15,000 marks to retrieve their lands unless they were able to persuade the French king to return to the peace.[102] We know that war subsequently continued until a truce was concluded in 1197, but Howden does not divulge what actually happened to the property of the sureties. Did the abbots pay the 15,000 marks to receive their lands back, or were these properties granted to someone else and held in custody? Were they given back after the new truce had been concluded? How did the sureties go about getting the parties back to the negotiating table, assuming that this is what they did? Howden is silent on all of these matters. Ralph de Diceto, however, quoting a letter of the archbishop of Rouen, Walter of Coutances, states that the archbishop later insisted on the restoration of these properties.[103] More puzzling, however, is the fact that Howden's details of these sureties are not corroborated by the text of the treaty. The treaty stipulates that there were only sureties to enforce that certain named individuals handed over specific properties, and not sureties to ensure that Richard and Philip kept their treaty, which was guaranteed by the oath of both kings.[104] John Baldwin has suggested that on this occasion the archbishop of Rouen acted as a surety, but Walter of Coutances himself states in a letter to Ralph de Diceto that he had refused to stand surety for Richard.[105] Whether or not the archbishop did in the end act as a surety is unclear, but, as with Howden's statement, his involvement in such a capacity cannot be corroborated by close reading of the text of the treaty. This is problematic because, if we believe Howden's statement, potentially there could have been other treaties that also used sureties, even though this was not mentioned in the treaty. Furthermore, if we know how some sureties were intended to work, we know precious little about the long-term implications for sureties, whether real or personal. Indeed treaties never stipulate more than how they were supposed to work, and narrative sources rarely touch upon this subject; Howden's account of how the properties of the 1196 sureties were seized is a rare example. Another may be found in the statement by William the Breton that, upon King John's refusal to attend Philip Augustus' court, the French king confiscated the castles that John had previously given as sureties.[106] This might indicate that, just as oaths often were, sureties were intended to serve as deterrents and that Richard in 1196 and Philip in 1202 were taking the unusual step of actually making use of the surety provisions. Without some further research into this area it is impossible to speculate as to the usage of such provisions, though a comparison with cases found within dispute settlement reveals that they were put into use at least occasionally.[107] One problem with this comparison is, however, that the type of sureties that were most often put into use in dispute settlement were those given to ensure payment of debts of varying nature, and those kinds of sureties we do not meet very often in peacemaking between rulers.

Hostages and sureties were inextricably linked to the ideals and practice of kingship. However, it was not an easy path to tread for a medieval king. Giving hostages was perceived as a sign of weakness, whereas taking hostages could be construed as tyrannical.[108] Similarly, harming hostages, even when an agreement had been broken, could be regarded as cruel, whereas showing leniency was the hallmark of a weak ruler. In light of this, it is hardly surprising that rulers more readily came to use sureties than hostages. Yet historians know very little about the practical use of sureties in peacemaking and diplomacy or about the socio-cultural, economic and symbolic aspects. One thing seems certain, however: the move towards guaranteeing agreements through sureties rather than hostages ran parallel to the revival of Roman law, the greater output in written records and the heightened status and ability of the papal court to act as an 'international' tribunal: themes that will be explored in the next chapter.

Notes

1 Ryan Lavelle, 'The Use and Abuse of Hostages in Later Anglo-Saxon England', *Early Medieval Europe*, 14 (2006), 269. Adam Kosto has also noted that, in Ireland, the possession of hostages was an index of royal status. Adam J. Kosto, 'Hostages in the Carolingian World (714-840)', *Early Medieval Europe*, 11 (2002), 137.

2 The best introduction on medieval hostages is Kosto, 'Hostages in the Carolingian World', 123-47.

3 For instance Thomas Madden's description of the 'hostage crisis' between Venice and Byzantium towards the end of the twelfth century is erroneous in that this crisis was concerned not with the provision of hostages to seal and confirm an agreement but with the release of captured Venetians for whom, incidentally, no hostages were given. Thomas F. Madden, 'Venice's Hostage Crisis: Diplomatic Efforts to Secure Peace with Byzantium between 1171 and 1184', in *Medieval and Renaissance Venice*, ed. Ellen E. Kittell and Thomas F. Madden (Chicago, 1999), 96-108.

4 Stones, *Anglo-Scottish Relations 1174-1328*, 2-4.

5 Howden, *Chronica*, iii, 216. Richard's ransom was in fact negotiated through three different treaties. For the initial agreements, see Ansbert, *Historia de expeditione Friderici*, ed. A. Chroust, MGH SRG, n.s. 5, 103-5; MGH Const. i, Heinrich VI, no. 354 (pp. 502-4); Howden, *Chronica*, iii, 199, 205. For a summary of the events and the secondary literature, see Gillingham, *Richard I*, 233-48.

6 Howden, *Chronica*, iii, 215-16.

7 Howden, *Chronica*, iii, 216. The text does not set out exactly what this 'promise' regarding Henry the Lion was, but it must be assumed that it concerned the restoration of lands and title to the exiled duke himself or his heir.

8 Howden, *Chronica*, iii, 216.
9 Stones, *Anglo-Scottish Relations 1174–1328*, 4.
10 *Ibid.*, 4–8.
11 For the symbolic use of hostages in the early medieval period, see Lavelle, 'The Use and Abuse of Hostages', 270, 274, 279–82, 295.
12 *Arnoldi Chronica Slavorum*, VI:xvii. According to one annalist, the Danish king also received the castle of Lovenburg as a pledge of the count's faith. *Annales Stadenses*, 354.
13 *Arnoldi Chronica Slavorum*, III:iv.
14 For the background and consequences of this event, see Grethe Jacobsen, 'Wicked Count Henry: the Capture of Valdemar II (1223) and Danish Influence in the Baltic', *Journal of Baltic Studies*, 9 (1978), 326–38
15 *Diplomatarium Danicum*, I, vi, nos 16, 17, 42.
16 *Diplomatarium Danicum*, I, vi, no. 42.
17 For a good introduction, see Matthew Strickland, *War and Chivalry: The Conduct and Perception of War in England and Normandy 1066–1217* (Cambridge, 1996).
18 For the modern definition, see UN Doc. A/RES/34/146, 17 Dec. 1979, I§I.
19 Howden, *Chronica*, iii, 196, 207.
20 *Arnoldi Chronica Slavorum*, III:iv.
21 *Rec. des actes de Philippe Auguste*, ii, no. 517.
22 Compare with Kosto's definition that 'the hostage is thus distinct on the one hand from the captive (*captivus*), who is deprived of liberty, but is not a surety, and on the other from the guarantor (*fideiussor, warantus*), who is a surety, but is not deprived of liberty'. Kosto, 'Hostages in the Carolingian World', 128.
23 Timothy Reuter, 'Plunder and Tribute in the Carolingian Empire', *TRHS*, 5th ser., 35 (1985), 75–8; Kershaw, 'Rex Pacificus', 128.
24 For two examples, see *Annales Fuldenses*, s.a. 849, 882.
25 Saxo, *DRHH*, ii, 438–9.
26 Saxo, *DRHH*, ii, 476–7.
27 Saxo, DRHH, ii, 438–9, 447–9, 476–7, 480–1, 502–3, 622–3; *Helmoldi Chronica Slavorum*, 97; *Arnoldi Chronica Slavorum*, III:iv, III:vii.
28 *Brut y Tywysogyon*, 61; *Ann. Mon.*, iv, 30; *Gervase of Canterbury*, i, 165–6; *Torigni*, 218.
29 *Brut y Tywysogyon*, 85.
30 *Brut y Tywysogyon*, 66–8. It is possible that Hywel is the hostage 'Howellum' mentioned in the *Annals of Osney* under the year 1157, in which case he would have been a hostage for fourteen years by 1171. *Ann. Mon.*, iv. 30. However, it is equally possible that he was given as a hostage in 1163 or 1165, making the length of his imprisonment shorter. What is clear is that Hywel received the epithet Sais ('Englishman') after his long stay at the English court. Frederick C. Suppe, 'Who Was Rhys Sais? Some Comments on Anglo-Welsh Relations before 1066', *HSJ*, 7 (1995), 67–8. Lavelle has explored the phenomenon of the aristocratic hostage at court in the Anglo-Saxon period and there are also examples of this in Scandinavian literature. Lavelle, 'The Use and Abuse of Hostages', 284–6.

For other early medieval examples, see also Kosto, 'Hostages in the Carolingian World', 133.

31 On the background to the events of 1171/72 and the relationship between Henry II and the Lord Rhys, see Chapter 2, 50–1. Both Rees Davies and Huw Pryce have argued that submission to the English king may have served as a strategy by the Welsh princes to increase their power and status vis-à-vis other native rulers, marcher lords and primarily the nobility within their own territories. Davies, *Domination and Conquest*, 59–60; Huw Pryce, 'Welsh Rulers and European Change, c. 1100–1282', in *Power and Identity in the Middle Ages. Essays in Memory of Rees Davies*, ed. Huw Pryce and John Watts (Oxford, 2007), 45. On cultural transmission in general, see Adam J. Kosto, 'L'otage comme vecteur d'échange culturel du 4e au 15e siècle', in *Les prisonniers de guerre dans l'histoire: contacts entre peuples et cultures*, ed. Sylvie Caucanas et al. (Toulouse, 2003).

32 Holt, *Magna Carta*, 82, 101, 191, 194.

33 Kershaw, 'Rex Pacificus', 131. Only Roger of Howden among the English chroniclers seems to have refrained from giving such unfavourable views of the Welsh. For a discussion of his views of the Welsh, see J. Gillingham, 'The Travels of Roger of Howden and His View of the Irish, Scots and Welsh', 83.

34 *Gesta Stephani*, 9.

35 *Newburgh*, i, 145.

36 *Torigni*, 222.

37 *Giraldi Cambrensis Opera Omnia*, vi, 206–7.

38 *The Correspondence of Thomas Becket*, i, 200–1, no. 45.

39 *De Nugis Curialium*, 182–3.

40 *Heinrici Chronicon Lyvonie*, 246–7, 270. For an outline of the background to these events and the life of Henry of Livonia, see *The Chronicle of Henry of Livonia*, 2nd edn, tr. James A. Brundage (New York, 2003) xi–xxxiv, 3–21.

41 *Helmoldi Chronica Slavorum*, 58, 60–1, 66, 80–1, 84, 92, *Arnoldi Chronica Slavorum*, III:iv–vii. Helmold did, however, take a great interest in describing the idolatry and rites of the Slavs, for which see *Helmoldi Chronica Slavorum*, 52, 66, 75–6, 96–7.

42 Saxo, *DRHH*, ii, 372.

43 Saxo, DRHH, ii, 476–7.

44 *Annales Ryenses*, 403; Saxo, *DRHH*, ii, 485; Sawyer, 'Valdemar, Absalon and Saxo: Historiography and Politics in Medieval Denmark', 693.

45 Chaplais, *EMDP*, ii, no. 287; Howden, *Chronica*, iii, 217–20.

46 Howden, *Gesta*, ii, 70. Instead of hostages, Philip and Richard were to hold certain castles as pledges of the agreement.

47 *Diplomatarium Danicum*, I:1, no. 110; *Gesta Friderici*, 158.

48 John France, 'Siege Convention in Western Europe and the Latin East', in *War and Peace in Ancient and Medieval History*, ed. Philip de Souza and John France (Cambridge, 2008), 161.

49 Gillingham asserts that the perception of Celtic societies as barbarous functioned in part as an ideology of conquest. John Gillingham, 'The Beginnings of

English Imperialism', in his *The English in the Twelfth Century* (Woodbridge, 2000), 17.

50 John Gillingham, 'Conquering the Barbarians: War and Chivalry in Twelfth-century Britain and Ireland', in his *The English in the Twelfth Century*, 54–8. For a summary of some of the economic and cultural differences between the Welsh, the Scots and the English, see Davies, *The First English Empire*, 120–7

51 For a discussion of this, see pp. 166–8.

52 For a very good summary on the differences between the central western kingdoms and those on the fringes of the medieval West in this period, see Robert Bartlett, *The Making of Europe. Conquest, Colonization and Cultural Change 950–1350* (London, 1993), 15–23, 70–84, 200–1, 304–6. For a short survey of castle building in Denmark in the twelfth century, see Hans Stiesdal, 'Types of Public and Private Fortifications in Denmark', in *Danish Medieval History: New Currents*, ed. Niels Skyum-Nielsen and Niels Lund (Copenhagen, 1981), 209–12. For one possible castle surety received by the Danish king from the men of Holstein, see *Annales Stadenses*, 354.

53 For these changes, see Gillingham, 'Conquering the Barbarians', 54.

54 Saxo, *DRHH*, ii, 516–17. More famously, in 1016 Edmund Ironside exchanged hostages with the Viking leader Cnut to ensure the safety of both kings while conferring on an island in the river Severn. *The Chronicle of John of Worcester*, ii, 493. For one other eleventh-century example see Thietmar, *Chronicon*, 186.

55 Holdsworth, 'Peacemaking in the Twelfth Century', 5.

56 For some examples from the earlier Middle Ages and one example where the most treacherous individuals were given, see Kosto, 'Hostages in the Carolingian World', 134–5.

57 *Brut y Tywysogyon*, 63–4.

58 *Arnoldi Chronica Slavorum*, VI:xvii.

59 Kosto speaks of this as being symbolically important and cites examples both from the early medieval period and from Roman history. Kosto, 'Hostages in the Carolingian World', 137.

60 Pryce, *The Acts of Welsh Rulers*, 387, no. 233.

61 Smith, 'Magna Carta and the Charters of the Welsh Princes', 355. Compare the Carolingian example of Lambert, who was given as a hostage by his father Aganus in the 760s. In the 820s, Lambert petitioned the Emperor Louis the Pious for the restoration of his freedom and his patrimony in Aquitaine, proving that Lambert 'was living with the consequences of his father's actions well into his sixties'. Kosto, 'Hostages in the Carolingian World', 141–2.

62 *Arnoldi Chronica Slavorum*, VI:xvii; *Oeuvres de Rigord et de Guillaume le Breton*, i, 299.

63 *Magna Carta*, cap. 58.

64 *Rot. Litt. Pat.*, 131, 132. For the context of this release, see Smith, 'Magna Carta and the Charters of the Welsh Princes', 352–3.

65 Pryce, *The Acts of Welsh Rulers*, no. 576.

66 *Brut y Tywysogyon*, 63–4. Gerald of Wales says that Henry murdered the hostages out of hand. *Giraldi Cambrensis Opera Omnia*, vi, 143; vii, 217.

67 *Brut y Tywysogyon*, 86.

68 *Flores Historiarum*, ii, 61.

69 *Heinrici Chronicon Lyvonie*, 312.

70 Saxo, *DRHH*, ii, 474–5; iii, 819, fn. 403; *Helmoldi Chronica Slavorum*, 84–5, 89–90.

71 Saxo, *DRHH*, ii, 454–5.

72 Paul Latimer, 'Henry II's Campaign against the Welsh in 1165', *Welsh History Review*, 14 (1989), 533.

73 For examples, see *Two of the Saxon Chronicles Parallel*, i, 145; *Hemingi Chartularium Ecclesiae Wigorniensis*, 2 vols, ed. T. Hearne (Oxford, 1723), i, 259–60.

74 D. Crouch, *William Marshal: Court, Career and Chivalry in the Angevin Empire 1147–1219* (London, 1990), 16–17.

75 Howden, *Chronica*, iii, 233. Robert had in fact turned up in Germany as an envoy carrying letters from John. Robert's refusal was said to have made Richard so furious that he immediately ordered that he be thrown into prison at Dover. Despite the fact that most of John's followers were pardoned in March 1195, Robert was not released, which might illustrate the importance that Richard attached to this breach of faith. Robert did, however, die in prison during that same year and this could thus plausibly have been another reason why he was not released. Howden, *Chronica*, iii, 287.

76 For the view that hostage giving was a light undertaking see Kershaw, 'Rex Pacificus', 128–31.

77 For examples of pledges in dispute settlement see articles by Ian Wood, Janet L. Nelson, Roger Collins and Chris Wickham in *The Settlement of Disputes in Early Medieval Europe*, ed. Wendy Davies and Paul Fouracre. See also Wendy Davies, 'Suretyship in the *Cartulaire de Redon*', in *Lawyers and Laymen*, ed. T. M. Charles-Edwards, Morfydd E. Owen and D. B. Walters (Cardiff, 1986); J. Yver, 'Les sûretés personelles en Normandie', in *Les sûretés personnelles*, 3 vols, Recueil de la société Jean Bodin pour l'histoire comparative des institutions 29 (Brussels, 1969–74), ii, 221–61. For a possible eleventh-century example of sureties see the terminology used in the *ASC* for the 1016 agreement between Edmund Ironside and Cnut. According to the *ASC* the agreement was confirmed 'ge mid wedde ge mid aðe'. *Two of the Saxon Chronicles Parallel*, i, 153.

78 Jehan de Malafosse, 'Contribution à l'étude du crédit dans le Midi aux Xe et XIe siècles: les sûretées réelles', *Annales du Midi*, 63 (1951), 105–48; Kosto, *Making Agreements in Medieval Catalonia*, 124–5.

79 Yver, 'Les sûretés personelles en Normandie', 221–61; John Gilissen, 'Esquisse d'une histoire comparée des sûretés personnelles: essai de synthèse général', in *Les sûretés personnelles*, i, 50–69; Kosto, *Making Agreements in Medieval Catalonia*, 125.

80 Kosto, *Making Agreements in Medieval Catalonia*, 125.

81 *Rec. des actes de Philippe Auguste*, i, 465–6, no. 376. For a discussion of this treaty see Powicke, *The Loss of Normandy*, 83–7; Landon, *The Itinerary of King*

Richard I, 227–32. On the identification of one of the sureties as William de Boury, see Daniel Power, *The Norman Frontier*, 418, fn. 26.

82 Kosto, *Making Agreements in Medieval Catalonia*, 126.

83 Stones, *Anglo-Scottish Relations 1174–1328*, 3. See also discussion above, pp. 156–7.

84 In 1193 the treaty concluded with Philip Augustus by Richard's envoys specified that the four castles pledged for the observance of the terms would be maintained at Richard's expense. *EMDP*, ii, no. 287.

85 *Rec. des actes de Philippe Auguste*, i, 464, no. 376; *Dip. Docs*, i, no. 5. The text of the treaty can be found in the PRO, in the form of an English fourteenth-century copy probably made by, or on the instruction of, John de Burton, keeper of the Rolls from 1386 to 1394. The roll on which the treaty appears further contained another two Anglo-French treaties. *Dip. Docs*, i, 15–16.

86 Gillingham, *Richard I*, 142. The French contemporary Rigord omits all mention of the treaty, though he supplies some interesting information on the events leading up to its conclusion that make this historian, at least, concur with Gillingham's conclusion. *Ouevres de Rigord et de Guillaume le Breton*, i, 107–8. John Baldwin in his semi-biography of the French king states that the treaty can be 'ignored' since most of its provisions 'were abrogated by subsequent actions'. Baldwin, *The Government of Philip Augustus*, 78.

87 Howden, *Gesta*, ii, 134; Howden, *Chronica*, iii, 61–2.

88 Howden, *Gesta*, ii, 136; Howden, *Chronica*, iii, 64–5.

89 *Dip. Docs*, i, 20–23; *Rec. des actes de Philippe Auguste*, ii, no. 633. Also the treaty of 1195/96 between these two kings survives in the form of letters patent issued by each king. *Dip. Docs*, i, 16–18.

90 These changes are noted in Chaplais's edition as references to manuscript O. *Dip. Docs*, i, 20–23.

91 *Dip. Docs*, i, 23; *Rec. des actes de Philippe Auguste*, ii, no. 633, §21–2.

92 *Dip. Docs*, i, 3–4; van Houts, 'The Anglo-Flemish Treaty of 1101', §17, 19. The reason why one of Henry's guarantors had to pay 200 instead of 100 marks was simply that Henry only had eleven guarantors. Kosto refers to these types of personal sureties as 'conditional hostages'. Adam J. Kosto, 'Les otages conditionnels en Languedoc et en Catalogne au XIe siècle', *Annales du Midi*, 118 (2006), 387–403.

93 *Dip. Docs*, i, 3–4; van Houts, 'The Anglo-Flemish Treaty of 1101', §19.

94 *Dip. Docs*, i, 11–12

95 *Dip. Docs*, i, nos 2–3, 7; Orderic, *HE*, vi, 378–9; Galbert of Bruges, *Histoire du meurtre de Charles le Bon*, 176 (cap. 122); Howden, *Gesta*, i, 246; Howden, *Chronica*, iv, 20; *Diceto*, ii, 152–3 Renée Nip, 'The Political Relations between England and Flanders (1066–1128)', *ANS*, 21 (1999), 158, 165.

96 *Dip. Docs*, i, 7.

97 *Dip. Docs*, i, no7.

98 Howden, *Gesta*, i, 36–41

99 Howden, *Gesta*, ii, 136.

100 *Dip. Docs*, i, 23; *Rec. des actes de Philippe Auguste*, ii, no. 633.

101 *Rot. Chart.*, I, 30; H. Malo, *Un grand feudataire*, 259.

102 Howden, *Chronica*, iv, 4–5.

103 *Diceto*, ii, 145. For a discussion of the circumstances, see Powicke, *The Loss of Normandy*, 113–15.

104 For a good discussion of the surety provisions of 'a contract within a contract', that is the surrender of the castelry of Pacy to the French king and the earl of Leicester's provision of three French magnates as sureties to this effect, see Daniel Power, 'L'aristocratie Plantagenêt face aux conflits capétiens-angevins: l'example du traité de Louviers', in *Noblesses de l'espace Plantagenêt (1154–1224)*, ed. Martin Aurell (Poitiers, 2001), 121–37. For a discussion on the political context and consensual nature of suretyship among the aristocracy of the Norman frontier region, see Power, *The Norman Frontier*, 250–62.

105 Baldwin, *The Government of Philip Augustus*, 267; *Diceto*, ii, 136.

106 *Oeuvres de Rigord et de Guillaume le Breton*, i, 207. Another example, though not strictly concerned with peacemaking between rulers can be found in the *Brut y Tywysogyon*. According to this source, Henry II had given sureties to the king of France for the restoration of peace with Archbishop Thomas Becket. Upon the murder of Becket, Pope Alexander sent letters to the French king and the sureties to compel Henry II to come to the Papal Court to make amends for the death of the archbishop. *Brut y Tywysogyon*, 66.

107 For a good discussion of the use of sureties in dispute settlement see Davies, 'Suretyship in the *Cartulaire de Redon*'. See also Kosto, *Making Agreements in Medieval Catalonia*, 134–7.

108 I am grateful to Björn Weiler for pointing this out to me. For examples, see his *Kingship, Rebellion and Political Culture. England and Germany c. 1215–c. 1250* (Basingstoke, 2007).

PART V

Peacemaking and the written word

8

Treaties, terminology and the written word

It has been argued by historians that even as late as the twelfth century many treaties were still oral agreements.[1] This theory has been backed up in part by the fact that no early medieval treaty survives in what can be shown to have been its original form. Despite this fact, some authorities such as Paul Kershaw and Ryan Lavelle have preferred to take a different view. Kershaw, for instance, has suggested that those written treaties that have survived for the earlier medieval period are but a small portion of the total once extant.[2] Certainly it is true that the absence of written records of peacemaking does not necessarily mean that they were never made. As expected, there are many reasons why such documents may over a long period of time have disappeared, the one usually cited by historians being that political events quickly outstripped an agreement's terms. Most revealingly, Rosemary Morris has noted the irony of the fact that so few administrative documents have survived from Byzantium, one of the most bureaucratic states of the medieval world. 'We know', Morris argues, 'that instructions were given to file duplicate or even triplicate copies in the offices of governmental bureaus, yet most of these originals have disappeared without a trace.'[3]

If we look specifically for twelfth- and early thirteenth-century treaties from England – perhaps the 'most bureaucratic' of the twelfth-century Western European polities – we find that only one Anglo-French treaty survives from the reigns of Henry I and Stephen, and the early part of Henry II's reign, despite the fact that we know that peace was made at least eight times in the period between 1100 and 1177. Between 1177 and 1200 a number of treaties do survive in the two recensions of the chronicle attributed to Roger of Howden and in the chronicle of Ralph de Diceto. However, the texts of agreements copied into the work of Diceto are often abridged versions, and, though Howden in general seems to have included the full texts in his two works, he copied at least one treaty in a shortened form.[4] Moreover some treaties that we know were made are not found in these chronicles but have come down to us in a written form from later copies. One such is the so-called Treaty of Messina of 1191 where historians know the text of the agreement through a fourteenth-century copy.[5] Not only are there few Anglo-French treaties but we have virtually no texts of any treaty involving an English king prior to 1173, when Howden inserted the text of the agreement concluded between King Henry II and the count of Maurienne into his *Gesta*.[6] During John's reign several treaties were enrolled, but even this was not done consistently since we know of at least one lost treaty from this reign: the Anglo-Scottish treaty of 1209.[7] It is apparent from a document of August 1209 that William the Lion, king of Scots, had bound himself to pay John 15,000 marks for his goodwill and for fulfilling the agreement that had been made between them, an agreement that had been confirmed by charters.[8] These charters, however, have not been enrolled, or been copied into any surviving chronicle account. It is thus clear that our knowledge of the written records of peacemaking involving the English king is limited prior to John's reign and is primarily dependent upon the interests and recording methods of particular chroniclers.

By comparison the survival of treaties from Denmark is even more negligible. Only four written treaties survive from our period, and they are all concerned with the same matter: the release from captivity of Valdemar II and his son in the 1220s.[9] We certainly know that a number of treaties were concluded between Danish kings and neighbouring princes in the period c. 1157 to c. 1241. For instance in 1203 Pope Innocent III wrote to Valdemar II confirming the agreements ('conventiones') between the Danish king and the imperial candidate Otto of Brunswick and his brothers.[10] We know that one treaty had initially been agreed in 1202 by King Cnut VI and Otto, and that it was solemnised through the marriage of the Danish king's sister, Helen, to William of Lüneburg, the brother of Otto.[11] As Cnut VI died in that same year and was succeeded on the throne by his brother Valdemar II, the agreement was evidently renewed at some point before Innocent's letter of confirmation of December 1203. It would thus seem that at least two treaties had been concluded, yet neither has survived into modern times. We also know from a letter of Otto to Innocent III that an agreement between Cnut VI and the German king existed before 1202. Otto wrote to the pope in the spring of 1200 explaining that Cnut VI was expected to fall into Saxony, 'in auxilium nostrum', to fight

Otto's enemies.[12] It is highly unlikely that Otto would have held such expectations without the existence of a formal treaty, either written or oral. There is, furthermore, ample evidence from narrative sources of treaties concluded between Valdemar I and Duke Henry the Lion in the 1160s and 1170s, but none of these contemporary writers included a copy of the text of such an agreement. However, Helmold's statement that Henry the Lion sent messengers to the cities and kingdoms of the north – Denmark, Sweden, Norway and Russia – offering them peace and free access to his city of Lübeck can be confirmed by extant treaties, or fragments thereof.[13] Among non-Danish sources, one of the most well known Danish agreements of this period, and certainly the one in which contemporaries held most interest, is the alliance of 1193 between Cnut VI and Philip of France, whereby the French king was to marry Cnut's sister Ingeborg, an alliance for which it is perhaps possible, but unlikely, that a written agreement did not exist.[14] In another example, Saxo relates how the terms of the treaty concluded between Valdemar I and Jarl Erling Skakke, regent of Norway, were afterwards published by the jarl in the Norwegian assembly.[15] It is difficult to imagine how this would have been done without the existence of a written copy of these terms, but again, if there was such an original, it has not survived into modern times.

A further indication that more agreements originally existed than have survived until modern times is the letter of October 1240 in which Valdemar II announced the renewal of the 'amicicia' between the Danes and the count and the men of Flanders. In this letter Valdemar refers to agreements struck at least forty years earlier.[16] Furthermore, in 1187, the Emperor Frederick Barbarossa wrote to his son Henry warning him about the friendship between the archbishop of Cologne, the kings of England and Denmark and the count of Flanders. This might indicate that at this point there was a more formal relationship between some of these princes and the king of Denmark which had been set down in writing, or it might merely reflect that they were all supporters of Barbarossa's arch-rival Duke Henry the Lion.[17] Another example, the so-called 'Golden Bull' of 1214, sets out that Frederick II had concluded 'a perpetual friendship' for the preservation of peace with Valdemar II. This document, however, is fraught with difficulties in terms of dating and it is not clear to what extent it was preceded by negotitations.[18] A similar announcement of an agreement can also be found in 1218, when Archbishop Gerhard of Bremen declared that he agreed to support Valdemar II against any enemy.[19] It is thus clear that there were a number of agreements concluded with the Danish kings in this period, even though the survival of the actual treaties is negligible. The issue of the survival of written treaties from the Danish kingdom is further complicated by the fact that a number of agreements were concluded with the Slavs, some of whom were not Christians, and it is uncertain whether these agreements would have been committed to writing.

One problem with the survival of treaties is that kings do not seem to have had well-kept royal archives or chancellery registers prior to the thirteenth century. In many cases there would have been few incentives to keep an agreement that had ceased to be valid. We know, for instance, that, at the council of Oxford in July 1215, the 1211 submission charter of Llywelyn was annulled, which presumably meant that it was destroyed or handed back to Llywelyn, and it seems likely that this was also the fate of other treaties that were no longer valid.[20] Moreover, the church, the main preserver of documentation, had little incentive to keep copies of treaties that did not refer to church property, although there is at least one example, from 1225, where the intention of the parties, namely King Henry III and Count Raymound VII of Toulouse, was to deposit a treaty in a religious house, and one can only assume from the manner in which this suggestion was made that the practice was not a novelty.[21] In England treaties and other such documents were kept at the treasury from at least the twelfth century.[22] For instance the text of the 1101 Anglo-Flemish agreement was evidently kept at a place where it could be easily retrieved, since the texts of the renewal of the agreement in 1110 and 1163 follow almost word for word the earlier text. It seems unreasonable to assume that other treaties were not taken care of in the same way. None the less, there is one example from the late thirteenth century where those who were supposed to look after the texts of an Anglo-German alliance seem to have mislaid them within three years of the agreement having been concluded, prompting Edward I to write desperately to the treasurer and the barons of the Exchequer asking them to search for these documents in the treasury and elsewhere.[23]

Michael Clanchy has argued that 'making records was a product of mistrust rather than social progress'.[24] However, a written record of an agreement between two rulers would have served little function unless there was somewhere an injured party could produce such a document in order to appeal against any breaches of the terms contained within it. We know that there were occasions when rulers offered their disputes to arbitration and in the process offered written documents as proof. The court supreme in the Middle Ages was the papal court, which, according to Ullmann, had compulsory jurisdiction, authoritatively laying down, explaining, interpreting and developing the law, and which could reasonably anticipate the enforcement of its decision.[25] Ullmann further argues that 'the exercise of practical judicial functions by the papacy as the supreme court of Western Christendom was contingent upon the availability of a body of law that was capable of being administered and applied by the papacy'.[26] This contingency occurred only from the mid-twelfth century, which could partly explain the greater drive to preserve documents that begins after this date.

A letter of 1198 from Pope Innocent III to the French king sums up the complaints in one case that was submitted to the papal court. According to this letter, both Richard I and Philip Augustus had complained to the pope about the conduct of the other, at the heart of which stood the surrender of the Norman Vexin at Messina in 1191.[27] One would have thought that this case was clear-cut. After all the text of the Treaty of Messina was still extant in 1322 and it has come down to us through a fourteenth-century copy. However, it is clear that Innocent's letter shows that there existed some doubt over the exact terms on which Richard obtained release from his contract to marry Alice, the sister of Philip Augustus.[28] It is also evident, as Landon has argued, that the later document that purports to be the text of the original Treaty of Messina is at variance with various subsequent events that should have been governed by the treaty's terms. Landon suggested that one such variant was Philip's demand for the restoration of Alice and with her the castle of Gisors, and the counties of Aumale and Eu, within a month of his own return, whilst Richard was still in the Holy Land. To support his demands Philip produced a copy of the treaty at a meeting with the representatives of the English king. The seneschal of Normandy, William fitz Ralph, and the Norman barons refused both demands, saying that they had not received a mandate to this effect from their king.[29] The story here related by Howden agrees with the terms of the extant Treaty of Messina with the exception that the counties of Aumale and Eu are not mentioned in the text.[30] Consequently, if the French king did show such a document to the Norman seneschal, it could not have been the text of the treaty as we now have it. Not only does this show the limitation of trying to offer written proof of treaties in order to make claims or to facilitate a final judgement before the matter was submitted to the papal court, it also highlights the fundamental problem of independent arbitration: how to make both sides accept the judgement even if there are written records.

Ullmann has argued not only that the papal court had compulsory jurisdiction but also that, by virtue of the universality of papal law, the rulings of the court applied to all Christians. According to Ullmann, 'one of the most conspicuous features of the papal judicial decisions was that they denied the personal sovereignty of those rulers they affected'.[31] True though this may be in theory, it is clear that the actual practice of papal arbitration in the late twelfth and early thirteenth centuries by no means involved simply the issuing of papal commands followed by local obedience to such commands. For instance the distance of northern Europe from Rome meant that negotiations were often long and drawn out, and the death or defeat of one party could halt papal intervention. This was, of course, what happened in the case of the dispute over the surrender of the Norman Vexin, as, although a papal legate was despatched and managed to negotiate a truce, Richard died before a formal peace could be concluded. Furthermore, the pope himself, like any other medieval ruler, could be involved in international diplomacy and this could hinder, delay or bias any final judgement. For example, in 1189 when the papal legate sent to mediate between Henry II and Philip Augustus threatened the French king with excommunication, Philip simply replied that he was not frightened and that the legate threatened him only because he loved pounds sterling.[32] Another well-known example is the 1193 marriage alliance between Philip Augustus and Ingeborg, sister of Cnut VI of Denmark, which was concluded in the midst of the negotiations for the release from captivity of Richard I, Philip's arch-enemy. This case was submitted to papal arbitration after Philip repudiated his wife, 'after one night only', and then attempted to annul the marriage on grounds of consanguinity.[33] Despite the fact that the French king's lands were twice placed under interdict on account of his refusal to honour the marriage agreement, the matter was not finally resolved until 1214 when Philip took back his Danish bride with the clear intention of again gaining Danish support to counter the alliance between King John and the Emperor Otto IV. In this case papal jurisdiction and enforcement by interdict were clearly not enough to encourage the French king to accept the pope's decision, and, most importantly, the pope was limited in his ability to act upon this matter after 1197 with the double election of Philip of Swabia and Otto of Brunswick to the German throne.[34] Whilst it is clear that agreements between rulers were increasingly drawn up and preserved in order that a ruler would be able to offer written proof, documents and formal papal judgements did not outweigh other considerations guiding a ruler's actions.

The intervention of the papacy was not the only way to secure a judgement on a long-standing dispute. There are a number of examples from this period of cases that were submitted to independent arbitration. Most famously, in 1177, the kings of Castile and Navarre called upon the intervention of the English king in their dispute over the land and castles of Burona.[35] Sancho VI of Navarre and Alfonso VIII of Castile sent a large embassy to the court of Henry II, at Windsor, and here, on 9 March, the English king was presented with a document drawn up in August 1176 in which the two Spanish kings agreed to refer their dispute to Henry. A number of castles had been pledged by each side to guarantee that the terms would be carried out and a seven-year truce had also been agreed while the matter was being referred – the kings were evidently convinced that arbitration was not a quick option. The agreement, furthermore, stated that if the king of England should have died before the envoys reached his court, they were then to proceed to the court of the French king.[36] Having seen this agreement, Henry II summoned his barons and bishops to a council in London on 13 March where the matter would be discussed and, at this council, the English king asked for the allegations in writing, with documents being presented to support the claims, among which was a treaty concluded between the two Spanish kings in 1167 which Sancho of Navarre claimed had been broken by Alfonso. In addition to this, the envoys had to take oaths on behalf of their masters, promising that the kings of Castile and Navarre would adhere to Henry's decision. The court then discussed the matter and made an adjudication that recommended restitutions on both sides. Finally, letters setting out the claims and the adjudication were sent to both Sancho and Alfonso.[37]

Henry II can hardly be considered an independent arbiter in this case. He had given his daughter Eleanor's hand in marriage to Alfonso of Castile in the mid-1170s and, as duke of Aquitaine, he was the neighbour of the king of Navarre who, together with the king of Aragon and the count of Toulouse, had been present at the conference at Limoges in 1173. We also know that Henry was an ally of the king of Aragon, who, in turn, was at times both the friend and the adversary of the king of Castile. The English king was thus familiar with some of the rights, claims, lordships and disputes of these three kings, and it seems likely that this was the reason why Henry II had been chosen by the two Spanish kings as the adjudicator in their dispute, ahead of his French counterpart. Henry's involvement in this dispute seems to have been primarily as a 'friend', possibly performing one of those duties that came under the phrase *auxilium et consilium*, even though, to our knowledge, there were no documents formalising such a relationship with either the king of Castile or the king of Navarre. In his letter informing the Spanish kings of his decision, Henry did, however, address them as 'his dearest friends' ('carissimis amicis suis').[38] After this successful arbitration, Henry was called upon as an arbiter friend in other disputes. We know, for instance, that in the 1180s, the English king attempted to mediate in the many disputes between the count of Flanders and the French king.[39]

Another remarkable thing about Henry's arbitration in the Navarre–Castile case is that both the testimony of the envoys and the written word played such a large role. Henry II was not content with just hearing the claims and allegations of the various envoys; he also wanted them in writing, allegedly because the king and his council were unable to understand the Spanish envoys. Furthermore, both sides had brought documents to support their claims, and the envoys also took oaths promising that their masters would adhere to Henry's decision. All of this quite clearly tells the historian that asking for intervention in this way was not a new phenomenon. Both the envoys and King Henry seem to have known the procedure and they also knew the possible outcomes. Why else would the envoys have also brought with them two champions to decide the dispute by single combat, should it prove necessary?[40] Here, there is a clear parallel to be drawn with the settlement of disputes and peacemaking at the lower levels of society. Stephen D. White, in particular, has drawn our attention to the fact that peacemaking on a local, lower level was often a process of self-regulation that operated outside the established structures for dispute settlement.[41] In this type of peacemaking, friends, compromise and negotiations loom large, and the agreements concluded were usually known as *pax, amicitia, concordia* or *conventus*.[42] Despite some obvious parallels, it is also evident that peacemaking between rulers ultimately relied upon faith, and adherence to any decision, whether made by the pope or through the mediation of friends, depended on the willingness of rulers, witnesses and sureties to keep their oaths.

In order to be able to submit their disputes to arbitration or to make claims of breaches or restitutions, rulers needed to have (near) exact copies of the terms of any agreement drawn up, exchanged and announced. According to Chaplais, all of the extant treaties from the reign of Henry II are in the form of final agreements, drawn up in duplicate, in the joint names of the two contracting parties. The two exemplars were then sealed interchangeably, the exemplar sealed by the king of England being delivered to the foreign ruler and vice versa.[43] From the reign of Richard I, Anglo-French treaties were no longer issued in the joint names of the rulers, but were drawn up in the form of individual letters patent and subsequently exchanged.[44] Esther Pascua has noted that the stronger of the kings making peace usually comes first in the texts of twelfth-century treaties.[45] However, with regard to the Anglo-French agreements, this is unlikely to have been the case, as each king probably issued a text in which he likely named himself first.[46]

From the lack of evidence it would be difficult to make a comparison here with how Danish treaties were drawn up and exchanged. The treaties pertaining to the ransom and release of King Valdemar II and his son all bear evidence of practices current in the German empire. For instance the phrase 'hec est forma compositionis/liberationis' is one that we meet also in the ransom treaty between the Emperor Henry VI and Richard I in the 1190s.[47] These phrases also bear witness to the fact that most of these agreements were intended as proposals and were not ratified final treaties.[48] Furthermore, none of these agreements is given in the name of the Danish king and most of them are drawn up in a German hand. This includes the proposal submitted by the Danish and Holstein nobles in 1225, which was written by two scribes who came from the opposing, Count of Schwerin, party.[49] By contrast one of the proposals from 1224 is in a Danish hand and the seal attached to the document is that of the Danish lead negotiator, Count Albert of Holstein.[50] It is also noteworthy that unlike most of the English agreements, these particular documents were working, negotiating, copies and they contain erasures and amendments made in different hands.[51] Another thing to note about agreements involving the Danish king is that only one has come down to us in a copy bearing the characteristics of the Danish chancery.[52] Consequently the way in which these various Danish agreements, or proposed agreements, were drawn up seems different to Angevin practice, but this may merely reflect the random survival of documents and not genuine practice.

Chaplais has classified three different types of treaties in the medieval period: a peace treaty (ending war); treaties of alliance and friendship or confederations; and contracts of marriage.[53] He based his classification on how the first contacts between the two parties were established. According to Chaplais, in the case of alliances or marriage contracts, contacts were usually established directly by the sending of envoys to and fro, whereas peace treaties, because of the state of war, were usually preceded by the intervention of a third party.[54] Chaplais's classification, however, is better suited to documents of the late medieval period than to those of the twelfth and early thirteenth centuries. As Chapter 5 showed, for the twelfth century we know relatively little about how contacts between two parties were established and even less about the ability of third parties to intervene in conflicts or to conclude agreements to end hostilities. Furthermore, in contrast to the later medieval period, there are simply not enough documents from the late twelfth and early thirteenth centuries on which to base any comparisons. Consequently it has been necessary to adopt a different approach from that of Chaplais. Treaties of the late twelfth and early thirteenth centuries seem generally to have fallen into three categories: those made for peace (*pax*) following a period of warfare; those concluded with a more general aim of peace and friendship (*amicitia*); and those treaties agreed for an end to hostilities for a limited time (*treuga, inducia*). With these three categories in mind, a classification will be attempted by looking at the terminology used by contemporaries.

One might expect that any document or contemporary commentator that uses a terminology involving the word peace (*pax*) denotes an agreement concluded to mark the end of war (*guerra, bellum*). However, in this period, descriptions of hostilities, or of the outbreak of war, are actually referred to by means of a number of different phrases. Perhaps most common, among the Anglo-Norman chroniclers at least, is the wording 'orta est dissensio', but others, such as 'inimicitiae . . . orte sunt', 'discordia orta/mota/facta est', are also frequent.[55] Some chroniclers, however, merely noted that there was anger ('ira') between the two kings.[56] Only two of the chroniclers, Saxo Grammaticus and Rigord, use the words *bellum* and *guerra* regularly as the antonym of *pax* and, in the case of Saxo, at least, this is a reflection of his strong classical style, rhetoric and borrowings.[57] The nature of warfare in this period further means that, at times, hostilities are not referred to by any specific phrase but merely indicated by the large number of attempts to capture strongholds. Consequently it is evident that it would be difficult to narrow the usage of the term *pax* to being simply the opposite of *guerra/bellum*, when hostility carried a very varied terminology.[58]

Peace treaties of the late twelfth and early thirteenth centuries were commonly denoted by the phrase *pax et finalis concordia*. Howden, for example, records at least seven such agreements between 1153 and 1201, all concluded to mark the end of hostilities.[59] In 1191 the Treaty of Messina established peace (*pax firma*) between Richard I and Philip Augustus after a short period of animosity, even though the circumstances would possibly not allow us to speak of hostilities.[60] Both Rigord and William the Breton use the single word *pax* to describe a number of agreements between rulers. This is, for instance, how they denote the agreements between Henry II and Philip Augustus that ended the hostilities of 1188 and those of early July 1189; the agreement between Richard I and Philip of 22 July 1189, which was merely a renewal of that of 4 July and thus not preceded by hostilities; and the 1195/96 treaty of Louviers between Richard and Philip, which was concluded in the space between their two armies.[61] Though Howden, and his diplomatic source, often used the word *concordia* to denote an agreement for peace, other contemporaries used a different terminology. Saxo, for instance, uses either *pactio* or *pactum* to denote peace treaties with the Slavs.[62] Similarly, when Helmold of Bosau described one peace (*pax*) concluded between Valdemar I and Duke Henry the Lion, he used the term *pactum* to describe the treaty whereby they agreed to divide the tribute accrued from subjugated lands.[63]

Amicitia is a term used in narrative sources and documents about peacemaking to describe a number of different relationships, circumstances and, hence, agreements.[64] For instance, though King John's 1201 treaty with Sancho of Navarre was said to make and confirm peace and true friendship between the two kings, the treaty is primarily concerned with the latter of the two. According to the text of the treaty, Sancho would give King John and his heirs 'auxilium et consilium' against all men (except the king of Morocco) and he promised not to make any peace, truce or other agreement without consulting the English king. The treaty further stipulated that mutual assistance could and should be offered in every way, whether in men or money, and this leaves the historian in no doubt that this was a friendship concluded for military purposes.[65] In fact, in the confirmation of this treaty, the peace and friendship are accompanied by the term *confederatio*, which we know from the work of Voss replaced *amicitia* towards the end of the twelfth century, especially in agreements that had a specific military purpose.[66] The 1212 alliance between Philip Augustus and Llywelyn ap Iorwerth is another such example. This agreement was endorsed 'confederacio Loelini principis Norwallie cum domino rege Francie', and it is specifically aimed at the English king.[67] Llywelyn promised to be a friend to Philip's friends and an enemy to his enemies ('vestris amicis amici erimus et inimici inimicis'), and further specified that he would not make any peace or truce with the English without consulting the French king.[68] A third example can be found with the Anglo-Flemish treaty of 1197. This treaty falls into the same category as the first two examples, even though neither of the terms *confederatio* or *amicitia* appears in the text, nor are there any references to the word *amicus*. Instead, King Richard and Count Baldwin are said to have made a 'fedus et conventio'.[69] The content of this agreement is, nevertheless, the same as those discussed above: Baldwin and Richard promised not to make any peace or truce with the French king and to give each other mutual assistance, both during and after the war.[70]

The *conventio* is commonly thought by modern historians to have denoted a 'feudal' agreement, that is, it was formed on the basis of an oath of fealty, the act of homage and service. Both Chaplais and Ganshof have argued that the twelfth-century Anglo-Flemish treaties, that is those of 1101, 1110 and 1163 fall into such a category.[71] This is, of course, a problematic concept since we know that these treaties all specifically state that the Flemish count will aid the English king as a friend, and that they bear all the hallmarks of mutual agreements.[72] Compare this also to a number of *conventiones* of the early thirteenth century that have a similar content to the treaties (*confederationes*) of Sancho and John, and of Philip and Llewelyn, but, just as in the case of the 1197 Anglo-Flemish treaty, there is a complete absence of friendship terminology.[73] These agreements were clearly not merely *conventiones* but also *confederationes*. The differences between all of these agreements are by degree rather than kind – they are all in some way embraced by the term *amicitia* – yet something sets the *conventio* aside from the *confederatio* and it would be difficult not to concur with Chaplais and Ganshof that this something was the homage, fealty and service owed by one party to the other. It is clear, however, that not all *conventiones* were contracts for homage and fealty in return for annual payments; some were quite simply peace treaties. One example is the treaty between Henry II and Louis VII of 1160, and another is the 1191 Treaty of Messina.[74] Furthermore, the agreement whereby the kings of Castile and Navarre agreed to submit their dispute to the arbitration of the English king was a *conventio*, as well as a *pactum* of truce.[75]

Amicitia, *conventio* and *confederatio* were not the only ways in which contemporaries denoted various forms of friendship agreements. For example, *foedus* was often used in the sense of 'agreement' or 'treaty', though occasionally it had the more narrow interpretation of 'alliance'. When the French historian Rigord commented on how Richard, count of Poitou, had switched his allegiance from his father, Henry II, to the French king in 1188, it would seem that he used the word *fedus* to show that this agreement was distinctly different from other agreements (*pactiones*) that he commented on.[76] Saxo, by contrast, used *pactio* ('agreement', 'contract') to denote the agreement whereby Erling of Norway became Valdemar's man ('miles regis'), and in the narrative of Arnold of Lübeck, the ill-fated Dano-imperial marriage agreement of the 1180s is described with the same word.[77] Furthermore, it is evident that some treaties fall into more than one of these two categories of peace and friendship. For example, the treaty between Richard I and Tancred of Sicily was a peace (*pax*), because it ended hostilities, but it was also an alliance ('fedus amicitie') that was characterised by promises of specified mutual assistance: Richard, while he remained in Sicily, was to help Tancred defend his territories against any invader, wheras Tancred offered support in terms of materials and supplies for Richard's crusade.[78] Similarly, when Valdemar II announced the 'amicicia' concluded with the count and men of Flanders, he also made it clear that the agreement had been made for the preservation of peace, primarily, it would seem, in order to facilitate commercial activity.[79] It is clear from these examples that it can be very difficult to try to see any consistent usage in the different terms found in narrative and documentary sources.

Another term for alliance, one used most commonly to denote 'rebel alliances', is *conjuratio*. Althoff has noted that *conjurationes* as a rule encompassed larger groups of people, while *amicitia* usually only applied to a relationship between two people.[80] This interpretation certainly seems to fit the contemporary evidence. For example, *conjuratio* was the term that Gervase of Canterbury used to describe the agreement(s) between those English barons who joined the rebellion of Henry the Young King in 1173/74.[81] *Conjuratio* also appears in documents or narratives recording agreements concluded under the auspices of the Peace of God movement, one such example being the collective oath-swearing to keep the peace undertaken at Le Puy in 975.[82] This again reinforces the idea that this term was usually applied to a relationship between larger groups of people, but without necessarily linking it to rebellion.

Unlike agreements concluded for peace (*pax*) and/or friendship (*amicitia*), the truce (*treuga*, *induciae*), as laid out in the Council of Rouen, 1096, limited war at specific times of the year: 'From Septuagesima Sunday until dawn on the Monday after the octave of Pentecost, and from sunset on the Wednesday before Advent until the octave of Epiphany, and in every week throughout the year from sunset on Wednesday until dawn on Monday, and on all the feasts of St Mary with their vigils, and on all the feasts of the apostles with their vigils'.[83] There is plentiful evidence of truces being observed over the Christmas or Easter periods, and of peace conferences being held on certain days specified as days when a general truce was to be observed, such as the feast day of St Hilary (13 January).[84]

Jocelyn G. Russell has defined the truce as 'a condition of war, a state of suspended hostilities', during which the status quo was to be rigorously preserved.[85] A truce was broken by any act of war, in which case the hostilities could be restarted without any official renunciation of the truce.[86] According to the fourteenth-century writer Honoré Bouvet, the truce was a royal surety signifying three things: surety to persons, surety to goods and hope of peace. During the truce, argues Bouvet, ways and means of reconciling and of pacifying the two sides should be sought.[87] Bouvet's definition has a clear connection with the promotion of peace. In the twelfth and thirteenth centuries some writers had similar ideas as to the nature and purpose of a truce. For instance, Gervase of Canterbury noted that when King John and Philip Augustus met and concluded a truce (*induciae*) in 1199, this was done with the hope of future peace (*pax*).[88]

The notion that a truce was a period during which attempts for a more permanent peace should be made perhaps explains why the difference in terminology between peace (*pax*) and truce (*treuga*, *induciae*) is not always clear-cut in the works of contemporaries. Rigord, for example, refers to an 1187 agreement (*pactio*) between Henry II, Philip Augustus and Richard, count of Poitou.[89] *Pactio* is a rather vague term and could perhaps be referring to either a formal peace or a truce, or, indeed, any other agreement. Though working on the assumption that *pactio* is derived from *pax*, one would perhaps prefer to exclude the word truce from the list of interpretations. However, none of the English chroniclers record a formal peace concluded in 1187, but merely a truce for two years.[90] Similarly, the peace treaty ('carta pacis et concordiae') between the kings of Castile and Navarre, concluded in 1167, was seemingly a truce (*treugae*) intended to last for ten years.[91] In another example, Howden uses the word peace (*pax*) to describe what could reasonably be seen as a truce. According to Howden, in December 1195, Richard and Philip Augustus met near Issoudun and an agreement ('pax et concordia') was agreed to last from the Saturday next after the feast of St Nicholas (6 December) until the feast of St Hilary (13 January). When the parties met again on the agreed day, they concluded 'pacem et finalem concordiam'.[92] The time period of the initial peace is one commonly encountered as a period of truce among the sources, and it is curious why Howden on this occasion preferred to call it a peace. Possibly his terminology here portrays that the initial agreement was in fact a number of articles of peace agreed orally, which had not yet been ratified or put into writing. Such careful use of terminology certainly fits with the accounts of these two agreements given by other contemporaries.[93]

Some chroniclers also make a distinction in their choice of terminology between *treuga* and *inducia*. Gervase of Canterbury, for instance, always refers to truces as *induciae*, not once using the term *treuga*.[94] Howden, however, uses both terms, but he seems to prefer *treuga* in referring to truces on the continent, and *induciae* for truces in England, in particular those given by the king's representatives.[95] Hence he refers to the *treuga* between Richard and Philip of 1194, but to the *induciae* agreed with Count John by Walter of Coutances and the other guardians of Richard's lands during his absence on the Third Crusade.[96] This seems to be a very specific usage of these two terms.

It is clear from this discussion of the various terms used to describe agreements that it is extremely difficult to equate the terminology used by chroniclers with that employed in actual documents, and in trying to use terminology, whether in documents or in narratives, to unravel the nature of agreements. Consequently it is impossible to conclude that certain terms were used for certain types of treaties, because, as the example of *pactio* has shown, contemporaries could use it for marriage agreements, truces, acts of reconciliations and a number of other forms of agreement. This is probably why in the treaty of 1185 (or 1186) between King Alfonso of Aragon and Richard, count of Poitou, neither party was to be allowed to make any 'treugas, pacem, concordiam, sive aliquam composicionem' without the other's approval.[97] The intention was clearly to cover as many potential names of agreements and different relationships as possible. Most of the terms discussed in this chapter did not have exact meanings and the circumstances in which the agreements were concluded and the relationships they conveyed varied greatly.

Some historians have distinguished between agreements such as alliances, non-aggression pacts, peace treaties, marriage agreements and commercial treaties. Using the evidence of terminology it would seem, however, that such distinctions are fraught with difficulties. Often documents and chroniclers alike used a combination of terms. What is clear from the evidence is that peace in the late twelfth and early thirteenth centuries was often seen in the context of ensuring peaceful relations and that this could be done in a number of different ways: by marriage, commerce, friendship, joint military action and conquest, to name but a few. Whereas historians may want to distinguish between these and to limit peacemaking to agreements concluded after a period of hostilities, such a classification is wholly artificial and, moreover, was not a distinction that contemporaries always made.[98] Terminology and classification of treaties were clearly subject to geographical and periodical variations, and, with regards to narrative sources, were also subject to the language, rhetoric and flourishes of individual authors. However, if the historian is to claim that the medieval treaty was a distinct documentary type, as some historians of the earlier medieval period have done, it is clear that terminology cannot be used as evidence upon which to base such an assumption.[99]

Notes

1 Holdsworth, 'Peacemaking in the Twelfth Century', 3; Lund, 'Peace and Non-peace in the Viking Age', 257.
2 Kershaw, 'Rex Pacificus', 35, 243.
3 Rosemary Morris, 'Dispute Settlement in the Byzantine Provinces in the Tenth Century', in *The Settlement of Disputes in Early Medieval Europe*, 125. See also Graham Loud's recent discussion about the chancery of the kings of Sicily in the twelfth century, which, despite being regarded as one of the most advanced in Europe, have fewer surviving documents than those of the French and German kings. G. A. Loud, 'The Chancery and Charters of the Kings of Sicily (1130–1212)', *EHR*, 124 (2009), 783–4.
4 Howden, *Gesta*, ii, 102–4.
5 *Dip. Docs*, i, 14–16, no. 5.
6 Howden, *Gesta*, i, 36–41. The exception is, of course, the Anglo-Flemish agreements of 1101, 1110, and 1163. For these, see *Dip. Docs*, i, nos 1–3.
7 I have here not included the lost 1212 Anglo-Scottish marriage agreement that was discussed by E. L. G. Stones, because it seems to me that it is not clear whether there are any precise references to it. Anyway, the references cited by Stones do not specifically mention any written agreement. Stones, *Anglo-Scottish Relations 1174–1328*, xlvi–xlvii.
8 Rymer, *Foedera*, I, i, 103; *Flores Historiarum*, ii, 50; Stones, *Anglo-Scottish Relations 1174–1328*, xlv.
9 *Diplomatarium Danicum*, I:5, no. 217; I:6, nos 16, 17, 42.
10 *Diplomatarium Danicum*, I:4, no. 89.
11 *Arnoldi Chronica Slavorum*, VI:xv; *Annales Stadenses*, 353.
12 *Diplomatrium Danicum*, I:4, no. 4.
13 *Helmoldi Chronica Slavorum*, 79; *Urkunden Heinrich des Löwen*, ed. Karl Jordan (Stuttgart, 1957–60), nos 48, 115, 116.
14 *Newburgh*, i, 368; Howden, *Chronica*, iii, 224; *Gervase of Canterbury*, i, 529.
15 Saxo, *DRHH*, ii, 516–17. Heimskringla also has an account of Dano-Norwegian diplomacy and agreements, for which see Magnus Erlingson's Saga in *Heimskringla*, cap. 2, 23–4, 27–30.
16 *Diplomatarium Danicum*, I:7, no. 59.
17 *Diplomatarium Danicum*, I:3, no. 145.
18 *Diplomatarium Danicum*, I:5, no. 48; *Danmarks Riges Breve*, I:5, no. 48.
19 *Diplomatarium Danicum*, I:5, no. 146.
20 Smith, 'Magna Carta and the Charters of the Welsh Princes', 351. For Richard I's annulment of the treaty between William the Lion and Henry II, see Howden, *Gesta*, ii, 102–3; Howden, *Chronica*, iii, 25–6.
21 Langeli, 'Private Charters', 207; Chaplais, *EMDP*, i, no. 2.
22 Johnson, *Dialogus de Scaccario*, 62.
23 Chaplais, *EMDP*, ii, no. 354. For a discussion of similar problems in the kingdom of Sicily, see Loud, 'The Chancery', 799–800.
24 Clanchy, *From Memory to Written Record*, 6.

25 Ullmann, 'The Medieval Papal Court as an International Tribunal', repr. in his *The Papacy and Political Ideas in the Middle Ages*, 356.

26 Ullmann, 'The Medieval Papal Court as an International Tribunal', 361.

27 *RHF*, xix, 360; Powicke, *The Loss of Normandy*, 84; Landon, *Itinerary*, 233–4.

28 Landon, *Itinerary*, 233–4.

29 Howden, *Gesta*, ii, 236; Landon, *Itinerary*, 231–2.

30 *Dip. Docs*, i, no. 5; Landon, *Itinerary*, 232.

31 Ullmann, 'The Medieval Papal Court as an International Tribunal', 362.

32 Howden, *Gesta*, ii, 66–7. Similarly, in 1203, Pope Innocent III tried to mediate between John and Philip, but the French king argued that he was not obliged to answer to the pope in a dispute over feudal rights. Brenda Bolton, 'Philip Augustus and John: Two Sons in Innocent III's Vineyard?', *Studies in Church History*, 9 (1991), 120.

33 *Oeuvres de Rigord et de Guillaume le Breton*, i, 124–5, 195; Howden, *Chronica*, iii, 224–5; Newburgh, i, 369; Baldwin, *The Government of Philip Augustus*, 82–7; Bradbury, *Philip Augustus*, 179–85; Riis, 'Autour du mariage de 1193', 341–61.

34 For a discussion of this particular marriage alliance see my 'Philip Augustus and the Angevin Empire: The Scandinavian Connexion'. The best discussion of this marriage and the surrounding politics is still Robert Davidsohn, *Philipp II August von Frankreich und Ingeborg* (Stuttgart, 1888).

35 For this dispute and the arbitration, see also Fernando L. Corral, 'Alfonso VIII of Castile's Judicial Process at the Court of Henry II of England: an Effective and Valid Arbitration?', *Nottingham Mediaeval Studies*, 50 (2006), 22–42.

36 Howden, *Gesta*, i, 139–43; Howden, *Chronica*, ii, 120–2; *Diceto*, i, 418–20. Gervase merely states that the envoys brought their masters' claims before Henry II in Lent and that the king gave them his decision after Easter. *Gervase of Canterbury*, i, 261.

37 Howden, *Gesta*, i, 143–54; Howden, *Chronica*, ii, 122–31. Gerald of Wales specifically comments upon Henry's resolve to walk by a middle course, in giving his decision. *Giraldi Cambrensis Opera Omnia*, viii, 218.

38 Howden, *Gesta*, i, 151.

39 Howden, *Gesta*, i, 277, 285–6, 311–12, 334–5; *Diceto*, ii, 10, 38, 40.

40 Howden, *Gesta*, i, 139. The idea of war and disputes between kings being settled through a judicial battle between four knights is a recurring theme in the *History of William Marshal*. For one example, see *The History of William Marshal*, ll. 7503–650.

41 S. D. White, 'Feuding and Peacemaking in the Touraine around the Year 1100', *Traditio*, 42 (1986), 195–263; ' "Pactum . . . legem vincit et amor judicium": the Settlement of Disputes by Compromise in Eleventh-century Western France', *American Journal of Legal History*, 22 (1978), 281–308; 'Proposing the Ordeal and Avoiding it: Strategy and Power in Western French Litigation, 1050–1110', in *Cultures of Power: Lordship, Status, and Processes in Twelfth-century Europe*, ed. Thomas N. Bisson (Philadelphia, 1995). See also Patrick J. Geary, 'Vivre en conflit dans une France sans état: Typologie des mécanismes de règlement des conflits , 1050–1200', *Annales: Economies, Sociétés, Civilisations*, 41 (1986), 1107–33.

42 Geary, 'Vivre en conflit', 1120; White, ' "Pactum . . . legem vincit et amor judicium"', 300–1.

43 Chaplais, 'English Diplomatic Documents to the End of Edward III's Reign', 24.

44 Chaplais, 'English Diplomatic Documents to the End of Edward III's Reign', 25.

45 Esther Pascua, 'Peace among Equals: War and Treaties in Twelfth-century Europe', in *War and Peace in Ancient and Medieval History*, ed. Philip de Souza and John France (Cambridge, 2008), 194.

46 Furthermore, the word strength is subjective and could be made to mean a myriad of things. Hence, it would be difficult to determine which king was the 'stronger'.

47 Howden, *Chronica*, iii, 215.

48 For instance, what seems like the final agreement of November 1225 envisaged that it would have a number of seals attached to it, including those of the Danish king and his sons, eight from the Danish bishops and some from the Danish nobles. In the end, however, the document was sealed only by four people, one of whom, Archbishop Gerhard of Bremen, was not a party to the negotiations. It is thus doubtful if this agreement should be viewed as ratified. *Diplomatarium Danicum*, I:6, 59–60.

49 *Diplomatarium Danicum*, I:6, no. 42, pp. 59–60. At least one of the other agreements was also written by a scribe from the Count of Schwerin's chancery, for which see *Diplomatarium Danicum*, I:6, no. 16, p. 24.

50 *Diplomatarium Danicum*, I:6, no. 17, pp. 30–2.

51 *Diplomatarium Danicum*, I:5, no. 217; I:6, nos 16, 17, 42. One possible English example is the 1201 Anglo-Welsh agreement which was seemingly never ratified and contains that same phrase 'hec est forma compositionis'. Pryce, *The Acts of Welsh Rulers*, no. 221.

52 *Diplomatarium Danicum*, I:7, no. 59.

53 Pierre Chaplais, 'The Making of the Treaty of Paris', 237.

54 Chaplais, 'The Making of the Treaty of Paris', 237.

55 *Coggeshall*, 17, 76; *Torigni*, 203, 230, 302, 311.

56 *Newburgh*, i, 130.

57 For two examples, see Saxo, *DRHH*, ii, 447; *Oeuvres de Rigord et de Guillaume le Breton*, i, 132. The author of the *History of William Marshal* uses the French equivalent to *pax* and *guerra/bellum* at least once, specifying that the 'pais' had ended the 'guerre' of 1173–4. *The History of William Marshal*, ll. 2358–68. On Saxo's classical reference points, see Karsten Friis-Jensen, *Saxo Grammaticus as Latin Poet: Studies in the Verse Passages of the Gesta Danorum*, Analecta Romana, Instituti Danici, Supplementum, 14 (Rome, 1987); Giorgio Brugnoli, 'Gli auctores di Saxo', in *Saxo Grammaticus: Tra storiografia e letteratura*, ed. Carlo Santini (Rome, 1992), 27–45; Giovanni Polara, 'Tra fantasmi e poeti: Coincidenze e reminiscenze classiche nelle parti in versi dei *Gesta Danorum*', in ibid., 261–80.

58 Wolfthal, 'Introduction', xvi.

59 Howden, *Chronica*, i, 219; ii, 79, 143, 288; iii, 305; iv. 148; Howden, *Gesta*, i, 77.

60 *Dip. Docs*, i, no. 5; Howden, *Gesta*, ii, 160–1; *Rec. des actes de Philippe Auguste*, i, no. 376.

61 *Oeuvres de Rigord et de Guillaume le Breton*, i, 97, 132–3, 190, 199.

62 Saxo, *DRHH*, ii, 506–7, 476–7.

63 *Helmoldi Chronica Slavorum*, 92.

64 Pascua has recently pointed out that Latin writers in the twelfth century use, among other terms, *amor, caritas, dilectio, affectus, intellectus* and *amicitia* 'to name the same or different aspects of a personal relationship to God, love of humankind, friendship of fellow Christians and spiritual friendship'. Pascua, 'Peace among Equals', 195 fn. 4.

65 *Foedera*, I, i, 126–7.

66 Voss, *Herrschertreffen*, 188–9.

67 T. Matthews, *Welsh Records in Paris* (Carmarthen, 1910), 3–4. For a discussion of this alliance, see Trehane, 'The Franco-Welsh Treaty of Alliance in 1212', 60–75.

68 Matthews, *Welsh Records in Paris*, 3–4.

69 *Dip. Docs*, i, no. 7.

70 *Dip. Docs*, i, 18–19.

71 Chaplais, *EDP*, 42; Ganshof, 'Note sur le premier traité anglo-flamand de Douvres', 250.

72 For a discussion of this, see Chapter 4, pp. 102–5.

73 *Foedera*, I, i, 156–8, 168–9.

74 Landon, *Itinerary*, 221–2; *Rec. des actes de Philippe Auguste*, i, no. 376; *Dip. Docs*, i, no. 5.

75 Howden, *Gesta*, i, 140.

76 *Oeuvres de Rigord et de Guillaume le Breton*, i, 93.

77 Saxo, *DRHH*, ii, 516–17; *Arnoldi Chronica Slavorum*, III:ii.

78 Howden, *Gesta*, ii, 134, 137, 159.

79 *Diplomatarium Danicum*, I:7, no. 59.

80 Althoff, *Verwandte, Freunde und Getreue*, 119–33.

81 *Gervase of Canterbury*, ii, 80.

82 Bernard S. Bachrach, 'The Northern Origins of the Peace Movement at Le Puy in 975', *Historical Reflections*, 14 (1987), repr. in his *State-building in Medieval France: Studies in Early Angevin History* (Aldershot, 1995), 414.

83 Orderic, *HE*, v, 20–1.

84 For some brief examples, see Howden, *Gesta*, i, 63–4, 312; Howden, *Chronica*, iii, 305. For a discussion of conferences held on specific feast days, see Voss, *Herrschertreffen*, 112–13; Kolb, *Herrscherbegegnungen*, 71–3.

85 Russell, *Peacemaking in the Renaissance*, 83. According to Poly and Bournazel, the *treuga* was originally an oath which halted for a period the feuding (*faida*) between relations. J. P. Poly and B. Bournazel, *The Feudal Transformation 900–1200*, tr. Caroline Higgitt (London, 1991), 155.

86 Russell, *Peacemaking in the Renaissance*, 84.

87 *The Tree of Battles of Honoré Bonet*, tr. G. W. Coopland (Liverpool, 1949), 189–90.

88 *Gervase of Canterbury*, ii, 92.

89 *Oeuvres de Rigord et de Guillaume le Breton*, i, 90.

90 Howden, *Gesta*, ii, 7; *Diceto*, ii, 49.

91 Howden, *Chronica*, ii, 125.

92 Howden, *Chronica*, iii, 305.

93 *Newburgh*, ii, 461.

94 *Gervase of Canterbury*, i, 246, 309, 435, 439, 532, 544; ii, 92.

95 Howden, *Chronica*, ii, 56, 66, 314-15, 317, 355; iii, 184, 207, 254, 257, 276; iv, 24, 68, 80, 93, 97.

96 Howden, *Chronica*, iii, 207, 257.

97 R. Benjamin, 'A Forty Years War: Toulouse and the Plantagenets, 1156-96', 283 (appendix).

98 See also Althoff's conclusion on the different types of social bonds, in which he determines that in many ways 'foedera, pacta, amicitiae, coniunctiones, coniurationes and other associations . . . were all basically the same'. Althoff, *Family, Friends and Followers*, 101.

99 Keynes, 'Royal Government and the Written Word in Anglo-Saxon England', 233-4; M. Wielers, 'Zwischenstaatliche Beziehungsformen im frühen Mittelalter (*Pax, Foedus, Amicitia, Fraternitas*), unpublished Ph.D. thesis (Münster, 1959), 14ff; Kershaw', 'Rex Pacificus', 36-9.

Conclusion

So far, we have surveyed the mechanism and principles which under-lay medieval peacemaking. To conclude, it may be useful to ask how successful were the attempts to bring about peace which were made in this period. If we believe that peacemaking refers only to those treaties concluded in the aftermath of hostilities and that peace simply meant an absence of war, then the answer to this question is almost without exception negative. Few of the agreements mentioned in this book lasted longer than five years, and only three – the peace between Henry II and the Lord Rhys of 1171/72, the submission treaty of the king of Scots concluded in 1174, and the submission of Bogiszlav to Cnut VI in 1184/85 – were still in effect after ten years. Some individual treaties solved the issues at stake, yet, within a few months or years, war broke out again (though not always over the same issue). However, terminology, the actions of those involved in peacemaking, and the language and rhetoric of contemporary commen-tators have shown that peacemaking was much more than simply those treaties concluded after a period of hostility and that the meaning of peace is not restricted to being the antonym of war.

A more useful way of approaching success or failure is to view peace-making and diplomacy as a web of different relationships that contributed to ultimate success or failure. Althoff has already explored this phenom-enon in terms of group bonds and *personenverbandsstaat* and his conclu-sions are clearly applicable to peacemaking because, in a period without nation states, the focus of making peace was the relationship(s) between individual rulers. According to Althoff it was in the interest of almost all medieval people to be part of as large a network as possible to guarantee protection and help in all aspects of life.[1] In the modern period histori-ans would term such networks between different countries international relations, but for the twelfth and early thirteenth centuries peace and peacemaking are appropriate terms because of the focus on the individual rulers. Peace was thus always the ultimate goal of rulers just as theologically it was the ultimate goal of each individual, but the means by which one achieved this goal varied greatly.[2] Being a leader in both peace and war stands at the heart of this and cannot be viewed as two separate duties of a medieval prince. Moreover, historians cannot look for some sort of coherent policy of peace or war, because coherence was dependent on the aims and goals of each ruler at any one specific time. Consequently, successful peacemaking was not a matter of longevity, but rather to what extent it satisfied an individual ruler's hopes and needs at times of specific action, be this war, concluding agreements of varying kinds, negotiating or doing nothing.

By investigating the reasons why the English and Danish kings went to war and how the issues at stake were eventually resolved, it is possible to offer an explanation as to whether or not disagreements were resolved successfully. It is not possible to do this for every single dispute, war, agreement or treaty covered by this book, nor is it necessary. A few examples will aptly illustrate the problems and possibilities, starting with events of 1177. In this year Henry II of England and Louis VII of France concluded a treaty following a dispute about the proposed marriage between Louis's daughter Alice and Henry's son Richard. This marriage had been negotiated in 1168 with the intention of solving the long-standing dispute between the kings of England and France over the duchy of Aquitaine and its neighbouring regions.[3] The duchy had been acquired by Louis VII upon his marriage to the heiress Eleanor of Aquitaine, but the couple divorced in 1152 and the vast lands of the duchy reverted back to Eleanor, who then made a swift new marriage to Henry. At the time Henry was only duke of Normandy, but was also waiting for the right opportunity to press his claim to the English throne. Quite naturally, this new match set alarm bells ringing for the French king, who was faced with a rival with claims to more than half of the kingdom of the French and, over the next few years, Louis was only too happy to aid any barons or lords with a complaint against Henry II. In 1168, following a rebellion by a number of Aquitainian nobles supported by Louis, the idea behind negotiating the marriage was that Richard, as Henry's second son, would be invested with the duchy of Aquitaine and thus any heir from his marriage to the French princess would be as closely tied to the king of France as they were to the king of England. Alice may initially have had a marriage portion, possibly the city of Bourges, a city in the Berry the rights to which were disputed by both kings. But, when the betrothal was finalised at Montmirail in January 1169, it was agreed that Alice would come without a marriage portion.[4] This agreement then seemingly settled various issues that had smouldered for a while between the two kings, but, as is so often the case with even the best-laid plans, this one certainly went awry and the proposed marriage, rather than promoting peace, itself became a source of renewed hostilities.

One such period of hostility occurred in 1177. In June of this year, following a number of skirmishes in the Berry and Auvergne regions, Henry II decided that he wanted to settle these disputed rights and claims once and for all and sent envoys to the French king to demand that Louis VII would honour the agreements he had made concerning Alice's marriage to Richard as well as that of Henry's oldest son, also named Henry, to Louis's daughter Margaret. Furthermore, he asked that the French king would endow Alice with Bourges and its appurtenances and that Louis hand over the French Vexin on the Norman border as the remainder of Margaret's dowry. In response Louis argued that it was Henry who had broken the agreement by keeping Alice in his custody without marrying her to Richard as promised. To add clout to his argument, Louis also persuaded a papal legate to publish the fact that he had been instructed by Pope Alexander III to lay all of Henry's dominions under interdict unless the marriage between Alice and Richard was celebrated.[5]

What is interesting about all of this is that the treaty that eventually came out of these negotiations completely bypasses the issue at the heart of the hostilities: the proposed marriage. Instead, the two kings promised to remove all discord between them and to henceforth remain friends.[6] The disputed rights and claims in Berry were to be settled through the arbitration of six men from either side, whereas the lands of Auvergne and Châteauroux were not to be included in the peace. Henry and Louis also promised to go on a crusade together, and, almost as if it was an afterthought, the text of the treaty states that men and merchants from both sides would be able to enjoy peace while in the territories of either one of the kings.[7]

One of the most interesting aspects of the 1177 treaty lies in its perception of what constituted war and what was regarded as peace. The treaty established a general peace and firm friendship between Henry and Louis, yet there were issues that remained unresolved and others which specifically are stated to be outside this peace. On the basis of the terms of the treaty, it was seemingly possible to continue the war on some issues while also observing the peace on others. Exactly how well this worked in practice is not entirely clear. We know that, within weeks of concluding this treaty, Henry II renewed his attack on Châteauroux, and that he also sent his son Henry into Berry to attack the king's enemies. In 1179 the English and French kings furthermore mustered their forces, but without actually engaging in any fighting. Despite this, neither king seems to have considered these instances to be a breach of the terms and in fact the treaty was reconfirmed twice in 1180.[8] In 1177 peace and war seemingly existed side by side as strategies by which a king could achieve different goals and were not opposing theoretical concepts.

Was the treaty of 1177 successful? In terms of solving the issue of the marriage, the answer is clearly negative. Yet the English and French kings certainly attempted to solve some of the other outstanding issues, and most importantly, for a time, they found it more expedient to appear to keep a semblance of peace between them. Had either king thought this to be unsuccessful peacemaking, they could have started up formal hostilities again, but, despite some false starts, this did not happen until 1183.[9] In 1177 the treaty thus satisfied what both kings wanted to achieve at that particular time.

Another example of the complexities involved in analysing the success of peacemaking in this period can be found with the so-called Treaty of Le Goulet, concluded between King John and Philip Augustus in May 1200. The English exemplar of this treaty survives in the original in France, while the French version, though still extant in 1322 when it was listed in the Gascon calendar, survives only in a copy.[10] The treaty is based on two earlier agreements between John's predecessor on the English throne, Richard I, and Philip of France, which were intended to divide the territories between the two kings following years of almost continuous warfare. In 1193 Philip Augustus had invaded the lands of King Richard while he was away on the Third Crusade, justifying his action by stating that Richard had broken his promises with regards to his betrothal to Philip's sister Alice. Richard, as is well known, had suffered shipwreck while on his way home from the Third Crusade and was captured by the Duke of Austria as he tried to make his way home through imperial lands and handed over to the Emperor Henry VI. Henry then kept Richard in captivity until February 1194, during which time Philip had allied himself to Richard's brother John and invaded and captured large parts of Normandy. Unsurprisingly, warfare then continued between the two kings until a peace was brokered in December 1195. The agreement lasted only a few weeks before war recommenced and then continued intermittently until January 1200.[11] However, shortly before Richard's death in April 1199 a new treaty had been proposed, which envisaged leaving

Gisors in Philip's hands while Richard would receive the rights over the church of Tours.[12] These two treaties then served as the basis from which the peace of Le Goulet was negotiated. The treaty of 1195 gives a clear indication of the nature of warfare in this period because the main concern of the two kings was not to draw up an exact boundary between their two territories but rather to set out in writing the allegiance of certain Norman marcher castles and their lords, including Gournai, Vernon and Vaudreuil.[13] The Treaty of Le Goulet shows a similar concern even though some boundaries were also set.[14] To further solve some of the disputed lands, John and Philip also decided to marry Philip's son, Louis, to John's niece, Blanche of Castile, and the youngsters were given the disputed territories of Berry, Auvergne and those parts of Normandy held by Philip Augustus as their marriage portion, which were to be returned to John if no heir materialised from the marriage.[15]

Apart from the disputed lands, the peace of Le Goulet also resolved a number of other issues. For instance, John was recognised as the rightful heir to his brother Richard I. According to Roger of Howden, Richard had named John as his successor upon his death in 1199, but variations in custom and practice across the vast lands of the Angevin empire meant that some accepted John as successor whereas others argued that the fifteen-year-old Arthur of Brittany, as the son of John's deceased older brother Geoffrey, had a better claim and they sought military and moral support for this from the French king.[16] In the treaty, however, Philip Augustus agreed that he would not recognise Arthur's claims to the continental possessions of the English king, and, furthermore, that Arthur would hold Brittany from his uncle and not from the French king. The treaty also stipulated that the counts of Flanders, Boulogne and Ponthieu, who had been allied to the English king since 1197, were to hold their lands from the French king.[17] Furthermore, John agreed to abandon his alliance to the emperor-elect Otto. This particular alliance had been a significant threat to the French king, because imperial lands bordered France and thus the English king's alliance with Otto had threatened to squeeze Philip's domains in a sort of pincer movement.[18] The peace concluded between John and Philip near Le Goulet thus did what one would perhaps expect from a peace treaty. No issues were left unresolved and there is no notion here that hostilities could continue while at the same time keeping the peace intact.

The Treaty of Le Goulet was arguably the most successful Anglo-French attempt to make peace in this period. Contemporaries certainly seemed to think that the peace was significant. Ralph of Coggeshall for instance described how John with this treaty tried to keep the kingdom away from the hostility that had proved so injurious to his father and brother.[19] Similarly Gervase of Canterbury angrily reported that the opponents to the peace called John 'Softsword'.[20] By contrast, most modern commentators have not viewed the peace as a success: certainly, it has not been seen as a success from an English point of view. John Gillingham has argued that, in abandoning his alliance with Otto, John was left isolated on the European diplomatic stage. Furthermore, Gillingham argues that John's personal traits also stood in stark contrast to those of his brother (Richard I) and that those around him feared that John would behave treacherously.[21] Similarly Powicke commented that events had forced Philip Augustus to make peace on terms that might have proved lasting if only John had acted with 'ordinary prudence'.[22] Powicke further pointed out that, in the treaty, John agreed to pay the French king 20,000 marks of silver as a relief ('rachatum') for his lands and as payment for the recognition of his overlordship in Brittany. To Powicke and others this was the most significant part of the treaty because it recognised the supremacy of the French court and it was this court which in 1202 would confiscate all of John's continental possessions.[23]

The problem with these interpretations is that they view the treaty in light of subsequent events, in particular the events leading up to the loss of Normandy to the French king in 1204. According to some historians, the Treaty of Le Goulet played a significant part in this loss because some of its terms left John in a very weak position towards the French king. However, it would be quite difficult to pinpoint exactly how the treaty contributed to the loss of Normandy. For instance, Gillingham's complaint about John agreeing to abandon the alliances of his brother is problematic, because by 1202 some of those former allies, such as the count of Flanders, had sailed off on the Fourth Crusade and would have been no help to John even if the treaty had stipulated that they should still be allied to the English king. Similarly, it is perhaps questionable whether Otto, the imperial candidate, would have been in a position to lend aid to John, as his own position within Germany was precarious and his foremost concern with regards to allies seems to have been the other German princes, the pope and the Danish king. It is in any case clear that John and Otto renewed their alliance almost immediately upon the renewal of war in France, and that John also had a number of other allies, including Sancho of Navarre.[24]

The issues of the payment to Philip and the subjection of John to the French king's court fare little better. The relief paid to Philip Augustus was similar to that paid by Richard I in 1189 upon his accession to the

English throne, yet no historian has suggested that this payment made Richard subject to Philip's court.[25] Furthermore, rarely in this period did legality outweigh politics. Theoretically, as duke of Normandy, count of Anjou and duke of Aquitaine, the English kings had always been subject to the French king's judgement. Certainly, the availability of an alternative source of appeal had often lured disaffected nobles to the French king's side, but enforcing such a judgement was much harder and was usually attempted by military might.[26] It would thus appear that what was new in the campaigns of 1202–4 was the result not of the terms of the treaty but rather of the English king's inability to win the war. Most conclusively, the treaty was not a direct cause of the war that led to the loss of the English king's continental lands. Instead this was attributed by contemporaries to a series of events started off by the Poitevins and the Lusignan family.[27] It is difficult to imagine how the two kings in 1200 could have made peace on terms that two years later could forestall certain members of the aristocracy being unhappy about various matters, not all of which were regulated by the treaty. Furthermore, it could be argued on the evidence in contemporary sources that the loss of the continental lands was the result of John's treatment of his nephew Arthur after 1202 and not the outcome of the rebellion and the judgement in Philip's court, because this had been settled by John's victory and capture of his enemies at Mirebeau in the summer of 1202.[28]

It is evident that the problem with determining if peacemaking was successful or not often lies in how historians view its impact in the longer term. Yet historians do not always judge success in war by longevity. If we did, Richard I could hardly be judged a successful military leader, as his reign saw almost continuous warfare, none of which had any lasting effect.[29] Similarly Valdemar II's epithet 'Sejr', the Victorious, would be wholly inapt as the last twenty years of his reign were marred by his captivity and the eventual loss of most of the Danish conquests between the Eider and the Elbe.[30] Peace through victory is often seen as the most preferable way to secure peace. Yet even such a peace cannot be considered successful if we judge it by longevity. For instance, historians usually view Henry II's defeat of William king of Scots in 1174 as a great success for the English king. It was, but only in terms of ensuring that Henry could deprive his sons of an ally and thereby defeat them. The long-term impact of the victory was negligible.[31] Likewise, although Cnut VI's conquest of the Slavs in 1184/85 was hailed by the Danish contemporaries Sven Aggesen and Saxo Grammaticus, modern commentators have been more cautious in judging this event as a success.[32]

The main question is, of course, how long is required to judge success? One year? Five? Fifty? The lifetime of a king? For ever? If a treaty solves a disputed issue over two pieces of land, but two years later the two kings go to war over a different piece of land, does this make the initial peace unsuccessful? For instance, following Henry the Young King's death in 1183, hostilities broke out between the English and French kings over the dower of Henry's wife Margaret, sister of Philip of France. The issue was settled in 1186, but shortly after hostilities broke out again between the two kings. However, the hostilities of late 1186 and early 1187 had little to do with the issues over Margaret's dower and thus it would be difficult to regard the peacemaking of 1186 as unsuccessful on account of a dispute over a different matter.[33] Similarly, in 1211, John invaded Llywelyn's lands in north Wales and forced him to a humiliating defeat.[34] Does Llywelyn's renewal of hostilities in 1212 make the earlier victory 'unsuccessful'? There are clearly some inherent problems in using longevity as a yardstick by which to judge success in peace, or, for that matter, war. However, this is not to say that longevity or durability was unimportant, but merely to highlight that, if historians use this particular measurement alone, we lose some of the immediate context in which an agreement was concluded.

Success in the medieval period, as today, is usually about the public perception of a ruler's ability to lead a war to a satisfactory conclusion, to resolve matters of dispute and restore order, or to prevent hostilities from breaking out at all. But this is infinitely more difficult to measure because of the nature of our sources. For instance, Sven Aggesen describes the Danish conquest and public submission of the Slav leader Bogiszlav in the most glorious of terms: Sven was, after all, writing about an event to which he had been a witness. Yet the very last two sentences in his history reveal an uncertainty about the relative success of the agreement: 'When that was concluded, we rowed homeward with immense jubilation. May the ruler of all things order this conclusion in His peace!'[35] As Eric Christiansen has pointed out, this is reflecting an anxiety about what was going to happen, because at the time of Sven writing his history – probably in 1188 – tension continued between the Danes and the Slavs and no final settlement had been worked out.[36] By contrast, Saxo, writing later but almost certainly before 1202, responded to some of this anxiety by recording that Bogiszlav remained loyal to Cnut VI until his death in 1187 and that the king afterwards acted as guardian to the duke's two young sons.[37] The success of the agreement between Cnut and Bogiszlav concluded in 1184/85 hence depends on whether we are looking at it in the context of events in 1184/85, c. 1188, in the 1190s, or in the context of even later events and sources.

As successful peacemaking was about public perception, a public event was necessary. Thus, when it comes to asking how successful peacemaking was, we should perhaps not look at how long these treaties lasted but rather at how the event was perceived by contemporaries. Abels argues that peacemaking was successful if it ended a process of negotiation with a public event declaring the peace; a so-called 'liminal' event. In this process, hostility was converted by 'ritual' into peace, and enemies transformed into friends.[38] Although Abels was referring specifically to the earlier medieval period, the concept translates equally well into the twelfth and early thirteenth centuries. For instance, this is why, during the 1180s and 1190s, so many meetings were held between the French and English kings and the reason why so many treaties were concluded. As the opportunities for dispute increased, so did also the number of conferences – that is, those public events that symbolised the beginning of a new relationship. Furthermore, treaties eventually came to symbolise these particular events, hence their increased importance throughout this period.

War in the medieval period, as in others, broke out because participants thought that they had more to gain from war than from keeping the peace. Nevertheless, the ultimate aim was always peace and this could be achieved through warfare as well as by diplomacy. The only real constants in these continuously changing networks lie in the durability of the mechanics of how to make peace, that is, those principles that were an essential part of the public, liminal, event: the meeting places, the envoys, the ceremonies, the guarantees, the treaties. Successful peacemaking in the twelfth century was thus, in many ways, more about how to make peace than it was about the longevity of the terms of individual agreements. To many contemporaries the most important thing was simply to record that the king had made peace. Through the various ceremonies and gestures, the public event thus signified that each ruler had fulfilled his duties to ensure future peace and the restoration or confirmation of societal order.[39] In the tenth and eleventh centuries, contemporaries provided full descriptions of the many ceremonies and gestures surrounding the making of peace, but rarely did they include descriptions of what was concluded. By the late twelfth century, however, treaties symbolised the event and the ceremonies, and, furthermore, provided proof of what had been agreed which could be used to challenge any future hostile claims. The establishment and maintenance of peace, alongside success in war, was thus a key way for rulers to demonstrate that their authority was ordained and approved by God.[40]

It seems certain that contemporaries recognised that *realpolitik* meant that agreements did not always last very long. Yet the recurrence of the principles of how to make peace is enough to suggest that rulers considered them to be successful. There was also recognition that not every way or means of securing peace was appropriate on every occasion and that the principles could change. For instance, in or around 1159, Henry the Lion procured a peace between himself, Valdemar I and certain leaders of the Slavs. As hostages and tribute had not previously been successful in securing a long-term agreement with the Slavs, Henry decided that this treaty was to be guaranteed by different means, namely the delivery of all Slav ships, thereby curtailing their ability to undertake raids. The principle of guaranteeing the peace thus remained the same, but the actual guarantee was altered in an attempt to rectify previously unsuccessful attempts at peacemaking. Unfortunately, also this attempt was futile, though this may have had less to do with the means by which the treaty was guaranteed and more to do with the fact that Valdemar's two German neighbours and allies were absent in Italy and Normandy shortly after the conclusion of the peace and Valdemar was then unable to curtail the Slavs by himself.[41]

Peacemaking involving the Danish kings further shows that the principles and practice altered slightly over the course of the medieval period. Quite naturally, what was successful in the ninth century might not necessarily be so in the twelfth. One example is sponsorship at baptism of non-Christians, which played such a large part of the peacemaking strategies of western rulers with the Vikings in the ninth and tenth centuries. The notion that successful peacemaking in the Viking period rested on a shared concept of peace through Christianity, achieved mainly through sponsorship at baptism or at confirmation, is a well-attested phenomenon in early medieval Europe.[42] According to Richard Abels, Christian sponsorship developed in Western European rulers' relations with non-Christians essentially because of the failure of other attempts to bind them to their oaths. Central to this argument is the shared Christian belief that divine retribution would befall oath-breakers.[43] Although political subordination was at the heart of the relationship created, Lynch has argued that the blow was softened by 'the sacred and honourable bond of spiritual kinship'.[44]

By the time we get to the twelfth century, however, a different picture emerges of how Western rulers made peace with non-Christians. For instance, despite the fact that Duke Henry the Lion and successive Danish kings launched several expeditions against the non-Christian Slavs in the second half of the twelfth century and although peace was made several times, sponsorship at baptism does not seem to have been a feature of this peacemaking. Conversion to Christianity remained, but there were no elaborate sponsorship scenes where the king or the duke stood sponsor to the vanquished leaders and showered them with gifts. When Helmold recorded a peace made by 'our men' with the Slavs in the late 1140s, he merely stated that they 'embraced Christianity': a strange omission for someone who, according to Eric Christiansen, was chiefly concerned with recording the conversion of these peoples.[45] Similarly, when Valdemar I conquered the Rugians in c. 1169, Saxo records how they received Christianity and then provides an elaborate account of the destroying of Slav idols.[46] On these occasions, however, there was a compelling reason why there were no elaborate scenes of sponsorship at baptism: the non-Christian Slavs were conquered. During the sponsorship scenes of the Viking period, the Christian rulers were in a position whereby they needed the co-operation of the non-Christians in order to make peace and either to settle them as an integrated part of Christian society or to make them return from where they had come. In the twelfth century the peacemaking strategies of Henry the Lion and the Danish kings with the Slavs were enforced through military might and consequently the baptism and conversion were symbolic as gestures of political submission, yet without needing to 'soften the blow' by creating a bond of spiritual kinship.

The principles of how to make peace are easily recognisable throughout history. In the modern period the shaking of hands has come to symbolise agreement and concord, and there are many examples of this gesture from the medieval period, even though its importance and interpretation have been overshadowed by the large literature on the related gesture of homage.[47] Similarly a number of historians have recently highlighted the considerable emphasis in classical Greece and late antiquity on gift giving as a strategy to influence negotiations and to honour the other party; a strategy which is found also among medieval rulers.[48] However, it is not only the gestures and symbolism surrounding the making of peace or the sites where rulers met that are easily recognisable throughout history. That essential element of the concept of peace and peacemaking is also evident. When Churchill, Roosevelt and Stalin claimed at the end of the conference in Tehran in 1943 that their nations would work together in war and in the peace that followed and that they parted as friends in fact, spirit and purpose, it was not unlike the claims and aims of many twelfth and early thirteenth-century treaties.[49] In many ways then, medieval notions of war and peace bear a strong likeness to those of the ancient world, as well as those of more modern periods.

However, peacemaking in the twelfth century was intensely personal. Most negotiations were still conducted face-to-face and the issues in dispute and how they were solved involved the ruler directly: succession, marriage, loyalty of the greater lords, control of castles, personal ambition and so on. Furthermore, kings could not discharge their duty as peacemakers on to someone else. Truces could be negotiated by deputies, but the conclusion of peace or friendship was the exclusive preserve of the ruler in this period. There are very few exceptions to this and they usually take place in very specific circumstances. For instance the 1193 Anglo-French treaty was negotiated and concluded by Richard I's deputies while the king himself was imprisoned in the Empire. By contrast, leading troops into battle, another royal duty, was often done by others because the king could simply not be in several places at the same time. It is clear that in peacemaking a number of functions of a medieval king converged. Not only did the king have to take the lead in matters of war, but as a Christian prince the king also needed to show *caritas* (love, charity) and humility (*humilitas*) and that he was able to set aside pride and anger and instead foster unity. Many of the gestures and ceremonies surrounding the making of peace are specifically concerned with conveying these notions, as well as showing the power and prestige of royal majesty. Moreover, the medieval prince had to show that he was a provider of justice and consequently terms of treaties are often expressed within a legal framework, i.e. they determine rights and possessions, use guarantees, and/or afford protection to certain sections of society. In addition, many of the activites surrounding the making of peace relied upon the personality and personal relationships of the king. Kin, closest advisers and friends acted as envoys, guarantors and oath-takers, while, at the same time, there can be no doubt that making agreements could be greatly facilitated (or hindered) by the rulers involved knowing each other on a more personal basis.[50] For these, and for many other reasons, peacemaking was very much part of ruling.

Notes

1 Gerd Althoff, *Family, Friends and Followers*, 6–7.
2 The idea of peace always being the ultimate goal is one that appears in contemporary sources and it is based on the ideas of St Augustine that 'the lower forms of peace are stepping stones to the higher forms, the highest being the final peace in heaven'. Renna, 'The Idea of Peace', 147. For some contemporary views, see

The Works of Sven Aggesen, tr. Eric Christiansen (London, 1992) 22, 112 fn. 46; *Newburgh*, i, 282; *Giraldi Cambrensis Opera Omnia*, v, 303.

3 *Torigni*, 235–6; Landon, *Itinerary*, 223; Eyton, *Court, Household and Itinerary of King Henry II*, 112–13. Diceto places the proposal under 1167, for which see *Diceto*, i, 331.

4 *The Letters of John of Salisbury*, ii, no. 288 (pp. 648–9). Torigni has a detailed description of the events leading up to the peace negotiations and then says very little about what was agreed. *Torigni*, 237–8, 240. For a discussion about the negotiations surrounding the betrothal, see John Gillingham, 'The Meetings of the Kings of France and England, 1066–1204', in *Normandy and Its Neighbours, 900–1250*, ed. David Crouch and Kathleen Thompson (forthcoming, 2010).

5 Howden, *Gesta*, i, 127, 132, 168–9, 180–1; Howden, *Chronica*, ii, 147; *Torigni*, 274. Gerald of Wales has a story about Henry II dishonouring Alice after the death of his concubine Rosamund and that, after the rebellion of 1173–74, Henry devised a plan to divorce Eleanor and marry Alice. Landon believed that this might have been the reason why Henry invited papal legates to Normandy in 1176. *Giraldi Cambrensis Opera Omnia*, viii, 232; Landon, *Itinerary*, 223–4.

6 Howden, *Gesta*, i, 191; Howden, *Chronica*, ii, 144; *Gervase of Canterbury*, i, 272.

7 Howden, *Gesta*, i, 191–4; Howden, *Chronica*, ii, 144–6; *Gervase of Canterbury*, i, 272–4. Torigni records only the promise to go on crusade. *Torigni*, 276–7.

8 In June 1180, Henry acted as mediator between Philip, his family and advisors, and it was at this point that the treaty was first renewed. It was then renewed a second time after the death of Louis VII. Howden, *Gesta*, i, 194–6; 244–50; Howden, *Chronica*, ii, 147, 198–9; *Torigni*, 274, 289–90; *Diceto*, ii, 6.

9 One such false start happened in 1180, when Diceto records that Henry prevented an attack by Philip by sending envoys. *Diceto*, ii, 4.

10 The Gascon calendar is the result of the cataloguing of documents in the English exchequer and the wardrobe. Although most of its content dates from the reign of Edward I and concerns Anglo-French negotitations involving the duchy of Aquitaine, the catalogue contains documents for the whole period 1187–1331, most of which bear witness to the English administration of the duchy. *The Gascon Calendar of 1322*, ed. G. P. Cuttino (London, 1949).

11 For a convenient summary of the chronology of these events, see Gillingham, *Richard I*, 283–320.

12 Howden, *Chronica*, iv, 80–1.

13 *Dip. Docs*, i, 16–18.

14 *Dip. Docs*, i, 20–1.

15 *Dip. Docs*, i, 21; *Diceto*, ii, 168; Howden, *Chronica*, iv, 115. The marriage had been part of the proposals of 1199. Howden, *Chronica*, iv, 80–1.

16 Howden, *Chronica*, iv, 83, 87; *Coggeshall*, 99.

17 *Dip. Docs*, i, 22.

18 For a short summary of this problem in the twelfth-century, see Benham, 'Philip Augustus and the Angevin Empire', 38–9.

19 *Coggeshall*, 101.

20 *Gervase of Canterbury*, ii, 92–3.

21 Gillingham, *Richard I*, 335–8.

22 Powicke, *The Loss of Normandy*, 134.

23 Powicke, *The Loss of Normandy*, 137; W. L. Warren, *King John* (London, 1961), 70–1; Jacques Boussard, 'Philippe Auguste et les Plantagenêts', in *La France de Philippe Auguste: le temps des mutations*, ed. R.-H. Bautier (Paris, 1982), 279; *Dip. Docs*, i, 22.

24 *Rot. Litt. Pat.*, 5a; Rymer, *Foedera*, I, i, 85–7; Poole, 'Richard the First's Alliances', 90–99; Hans-Eberhard Hilpert, 'Zwei Briefe Kaiser Ottos IV. an Johann Ohneland', *DA*, 38 (1982), 125; Natalie Fryde, 'King John and the Empire', in *King John: New Interpretations*, ed. S. D. Church (Woodbridge, 1999), 336, 341.

25 According to Howden, at a conference on 22 July 1189, Richard paid Philip 4,000 marks of silver 'pro expensis suis' in addition to honouring the payment of 20,000 marks that Henry II had promised the French king just a few days before on 4 July. As the actual texts of these two treaties do not survive, unlike the Treaty of Le Goulet, it would be difficult to dismiss these payments on grounds of terminology. Certainly, the circumstances indicate that Henry agreed to make the payment as the price for peace and, following his death, Richard then paid that same sum and the additional 4,000 marks as the price to succeed his father. Howden, *Gesta*, ii, 69–71, 74. Furthermore, the payment had formed part of the proposals made to Richard in 1199. Howden, *Chronica*, iv, 80–1.

26 For instance, in the late 1150s the count of Toulouse made such an appeal to the French king following Henry's assertion to his rights in the county as duke of Aquitaine. *Torigni*, 201–3; *Continuatio Beccensis*, 321–2.

27 Contemporaries did not see events of 1201–4 as one continuous chain, but rather there were two distinct phases of rebellions, one in 1201–2 and another in 1203–4. The sources are not in complete agreement about the cause(s) of the first rebellion. According to Howden the men of Poitou rose in rebellion and laid siege to John's castles, but Philip raised the sieges after hearing of John's impending return and in the end John never actually left England. Howden, *Chronica*, iv, 160–1. Diceto merely states that many disputes broke out between Hugh de Lusignan and King John. *Diceto*, ii, 170. Ralph of Coggeshall records that Hugh de Lusignan rose against John because the king had married the daughter of the count of Angoulême, who had previously been betrothed to Hugh and in his keeping. *Coggeshall*, 128–9, 135. The author of the *History of William Marshal* also follows this version of events, only to connect the resolution of this dispute to the Peace of Le Goulet, which had in fact been concluded before John's marriage to Isabella. A little later the author then states that it was Philip's unreasonable behaviour that led to war. *The History of William Marshal*, ll. 11996–12000, 12011–18, 12023–43. Gervase of Canterbury, on the other hand, recalls that the whole war was started on account of Philip Augustus asking John to surrender three Norman castles, which was contrary to the terms of the peace. *Gervase of Canterbury*, ii, 93.

28 *Coggeshall*, 137–8; *The History of William Marshal*, ll. 12059–110. Most sources agree that the second phase of the war in 1203–4 occurred following John's

treatment, and possibly murder, of his nephew Arthur of Brittany. *Coggeshall*, 139, 143–5; *Gervase of Canterbury*, ii, 94; *Ann. Mon.*, i, 27.

29 For Richard's reputation as a military leader, see Gillingham, *Richard I*, 3–7, 331–4, 348; M. Markowski, 'Richard Lionheart: Bad King, Bad Crusader', *JMH*, 23 (1997), 351–65.

30 Jacobsen, 'Wicked Count Henry', 326–36; N. G. Heine, 'Valdemar II's udenrigspolitik. Kampen om Østersøvaeldet', in *Østersøproblemer omkring 1200*, ed. N. G. Heine (Aarhus, 1941), 58–85.

31 Duncan, 'John King of England and the Kings of Scots', 250–1.

32 Nils Hybel and Bjørn Poulsen, *The Danish Resources c. 1000–1550* (Leiden, 2007), 135–6.

33 Landon, *Itinerary*, 224–6; Howden, *Gesta*, i, 306; Howden, *Chronica*, ii, 281; *Diceto*, ii, 40.

34 *Brut y Tywysogyon*, 85; *Annales Cambriae*, 67–8; *The Annals of Margam*, in *Ann. Mon.*, i, 31; *Memoriale Fratris Walteri de Coventria*, ii, 203; *Flores Historiarum*, ii, 58; Pryce, *The Acts of Welsh Rulers*, no. 233.

35 *A Short History of the Kings of Denmark*, 74; Sven Aggesen, *Brevis Historia*, 141.

36 *The Works of Sven Aggesen*, 25–6.

37 Saxo, *DRHH*, ii, 624–5; *Knytlingasaga*, cap. 130.

38 Abels, 'Paying the Danegeld', 179. On the concept of liminality, see Victor Turner, *The Ritual Process: Structure and Anti-Structure* (Ithaca, 1969), 94–130, 166–78.

39 In much, this agrees with Fasoli's definition of peace (*pax/pak*) as an agreement that symbolised the maintenance of a new situation. See Introduction, 3.

40 Pascua similarly notes that treaties were backed not by international law but 'by divine providence through the eyes and testimony of those who were present at the event'. Pascua, 'Peace among Equals', 196. An interesting discussion can also be found in Hermann Kamp, *Friedensstifter und Vermittler im Mittelalter* (Darmstadt, 2001)

41 *Helmoldi Chronica Slavorum*, 170.

42 For some early medieval examples of sponsorship at baptism, see Ermold le Noir, *Poème sur Louis le Pieux*, ll. 2165–2528; *Annales Xantenses*, 6–7; *De Moribus*, 170; *ARF*, 56. The essential study on this topic is Joseph H. Lynch, *Godparents and Kinship in Early Medieval Europe* (Princeton, 1986). See also Joseph H. Lynch, *Christianizing Kinship. Ritual Sponsorship in Anglo-Saxon England* (Ithaca, 1998). For a more specific discussion of this ceremony within the context of peacemaking in the early medieval period, see Nelson, 'The Lord's Anointed and the People's Choice: Carolingian Royal Ritual', 137–80; Abels, 'King Alfred's Peace-making Strategies with the Vikings', 27–32; Ian Wood, 'Christians and Pagans in Ninth-century Scandinavia', in *The Christianization of Scandinavia*, ed. Birgit Sawyer, Peter Sawyer and Ian Wood (Alingsås, 1987), 36–67; T. M. Andersson, 'The Viking Policy of Ethelred the Unready', *SS*, 59 (1987), 284–95; Peter Sawyer, 'Ethelred II, Olaf Tryggvason, and the Conversion of Norway', *SS*, 59 (1987), 299–307. For a discussion of the symbolism of baptism, see J. P. Bouhout, 'Explications du rituel baptismal à l'époque carolingienne', *Revue des*

études augustiniennes, 24 (1978), 278–301; F. W. Dillistone, *Christianity and Symbolism* (London, 1985), 185–99.

43 Abels, 'King Alfred's Peace-making Strategies with the Vikings', 27.

44 Lynch, *Godparents and Kinship in Early Medieval Europe*, 176; *Christianizing Kinship*, 206.

45 *Helmoldi Chronica Slavorum*, 60; Christiansen, *The Northern Crusades*, 61.

46 Saxo, *DRHH*, ii, 504–9.

47 For a few examples, see *The Annals of Fulda*, tr. T. Reuter (Manchester, 1992), 61, fn.13; Widukind, *Res Gestae Saxonicae*, 127, 145; *The Ruodlieb*, 13; *The Alexiad of Anna Komnena*, I:xi; Suger, *Vie de Louis VI*, 230–1; *The Letters of John of Salisbury*, ii, 636–8; Saxo, *DRHH*, ii, 593–4.

48 Lee, 'Treaty-making in Late Antiquity', 118–19; Rung, 'War, Peace and Diplomacy', 49.

49 *Foreign Relations of the United States, Diplomatic Papers, the Conferences at Cairo and Teheran*, 640–1.

50 For instance, it was no accident that Frederick Barbaross in 1152 awarded the disputed kingdom of Denmark to Svein rather than to Cnut, because Barbarossa had been Svein's 'socio militiae' during the reign of Conrad III. Saxo, *DRHH*, ii, 379. Similarly, the many disputes between the Angevin and Capetian kings in this period were perhaps heightened by the kings' personal experiences of, and with, one another. Richard and Philip Augustus were said to have been exceptionally close, united in their efforts against Henry II, but so their fallout after the Treaty of Messina was also bitter. Howden. *Gesta*, ii, 7. On the importance of the personalities of kings, see Gillingham, 'The Meetings of the Kings of France and England'.

BIBLIOGRAPHY

Manuscript sources

PRO, London, *E135/3/25*
Châteauroux, Bibliothèque municipale, MS 5, f. 225v
Marseilles, Archives départementales du Bouche-du-Rhône, *B337*

Printed sources

Actes concernant les vicomtes de Marseille et leur descendants, ed. H. de Gérin-Ricard (Monaco, 1926)

Actes de Philippe I, comte et marquis de Namur 1196–1211, ed. M. Walraet (Brussels, 1949)

Actes des comtes de Namur, 946–1196, ed. F. Rousseau (Brussels, 1937)

Actes des princes lorrains, 2 vols, ed. J. Laplace (Nancy, 1972–74)

The Acts of Welsh Rulers 1120–1283, ed. Huw Pryce (Cardiff, 2005)

Adalbertus Samaritanus Praecepta Dictaminum, ed. Franz-Josef Schmale (Weimar, 1961)

Adam Bremensis Gesta Hammaburgensis Ecclesiae Pontificum, 3rd edn, ed. B. Schmeidler, MGH SRG, 12 (Hanover, 1917)

Adam of Bremen, *History of the Archbishops of Hamburg-Bremen*, tr. F. J. Tschan (New York, 1959)

Adémar de Chabannes, Chronique, ed. J. Chavanon (Paris, 1897)

Aelfric's Lives of the Saints, ed. W. W. Skeat, Early English Text Society, 76 (London, 1881–85)

Alcuin, Operum pars septima – opera didascalia, in *PL 101*

Äldre Västgötalagen, ed. Herman Vendell (Helsingfors, 1897)

Äldre Västgötalagen, tr. Nat. Beckman (Uppsala, 1924; repr. Skara, 1974)

Ambroise, *Estoire de la guerre sainte*, in *The History of Holy War*, ed. and tr. Marianne Ailes and Malcolm Barber, 2 vols (Woodbridge, 2003)

Andreae Marchianensis Historia Regum Francorum, ed., G. Waitz, MGH SS, 26 (Hanover, 1882)

Anglo-Normannische Geschichtsquellen, ed. F. Liebermann, (Strasbourg, 1879)

Anglo-Saxon Charters, 2nd edn, ed. A. J. Robertson (Cambridge, 1956)

Anglo-Scottish Relations 1174–1328: Some Selected Documents, ed. E. L. G. Stones (London, 1965)

Annales Altahenses, ed. G. H. Pertz, MGH SRG, 4 (Hanover, 1868; repr. 1979)

Annales Augustini, ed. G. H. Pertz, MGH SS, 3 (Hanover, 1839; repr. Stuttgart, 1987)

Annales Bertiniani, ed. G. Waitz, MGH SRG, 5 (Hanover, 1883)

Annales Cambriae, ed. J. Williams ab Ithel (London, 1860)

Annales Cameracenses, ed. G. H. Pertz, MGH SS, 16 (Leipzig, 1925)

Annales de l'abbaye royale de Saint-Pierre de Jumièges, ed. J. Laporte (Rouen, 1954)

Annales Fuldenses, ed. F. Kurze, MGH SRG, 7 (Hanover, 1978)

Annales Magdeburgenses, ed. G. H. Pertz, MGH SS, 16 (Hanover, 1859)

Annales Marbacenses, ed. M. Bloch, MGH SRG, 9 (Hanover, 1907)

Annales Monastici, 5 vols, ed. H. R. Luard, Rolls Series, 36 (London, 1864–69)

Annales Palidenses, ed. G. H. Pertz, MGH SS, 16 (Stuttgart, 1994)

Gli Annales Pisani di Bernardo Maragone, ed. M. Lupo Gentile, RIS, 6, pt ii (Bologna, 1936)

Annales Quedlinburgenses, ed. G. H. Pertz, MGH SS, 3 (Hanover, 1839)

Annales Regni Francorum, ed. F. Kurze, MGH SRG, 6 (Hanover, 1895)

Annales Ryenses, ed. J. M. Lappenberg, MGH SS, 16

Les annales de Saint-Pierre et de Saint-Amand, ed. P. Grierson (Brussels, 1937)

Annales Sancti Disibodi, ed. G. Waitz, MGH SS, 17 (Leipzig, 1925)

Annales Stadenses, ed. J. M. Lappenberg, MGH SS, 16 (Stuttgart, 1994)

Annales Stederburgenses, ed. G. H. Pertz, MGH SS, 16 (Stuttgart, 1994)

Annales Valdemarii, in *Danmarks Middelalderlige Annaler*, ed. E. Kroman (Copenhagen, 1980)

Annales Xantenses et Annales Vedastini, ed. B. de Simson, MGH SRG, 12 (Hanover, 1909)

Annali Genovesi di Caffaro e de suoi continuatori, 4 vols, ed. L. T. Belgrano (Rome, 1890–1929)

The Annals of Fulda, tr. T. Reuter (Manchester, 1991)

The Annals of St Bertin, tr. Janet L. Nelson (Manchester, 1991)

Anselmi Gesta episcoporum Leodiensium, ed. R. Koepke, MGH SS, 7 (Leipzig, 1925)

Anselmi gestorum episcoporum Leodiensium recensione altera, MGH SS, 14 (Hanover, 1883)

Arnoldi Chronica Slavorum, tr. J. M. Lappenberg, MGH SS, 21 (Hanover, 1869; repr. Stuttgart, 1988)

Gli atti del commune di Milano, ed. C. Manaresi (Milan, 1919)

The Bayeux Tapestry, 2nd edn, ed. F. M. Stenton (London, 1965)

Beowulf, tr. Michael Alexander (London, 2003)

Boso's Life of Alexander III, tr. G. M. Ellis (Oxford, 1973)

Brunonis liber de bello Saxonico, MGH SS, 5, ed. G. H. Pertz (Stuttgart, 1985)

Brut y Tywysogyon or The Chronicle of the Princes, tr. T. Jones (Cardiff, 1952)

Calendar of Ancient Correspondence concerning Wales, ed. J. G. Edwards (Cardiff, 1935)

The Carmen de Hastingae Proelio, ed. Catherine Morton and Hope Muntz (Oxford, 1972)

Carolingian Chronicles, ed. B. W. Scholz (Minnesota, 1970)

Catalogue des actes des comtes de Toulouse, 4 vols, ed. E. G. Leonard (Paris, 1932)

Catherine of Siena, *The Orcherd of Syon*, ed. Phyllis Hodgson and Gabriel M. Liegey (Oxford, 1966).

The Charters of Duchess Constance of Brittany and Her Family 1171–1221, ed. J. Everard and M. Jones (Woodbridge, 1999)

Chartes et documents de Saint-Benigne de Dijon, 2 vols, ed. G. Chevrier, and M. Chaume (Dijon, 1943)

Chronica Magistri Rogeri de Hovedene, 4 vols, ed. W. Stubbs, Rolls Series, 51 (London, 1868–71)

Chronica Regia Colonienses, ed. G. Waitz, MGH SRG, 18 (Hanover, 1880)

The Chronicle of Battle Abbey, ed. E. Searle (Oxford, 1981)

The Chronicle of the Election of Hugh Abbot of Bury St Edmunds and Later Bishop of Ely, ed. R. M. Thomson (Oxford, 1974)

The Chronicle of Jocelyn of Brakelond, ed. H. E. Butler (London, 1949)

The Chronicle of John of Worcester, 3 vols, ed. R. R. Darlington and P. McGurk (Oxford, 1995–98)

The Chronicle of Melrose, ed. A. O. and M. O. Anderson (London, 1936)

The Chronicle of Richard of Devizes of the Time of King Richard the First, ed. John T. Appleby (London, 1963)

The Chronicle of Richard, Prior of Hexham, in *Chronicles of the Reigns of Stephen, Henry II and Richard I*, 4 vols, ed. R. Howlett, Rolls Series, 82 (London, 1884–89), iii, 139–78

The Chronicle of Robert Torigni, Abbot of Mont St Michel, in *Chronicles of the Reigns of Stephen, Henry II and Richard I*, 4 vols, ed. R. Howlett, Rolls Series, 82 (London, 1884–89), iv

Chronicle of the Third Crusade, tr. Helen J. Nicholson (Aldershot, 1997)

The Chronicles of Ralph Niger, ed. Robert Anstruther (New York, 1967)

Chronicles of the Vikings, ed. R. I. Page (London, 1995)

Chronicon Romualdi Salernitani, ed. C. A. Garufi, RIS, 7, pt I (Bologna, 1935–43)

Chronique des abbés de Fontenelle (Saint-Wadrille), ed. Pascal Pradié (Paris, 1999)

Chronique de Jordan Fantosme, in *Chronicles of the Reigns of Stephen, Henry II and Richard I*, 4 vols, ed. R. Howlett, Rolls Series 82 (London, 1884–89), iii, 202–377

La chronique de Saint Hubert, ed. K. Hanquet (Brussels, 1906)

Chronique de Saint-Pierre-le-Vif de Sens, dite de Clarius, ed. and tr. R.-H. Bautier (Paris, 1979)

Chronique des comtes d'Anjou et des seigneurs d'Amboise, ed. L. Halphen and R. Poupardin (Paris, 1913)

Chronique française des rois de France par un anonyme de Béthune, in *Recueil des historiens des gaules et de la France*, 24, pt 2, ed. M. Bouquet et al. (Paris, 1904)

La chronique de Gislebert de Mons, ed., L. Vanderkindere (Brussels, 1904)

La chronique de Saint-Hubert, ed. K. Hanquet (Brussels, 1906)

Close Rolls of Henry III, 1231–4 (London, 1902–38)

Codice diplomatico della repubblica di Genova, 4 vols, ed. C. Imperiale di Santangelo (Genoa, 1936–42)

Continuatio Beccensis, in *Chronicles of the Reigns of Stephen, Henry II and Richard I*, 4 vols, ed. R. Howlett, Rolls Series, 82 (London, 1884–89), iv, 317–27

The Correspondence of Pope Gregory VII, tr. E. Emerton (New York, 1966)

The Correspondence of Thomas Becket, Archbishop of Canterbury, 1162–1170, 2 vols, ed. and tr. Anne Duggan (Oxford, 2000)

Curia Regis Rolls of the Reigns of Richard I, John and Henry III Preserved in the Public Record Office, 18 vols (London, 1922–)

Danmarks middelalderlige annaler, ed. E. Kroman (Copenhagen, 1980)

Dialogus de Scaccario and Constitutio Domus Regis, ed. C. Johnson (Oxford, 1983)

Diplomatarium Danicum, vol. I, parts i–vii, ed. C. A. Christensen (Copenhagen, 1975–93)

Diplomatic Documents Preserved in the Public Record Office, 1101–1272, vol. I, ed. Pierre Chaplais (London, 1964)

Documents Illustrative of English History in the Thirteenth and Fourteenth Centuries, ed. H. Cole (London, 1844)

Domesday Book: seu liber censualis Wilhemi primi, inter archivos regni in domo capitulari Westmonasterii asservatus, 2 vols, ed. A. Farley (London, 1783)

Dudo of St Quentin, *History of the Normans*, tr. E. Christiansen (Woodbridge, 1998)

Eadmer, *History of Recent Events in England*, tr. G. Bosanquet (London, 1964)

Eadmeri Historia Novorum in Anglia, ed. M. Rule, Rolls Series, 81 (London, 1884)

The Ecclesiastical History of Orderic Vitalis, 6 vols, ed. and tr. M. Chibnall (Oxford, 1969–81)

Ekkehardi IV Casus sancti Galli, ed. H. F. Haefele, Ausgewählte Quellen zur deutschen Geschichte des Mittelalters, 10 (Darmstadt, 1980)

English Historical Documents, vol. I, ed. Dorothy Whitelock; vol. II, ed. Dorothy Whitelock and G. W. Greenaway; vol. III, ed. H. Rothwell; vol. IV, ed. A. R. Myers (London, 1955–69)

English Medieval Diplomatic Practice Part I: Documents and Interpretation, 2 vols, ed. Pierre Chaplais (London, 1982)

English Royal Documents. King John – Henry VI, 1199–1461, ed. Pierre Chaplais (Oxford, 1971)

Epistolarum Hugoni de Campo-Florido, in *RHF*, xvi

Ermold le Noir, *Poème sur Louis le Pieux*, ed. E. Faral (Paris, 1932)

Foedera, conventiones, litterae et cuiuscunque generis acta publica, 7 vols, ed. T. Rymer (London, 1816–69)

Flodoard, *Annales 919–966*, ed. Ph. Lauer (Paris, 1906)

Flores Historiarum Rogeri Wendoveri, ed. H. G. Hewlett, Rolls Series, 84 (London, 1886–89)

Foreign Relations of the United States, Diplomatic Papers, the Conferences at Cairo and Teheran, 1943 (Washington D.C., 1961)

The Fourth Book of the Chronicle of Fredegar with its Continuations, tr. J. M. Wallace-Hadrill (London, 1960)

Galbert of Bruges, *Histoire du meurtre de Charles le Bon*, ed. Henri Pirenne (Paris, 1891) Available in English as *The Murder of Charles the Good*, ed. J. B. Ross (Toronto, 1982)

The Gascon Calendar of 1322, ed. G. P. Cuttino (London, 1949)

Geoffrey of Monmouth, *The History of the Kings of Britain*, tr. L. Thorpe (London, 1966)

Geoffroi Villehardouin, *La Conquête de Constantinople*, in *Historiens et chroniqueurs du Moyen Âge*, tr. E. Pognon (Paris, 1952)

Gesta Chuonradi II Imperatoris Wiponis, in *Die Werke Wipos*, ed. H. Bresslau, 3rd edn, MGH SRG, 61 (Hanover, 1915, repr. 1977)

Gesta episcoporum Cameracensium, ed. L. C. Bethmann, MGH SS, 7 (Leipzig, 1925)

The Gesta Guillelmi of William of Poitiers, ed. and tr. R. H. C. Davis and M. Chibnall (Oxford, 1998)

The Gesta Normannorum Ducum of William of Jumièges, Orderic Vitalis and Robert of Torigni, ed. E. M. C. van Houts (Oxford, 1992–95)

Gesta Regis Henrici Secundi Benedicti Abbatis, 2 vols, ed. W. Stubbs, Rolls Series, 49 (London, 1867)

Gesta Stephani, ed. K. R. Potter (London, 1955)

Giraldus Cambrensis Opera, 8 vols, ed. J. S. Brewer et al., Rolls Series, 21 (London, 1861–91)

Gotifredi Viterbiensis Gesta Friderici I et Heinrici VI, ed. G. H. Pertz, MGH SRG, 30 (Hanover, 1978)

Les grandes chroniques de Saint Denis, 6 vols, ed. M. Paulin (Paris, 1836–38)

Gregorii Episcopi Turonensis Liber de miraculis beati Andreae Apostoli, ed. Max Bonnet, MGH SSRM, 1, part II (Hanover, 1951)

Gregorii Episcopi Turonensis Libri Historiarum X, ed. Bruno Krusch and Wilhelm Levison, MGH SSRM, 1, part I (Hanover, 1951)

Guillelmi I. Regis Diplomata, ed. H. Enzensberger (Cologue, 1996)

Hamburgisches Urkundenbuch, 3 vols, ed. J. M. Lappenberg et al. (Hamburg, 1842–1953)

Heinrici Chronicon Lyvonie, ed. Wilhelm Arndt, MGH SS, 23 (Hanover, 1874; repr. Stuttgart, 1986) Available in English as *Henricus Lettus, The Chronicle of Henry of Livonia*, tr. James A. Brundage (New York, 2003)

Helmold, *The Chronicle of the Slavs*, ed. F. J. Tschan (New York, 1966)

Helmoldi Presbyteri Bozoviensis Chronica Slavorum, 3rd edn ed. B. Schmeidler, MGH SRG, 32 (Hanover, 1937)

Hemingi Chartularium Ecclesiae Wigornensis, 2 vols, ed. T. Hearne (Oxford, 1723)

Henry of Huntingdon, *Historia Anglorum*, ed. Diana E. Greenway (Oxford, 1996)

Herimanni Augiensis Chronicon, ed. G. H. Pertz, MGH SS, 5 (Leipzig, 1925)

Histoire de Guillaume le Maréchal, 3 vols, ed. P. Meyer (Paris, 1891–1901)

Histoire des ducs de Normandie et des rois d'Angleterre, ed. F. Michel (Paris, 1840)

Historia de expeditione Friderici imperatoris et quidam alii rerum gestarum fonts eiusdem expeditionis, ed. A. Chroust, MGH SRG, new ser., 5 (Berlin, 1928)

The Historia Regum Britanniae of Geoffrey of Monmouth, ed. A. Griscom and tr. Robert Ellis Jones (London, 1929)

The Historia Rerum Anglicarum of William of Newburgh, in *Chronicles of the Reigns of Stephen, Henry II and Richard I*, 4 vols, ed. R. Howlett, Rolls Series (London, 1884–89); i–ii.

Historia Welforum, ed. Erich König (Stuttgart, 1938; repr. Sigmaringen, 1978)

The Historical Works of Gervase of Canterbury, 2 vols, ed. W. Stubbs, Rolls Series, 73 (London, 1879–80)

The Historical Works of Master Ralph de Diceto, 2 vols, ed. W. Stubbs, Rolls Series, 68 (London, 1876)

The History of the Archbishops of Hamburg-Bremen, ed. F. J. Tschan (New York, 1959)

The History of the Tyrants of Sicily by 'Hugo Falcandus' 1154–69, tr. Graham A. Loud and Thomas Wiedemann (Manchester, 1998)

The History of William Marshal, ed. A. J. Holden and S. Gregory (London, 2002)

Houts, E. M. C. van, 'The Anglo-Flemish Treaty of 1101', *ANS*, 21 (1999)

Hugh the Chanter, *The History of the Church of York 1066–1127*, ed. C. Johnson (Oxford, 1990)

Imperial Lives and Letters, tr. T. Mommsen, and K. F. Morrison (London, 1967)

Isidori Hispalensis Episcopi Etymologiarum sive originum libri XX, 2 vols, ed. W. M. Lindsay (Oxford, 1911)

Itinerarium Peregrinorum et Gesta Regis Ricardi, in *Chronicles and Memorials of the Reign of Richard I*, 2 vols, ed. W. Stubbs, Rolls Series, 38 (London, 1864), i.

Johannis de Fordun chronica gentis Scotorum, ed. W. Skene, 2 vols (Edinburgh, 1871–72)

John of Salisbury, *Historia Pontificalis*, tr. M. Chibnall (Oxford, 1965)

Knytlingasaga, tr. H. Pàlsson and P. Edwards (Odense, 1986)

Lamberti Hersfeldensis annales, MGH SS, 5, ed. G. H. Pertz (Stuttgart, 1985)

Leges Henrici Primi, ed. L. J. Downer (Oxford, 1972)

The Letters of John of Salisbury, 2 vols, ed. W. J. Millor and H. E. Butler; revised by C. N. L. Brooke (Oxford, 1979–86)

The Letters of Pope Innocent III concerning England and Wales. A Calendar with an Appendix of Texts, ed. C. R. Cheney and Mary G. Cheney (Oxford, 1967)

Le Liber Pontificalis, 3 vols, ed. L. Duchesne (Paris, 1886)

The Lives of Thomas Becket, tr. Michael Staunton (Manchester, 2001)

Loud, G. A., 'A Calendar of the Diplomas of the Norman Princes of Capua', in his *Conquerors and Churchmen in Norman Italy* (Aldershot, 1999)

Luchaire, A., *Louis VI, le gros. Annales de sa vie et de son règne (1081–1137)* (Paris, 1890)

Magna Carta, 2nd edn, ed. J. C. Holt (Cambridge, 1992)

Major Peace Treaties of Modern History, ed. A. Toynbee, F. L. Israel and E. Chill (New York, 1967)

Materials for the History of Thomas Becket, Archbishop of Canterbury, 7 vols, ed. J. C. Robertson, Rolls Series, 67 (London, 1875–85)

Matthaei Parisiensis Chronica Maiora, 7 vols, ed. H. R. Luard, Rolls Series, 57 (London, 1872–84)

Mémoires de sire Philippe de Commynes, in *Historiens et chroniqueurs du Moyen Âge*, ed. and tr. E. Pognon (Bruges, 1952)

Memoriale Fratris Walteri de Coventria, 2 vols, ed. W. Stubbs, Rolls Series, 58 (London, 1875)

Memorials of Saint Dunstan, Archbishop of Canterbury, ed. W. Stubbs, Rolls Series, 63 (London, 1874)

MGH Capitularia Regum Francorum, vol. i and ii, ed. A. Boretius and V. Krause (Hanover, 1840)

De Moribus et Actibus Primorum Normannorum Ducum auctore Dudone Sancti Quintini decano, ed. J. Lair (Caen, 1865)

Mubadele: An Ottoman–Russian Exchange of Ambassadors, ed. N. Itzkowitz and M. Mote (Chicago, 1970)

Nithard, *Histoire des fils de Louis le pieux*, ed. and tr. Ph. Lauer (Paris, 1964)

Nithard's Histories, in *Carolingian Chronicles*, tr. B. W. Scholz (Minnesota, 1972)

Odo of Deuil, *De profectione Ludovici VII in orientem*, ed. Virginia Gingerick Berry (New York, 1948)

Oeuvres de Rigord et de Guillaume le Breton historiens de Philippe-Auguste, 2 vols, ed. H. F. Delaborde (Paris, 1882–85)

Ottonis de Sancto Blasio Chronica, ed. A. Hofmeister, MGH SRG, 47 (Hanover, 1912)

Ottonis et Rahewini Gesta Friderici I Imperatoris, ed. G. Waitz, MGH SRG, 46 (Hanover, 1884) Available in English as *The Deeds of Frederick Barbarossa*, ed. C. C. Mierow (Toronto, 1994)

Ottonis Morena et continuatorum Historia Friderici I, ed. F. Güterbock, MGH SRG, new ser., 7 (Berlin, 1930)

De Pace Veneta Relatio, in R. M. Thomson, 'An English Eyewitness Account of the Peace of Venice, 1177', *Speculum*, 50 (1975)

Patrologia Latina, 221 vols, ed. J.-P. Migne, complete electronic version of 1st edition of Migne's *PL*, 1844–55 (Cambridge, 1995)

Philippi regis constitutiones, ed. L. Weiland, MGH Const., 2 (Hanover, 1896)

Pipe Rolls: Citations to Pipe Rolls are to the regnal years of the reigning kings and published by the Pipe Roll Society, London

The Poems of the Troubadour Bertran de Born, ed. W. D. Paden, T. Sankovitch and P. H. Stablein (Berkeley, 1986)

Radulphi de Coggeshall Chronicon Anglicanum, ed. J. Stevenson, Rolls Series, 66 (London, 1875)

Rangerius of Lucca, *Vita Metrica*, ed. E. Sackur, G. Schwartz and B. Schmeidler, MGH SS, 30, part ii (Leipzig, 1934)

Raoul Glaber, *Historiarum Libri Quinque*, in *Opera*, ed., J. France (Oxford, 1989)

De Rebus Gestis Rogerii Calabrie et Siciliae Comitis et Roberti Guiscardi Ducis fratris ejus auctore Gaufredo Malaterra, ed. E. Pontieri, RIS, 2 (Bologna, 1927)

Recueil des actes de Charles III le Simple, roi de France (893–923), ed. F. Lot and Ph. Lauer (Paris, 1949)

Recueil des actes d'Henri II roi d'Angleterre et duc de Normandie concernant provinces françaises et affaires de la France, 4 vols, ed. L. Delisle (Paris, 1906–27)

Recueil des actes de Louis VI, roi de France (1108–1137), 4 vols, ed. R.-H. Bautier and Jean Dufour (Paris, 1992)

Recueil des actes de Philippe Auguste, 4 vols, ed. H. F. Delaborde (Paris, 1916–79)

Recueil des actes des comtes de Ponthieu (1026–1279), ed. C. Brunel (Paris, 1930)

Recueil des actes des comtes de Provence appartenant à la maison de Barcelone. Alphonse II et Raimond Bérenger V, 2 vols, ed. F. Benoit (Monaco, 1925)

Recueil des actes des ducs de Normandie (911–1066), ed. Marie Fauroux (Caen, 1961)

Recueil des actes des ducs normands d'Italie. Le premier ducs (1046–1087), ed. L. R. Menager (Bari, 1980)

Recueil des historiens des gaules et de la France, 24 vols, ed. M. Bouquet et al. (Paris, 1840–1914)

Regesta Regum Anglo-Normannorum, vol. 1, ed. H. W. C. Davis and R. J. Whitwell; vol. 2, ed. C. Johnson and H. A. Cronne; vol. 3, ed. H. A. Cronne and R. H. C. Davis; vol. 4, ed. David Bates (Oxford, 1913–97)

Regestes de Thierry d'Alsace, comte de Flandre, ed. H. Coppieters Stochove (Gand, 1901)

Das Register Gregors VII, 2 vols, ed. F. Caspar, MGH Ep., 2 (Berlin, 1955)

Richer, Histoire de France 888–995, 2 vols, ed. R. Latouche (Paris, 1930–7)

Robert de Clari, *La Conquête de Constantinople*, ed. Ph. Lauer (Paris, 1924)

Rotuli Chartarum in Turri Londiniensi Asservati, 2 vols, ed. T. Duffus Hardy (London, 1837)

Rotuli de Liberate ac de Misis et Praestitis Regnante Johannes, ed. T. Duffus Hardy (London, 1844)

Rotuli Litterarum Clausarum in Turri Londiniensi Asservati, 2 vols, ed. T. Duffus Hardy (London, 1833–44)

Rotuli Litterarum Patentium in Turri Londiniensi Asservati, ed. T. Duffus Hardy (London, 1835)

The Ruodlieb, tr. Gordon B. Ford (Leiden, 1965)

Saxo Grammaticus, *Danorum Regum Heroumque Historia, Books X–XVI*, 3 vols, ed. Eric Christiansen, BAR International Series, 118 (Oxford, 1981)

Selected Letters of Pope Innocent III concerning England 1198–1216, ed. C. R. Cheney and W. H. Semple, (London, 1953)

Select Historical Documents of the Middle Ages, ed. E. F. Henderson (New York, 1965)

Sigeberti Continuatio Aquicincta, MGH SS, 6, ed. G. H. Pertz (Stuttgart, 1986)

The Song of Roland, tr. D. D. R. Owen (London, 1972)

Stephani Rotomagensis monachi Beccensis poema cui titulus Draco Normannicus, in *Chronicles of the Reigns of Stephen, Henry II and Richard I*, 4 vols, ed. R. Howlett, Rolls Series, 82 (London, 1884–89), ii, 589–779

Suger, *The Deeds of Louis the Fat*, tr. Richard Cusimano and John Moorhead (Washington, 1992)

Suger, *Vie de Louis VI le gros*, ed. Henri Waquet (Paris, 1964)

Symeon of Durham, *Opera Omnia*, ed. T. Arnold (London, 1882–85)

Tancredi et Willemi III Regum Diplomata, ed. H. Zielinski (Cologne, 1982)

Thietmari Merseburgensis Episcopi Chronicon, ed. R. Holtzmann, MGH SRG, n.s., 9 (Berlin, 1955)

Treaty Rolls preserved in the Public Record Office, vol. I, ed. Pierre Chaplais (London, 1972)

The Tree of Battles of Honoré Bonet, tr. G. W. Coopland (Liverpool, 1949)

Two of the Saxon Chronicles Parallel, 2 vols, ed. C. Plummer (Oxford, 1892–89; repr. 1952)

Die Urkunden Friedrichs I, 4 vols, ed. H. Appelt (Hanover, 1975–90)

Die Urkunden Heinrichs des Löwen, 2 vols, ed. K. Jordan (Stuttgart,1957–60)

Urkunden zur älteren Handels- und Staatsgeschichte der Republik Venedig, ed. G. L. Tafel and G. M. Thomas (Vienna, 1856–7; repr. Amsterdam: 1967)

Vita Heinrici IV. Imperatoris, ed. W. Eberhard, MGH SRG, 58 (Hanover, 1990)

Walter Map, *De Nugis Curialium*, ed. and tr. M. R. James, revised by C. N. L. Brooke and R. A. B. Mynors (Oxford, 1983)

Welsh Records in Paris, ed. T. Matthews (Carmarthen, 1910)

Widukindi monachi Corbeiensis Rerum Gestarum Saxonicarum Libri Tres, ed. H. E. Lohmann and Paul Hirsch, MGH SRG, 60 (Hanover, 1935)

William of Malmesbury, *Gesta Regum Anglorum*, ed. R. A. B. Mynors and M. Winterbottom (Oxford, 1998)

William of Malmesbury, *Historia Novella*, ed. K. R. Potter (London, 1955)

William of Newburgh, *The History of English Affairs, Book I*, ed. and tr. P. G. Walsh and M. J. Kennedy (Warminster, 1988)

The Works of Sven Aggesen, tr. Eric Christiansen (London, 1992)

Secondary works

Abels, Richard, 'Paying the Danegeld: Anglo-Saxon Peacemaking with the Vikings', in *War and Peace in Ancient and Medieval History*, ed. Philip de Souza and John France (Cambridge, 2008)

'King Alfred's Peace-making Strategies with the Vikings', *HSJ*, 3 (1991)

——*Lordship and Military Obligation in Anglo-Saxon England* (Berkeley, 1988)

Abulafia, D., *Italy in the Central Middle Ages 1000–1300* (Oxford, 2004)

——*Frederick II* (Cambridge, 1988)

Adolf, Antony, *Peace. A World History* (Cambridge, 2009)

Althoff, G., *Family, Friends and Followers. Political and Social Bonds in Early Medieval Europe* (Cambridge, 2004)

——'The Variability of Rituals in the Middle Ages', in *Medieval Concepts of the Past: Ritual, Memory, Historiography*, ed. Gerd Althoff, Johannes Fried and Patrick J. Geary (Cambridge, 2002)

——'Satisfaction: Amicable Settlement of Conflicts in the Middle Ages', in *Ordering Medieval Society. Perspectives on Intellectual and Practical Modes of Shaping Social Relations*, ed. Bernhard Jussen, tr. Pamela Selwyn (Philadelphia, 2001)

——'Friendship and Political Order', in *Friendship in Medieval Europe*, ed. J. Haseldine (Stroud, 1999)

——'*Amicitiae* [Friendships] as Relationships between States and People', in *Debating the Middle Ages*, ed. Lester K. Little and Barbara H. Rosenwein (Oxford, 1998)

——'Das Privileg der deditio. Formen gütlicher Konfliktbeendigung in der mittelalterlichen Adelsgesellschaft', in Althoff, *SP*

——'Demonstration und Inszenierung', in Althoff, *SP*

——'Königsherrschaft und Konlifktbewältigung im 10. und 11. Jahrhundert', in Althoff, *SP*

——*Spielregeln der politik im Mittelalter: Kommunikation in Frieden und Fehde* (Darmstadt, 1997)

——*Verwandte, Freunde und Getreue. Zum politischen Stellenwert der Gruppenbindung im früheren Mittelalter* (Darmstadt, 1990)

Amelotti, Mario, and Costamagna, Giorgio, *Alle origini del notariato italiano* (Rome, 1975)

Andersson, T. M., 'The Viking Policy of Ethelred the Unready', *SS*, 59 (1987)

Angenendt, Arnold, 'Das geistliche Bündnis der Päpste mit den Karolingern (754–796)', *Historisches Jahrbuch*, 100 (1980)

Arnold, B., *Princes and Territories in Medieval Germany* (Cambridge, 1991)

Arnoux, Mathieu, 'Before the *Gesta Normannorum Ducum* and Beyond Dudo: Some Evidence on Early Norman Historiography', *ANS*, 22 (2000)

Attreed, Lorraine, 'The Politics of Welcome. Ceremonies and Constitutional Development in Later Medieval English Towns', in *City and Spectacle in Medieval Europe*, ed. Barbara A. Hanawalt and Kathryn L. Reyerson (Minneapolis, 1994)

Aurell, Martin, 'Le meurtre de Thomas Becket: les gestes d'un martyre', in *Bischofsmord im Mittelalter*, ed. Natalie Fryde and Dirk Reitz (Göttingen, 2003)

Babcock, Robert S., 'Clients of the Angevin King: Rhys ap Gruffudd and Ruaidri Ua Conchobair Compared', in *Ireland and Wales in the Middle Ages*, ed. Karen Jankulak and Jonathan M. Wooding (Dublin, 2007)

Bachrach, Bernard S., 'The Northern Origins of the Peace Movement at Le Puy in 975', *Historical Reflections*, 14 (1987), repr. in his *State-building in Medieval France: Studies in Early Angevin History* (Aldershot, 1995)

Bagge, Sverre, 'On the Far Edge of Dry Land: Scandinavian and European Culture in the Middle Ages', in *Scandinavia and Europe 800–1350. Contact, Conflict, and Coexistence*, ed. Jonathan Adams and Katherine Holman (Turnhout, 2004)

——*Kings, Politics, and the Right Order of the World in German Historiography c.950–1150* (Leiden, 2002)

——'Ideas and Narrative in Otto of Fresing's *Gesta Friderici*', *JMH*, 22 (1996)

Baker, Derek, *Portraits and Documents: The Early Middle Ages 871–1216* (London, 1966)

Baldwin, John W., *The Government of Philip Augustus* (Los Angeles, 1986)

Barber, Malcolm, *The Two Cities: Medieval Europe 1050–1320* (London, 1992)

Barber, Richard, *Bestiary* (Woodbridge, 1999)

Barbour, N., 'The Embassy Sent by King John of England to Miramolin, King of Morocco', *Al-Andalus*, 25 (1960)

Barraclough, G., tr., *Medieval Germany 911–1250. Essays by German Historians*, 2 vols (Oxford, 1938)

Barrow, G. W. S., *The Kingdom of the Scots* (London, 1973)

Barrow, Julia, 'Friends and Friendship in Anglo-Saxon Charters', in *Friendship in Medieval Europe*, ed. J. Haseldine (Stroud, 1999)

Barthélemy, Dominique, *L'an mil et la paix de Dieu: la France chrétienne et féodale, 980–1060* (Paris, 1999)

——'La mutation feodale a-t-elle eu lieu?', *Annales: Economies, Sociétés, Civilisations*, 47 (1992)

Bartlett, Robert, *The Making of Europe. Conquest, Colonization and Cultural Change 950–1350* (London, 1993)

Bates, D., *Normandy before 1066* (London, 1982)

Bautier, R.-H., 'Anne de Kiev, reine de France, et la politique royale au XIe siècle', *Revue des études slaves*, 57 (1985)

——*La France de Philippe Auguste: le temps des mutations* (Paris, 1982)

Benediktsson, Jakob, 'Denmark', in *Medieval Scandinavia: An Encyclopedia*, ed. Phillip Pulsiano et al. (New York, 1993)

Benham, J. E. M., 'A Changing Perception of War: The Role of Peace Treaties from the Tenth to the Early Thirteenth Centuries', in *Battle and Bloodshed: Representations of War in the Middle Ages*, ed. Lorna Bleach and Katariina Närä (forthcoming, 2011)

——'Anglo-French Peace Conferences in the Twelfth Century', *ANS* 27 (2005)

——'Philip Augustus and the Angevin Empire: the Scandinavian Connexion', *Mediaeval Scandinavia*, 14 (2004)

——'Walter Map and Ralph Glaber: Intertextuality and the Construction of Memories of Peacemaking', *Citation, Intertextuality and Memory in the Middle Ages and Renaissance, 2: Cross-Disciplinary Perspectives on Medieval Culture*, ed. Giuliano di Bacco and Yolanda Plumley (forthcoming, 2011)

Benjamin, R., 'A Forty Years War: Toulouse and the Plantagenets, 1156–96', *Historical Research*, 61 (1988)

Benton, J. F., 'Suger's Life and Personality', in *Culture, Power and Personality in Medieval France*, ed. T. N. Bisson (London, 1991)

Berg, Dieter, *England und der Kontinent. Studien zur auswärtigen Politik der anglonormannischen Könige im 11. und 12. Jahrhundert* (Bochum, 1987)

Bernhardt, John, W., *Itinerant Kingship and Royal Monasteries in Early Medieval Germany c. 936–1075* (Cambridge, 1993)

Bertelli, Sergio, *The King's Body: Sacred Rituals of Power in Medieval and Early Modern Europe*, tr. R. Burr Litchfield (University Park, Pennsylvania, 2001)

Biddle, M., 'Seasonal Festivals and Residence: Winchester, Westminster and Gloucester in the Tenth to the Twelfth Century', *ANS*, 8 (1986)

Bijsterveld, Arnoud-Jan, 'The Medieval Gift as Agent of Social Bonding and Political Power: A Comparative Approach', in *Medieval Transformations. Texts, Power and Gifts in Context*, ed. Esther Cohen and Mayke B. de Jong (Leiden, 2001)

Bisson, T., 'The Organized Peace in Southern France and Catalonia, ca. 1140–ca. 1233', *American Historical Review*, 82 (1977)

Black, Jeremy, *Maps and Politics* (London, 1997)

Bloch, Marc, *Feudal Society*, tr. L. A. Manyon (London, 1961)

Boemeke, Manfred F., Feldman, Gerald D. and Glaser, Elisabeth, eds, *The Treaty of Versailles – A Reassessment after 75 Years* (Cambridge, 1998)

Bolton, Brenda, 'Philip Augustus and John: Two Sons in Innocent III's Vineyard?', *Studies in Church History*, 9 (1991)

Bossy, John, 'The Mass as a Social Institution', *Past & Present*, 100 (1983)

Bouard, Michel de, 'Sur les origines de la Trève de Dieu en Normandie', *Annales de Normandie*, 9 (1959)

Bouchard, C. B., *Strong of Body, Brave and Noble: Chivalry and Society in Medieval France* (London, 1998)

Bouhout, J. P., 'Explications du rituel baptismal à l'époque carolingienne', *Revue des études augustiniennes*, 24 (1978)

Boussard, Jacques, 'Philippe Auguste et les Plantagenêts', in *La France de Philippe Auguste: le temps des mutations*, ed. R. H. Bautier (Paris, 1982)

Boyer, M. N., *Medieval French Bridges* (Cambridge, 1976)

Bradbury, Jim, *Philip Augustus, King of France 1180–1223* (London, 1998)

——'Battles in England and Normandy, 1066–1154', in *Anglo-Norman Warfare*, ed. M. Strickland (Woodbridge, 1992)

——*The Medieval Siege* (Woodbridge, 1992)

Brooke, C. N. L., *The Medieval Idea of Marriage* (Oxford, 1989)

Brook-Shepherd, Gordon, *November 1918* (London, 1989)

Brooks, N., 'Medieval Bridges: a Window onto Changing Concepts of State Power', *HSJ*, 7 (1995)

Brown, E. A. R., '*La Grant Feste*. Philip the Fair's Celebration of the Knighting of His Sons in Paris at Pentecost 1313', in *City and Spectacle in Medieval Europe*, ed. Barbara A. Hanawalt and Kathryn L. Reyerson (Minneapolis, 1994)

Brown, E.A.R., 'The Tyranny of a Construct: Feudalism and Historians of Medieval Europe', *American Historical Review*, 79 (1974)

Brown, R. Allen, ed., *History of the King's Works*, 2 vols (London, 1963)

Brugnoli, Giorgio, 'Gli auctores di Saxo', in *Saxo Grammaticus: Tra storiografia e letteratura*, ed. Carlo Santini (Rome, 1992)

Brühl, C-R., *Fodrum, Gistum, Servitium Regis*, 2 vols (Cologne, 1968)

——*Palatium und Civitas: Studien zur Profantopographie spätantiker Civitates vom 3. bis zum 13. Jahrhundert*, 2 vols (Cologne, 1975)

Brundage, James, A., *Medieval Canon Law* (London, 1995)

—— *Law, Sex and Christian Society in Medieval Europe* (Chicago, 1987)

Buc, Philippe, *The Dangers of Ritual* (Princeton, 2001)

—— 'Political Rituals and Political Imagination in the Medieval West from the Fourth Century to the Eleventh Century', in *The Medieval World*, ed. Peter Linehan and Janet L. Nelson (London, 2001)

—— 'Martyre et ritualité dans l'Antiquité Tardive. Horizons de l'écriture médiévale des rituels', *Annales*, 48 (1997)

Bugge, A., *Norges Historie*, 2 vols (Oslo, 1909–17)

Bull, Marcus, ed., *France in the Middle Ages* (Oxford, 2002)

Bullough, D.A., 'Games People Played: Drama and Ritual as Propaganda in Medieval Europe', *TRHS*, 5th ser., 24 (1974)

—— *Friends, Neighbours and Fellow-drinkers: Aspects of Community and Conflict in the Early Medieval West*, H. M. Chadwick Memorial Lectures 1 (Cambridge, 1991)

Bumke, Joachim *Courtly Culture. Literature and Society in the High Middle Ages*, tr. Thomas Dunlap (London, 2000)

Bur, M., 'Recherches sur la frontière dans la région mosane aux XIIe et XIIIe siècles', *Actes du 103e Congrès National des Sociétés Savantes: Principautés et territoires et Études d'Histoire Lorraine* (Paris, 1979)

——'La frontière entre la Champagne et la Lorraine du milieu du Xe siècle la fin du XIIe siècle', *Francia*, 4 (1976)

Burns, Robert I., 'How to End a Crusade: Techniques for Making Peace in the Thirteenth-century Kingdom of Valencia', *Military Affairs*, 35 (1971)

Büttner, H., 'Friedrich Barbarossa und Burgund', *Vorträge und Forschungen herausgegeben vom kustanzer Arbeitskreis für mittelalterliche Geschichte*, 12 (1968)

Byock, J., *Feud in the Icelandic Saga* (Berkeley, 1982)

Caille, J., 'Les seigneurs de Narbonne dans le conflit Toulouse-Barcelone au XIIe siècle', *Annales du Midi*, 97 (1985)

Calasso, Francesco, *La convenientia: contributo alla storia del contratto in Italia durante l'alto medioevo*, Biblioteca della Rivista di storia del diritto italiano, 9 (Bologna, 1932)

Cameron, Averil, 'The Construction of Court Ritual: the Byzantine *Book of Ceremonies*', in *Rituals of Royalty*, ed. David Cannadine and Simon Price (Cambridge, 1987).

Campbell, Miles W., 'Earl Godwin of Wessex and Edward the Confessor's Promise of the Throne to William of Normandy', *Traditio*, 28 (1972)

Carlsson, S. and Rosén, J., ed. *Den svenska historien* (Stockholm, 1966)

Carpenter, D. A. *The Struggle for Mastery: Britain 1066–1284* (London, 2003)

——'Abbot Ralph of Coggeshall's Account of the Last Years of King Richard and the First Years of King John', *EHR*, 113 (1998)

——*The Minority of Henry III* (London, 1990)

Carr, A. D., *Medieval Wales* (Basingstoke, 1995)

——'Anglo-Welsh Relations 1066–1282', in *England and Her Neighbours, 1066–1453*, ed. Michael Jones and Malcolm Vale (London, 1989)

Carré, Yannick, *Le baiser sur la bouche au Moyen Âge* (Paris, 1992)

Chaplais, Pierre, *English Diplomatic Practice in the Middle Ages* (London, 2003)

——'The Making of the Treaty of Paris (1259) and the Royal Style', *EHR*, 67 (1952), repr. in his *Essays in Medieval Diplomacy and Administration* (London, 1981)

—— 'English Diplomatic Documents to the End of Edward III's Reign', in *The Study of Medieval Records: Essays in Honour of Kathleen Major*, ed. D. A. Bullough and R. L. Story (Oxford, 1971)

—— 'Review of *The Office of Ambassador in the Middle Ages*', *History*, 53 (1968)

—— 'The Anglo-Saxon Chancery: from the Diploma to the Writ', *Journal Society of Archivists*, 3 (1966)

Charles-Edwards, T., 'Alliances, Godfathers, Treaties and Boundaries', in *Kings, Currency and Alliances: History and Coinage of Southern England in the Ninth Century*, ed. Mark A. S. Blackburn and David N. Dumville (Woodbridge, 1998)

Cheney, C.R., *Notaries Public in England in the Thirteenth and Fourteenth Century* (Oxford, 1972)

——*Hubert Walter* (London, 1967)

——'The Eve of Magna Carta', *BJRL*, 38 (1955–56)

Chénon, É., 'Le rôle juridique de l'*osculum* dans l'ancien droit français', *Mémoirs de la Société National des Antiquaires de France*, 6 (1919-23)

Cheyette, F., 'Suum Cuique Tribuere', *French Historical Studies*, 6 (1970)

Christelow, Stephanie Mooers, 'Chancellors and Curial Bishops: Ecclesiastical Promotion and Power in Anglo-Norman England', *ANS*, 22 (2000)

Christensen, Aksel E., 'Denmark between the Viking Age and the Time of the Valdemars', *Mediaeval Scandinavia*, 1 (1968)

Christiansen, Eric, *The Northern Crusades* (London, 1980)

Church, S. D., *The Household Knights of King John* (Cambridge, 1999)

——*King John: New Interpretations* (Woodbridge, 1999)

Cipollone, Giulio, 'Les trinitaires, redempteurs des captifs (1198)', in *La guerre et la violence au Moyen Age*, ed. Philippe Contamine and Olivier Guyotjeannin (Paris, 1996)

Clanchy, Michael, *From Memory to Written Record. England 1066-1307*, 2nd edn (London, 1992)

——'Law and Love in the Middle Ages', in *Disputes and Settlements: Law and Human Relations in the West*, ed. J. Bossy (Cambridge, 1983)

Clementi, D. R., 'The Relations between the Papacy, the Western Roman Empire and the Emergent Kingdom of Sicily and South Italy, 1050-1156', *Bulletino del istituto storica italiano per il Medio Evo*, 80 (1968)

——*Some Unnoticed Aspects of Emperor Henry VI's Conquest of the Norman Kingdom of Sicily* (Manchester, 1954)

Cleve, T.C. van, *The Emperor Frederick II of Hohenstaufen* (Oxford, 1972)

Coleman, Edward, 'Cities and Communes', in *Italy in the Central Middle Ages 1000-1300*, ed. David Abulafia (Oxford, 2004)

Contamine, Philippe, *La guerre au Moyen Âge* (Paris, 1980)

Cooper, Alan, ' "The feet of those who bark shall be cut off": Timorous Historians and the Personality of Henry I', *ANS*, 23 (2000)

Cooper, J. C., ed., *Brewer's Book of Myth and Legend* (London, 1992)

Corral, Fernando Luis, 'Alfonso VIII of Castile's Judicial Process at the Court of Henry II of England: an Effective and Valid Arbitration?', *Nottingham Mediaeval Studies*, 50 (2006)

Corner, D., 'The *Gesta Regis Henrici Secundi* and *Chronica* of Roger, Parson of Howden', *BIHR*, 56 (1983)

Cronne, H. A., *The Reign of Stephen 1135-54* (London, 1970)

Crouch, D., 'A Norman *conventio* and Bonds of Lordship in the Middle Ages', in *Law and Government in Medieval England and Normandy: Essays in Honour of Sir James Holt*, ed. G. Garnett and J. Hudson (Cambridge, 1994)

—— 'Earls and Bishops in Twelfth-century Leicestershire', *Nottingham Medieval Studies*, 37 (1993)

——*William Marshal: Court, Career and Chivalry in the Angevin Empire 1147-1219* (London, 1990)

Cuttino, G. P., *English Medieval Diplomacy* (Bloomington, 1985)

——*English Diplomatic Administration 1259-1339* (Oxford, 1971)

Dalton, Paul, 'Sites and Occasions of Peacemaking in England and Normandy, c. 900–c. 1150', *HSJ*, 16 (2005)

—'Churchmen and the Promotion of Peace in King Stephen's Reign', *Viator*, 31 (2000)

—— 'Civil War and Ecclesiastical Peace in the Reign of King Stephen', in *War and Society in Medieval and Early Modern Britain*, ed. Diana Dunn (Liverpool, 2000)

Davidsohn, Robert, *Philipp II August von Frankreich und Ingeborg* (Stuttgart, 1888)

Davies, J. D., ed., *A New Dictionary of Liturgy and Worship* (London, 1986)

Davis, R. H. C., 'Treaty between William earl of Gloucester and Roger Earl of Hereford', in *A Medieval Miscellany for Doris Mary Stenton*, ed. P. M. Barnes and C. F. Slade (London, 1962)

Davies, R. R, *From Medieval to Modern Wales. Historical Essays in Honour of Kenneth O. Morgan and Ralph A. Griffiths*, ed. R. R. Davies and Geraint H. Jenkins (Cardiff, 2004)

—— *The First English Empire. Power and Identities in the British Isles 1093–1343* (Oxford, 2000)

—'Frontier Arrangements in Fragmented Societies: Ireland and Wales', in *Medieval Frontier Societies*, ed. R. Bartlett and Angus MacKay (Oxford, 1989)

—*Conquest, Coexistence, and Change: Wales 1063–1415* (Oxford, 1987)

—— 'Henry I and Wales', in *Studies in Medieval History Presented to R. H. C. Davis*, ed. H. Mayr-Harting and R. I. Moore (London, 1985)

—— 'Law and National Identity in Thirteenth-century Wales', in *Welsh Society and Nationhood: Historical Essays Presented to Glanmor Williams*, ed. R. R. Davies, R. A. Griffiths et al. (Cardiff, 1984)

—— 'Kings, Lords and Liberties in the March of Wales, 1066–1272', *TRHS*, 5th Ser., 29 (1979)

Davies, Wendy and Fouracre, Paul, eds, *The Settlement of Disputes in Early Medieval Europe* (Cambridge, 1992)

Davies, Wendy, 'Suretyship in the *Cartulaire de Redon*', in *Lawyers and Laymen*, ed. T. M. Charles-Edwards, Morfydd E. Owen and D. B. Walters (Cardiff, 1986)

Deák, Francis, *Hungary at the Paris Peace Conference* (New York, 1972)

Dhondt, J., 'Henri Ier, l'Empire et l'Anjou (1043–1056)', *Revue belge de philologie et d'histoire*, 25 (1947).

—— 'Les relations entre la France et la Normandie sous Henri Ier', *Normannia*, 12 (1939)

Diggelmann, Lindsay, 'Marriage as a Tactical Response: Henry II and the Royal Wedding of 1160', *EHR*, 119 (2004)

Dillistone, F. W., *Christianity and Symbolism* (London, 1985)

Dillon, Viscount, 'Ransom', *Archaeological Journal*, 61 (1904)

Dockrill, Michael, and Fisher, John, ed., *The Paris Peace Conference, 1919. Peace without Victory?* (Basingstoke, 2001)

Douglas, D. C., 'The Rise of Normandy', in his *Time and the Hour: Some Collected Papers of David C. Douglas* (London, 1977)

——'Edward the Confessor, Duke William of Normandy and the English Succession', *EHR*, 68 (1953)

Duby, Georges, *The Legend of Bouvines*, tr. Catherine Tihanyi (Cambridge, 1990)

Duffy, Eamon, *The Stripping of the Altars* (New Haven, 1992)

Dunbabin, Jean, 'Henry II and Louis VII', in *Henry II: New Interpretations*, ed. Christopher Harper-Bill and Nicholas Vincent (Woodbridge, 2007)

——*France in the Making 843–1180* (Oxford, 1985)

Duncan, A. A. M., 'John King of England and the Kings of Scots', in *King John: New Interpretations*, ed. S. D. Church (Woodbridge, 1999)

Dupont, Florence, *Daily Life in Ancient Rome*, tr. C. Woodall (Oxford, 1992)

East, Gordon W., *An Historical Geography of Europe*, 4th edn (London, 1962)

Edmonds, Robin, *The Big Three: Churchill, Roosevelt and Stalin* (London, 1991)

Eickels, Klaus van, *Vom inszenierten Konsens zum systematisierten Konflikt* (Stuttgart, 2002)

——'*Homagium* and *Amicitia*: Rituals of Peace and Their Significance in the Anglo-French Negotiations of the Twelfth Century', *Francia*, 24 (1997)

Engels, Odilo, 'Friedrich Barbarossa und Dänemark', in *Friedrich Barbarossa. Handlungsspielräume und Wirkungsweisen des staufischen Kaisers*, ed. A. Haverkamp (Sigmaringen, 1992)

Enright, M. J., 'Lady with a Mead-cup: Ritual, Group Cohesion and Hierarchy in the Germanic Warband', *Frühmittelalterliche Studien*, 22 (1988)

Ermini, G., 'I trattati della guerra e della pace di Giovanni da Legnano', *Studi e memorie per la storia dell'Università di Bologna*, 8 (1923)

Everard, J., *Brittany and the Angevins: Province and Empire 1158–1203* (Cambridge, 2000)

Eyton, Robert W., *Court, Household and Itinerary of King Henry II* (Hildesheim, 1974)

Farrer, W., 'An Outline Itinerary of King Henry the First', *EHR*, 34 (1919)

Fasoli, Gina, 'Pace e guerra nell'alto medioevo', *Settimane di studio del centro italiano di studi sull'alto medioevo, XV, Ordinamenti militari in Occidente nell'alto medioevo* (Spoleto, 1968), repr. in her *Scritti di storia medievale* (Bologna, 1974)

——'Federico Barbarossa e le città lombarde,' *Vorträge und Forschungen*, 12 (1967), 121–42, repr. in *Scritti di storia medievale*

Ferguson, W., *Scotland's Relations with England. A Survey to 1707* (Edinburgh, 1977)

Fernandez-Armesto, F., 'Food, Glorious Food', *Sunday Times*, 22 December, 2002

Fichtenau, H., *Lebensordnungen des 10. Jahrhunderts*, 2 vols (Stuttgart, 1984) Available in English as *Living in the Tenth Century*, tr. Patrick J. Geary (Chicago, 1991)

Ficker, Julius, *Reinald von Dassel: Reichskanzler und Erzbischof von Köln 1156–1167* (Aalen, 1966)

Firth, Raymond, 'Verbal and Bodily Rituals of Greeting and Parting', in *The Interpretation of Ritual*, ed. J. S. La Fontaine (London: Tavistock, 1972)

Fleckenstein, Josef, *Early Medieval Germany*, tr. Bernard S. Smith (Oxford, 1978)

Flori, Jean, *L'Essor de la Chevalerie* (Geneva, 1980)

Folz, Robert, 'Eighth Century Concepts about the Roman Empire', in *The Coronation of Charlemagne. What Did It Signify?*, ed. Richard E. Sullivan (Boston, 1959)

Fouracre, P., 'Space, Culture and Kingdoms in Early Medieval Europe', in *The Medieval World*, ed. Peter Linehan and Janet L. Nelson (London, 2001)

—— '*Placita* and the Settlement of Disputes in Later Merovingian Francia', in *The Settlement of Disputes in Early Medieval Europe*, ed. Wendy Davies and Paul Fouracre (Cambridge, 1992)

Frame, Robin *The Political Development of the British Isles, 1100–1400* (Oxford, 1990)

France, John, 'Siege Convention in Western Europe and the Latin East', in *War and Peace in Ancient and Medieval History*, ed. Philip de Souza and John France (Cambridge, 2008)

——'Rodulfus Glaber and French Politics in the Early Eleventh Century', *Francia*, 16 (1989)

Friis-Jensen, Karsten, *Saxo Grammaticus as Latin Poet: Studies in the Verse Passages of the Gesta Danorum*, Analecta Romana, Instituti Danici, Supplementum, 14 (Rome, 1987)

Fryde E. B. e t al., eds. *Handbook of British Chronology*, 3rd edn (London, 1986)

Fryde, Natalie, 'King John and the Empire', in *King John: New Interpretations*, ed. S. D. Church (Woodbridge, 2000)

Ganshof, F.-L., *Feudalism*, 3rd edn (London, 1979)

——*The Middle Ages: A History of International Relations*, tr. R. I. Hall (London, 1971)

—— 'Note sur le premier traité Anglo-Flamand de Douvres', *Revue du Nord*, 40 (1958)

Geary, Patrick J., 'Land, Language and Memory in Europe 700–1100', *TRHS*, 6th ser., 9 (1999)

—— 'Sacred Commodities: the Circulation of Medieval Relics', in his *Living with the Dead in the Middle Ages* (Ithaca, 1994)

—— 'Vivre en conflit dans une France sans état: Typologie des méchanismes de règlement des conflits, 1050–1200', *Annales: Economies, Sociétés, Civilisations*, 41 (1986)

—— 'The Humiliation of Saints', in *Saints and their Cults*, ed. Stephen Wilson (Cambridge, 1983)

Gelling, M., *Signposts to the Past* (London, 1978)

Génicot, L., 'La ligne et zone: la frontière des principautés médiévales', in *Études sur les principautés lotharingiennes* (Louvain, 1975)

George, W. and Yapp, B., *The Naming of the Beasts: Natural History in the Medieval Bestiary* (London, 1991)

Gibson, Margaret and Nelson, Janet L., ed., *Charles the Bald: Court and Kingdom*, BAR International Series, 101 (Oxford, 1981)

Gilissen, John, 'Esquisse d'une histoire comparée des sûretés personnelles: essai de synthèse général', in *Les sûretés personnelles*, 3 vols, Recueil de la société Jean Bodin pour l'histoire comparative des institutions, 29 (Brussels, 1969–74)

Gillingham, John, 'The Meetings of the Kings of France and England, 1066–1204', in *Normandy and Its Neighbours, 900–1250*, ed. David Crouch and Kathleen Thompson (forthcoming, 2010)

——'The King and the Castle: How Henry II Rebuilt His Reputation', *BBC History Magazine*, August (2009)

——'Doing Homage to the King of France', in *Henry II: New Interpretations*, ed. Christopher Harper-Bill and Nicholas Vincent (Woodbridge, 2007)

——'The Historian as Judge: William of Newburgh and Hubert Walter', *EHR*, 119 (2004)

——*The English in the Twelfth Century* (Woodbridge, 2000)

——'Conquering the Barbarians: War and Chivalry in Twelfth-century Britain and Ireland', in his *The English in the Twelfth Century* (Woodbridge, 2000)

——'Royal Newsletters, Forgeries and English Historians: Some Links between Court and History in the Reign of Richard I', in *La cour plantagenêt (1154–1204)*, ed. Martin Aurell (Poitiers, 2000)

——'The Beginnings of English Imperialism', in his *The English in the Twelfth Century* (Woodbridge, 2000)

——*Richard I* (New Haven, 1999)

——'Historians Without Hindsight: Coggeshall, Diceto and Howden on the Early Years of John's Reign', in *King John: New Interpretations*, ed. S. D. Church (Woodbridge, 1999)

—— 'The Travels of Roger of Howden and His Views of the Irish, Scots and Welsh', *ANS*, 20 (1998)

—— 'Henry II, Richard I and the Lord Rhys', *Peritia*, 10 (1996)

—— *Richard Coeur de Lion. Kingship, Chivalry and War in the Twelfth Century* (London, 1994)

—— 'Roger of Howden on Crusade', in his *Richard Coeur de Lion* (London, 1994)

—— 'The Context and Purposes of Geoffrey of Monmouth's *History of the Kings of Britain*', *ANS*, 13 (1990)

—— 'Richard I and the Science of War in the Middle Ages', in *War and Governement in the Middle Ages*, ed. J. Gillingham and J. C. Holt (Woodbridge, 1984), repr. in his *Richard Coeur de Lion* (London, 1994)

Gillmor, C. 'The Logistics of Fortified Bridge Building on the Seine under Charles the Bald', *ANS*, 11 (1988)

Gobry, Ivan, *Louis VII Père de Philippe Auguste* (Paris, 2002)

Goebel, J., *Felony and Misdemeanor. A Study in the History of the Common Law* (Philadelphia, 1976)

Goetz, Hans-Werner, '"Beatus homo qui invenit amicum". The Concept of Friendship in Early Medieval Letters of the Anglo-Saxon Tradition on the Continent', in *Friendship in Medieval Europe*, ed. J. Haseldine (Stroud, 1999)

Goez, Werner, '". . .. *iuravit in anima regis*"; Hochmittelalterliche Beschränkungen königlicher Eidesleistung', *DA*, 42 (1986)

Gordon, E. V., 'The Date of Aethelred's Treaty with the Vikings: Olaf Tryggvason and the Battle of Maldon', *Modern Language Review*, 32 (1937)

Grabois, A., 'De la trève de Dieu à la paix du roi. Étude sur la transformation du mouvement de paix au XIIe siècle', in *Cahiers de civilisation médiévale. Mélanges offert à René Crozet*, 2 vols, ed. Pierre Gallais and Yves-Jean Riou (Poitiers, 1966)

Gransden, A., *Historical Writing in England c. 550 to c. 1307* (London, 1996)

Green, Judith A., 'David and Henry I', *SHR*, 75 (1996)

—— 'Anglo-Scottish Relations 1066–1174', in *England and Her Neighbours, 1066–1453: Essays in Honour of Pierre Chaplais*, ed. Michael Jones and Malcolm Vale (London, 1989)

Grierson, Philip, 'Commerce in the Dark Ages: A Critique of the Evidence', *TRHS*, 5th ser., 9 (1959)

Hajdu, R., 'Castles, Castellans and the Structure of Politics in Poitou 1152–1271', *JMH*, 4 (1978)

Hamilton, Sarah, 'The Unique Favour of Penance: the Church and the People c. 800-c. 1100', in *The Medieval World*, ed. Peter Linehan and Janet L. Nelson (London, 2001)

Hanawalt, Barbara A. and Reyerson, Kathryn L., ed. *City and Spectacle in Medieval Europe* (Minneapolis, 1994)

Head, Thomas and Landes, Richard, *The Peace of God: Social Violence and Religious Response in France around the Year 1000* (Ithaca, 1992)

Heine, N. G., 'Valdemar II's udenrigspolitik. Kampen om Østersøvaeldet', in *Østersøproblemer omkring 1200*, ed. N. G. Heine (Aarhus, 1941)

Helmerichs, R., ' "Ad tutandos patriae fines": the Defence of Normandy, 1135', in *The Normans and Their Adversaries at War*, ed. R. P. Abels and B. S. Bachrach (Woodbridge, 2001)

——'King Stephen's Norman Itinerary, 1137', *HSJ*, 5 (1993)

Henisch, Bridget Ann, *Fast and Feast. Food in Medieval Society* (Philadelphia, 1976)

Henneman, John, Bell, *Royal Taxation in Fourteenth-century France: The Captivity and Ransom of John II, 1356–1370* (Philadelphia, 1976)

Hermann-Mascard, Nicole, *Les reliques des saints. Formation coutumière d'un droit* (Paris, 1975)

Hermanson, Lars, 'Vänskap som politisk ideologi i Saxo Grammaticus *Gesta Danorum*', *Historisk Tidskrift* (Sverige), 4 (2003)

——'Friendship and Politics in Saxo Grammaticus' *Gesta Danorum*', *Revue belge de philologie et d'histoire*, 83 (2005)

Heyn, U., *Peacemaking in Medieval Europe: An Historical and Bibliographical Guide* (Claremont, 1997)

Hill, Boyd H., *Medieval Monarchy in Action* (London, 1972)

Hill, David, *An Atlas of Anglo-Saxon England* (Oxford, 1981)

Hilpert, Hans-Eberhard, 'Zwei Briefe Kaiser Ottos IV. an Johann Ohneland', *DA*, 38 (1982)

Hoffman, Erich, 'The Unity of the Kingdom and the Provinces in Denmark during the Middle Ages', in *Danish Medieval History: New Currents*, ed. Niels Skyum-Nielsen and Niels Lund (Copenhagen, 1981)

Hoffmann, H., 'Zur mittelalterlichen Brieftechnik', in *Spiegel der Geschichte: Festgabe für Max Braubach*, ed. Konrad Repgen (Münster, 1964)

Holdsworth, C. W., 'Peacemaking in the Twelfth Century', *ANS*, 19 (1998)

Hollister, C. Warren, 'War and Diplomacy in the Anglo-Norman World: the Reign of Henry I', *ANS*, 6 (1984)

—— 'Henry I and the Invisible Transformation of Medieval England', in *Studies in*

Medieval History Presented to R. H. C. Davis, ed. Henry Mayr-Harting and R. I. Moore (London, 1985)

—— 'Royal Acts of Mutilation: the Case Against Henry I', *Albion*, 10 (1978)

Hollister, C. Warren, and Keefe, T. K., 'The Making of the Angevin Empire', *Journal of British Studies* 12 (1973)

Holmes, Catherine, 'Treaties between Byzantium and the Islamic World', in *War and Peace in Ancient and Medieval History*, ed. Philip de Souza and John France (Cambridge, 2008)

Holt, J. C., *Colonial England 1066–1215* (London, 1997)

—— *Magna Carta*, 2nd edn (Cambridge, 1992)

Holt, Peter, M., 'Qalawun's Treaty with Genoa in 1290', *Der Islam*, 57 (1980)

Holtzmann, W., 'Sui rapporti fra Normanni e Papato', *Archivio Storico Pugliese*, 11 (1958)

Houts, E. M. C. van, 'The Norman Conquest through European Eyes', *EHR*, 110 (1995)

Hubert, J., 'Le miracle de Déols et la trève conclue en 1187 entre les rois de France et d'Angleterre', *Bibliothèque de l'École des Chartes*, 96 (1935)

Hudson, Benjamin T., 'Cnut and the Scottish Kings', *EHR*, 107 (1992)

Hyams, P. R., 'Warranty and Good Lordship in Twelfth Century England', *Law and History Review*, 5 (1987)

Hybel, Nils and Poulsen, Bjørn, *The Danish Resources c. 1000–1550* (Leiden, 2007)

Hørby, Kai, 'The Social History of Medieval Denmark', in *Danish Medieval History: New Currents*, ed. Niels Skyum-Nielsen and Niels Lund (Copenhagen, 1981)

Jacobsen, Grethe, 'Wicked Court Henry: The Capture of Valdemar II (1223) and Danish Influence in the Baltic', *Journal of Baltic Studies*, 9 (1978)

Johns, Jeremy, 'The Norman Kings and the Fatimid Caliphate', *ANS*, 15 (1992)

Johnsen, Arne Odd, *Kong Sverre og England 1199–1202* (Oslo, 1970)

Joliffe, J. E. A., *Angevin Kingship* (London, 1970)

Jones, Michael and Vale, Malcolm, ed., *England and Her Neighbours, 1066–1453* (London, 1989)

Jordan, K., *Henry the Lion* (Oxford, 1986)

Jungmann, Joseph A., *The Mass of the Roman Rite. Its Origins and Development*, 2 vols, tr. Rev. Francis A. Brunner (Westminster, 1986)

Kamp, Hermann, *Friedensstifter und Vermittler im Mittelalter* (Darmstadt, 2001)

Keefe, Thomas K., 'Shrine Time: King Henry II's Visits to Thomas Becket's Tomb', *HSJ*, 11 (1998)

Keen, M. H., *Medieval Warfare – A History* (Oxford, 1999)

—— *The Laws of War in the Late Middle Ages* (London, 1965)

Keynes, Simon, 'Royal Government and the Written Word in Late Anglo-Saxon England', in *The Uses of Literacy in Early Medieval Europe*, ed. Rosamond McKitterick (Cambridge, 1990)

—— 'Regenbald the Chancellor (sic)', *ANS*, 10 (1987)

—— *The Diplomas of King Aethelred 'the Unready' 978–1016* (Cambridge, 1980)

Kienast, Walther, *Die deutschen Fürsten im Dienste der Westmächte bis zum Tode Philipps des Schönen von Frankreich*, 2 vols (Utrecht, 1924–31)

Kitsikés, Démétrios, *Propagande et pressions en politique internationale: La Grèce et ses revendications a la Conférence de la Paix* (Paris, 1963)

Koch, Hal, ed., *Danmarks Historie*, vol. 3 (Copenhagen, 1969)

Koch, Walter, 'Die Reichskanzlei unter Kaiser Friedrich I', *Archiv für Diplomatik, Schriftgeschichte, Siegel- und Wappenkunde*, 31 (1985)

Kolb, Werner, *Herrscherbegegnungen im Mittelalter* (Frankfurt, 1988)

Kolmer, Lothar, *Promissorische Eide im Mittelalter*, Regensburger Historische Forschungen, 12 (Kallmünz, 1989)

Körner, S., *The Battle of Hastings, England and Europe 1053–1066* (Lund, 1964)

Kosto, Adam J., 'Les otages conditionnels en Languedoc et en Catalogne au XIe siècle', *Annales du Midi*, 118 (2006)

—— 'L'otage comme vecteur d'échange culturel du 4e au 15e siècle', in *Les prisonniers de guerre dans l'histoire: contacts entre peuples et cultures*, ed. Sylvie Caucanas et al. (Toulouse, 2003)

——'Hostages in the Carolingian World (714–840)', *Early Medieval Europe*, 11 (2002)

——*Making Agreements in Medieval Catalonia* (Cambridge, 2001)

—— 'The *convenientia* in the Early Middle Ages', *Mediaeval Studies*, 60 (1998)

Koziol, G., 'Political Culture', in *France in the Middle Ages*, ed. Marcus Bull (Oxford, 2002)

——'England, France and the Problem of Sacrality in Twelfth-century Ritual', in *Cultures of Power*, ed. Thomas N. Bisson (Philadelphia, 1995)

——*Begging Pardon and Favor* (New York, 1992)

—— 'Monks, Feuds and the Making of Peace in Eleventh Century Flanders', *Historical Reflections*, 14 (1987)

Laidlaw, J., 'A Free Gift Makes No Friends', *Journal of the Royal Anthropological Institute*, 6 (2000)

Landon, L., *The Itinerary of King Richard I* (London 1935)

Langeli, A. B., 'Private Charters', in *Italy in the Early Middle Ages*, ed. Christina La Rocca (Oxford, 2002)

Latimer, Paul, 'Henry II's Campaign against the Welsh in 1165', *Welsh History Review*, 14 (1989)

Lavelle, Ryan, 'The Use and Abuse of Hostages in Later Anglo-Saxon England', *Early Medieval Europe*, 14 (2006)

——'Towards a Political Contextualization of Peacemaking and Peace Agreements in Anglo-Saxon England', in *Peace and Negotiation: Strategies for Coexistence in the Middle Ages*, ed. D. Wolfthal, Arizona Studies in the Middle Ages and the Renaissance, 4 (Turnhout, 2000)

Lee, A. D., 'Treaty-making in Late Antiquity', in *War and Peace in Ancient and Medieval History*, ed. Philip de Souza and John France (Cambridge, 2008)

Le Goff, Jacques, 'The Symbolic Ritual of Vassalage', in his *Time, Work and Culture in the Middle Ages*, tr. Arthur Goldhammer (Chicago, 1980)

—— *La naissance du purgatoire* (Paris, 1981)

Le Jan, Régine, 'Frankish Giving of Arms and Rituals of Power: Continuity and

Change in the Carolingian Period', in *Rituals of Power*, ed. Frans Theuws and Janet L. Nelson (Leiden, 2000)

Lemarignier, J. F., *Recherches sur l'hommage en marche et les frontières féodales* (Lille, 1945)

Leron-Lesur, P., *Colombiers et pigeonniers en France* (Paris, 1986)

Leyser, Karl, *Communications and Power in Medieval Europe: The Carolingian and Ottonian Centuries*, ed. Timothy Reuter (London, 1994)

—— 'Ritual, Ceremony and Gesture: Ottonian Germany', in his *Communications and Power in Medieval Europe: The Carolingian and Ottonian Centuries*, ed. Timothy Reuter (London, 1994)

—— 'Frederick Barbarossa: Court and Country', in his *Communications and Power in Medieval Europe: The Gregorian Revolution and Beyond*, ed. Timothy Reuter (London, 1994)

——'Frederick Barbarossa, Henry II and the Hand of St James', *EHR*, 90 (1975)

Liestøl, Aslak, 'Correspondence in Runes', *Mediaeval Scandinavia*, 1 (1968)

Lind, John, 'The Russian-Swedish Border according to the Peace Treaty of Nöteborg (Orekhovets-Pähkinälinna) and the Political Status of the Northern Part of Fennoscandia', *Mediaeval Scandinavia*, 13 (2000)

Little, Lester K., *Benedictine Maledictions. Liturgical Cursing in Romanesque France* (Ithaca, 1993)

——*Religious Poverty and the Profit Economy in Medieval Europe* (Ithaca, 1978)

Lloyd, J. E., *A History Wales from the Earliest Times to Edwardian Conquest*, 2 vols (London, 1912)

Lo Prete, Kimberley A., 'The Anglo-Norman Card of Adela of Blois', *Albion*, 22 (1990)

Lot, F., *Fidèles ou vassaux? Essai sur la nature juridique du lien qui unissait les grands vassaux à la royauté depuis le milieu du IXe jusqu'à la fin du XIIe siècle* (Paris, 1904)

Loud, G. A., 'The Chancery and Charters of the Kings of Sicily (1130–1212)', *EHR*, 124 (2009)

Luckau, Alma M., *The German Delegation at the Paris Peace Conference* (New York, 1971)

Lund, N., 'Peace and Non-peace in the Viking Age – Ottar in Biarmaland, the Rus in Byzantium, and the Danes and Norwegians in England', in *Proceedings of the Tenth Viking Congress*, ed. J. E. Knirk (Oslo, 1987)

Lynch, Joseph H., *Christianizing Kinship. Ritual Sponsorship in Anglo-Saxon England* (Ithaca, 1998)

——*Godparents and Kinship in Early Medieval Europe* (Princeton, 1986)

Lyon, Bryce, D., 'The Money Fief under the English Kings', *EHR*, 66 (1951)

MacMillan, Margaret, *Peacemakers: The Paris Conference of 1919 and Its Attempt to End War* (London, 2001)

Madden, Thomas F., 'Venice's Hostage Crisis: Diplomatic Efforts to Secure Peace with Byzantium between 1171 and 1184', in *Medieval and Renaissance Venice*, ed. Ellen E. Kittell and Thomas F. Madden (Chicago, 1999)

Magnou-Nortier, E., *Foi et Fidelité: Recherches sur l'évolution des liens personnels chez les francs du viie au ixe siècle* (Toulouse, 1976)

Major, J. R., '"Bastard Feudalism" and the Kiss', *Journal of Interdisciplinary History*, 17 (1987)

Malafosse, Jehan de 'Contribution à l'étude du crédit dans le Midi aux Xe et XIe siècles: les sûretées réelles', *Annales du Midi*, 63 (1951)

Malmros, R., 'Blodgildet i Roskilde historiografiskt belyst', *Scandia*, 45 (1979)

Malo, H., *Un grand feudataire: Renaud de Dammartin et la coalition de Bouvines* (Paris, 1898)

Mansfield, Mary C., *The Humiliation of Sinners. Public Penance in Thirteenth-century France* (Ithaca, 1995)

Maquet, J., *Pouvoir et société en Afrique* (Paris, 1970)

Mariotte, J.-Y., 'Le royaume de Bourgogne et les souverains allemands du haut Moyen-Âge 888–1032', in *Mémoirs de la société pour l'histoire du droit et des institutions des anciens pays bourguignons, comtots et romands*, 23 (1962)

Markowski, M., 'Richard Lionheart: Bad King, Bad Crusader', *JMH*, 23 (1997)

Martin, R. P., *Reconciliation. A Study of Paul's Theology* (London, 1980)

Martindale, J., 'Dispute Settlement and Orality in the *Conventum inter Guillelmum Aquitanorum comitem et Hugonem Chiliarchum*: a Postscript to the Edition of 1969', in her *Status, Authority and Regional Power* (Aldershot, 1997)

—— '"His Special Friend?" The Settlement of Disputes and Political Power in the Kingdom of the French (Tenth to Mid-twelfth Century)', *TRHS*, 6th ser., 5 (1995)

——'Peace and War in Early Eleventh-century Aquitaine', in *Medieval Knighthood IV: Papers from the Fifth Strawberry Hill Conference 1990*, ed. Christopher Harper-Bill and Ruth Harvey (Woodbridge, 1992)

——'Succession and Politics in the Romance-Speaking World, c. 1000–1140', in *England and Her Neighbours, 1066–1453: Essays in Honour of Pierre Chaplais*, ed. Michael Jones and Malcolm Vale (London, 1989)

——'The Kingdom of Aquitaine and the Dissolution of the Carolingian Fisc', *Francia*, 11 (1985)

——'*Conventum inter Guillelmum Aquitanorum comitem et Hugonem Chiliarchum*', EHR, 84 (1969); repr. in her *Status, Authority and Regional Power* (Aldershot, 1997)

Maschke, Erich, 'Die Brücke im Mittelalter', *Historische Zeitschrift*, 224 (1977)

Mason, E., 'The Hero's Invincible Weapon: an Aspect of Angevin Propaganda', in *The Ideals and Practice of Medieval Knighthood, III*, ed. C. Harper-Bill and Ruth Harvey (Woodbridge, 1990)

Matthew, D., *Atlas of Medieval Europe* (Oxford, 1983)

Maund, K. L., 'Owain ap Cadwgan: a Rebel Revisited', *HSJ*, 13 (2004)

Mauss, M., *The Gift: Forms Functions and Exchange in Archaic Societies*, tr. Ian Cunnison (London, 1954)

Mažeika, Rasa, 'When Crusader and Pagan Agree: Conversion as a Point of Honour in the Baptism of King Mindaugas of Lithuania (c. 1240–63)', in *Crusade and Conversion on the Baltic Frontier 1150–1500*, ed. Alan V. Murray (Aldershot, 2001)

McGuire, Brian Patrick, 'Friendship and Peace in the Letters of Gerbert, 982–97', in his *War and Peace in the Middle Ages* (Copenhagen, 1987)

McKitterick, Rosamond, 'Latin and Romance: an Historian's Perspective', in her *The Frankish Kings and Culture in the Early Middle Ages* (Aldershot, 1995)

—— *The Uses of Literacy in Early Medieval Europe* (Cambridge, 1990)

——*The Carolingians and the Written Word* (Cambridge, 1989)

Mead, W. E., *The English Medieval Feast* (London, 1967)

Mierow, C. C., 'Otto of Freising: a Medieval Historian at Work', *Philological Quarterly*, 14 (1935)

Miller, W., *Bloodtaking and Peacemaking: Feud, Law and Society in Saga Iceland* (Chicago, 1990)

Mitteis, Heinrich, *Lehnrecht und Staatsgewalt. Untersuchungen zur mittelalterlichen Verfassungsgeschichte* (Weimar, 1958)

Moeglin, Jean-Marie, 'Rituels et *Verfassungsgeschichte* au Moyen Âge', *Francia*, 25 (1998)

Moreau, J., *Dictionnaire de géographie historique de la Gaule et de la France* (Paris, 1972)

Morris, C., *The Papal Monarchy: The Western Church from 1050–1250* (Oxford, 1989)

Morris, Rosemary, 'Dispute Settlement in the Byzantine Provinces in the Tenth Century', in *The Settlement of Disputes in Early Medieval Europe*, ed. Wendy Davies and Paul Fouracre (Cambridge, 1992)

Munz, Peter, *Frederick Barbarossa* (London, 1969)

Murray, Alan V., 'The Danish Monarchy and the Kingdom of Germany, 1197–1319: the Evidence of Middle High German Poetry', in *Scandinavia and Europe 800–1350. Contact, Conflict, and Coexistence*, ed. Jonathan Adams and Katherine Holman (Turnhout, 2004)

Musset, Lucien, *Les peuples scandinaves au Moyen Âge* (Paris, 1951)

Nagy, Piroska, *Le don des larmes au Moyen Âge* (Paris, 2000)

Nelson, Janet L., 'Literacy in Carolingian Government', in *The Uses of Literacy in Early Medieval Europe*, ed. Rosamond McKitterick (Cambridge, 1995)

——*Charles the Bald: Court and Kingdom* (London, 1992)

——'Dispute Settlement in Carolingian West Francia', in *The Settlement of Disputes in Early Medieval Europe*, ed. Wendy Davies and Paul Fouracre (Cambridge, 1992)

—— 'The Lord's Anointed and the People's Choice: Carolingian Royal Ritual', in *Rituals of Royalty*, ed. David Cannadine and Simon Price (Cambridge, 1987).

Nip, Renée, 'The Political Relations between England and Flanders (1066–1128)', *ANS*, 21 (1999)

Norgate, K., *The Minority of Henry III* (London, 1912)

Odegaard, C. E., 'Carolingian Oaths of Fidelity', *Speculum*, 16 (1941)

Oexle, Otto Gerhard, 'Peace through Conspiracy', in *Ordering Medieval Society*, ed. Bernhard Jussen and tr. Pamela Selwyn (Philadelphia, 2001)

Olsson, G., 'Sverige och landet vid Göta Älvs mynning', *Göteborgs högskolas årsskrift*, 1, ix (1953)

Pacaut, Marcel, *Frederick Barbarossa* (London, 1970)

——*Alexandre III* (Paris, 1956)

Page, R. I., *Chronicles of the Vikings* (London, 1995)

Palmer, Alan, *Victory 1918* (London, 1998)

Paradisi, B., *Storia del diritto internazionale nell'alto medioevo* (Naples, 1956)

Parker, R. A. C., *Chamberlain and Appeasement* (Basingstoke, 1993)

Pascua, Esther, 'Peace among Equals: War and Treaties in Twelfth-century Europe', in *War and Peace in Ancient and Medieval History*, ed. Philip de Souza and John France (Cambridge, 2008)

Pastoureau, Michel, 'Pourquoi tant de lions dans l'occident médiéval?', *Micrologus*, 8 (2000)

Perella, N. J., *The Kiss Sacred and Profane* (Berkeley, 1969)

Petkov, Kiril, *The Kiss of Peace: Ritual, Self and Society in the High and Late Medieval West* (Leiden, 2003)

Petrucci, A., *Writers and Readers in Medieval Italy*, tr. Charles M. Radding (New Haven, 1995)

—— *Notarii: documenti per la storia del notariato italiano* (Milan, 1958)

Picasso, G., 'Roberto il Guiscardo *fidelis* della chiesa romana e di Gregorio VII', in *Roberto il Guiscardo tra Europa, Oriente e Mezzogiorno*, ed. C. D. Fonseca (Potenza, 1990)

Planhol, X. de, and Claval, P. *An Historical Geography of France*, tr. J. Lloyd (Cambridge, 1988)

Plescia, Joseph, *The Oath and Perjury in Ancient Greece* (Tallahassee, 1970)

Polara, Giovanni, 'Tra fantasmi e poeti: Coincidenze e reminiscenze classiche nelle parti in versi dei *Gesta Danorum*', in *Saxo Grammaticus: Tra storiografia e letteratura*, ed. Carlo Santini (Rome, 1992)

Poly, J. P. and Bournazel, E., *La mutation féodale: xe–xiie siècles* (Paris, 1980) Available in English as *The Feudal Transformation 900–1200*, tr. Caroline Higgitt (London, 1991)

Poole, A. L., 'Richard the First's Alliances with the German Princes in 1194', in *Studies in Medieval History: Presented to Frederick Maurice Powicke*, ed. R. W. Hunt et al. (Oxford, 1948)

——'England and Burgundy in the Last Decade of the Twelfth Century', in *Essays in History presented to R. L. Poole*, ed. H. W. C. Davis (Oxford, 1927)

Potts, C., 'Normandy or Brittany? A Conflict of Interests at Mont Saint Michel', *ANS*, 12 (1989)

Pounds, N. J. G., *An Historical Geography of Europe, 450 B.C. – A.D. 1330* (Cambridge, 1973)

Power, D. J., *The Norman Frontier in the Twelfth and Early Thirteenth Centuries* (Cambridge, 2004)

——'L'aristocratie Plantagenêt face aux conflits capétiens-angevins: l'example du traité de Louviers', in *Noblesses de l'espace Plantagenêt (1154–1224)*, ed. Martin Aurell (Poitiers, 2001)

——'King John and the Norman Aristocracy', in *King John: New Interpretations*, ed. S. D. Church (Woodbridge, 1999)

——'What Did the Frontier of Angevin Normandy Comprise?', *ANS*, 17 (1995)

Powicke, F. M., *The Loss of Normandy*, 2nd edn (Manchester, 1960)

Powicke, Michael R., 'War as a Means to Peace: Some Late Medieval Themes', in *Documenting the Past: Essays in Medieval History Presented to George Peddy*

Cuttino, ed. J. S. Hamilton and Patricia J. Bradley (Woodbridge, 1989)

Prestwich, J. O., 'Feudalism: a Critique', in his *The Place of War in English History 1066–1214*, ed. Michael Prestwich (Woodbridge, 2004)

Pryce, Huw, 'Welsh Rulers and European Change, c. 1100–1282', in *Power and Identity in the Middle Ages. Essays in Memory of Rees Davies*, ed. Huw Pryce and John Watts (Oxford, 2007)

——'Owain Gwynedd and Louis VII: the Franco-Welsh Diplomacy of the First Prince of Wales', *Welsh History Review*, 19 (1998)

Queller, Donald E., *The Office of Ambassador in the Middle Ages* (Princeton, 1967)

—— *Early Venetian Legislation on Ambassadors* (Geneva, 1966)

—— 'Thirteenth-century Diplomatic Envoys: *Nuncii* and *Procuratores*', *Speculum*, 35 (1960)

Qvistgaard Hansen, Jørgen '*Regnum et sacerdotium*: Forholdet mellem stat og kirke i Danmark 1157–70', in *Middelalder studier tilegnede Aksel E. Christensen på tresårsdagen* (Copenhagen, 1966)

Rackham, O., *The History of the Countryside* (London, 1997)

——*Ancient Woodland* (London, 1980)

Ragnow, Marguerite, 'Ritual Before the Altar: Legal Satisfaction and Spiritual Reconciliation in Eleventh-century Anjou', in *Medieval and Early Modern Ritual: Formalized Behaviour in Europe, China and Japan*, ed. Joëlle Rollo-Koster (Leiden, 2002)

Reeves, Compton, *Pleasures and Pastimes in Medieval England* (Stroud, 1995)

Renna, Thomas, 'The Idea of Peace in the West, 500–1150', *Journal of Medieval History*, 6 (1980)

Reuter, T., 'Assembly Politics in Western Europe from the Eighth Century to the Twelfth', in *The Medieval World*, ed. Peter Linehan and Janet L. Nelson (London, 2001)

——'The Making of England and Germany, 850–1050: Points of Comparison and Difference', in *Medieval Europeans*, ed. Alfred P. Smyth (Basingstoke, 1998)

——'Episcopi cum sua militia: the Prelate as Warrior in the Early Staufer Era', in *Warriors and Churchmen in the High Middle Ages. Essays Presented to Karl Leyser*, ed. T. Reuter (London, 1992)

——'Plunder and Tribute in the Carolingian Empire', *TRHS*, 5th ser., 35 (1985)

——*The Medieval Nobility* (Oxford, 1978)

Reynolds, A. *Later Anglo-Saxon England: Life and Landscape* (London, 1999)

Reynolds, R., 'Rites and Signs of Conciliar Decision in the Early Middle Ages', in *Segni e riti*, 2 vols, Centro Italiano di studi sull'alto medioevo, *Settimane*, 33 (1987)

Reynolds, S., 'Some Afterthoughts on *Fiefs and Vassals*', *HSJ*, 9 (1997)

——*Fiefs and Vassals* (Oxford, 1994)

Rich, J. W., 'Treaties, Allies and the Roman Conquest of Italy', in *War and Peace in Ancient and Medieval History*, ed. Philip de Souza and John France (Cambridge, 2008)

—— 'Augustus, War and Peace', in *The Representation and Perception of Roman Imperial Power*, ed. L. de Blois (Amsterdam, 2003)

Richardson, H. G. and Sayles, G. O., *The Governance of Medieval England from the Conquest to Magna Carta* (Edinburgh, 1974)

Richardson, M., *The Medieval Chancery under Henry V*, List and Index Society Special Series, 30 (London, 1999)

Rigby, S. H., *Wisdom and Chivalry: Chaucer's Knight's Tale and Medieval Political Theory* (Leiden, 2009)

Riis, T., 'Autour du mariage de 1193: l'épouse, son pays et les relations Franco-Danoises', in *La France de Philippe Auguste: le temps des mutations*, ed. R.-H. Bautier (Paris, 1982)

Riley-Smith, Jonathan, *What Were the Crusades?* (Basingstoke, 1989)

Rosenwein, Barbara H., *To Be the Neighbour of Saint Peter: The Social Meaning of Cluny's Property, 909–1049* (Ithaca, 1989)

Rowland, B., *Animals with Human Faces: A Guide to Animal Symbolism* (Knoxville, 1973)

Rowlands, Ifor W., 'The 1201 Peace between King John and Llywelyn ap Iorwerth', *Studia Celtica*, 24 (2000)

——'King John and Wales', in *King John: New Interpretations*, ed. S. D. Church (Woodbridge, 1999)

Rung, Eduard, 'War, Peace and Diplomacy in Graeco-Persian Relations from the Sixth to the Fourth Century BC', in *War and Peace in Ancient and Medieval History*, ed. Philip de Souza and John France (Cambridge, 2008)

Russell, F. H., *The Just War in the Middle Ages* (Cambridge, 1977).

Russell, J. G., *Peacemaking in the Renaissance* (London, 1986)

Sahlins, P., *Boundaries: The Making of France and Spain in the Pyrenees* (Berkeley, 1989)

Sawyer, B., 'The "Civil Wars" Revisited', *Historisk Tidskrift* (Norge), 82 (2003)

——'Saxo, Valdemar, Absalon', *Scandia*, 51 (1985)

—— 'Valdemar, Absalon and Saxo: Historiography and Politics in Medieval Denmark', *Revue belge de philologie et d'histoire*, 63 (1985)

Sawyer, Peter, 'Ethelred II, Olaf Tryggvason, and the Conversion of Norway', *SS*, 59 (1987)

Schmid, Karl, 'Unerforschte Quellen aus quellenarmer Zeit. Zur amicitia zwischen Heinrich I. und dem westfränkischen König Robert im Jahre 923', *Francia*, 12 (1984)

Schröder, Sybille, *Macht und Gabe: materielle Kultur am Hof Heinrichs II. von England* (Husum, 2004)

Schütte, Bernd, *König Philipp von Schwaben. Itinerar Urkundenvergabe Hof*, MGH Schriften, 51 (Hanover, 2002)

Scott, William, W., 'The March Laws Reconsidered', in *Medieval Scotland: Crown, Lordship and Community. Essays presented to G. W. S. Barrow*, ed. A. Grant and Keith J. Stringer (Edinburgh, 1993)

Shepard, Jonathan, 'Cross-Purposes: Alexius Comnenus and the First Crusade', in *The First Crusade: Origins and Impact*, ed. Jonathan Phillips (Manchester, 1997)

Skovgaard-Petersen, I., 'Saxo som samtidshistoriker. Det skånske oprör', *Scandia*, 56 (1990)

—— 'Saxo's *History of the Danes*: An Interpretation', *SJH*, 13 (1988)

Smith, J. Beverley, 'Magna Carta and the Charters of the Welsh Princes', *EHR*, 99 (1984)

——'The Treaty of Lambeth, 1217', *EHR*, 94 (1979)

Souza, Philip de, '*Parta victoriis pax*: Roman Emperors as Peacemakers', in *War and Peace in Ancient and Medieval History*, ed. Philip de Souza and John France (Cambridge, 2008)

Spiegel, Gabrielle M., 'The Cult of St Denis and Capetian Kingship', in *Saints and their Cults*, ed. Stephen Wilson (Cambridge, 1983)

Stenton, D. M. 'Roger of Howden and Benedict', *EHR*, 68 (1953)

Stiesdal, Hans, 'Types of Public and Private Fortifications in Denmark', in *Danish Medieval History: New Currents*, ed. Niels Skyum-Nielsen and Niels Lund (Copenhagen, 1981)

Strickland, M., *War and Chivalry: The Conduct and Perception of War in England and Normandy 1066–1217* (Cambridge, 1996)

—— *Anglo-Norman Warfare* (Woodbridge, 1992)

Stringer, K. J., *Earl David of Huntingdon. A Study in Anglo-Scottish History* (Edinburgh, 1985)

Suchan, Monika, *Königsherrschaft im Streit. Konfliktaustragung in der Regierungszeit Heinrichs IV* (Stuttgart, 1997)

Suppe, Frederick C., 'Who Was Rhys Sais? Some Comments on Anglo-Welsh Relations before 1066', *HSJ*, 7 (1995)

Suttor, Marc, 'Le fleuve, un enjeu politique et juridique. Le cas de la Meuse, du Xe au XVIe siècle', *Médiévales*, 36 (1999)

Tellenbach, Gerd, *Die westliche Kirchen vom 10. bis zum frühen 12. Jahrhundert* (Göttingen, 1988)

Testart, A., 'Uncertainties of the Obligation to Reciprocate: a Critique of Mauss', in *Marcel Mauss: A Centenary Tribute*, ed. W. James and N. J. Allen (New York, 1998)

Thomson, R. M., 'An English Eyewitness Account of the Peace of Venice, 1177', *Speculum*, 50 (1975)

Treharne, R. F., 'The Franco-Welsh Treaty of Alliance in 1212', *Bulletin of the Board of Celtic Studies*, 18 (1958–60)

Turner, Ralph V., 'Ricardus Dux Aquitanorum et Comes Andegavorum', *HSJ*, 13 (2004)

Turner, Victor, *The Ritual Process: Structure and Anti-Structure* (Ithaca, 1969)

Ullmann, Walter 'The Medieval Papal Court as an International Tribunal', *Virginia Journal of International Law*, 11 (1971), repr. in his *The Papacy and Political Ideas in the Middle Ages* (London, 1976)

Vacandard, E. F., *Vie de saint Bernard, abbé de Clairvaux*, 4th edn, 2 vols (Paris, 1927)

Vale, M., *Charles VII* (London, 1974)

Varrentrapp, C., *Erzbischof Christian I. von Mainz* (Berlin, 1867)

Verbruggen, J. F., *The Art of Warfare in Western Europe during the Middle Ages: From the Eighth Century to 1340*, 2nd edn (Woodbridge, 1997)

Villads Jensen, Kurt, 'The Blue Baltic Border of Denmark in the High Middle Ages: Danes, Wends and Saxo Grammaticus', in *Medieval Frontiers: Concept and Practices*, ed. David Abulafia and Nora Berend (Aldershot, 2002)

Vincent, Nicholas, C., 'Why 1199? Bureaucracy and Enrolment under John and His Contemporaries', in *English Government in the Thirteenth Century*, ed. Adrian Jobson (Woodbridge, 2004)

——'The Pilgrimages of the Angevin Kings of England 1154–1272', in *Pilgrimage: The English Experience from Becket to Bunyan*, ed. Colin Morris and Peter Roberts (Cambridge, 2002)

—— 'Some Pardoners' Tales: the Earliest English Indulgences', *TRHS*, 6th ser., 12 (2002)

——*The Holy Blood: King Henry III and the Westminster Blood Relic* (Cambridge, 2001)

——'Isabella of Angouleme: John's Jezebel', in *King John: New Interpretations*, ed. S. D. Church (Woodbridge, 1999)

——'The Origins of the Chancellorship of the Exchequer', *EHR*, 108 (1993)

Voss, Ingrid, *Herrschertreffen im frühen und hohen Mittelalter* (Cologne, 1987)

Walker, David *Medieval Wales* (Cambridge, 1990)

Walworth, A., *Wilson and His Peacemakers: American Diplomacy at the Paris Peace Conference, 1919* (New York, 1991)

Warner, D. A., 'Ritual and Memory in the Ottonian *Reich*: the Ceremony of *Adventus*', *Speculum*, 76 (2001)

Warren, Michelle R., *History on the Edge: Excalibur and the Borders of Britain, 1100–1300*, Medieval Cultures, 22 (Minneapolis, 2000)

—— 'Roger of Howden Strikes Back: Investing Arthur of Brittany with the Anglo-Norman Future', *ANS*, 21 (1999)

Warren, W. L., *Henry II* (New Haven, 2000)

——*The Governance of Norman and Angevin England 1086–1272* (London, 1987)

—— *King John* (London, 1961)

Webster, Bruce, *Medieval Scotland* (Basingstoke, 1997)

Weibull, C., 'Knytlingasagan och Saxo', *Scandia*, 42 (1976)

—— 'Den äldsta gränsläggningen mellan Sverige och Danmark', *Historisk Tidskrift från Skåneland*, 7 (1917–21)

Weiler, Björn, *Kingship, Rebellion and Political Culture. England and Germany c. 1215–c. 1250* (Basingstoke, 2007)

—— 'Knighting, Homage and the Meaning of Ritual: the Kings of England and Their Neighbours in the Thirteenth Century', *Viator*, 37 (2006)

Weinberger, Stephen, 'Cours judiciaires, justice et responsabilité sociale dans la Provence médiévale: IXe–XIe siècles', *Revue Historique*, 267 (1982)

Weiner, Annette, *Inalienable Possessions: The Paradox of Keeping While Giving* (Berkeley, 1992).

Weinfurter, Stefan *The Salian Century. Main Currents in an Age of Transition*, tr. Barbara M. Bowlus (Philadelphia, 1999)

White, Stephen, D., 'The Politics of Exchange: Gifts, Fiefs and Feudalism', in

Medieval Transformations. Texts, Power and Gifts in Context, ed. Esther Cohen and Mayke B. de Jong (Leiden, 2001)

—— 'From Peace to Power: The Study of Disputes in Medieval France', in *Medieval Transformations. Texts, Power and Gifts in Context*, ed. W. E. Conen and Mayke B. de Jong (Leiden, 2001)

——'Proposing the Ordeal and Avoiding it: Strategy and Power in Western French Litigation, 1050–1110', in *Cultures of Power: Lordship, Status, and Processes in Twelfth-century Europe*, ed. Thomas N. Bisson (Philadelphia, 1995)

—— 'Feuding and Peacemaking in the Touraine around the year 1100', *Traditio*, 42 (1986)

—— 'Pactum . . . legem vincit et amor judicium: the Settlement of Disputes by Compromise in Eleventh-century Western France', *American Journal of Legal History*, 22 (1978)

Williams, Ann, 'An Outing on the Dee: King Edgar at Chester A.D. 973', *Mediaeval Scandinavia*, 14 (2004)

Wilson, Stephen, *The Magical Universe. Everyday Ritual and Magic in Pre-modern Europe* (London, 2000)

Wolfthal, D., ed., *Peace and Negotiation: Strategies for Coexistence in the Middle Ages* (Turnhout, 2000)

Wood, Ian 'Disputes in Late Fifth- and Sixth-century Gaul', in *The Settlement of Disputes in Early Medieval Europe*, ed. Wendy Davies and Paul Fouracre (Cambridge, 1992)

—— 'Christians and Pagans in Ninth-century Scandinavia', in *The Christianization of Scandinavia*, ed. Birgit Sawyer, Peter Sawyer and Ian Wood (Alingsås, 1987)

Wormald, Patrick, 'Lex Scripta and Verbum Regis: Legislation and Germanic Kingship, from Euric to Cnut', in *Early Medieval Kingship*, ed. P. H. Sawyer and I. N. Woods (Leeds, 1977)

Yver, J., 'Les sûretés personelles en Normandie', in *Les sûretés personnelles*, 3 vols, Recueil de la société Jean Bodin pour l'histoire comparative des institutions, 29 (Brussels, 1969–74)

Unpublished works

Edwards, J. B., 'The English Royal Chamber and Chancery in the Reign of King John', unpublished Ph.D. thesis (Cambridge, 1974)

Kershaw, Paul, 'Rex Pacificus: Studies in Royal Peacemaking and the Image of the Peacemaking King', unpublished Ph. D. thesis (London, 1999)

Wielers, M., 'Zwischenstaatliche Beziehungsformen im frühen Mittelalter (*Pax, Foedus, Amicitia, Fraternitas*)', Unpublished Ph. D. thesis (Münster, 1956)

INDEX

Note: 'n.' after a page number indicates the number of a note on that page.

Lightning Source UK Ltd.
Milton Keynes UK
UKHW021813120419
340963UK00005B/254/P

9 781526 116680